MASSIMILIANO FERRARA'S CONTRIBUTIONS ON COVID-19 PANDEMIC DYNAMICS

Prof. Massimiliano Ferrara

Index of Sciences Ltd.
Kemp House,
160 City Road, London.
www.indexofsciences.com

Ordering Information:

Quantity sales. Special discounts are available on quantity purchases by corporations, associations, and others. For details, contact the publisher at the address above.

Printed in the United Kingdom
ISBN:979-8371054746

ISBN 979-8-3710-5474-6

9 798371 054746 >

Preface

In this book, different phases and management of COVID prediction modelling utilizing machine learning techniques and B-cell dataset are described and also studied the Infection with COVID-19 can be predicted using chest CT scans using ET-NET, a collection of transfer learning models. The areas covered in this book include the overview, clinical features, pathogenesis, diagnosis and treatment of COVID-19. Most of the chapters were retrieved from publications in peer-reviewed journals by my team and colleagues.

The areas covered in this book include the management of Identification of the leading risk factor associated with the spread of COVID-19 using the tentative fuzzy MCDM technique, as well as Mathematical Model of Fractal-Fractional Complexity to Address the Problem of Corona Virus in Pakistan. This book provides an overview of Pandemic Effects in The Society and New Future Challenges and discusses the Different types of nanomaterials and their impact on COVID-19 diagnosis, prevention, and treatment.

The straightforward format of this book makes it an easy read. It is written in a straightforward and clear style, making it accessible to a broad audience of Students, Academics, Researchers and Practionares

This is a fairly unique book in terms of the depth and complexity with which the subject is discussed. Tables, equations, and approximately one hundred illustrations are used to illustrate the data.

Acknowledgements

This work would not been possible if some Academic Institutions had not supported scientific production of the Decisions_Lab - UniRc - (http://www.decisionslab.unirc.it/it/).
Many thanks to ICRIOS - Bocconi University and Tecnovation s.r.l for their fundamental support to this Research which joining three Continents: Europe, Asia and Oceania. Two Universities - The National University of Malaysia and Bahcesehir University (Turkey) - were crucial in developing the two main research projects were promoted by Decisions_Lab:

1. Dynamics of transmission and control of COVID-19: A new mathematical modeling and numerical simulation;
2. Numerical simulations of non-Newtonian fluid behavior models with Multi-criterial decision making based on fuzzy picture parameters and applications to COVID-19.

I would to express my gratitude to a great Scientist and Friend who joined this seminal idea in promoting these research challenges - Dr. Ali Ahmadian - who was Visiting Professor at Dept DIGIES - Unirc in 2019. At that time born a great friendship and fruitful scientific platform that during the last three years have been producing a lot of results. My gratitude is extended to my favorite Ph.D Students Tiziana Ciano, Pasquale Fotia and Valentina Mallamaci and Decisions Lab Team. A special thanks to my Colleague and Friend Prof. Roberto Mavilia for his valuable support. Last but not least a warm sign of esteem to all co-authors of the collected paper which were involved in this Book. Without their joined efforts nothing would be not realized.

About the Author

Massimiliano Ferrara received the master's degree (cum laude) in economics from the University of Messina, the master's degree (cum laude) from the University of Naples Federico II, the master's degree (cum laude) from the Scuola Normale Superiore di Pisa, and the PhD degree (cum laude) from the University of Messina. He has been a Research Affiliate with the ICRIOS–Invernizzi Center for Research on Innovation, Organization, Strategy and Entrepreneurship, University Bocconi of Milan, since 2013, the President of the Scientific Committee of the MEDAlics Research Center, and the Scientific Director of the DECISIONS Lab. He was a General Counsel of the Fondazione Banco di Napoli, the Vice-Rector of the University for foreigners "Dante Alighieri'' of Reggio Calabria, and the Head of Region Calabria Department for Cultura, Research and Education. He was a Visiting Professor at Harvard University, Cambridge, MA, USA, Western Michigan University, USA, Morgan State University, Baltimora, MD, USA, the Northeastern University di Boston, USA, and recently with the Center for Dynamics of Dresden University of Technology, Germany. He is currently a Full Professor of mathematical economics, business analytics & decision theory, and applied economics with the Mediterranea University of Reggio Calabria, where he was also the Chairman of the Department of Law, Economics & Human Sciences, and a Member of the Academic Senate. He is an author of more than 220 research papers published in peer-reviewed Journals edited by Nature, IEEE, Elsevier, Springer, Wiley, etc. He has been *Knight Order of Merit* of the Italian Republic since 2010 "for international scientific merits". He also received the "*Hepites Award*" from the Romanian Academy of Science in 2010, the *Silver Medal from Universiti PUTRA Malaysia* on the occasion of Invention, Research and Innovation Exhibition (PRPI) in 2016, and recently he was listed as the *2% top scientists released by Stanford University- Elsevier* in 2022. He serves as Editor, Co-Editor, and Associate Editor of several Journals. In particular: NATURE-Scientific Reports (Editorial Board Member), Mathematics - MDPI Section Financial Mathematics (Editor in Chief), Applied Sciences (Editor), Soft Computing, Dynamic Games and Applications, Mathematical Problems in Engineerings (Associate Editor). He is serving as a Referee of over 200 international scientific journals in economics, pure and applied mathematics indexed by SCOPUS, WoS, and MathSciNet.

Contents

Preface 3

Acknowledgements 4

About the Author 5

PART ONE: Pandemic Dynamics Forecasting 8

Chapter 1 9

An examination of a novel corona virus nonlinear susceptible-exposed infected-quarantine-recovered pandemic model with delay effect 9

Chapter 2 22

Modeling of COVID using machine learning techniques from the B-cell dataset to make predictions 22

Chapter 3 41

Using the detection approach of the hesitant fuzzy multi-criteria decision-making of the primary risk factor linked to the transmission of the Coronavirus 41

Chapter 4 49

Prevention of COVID'19 disease outbreak by optimum surveillance: Fractional order compartment model control 49

Chapter 5 70

Modeling the impact of the delay strategy on HIV/AIDS disease transmission dynamics 70

Chapter 6 81

Mathematical Fractal-Fractional Model for the Pakistani Corona Virus Situation 81

Chapter 7 102

Perturbed collage theorem for solving an uncertain inverse issue in Fractional Dynamical Systems 102

Chapter 8 116

Prerequisites for a Globally Stable COVID-19-Free State 116

Part two: ARTIFICIAL INTELLIGENCE AND COVID-19 DETECTION SYSTEMS 129

Chapter 9 130

A hybrid meta-heuristic feature selection technique called MRFGRO is used to screen the COVID-19 using deep features 130

Chapter 10 147

CNN models are fused fuzzy rank-based employing the Gompertz algorithm to evaluate COVID-19 CT images 147

Chapter 11 159

Graph CovidNet: A neural network-based model for identifying COVID19 from chest CT images and X-rays 159

Chapter 12 174

Predicting COVID-19 infection from chest CT scans using ET-NET, an ensemble of transfer learning models 174

PART THREE: PANDEMIC EFFECTS IN THE SOCIETY AND NEW FUTURE CHALLENGES 190
Chapter 13 191
A Model of Emotional Care Based on Multimodal Text Analysis of COVID-19 191
Chapter 14 205
An evolutionary-optimized Padé approximation method for studying the crowding impact in the Covid-19 model 205
Chapter 15 219
Role of various nanomaterials in COVID-19 treatment, prevention, and diagnosis 219

PART ONE: Pandemic Dynamics Forecasting

Chapter 1

An examination of a novel corona virus nonlinear susceptible-exposed infected-quarantine-recovered pandemic model with delay effect[1]

Introduction

The respiratory syndrome, severe acute respiratory syndrome, and the common cold are all diseases brought on by the coronavirus family of viruses. The COVID-19 corona virus was first discovered in humans. This is the brand-new one that has never before been observed in humans. A novel coated RNA coronavirus-2 known as SARS coronavirus-2 (SARS-COV-2) was discovered as the antibiotic and has undergone emergent evolution similar to that of SARS-COV-3. Both in the hospital and at homes, cases of infected individuals have been documented. The corona virus disease of 2019 (COVID19) has recently been deemed a pandemic by the World Health Organization (WHO). We determined that an updated review of cases worldwide might aid in identifying the dynamics of the corona virus due to the rapid dissemination of COVID-19.

This new corona virus has caused a lot of deaths worldwide. Typhoid fever and hepatitis B stochastic analyses were looked into by Arif et al. The dynamics of influenza, which are essentially coronavirus symptoms in humans, were reported by Baleanu et al. in the context of ongoing vaccination campaigns. Li et al. investigated how the human population's brain waves are categorized. Under the premise of individual responses and governmental action, Lin et al. presented the coronavirus model in the Chinese population. The features of coronavirus in the human population were studied by Shereen et al. Shim et al. investigated the kinetics of the coronavirus in the South Korean populace.

The dynamics of Middle East respiratory syndrome in the general population were presented by Tahir et al. Zhao et al. researched prevention strategies for the coronavirus pandemic. The World Health Organization (WHO) deemed the coronavirus outbreak to be a global problem. This initiative provides a platform for all scholars to propose novel delayed mathematical modeling in order to comprehend the extinction and survival of coronavirus as a result of the pandemic. Therefore, there is a great demand for mathematical models that are biologically coherent to describe the dynamics and transmission of COVID-19. Ivorra et al. used undiscovered infections to study the mathematical modeling of coronavirus illness.

---

1 *Landmark paper: Ali Raza, Ali Ahmadian, Muhammad Rafiq, Soheil Salahshour, Massimiliano Ferrara, "An analysis of a nonlinear susceptible-exposed-infected-quarantine-recovered pandemic model of a novel coronavirus with delay effect", Results in Physics, Volume 21, 2021, 103771, ISSN 2211-3797, https://doi.org/10.1016/j.rinp.2020.103771.*

A mathematical model for a new coronavirus was presented by Yang et al. using the case study of Wuhan, China. Sameni described a unique situation involving Covid-19 while presenting the mathematical modeling of various pandemic diseases. In their investigation of the fractional order model for the coronavirus outbreak, Rajagopal et al. made predictions about various outcomes in the sphere of a fractional derivative. Baleanu et al. used the Caputo-Fabrizio derivative in the realm of a fractional derivative to provide the coronavirus model. Goufo et al. looked into the joint dynamical study of the mathematical equilibrium between HIV and COVID-19. The dynamics of the coronavirus pandemic model with an ideal control approach and its transmission were explored by Kouidere et al.

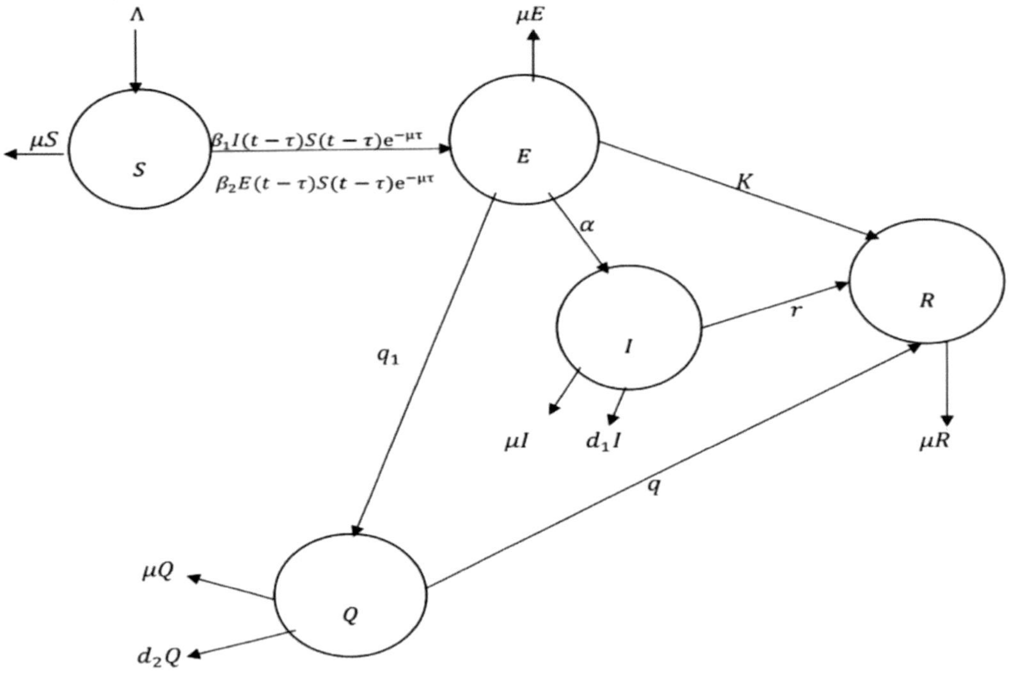

Fig. 1. Flow chart of the model.

Naveed et al. created a compartmentalized model of the coronavirus pandemic using delay techniques on a subgroup of humans who were exposed to it and then became systemically sick before recovering. In their study of the dynamics of the stochastic coronavirus model, Shatanawi et al. focused on the positivity, boundedness, consistency, and stability of the aforementioned goals. According to Atangana et al., the primary sources of the coronavirus pandemic's prevalence include the sea food market, asymptomatic people, and people with symptoms. How the fearsome virus might be eliminated with proper facemask use. On the other hand, a brilliant concept was presented by a scientist regarding the application of the fractal fractional derivative approach and the potential benefits of the lack-down strategy.

In the western African nations, Atangana et al. investigated the dynamics of the Ebola virus homologic fever. Give appropriate advice on how to treat such a terrible infection. The impact of delay strategies on the dynamics of HIV/AIDS transmission was investigated by Raza et al. Since there are no coronavirus vaccinations available anywhere in the globe, social isolation, quarantine, travel restrictions, extended holidays, and other delay factors have helped to contain the coronavirus epidemic. This is what drove us to create a coronavirus pandemic model with a delay strategy using mathematics. Due to the delay term, we have examined the delay differential equations in this work.

The following sections have guided the flow of the paper: Described the creation of the nonlinear delayed model and its equilibrium points in Section "Formulation of the Model." The local stability of the suggested model is covered in Section "Local stability." The proposed model's global stability is described in Section "Global stability." Before we conclude, we should mention the computer simulations in Section "Computer simulations" that use a different approach to solve the susceptible-exposed-infected-quarantine recovered pandemic models. The study's conclusion is offered in the end.

Formulation of the model

In this part, we took into account the entire human population, denoted by the number N. Define the population dynamics function $f:N \rightarrow [0,\infty]$, for allt$\in$ [-Ţ, 0], and $\tau \in [0, \infty)$. The susceptible human component is denoted by the letters S, exposed human component is denoted by the letters E, infected human component is denoted by the letters I, quarantined human component is denoted by the letters Q, and recovered human component is denoted by the letters R, as requested.

Assume that the model's nonnegative constants are Λ (which denotes the natural birth rate of humans), β_1 (which denotes the infection rate of infected humans who are interaction with susceptible humans), β_2 (which denotes the infection rate of exposed humans who are interaction with susceptible humans), q_1 (which denotes the rate of exposed humans who are directly moving to quarantine component), K (which denotes the rate of natural immunity),α (which denotes the rate of quarantine humans who are recovered), q (denotes the rate of quarantined people who recover), d_2 (denotes the rate of quarantined people who die after quarantine because they have a weak immune system or having disorders), and d_1 (denotes the rate of death of infected people owing to corona virus) μ(denotes the natural death rate of humans components). The dynamics using nonlinear delayed equations then go like this:

$$S'(t) = \Lambda - (\beta_1 I(t-\tau) + \beta_2 E(t-\tau))S(t)e^{-\mu\tau} - \mu S(t), \forall t \times \int [-\tau, 0], \tau \int [0, \infty). \quad (1)$$

$$E'(t) = (\beta_1 I(t-\tau) + \beta_2 E(t-\tau))S(t)e^{-\mu\tau} - q_1 E(t) - KE(t) - \alpha E(t) - \mu E(t), \forall t \in [-\tau, 0], \tau \in [0, \infty) \quad (2)$$

$$I'(t) = \alpha E(t) - rI(t) - \mu I(t) - d_1 I(t), \forall t \in [-\tau, 0]. \quad (3)$$

$$Q'(t) = q_1 E(t) - qQ(t) - \mu Q(t) - d_2 Q(t), \forall t \in [-\tau, 0]. \quad (4)$$

$$R'(t) = KE(t) + rI(t) + qQ(t) - \mu R(t), \forall t \in [-\tau, 0]. \quad (5)$$

with initial conditions $S_0 = S(0), E_0 = E(0), I_0 = I(0), Q_0 = Q(0), R_0 = R(0)$. Also, the feasible region of the equations (1) to (5) is $\Omega = \left\{(S, E, I, Q, R) : S+E+I+Q+R \leq \frac{\Lambda}{\mu}, S \geq 0, E \geq 0, I \geq 0, Q \geq 0, R \geq 0\right\}$. Note that, the solutions of a given system are positive and bounded, and lies in the feasible region.

Model Equilbria

According to the analysis, the system (1–5) has three different forms of equilibria: Virus absenteeism equilibrium (VAE) is represented by $C_1 = (S^\circ, E^\circ, I^\circ, Q^\circ, R^\circ) = (\Lambda/\mu, 0, 0, 0, 0)$, and virus incidence equilibrium (VIE) is represented by $C_2 = (S^1, E^1, I^1, Q^1, R^1)$,trivial equilibrium is represented by $C = (S, E, I, Q, R) = (0, 0, 0, 0, 0)$.

where, $S^1 = \frac{(q_1+K+\alpha+\mu)(r+\mu+d_1)}{\beta_1\alpha+\beta_2(r+\mu+d_1)e^{-\mu\tau}}$, $E^1 = \left(\frac{(\Lambda-\mu S^1)(r+\mu+d_1)}{\beta_1\alpha+\beta_2(r+\mu+d_1)S^1 e^{-\mu\tau}}\right)$, $I^1 = \frac{\alpha E^1}{r+\mu+d_1}$,

$Q^1 = \frac{q_1 E^1}{q+\mu+d_2}$ and $R^1 = \frac{KE^1+rI^1+qQ^1}{\mu}$.

Reproduction Number

In this section, we apply the next generation matrix (NGM) method to the systems (1) to (5) in order to calculate the transmission and transition matrices in order to determine the reproduction number:

$$\begin{bmatrix} E' \\ I' \\ Q' \\ R' \end{bmatrix} = \begin{bmatrix} \beta_2 Se^{-\mu\tau} & \beta_1 Se^{-\mu\tau} & 0 & 0 \\ 0 & 0 & 0 & 0 \\ 0 & 0 & 0 & 0 \\ 0 & 0 & 0 & 0 \end{bmatrix} \begin{bmatrix} E \\ I \\ Q \\ R \end{bmatrix} - \begin{bmatrix} (k+\alpha+\mu+q_1) & 0 & 0 & 0 \\ -\alpha & (r+\mu+d_1) & 0 & 0 \\ -q_1 & 0 & (q+\mu+d_2) & 0 \\ -k & -r & -q & \mu \end{bmatrix} \begin{bmatrix} E \\ I \\ Q \\ R \end{bmatrix}$$

After it, the virus absenteeism equilibrium (VAE) is C_1, followed by the transmission matrix F and transition matrix V,where

$$F=\begin{bmatrix} \frac{\beta_2 \Lambda e^{-\mu\tau}}{\mu} & \frac{\beta_1 \Lambda e^{-\mu\tau}}{\mu} & 0 & 0 \\ 0 & 0 & 0 & 0 \\ 0 & 0 & 0 & 0 \\ 0 & 0 & 0 & 0 \end{bmatrix}$$

$$V=\begin{bmatrix} (k+\alpha+\mu+q_1) & 0 & 0 & 0 \\ -\alpha & (r+\mu+d_1) & 0 & 0 \\ -q_1 & 0 & (q+\mu+d_2) & 0 \\ -k & -r & -q & \mu \end{bmatrix}.$$

Notice that, the spectral radius of FV^{-1}, is called reproduction number and $R_O = \frac{\Lambda e^{-\mu\tau}[\beta_2(r+\mu+d_1)+\beta_1\alpha]}{(k+\alpha+\mu+q_1)(r+\mu+d_1)}$.

Local Stability

In this part, we proved the well-posed theorem at both equilibria in the manner described below:

Theorem:. *The virus absenteeism equilibrium (VAE), $C_1 = (S^o, E^o, I^o, Q^o, R^o) = (\frac{\Lambda}{\mu}, 0, 0, 0, 0)$ is locally asymptotical stable (LAS) if $R_0 < 1$, forgiven $t \in [-\tau, 0]$ and $\tau \in [0, \infty)$.*

Proof:. *Considering the Jacobean matrix (JM) for the system (1–5) at C_1 is estimated as follows:*

$$J(C_1) = \begin{bmatrix} -\mu & -\frac{\beta_2 \Lambda e^{-\mu\tau}}{\mu} & -\frac{\beta_1 \Lambda e^{-\mu\tau}}{\mu} & 0 & 0 \\ 0 & \frac{\beta_2 \Lambda e^{-\mu\tau}}{\mu} - (k+\alpha+\mu+q_1) & \frac{\beta_1 S e^{-\mu\tau}}{\mu} & 0 & 0 \\ 0 & \alpha & -(r+\mu+d_1) & 0 & 0 \\ 0 & q_1 & 0 & -(q+\mu+d_2) & 0 \\ 0 & k & r & q & -\mu \end{bmatrix}$$

Notice that, two eigenvalues are repeated as, $\lambda_1 = -\mu < 0, \lambda_2 = -\mu < 0$ and third eigenvalue is

$\lambda_3 = -(q+\mu+d_2) < 0$

$$|J(C_1) - \lambda I| = \begin{vmatrix} \frac{\beta_2 \Lambda e^{-\mu\tau}}{\mu} - (k+\alpha+\mu+q_1) - \lambda & \frac{\beta_1 \Lambda e^{-\mu\tau}}{\mu} \\ \alpha & -(r+\mu+d_1) - \lambda \end{vmatrix} = 0.$$

$$\lambda^2 + \lambda(-\beta_2 a_1 + a_2 + a_3) + (a_3 a_2 - a_3 \beta_2 a_1 - \alpha \beta_1 a_1) = 0$$

where, $\frac{\Lambda e^{-\mu\tau}}{\mu} = a_1$, $(k+\alpha+\mu+q_1) = a_2$, $(r+\mu+d_1) = a_3$.

By using the second order Routh-Hurwitz Criterion as,

$a_3 + a_2 - \beta_2 a_1 > 0$, if $(k+\alpha+\mu+q_1) + (r+\mu+d_1) - \frac{\beta_2 \Lambda e^{-\mu\tau}}{\mu} > 0$, $R_0 = \frac{\beta_2 \Lambda e^{-\mu\tau}}{\mu(k+\alpha+2\mu+q_1+r+d_1)} < 1$ and $(a_3 a_2 - a_3 \beta_2 a_1 - \alpha \beta_1 a_1) > 0$, if $R_0 < 1$.

Hence, by Routh Hurwitz criteria, the given equilibria, C_1 is locally asymptotical stable because all eigenvalues are negative.

Theorem: The virus incidence equilibrium (VIE), $C_2 = (S^1, E^1, I^1, Q^1, R^1)$ is locally asymptotical stable (LAS) if $R_0 > 1$, forgiven $t \in [-\tau, 0]$ and $\tau \in [0, \infty)$.

Proof: Considering the Jacobean matrix (JM) for the system (1–5) at C_2 is estimated as follows: Notice that, the eigen values are, $\lambda 1 = -\mu < 0$, $\lambda 2 = -(q + \mu + d2) < 0$

$$J(C_2) = \begin{bmatrix} -\beta_1 I^1 e^{-\mu\tau} - \beta_2 E^1 e^{-\mu\tau} - \mu & -\beta_2 S^1 e^{-\mu\tau} & -\beta_1 S^1 e^{-\mu\tau} & 0 & 0 \\ \beta_1 I^1 e^{-\mu\tau} + \beta_2 E^1 e^{-\mu\tau} & \beta_2 S^1 e^{-\mu\tau} - (k+\alpha+\mu+q_1) & \beta_1 S^1 e^{-\mu\tau} & 0 & 0 \\ 0 & \alpha & -(r+\mu+d_1) & 0 & 0 \\ 0 & q_1 & 0 & -(q+\mu+d_2) & 0 \\ 0 & k & q & r & -\mu \end{bmatrix}$$

$$|J(C_2) - \lambda I| = \begin{vmatrix} -b_1 - \mu - \lambda & -b_2 & -b_4 \\ b_1 & b_2 - b_3 - \lambda & b_4 \\ 0 & \alpha & -b_5 - \lambda \end{vmatrix} = 0$$

$$\begin{aligned} &\lambda^3 + (b_1 - b_2 + b_3 + b_5 + \mu)\lambda^2 \\ &\quad + (b_1 b_3 + b_1 b_5 - b_2 b_5 + b_3 b_5 - b_2\mu + b_3\mu + b_5\mu - b_4\alpha)\lambda \\ &\quad + (b_1 b_3 b_5 - b_2 b_5 \mu + b_3 b_5 \mu - b_4 \alpha\mu) = 0 \end{aligned}$$

where, $b_1 = \beta_1 I^1 e^{-\mu\tau} + \beta_2 E^1 e^{-\mu\tau}$, $b_2 = \beta_2 S^1 e^{-\mu\tau}$, $b_3 = k + \alpha + \mu + q_1$, $b_4 = \beta_1 S^1 e^{-\mu\tau}$, $b_5 = r + \mu + d_1$ and $b_6 = q + \mu + d_2$.

By using third order Routh-Hurwitz Criterion,

$(b_1 - b_2 + b_3 + b_5 + \mu) > 0$, $(b_1 b_3 b_5 - b_2 b_5 \mu + b_3 b_5 \mu - b_4 \alpha\mu) > 0$, if $R_0 > 1$,

and

$(b_1 - b_2 + b_3 + b_5 + \mu)(b_1 b_3 + b_1 b_5 - b_2 b_5 + b_3 b_5 - b_2\mu + b_3\mu + b_5\mu - -b_4\alpha)\rangle(b_1 b_3 b_5 - b_2 b_5 \mu + b_3 b_5 \mu - b_4 \alpha\mu)$, if $R_0 > 1$.

Thus, we have concluded that all eigenvalues are negative and by Routh Hurwitz (RH) criteria, the given equilibria, C_2 is locally asymptotical stable.

Global stability

In this part, we proved the following well-known theorems at both equilibria:

-

Theorem:. *The virus absenteeism equilibrium (VAE), $C_1 = (S^o, E^o, I^o, Q^o, R^o) = (\frac{\Lambda}{\mu}, 0, 0, 0, 0)$ is globally asymptotical stable (GAS) if $R_0 < 1$, forgiven $t \in [-\tau, 0]$ and $\tau \in [0, \infty)$.*

Proof:. *Considering the Volterra Lyapunov function $V : \Omega \to R$, as well-defined:*

$$V = \left(S - S^o - S^o \log \frac{S}{S^o}\right) + E + I + Q + R, \forall (S, E, I, Q, R) \in \Omega.$$

$$\frac{dV}{dt} = \left(1 - \frac{S^o}{S}\right)\frac{dS}{dt} + \frac{dE}{dt} + \frac{dI}{dt} + \frac{dQ}{dt} + \frac{dR}{dt}.$$

$$\frac{dV}{dt} = (S - S^o)\left[\frac{\Lambda}{S} - (\beta_1 I + \beta_2 E)e^{-\mu\tau} - \mu\right] + (\beta_1 I + \beta_2 E)Se^{-\mu\tau} - (k + \alpha + \mu + q_1)E + \alpha E - (r + \mu + d_1)I + q_1 E - (q + \mu + d_2)Q + kE + rI + qQ - \mu R.$$

$$\frac{dV}{dt} = (S - S^o)\left[\frac{\Lambda}{S} - (\beta_1 I + \beta_2 E)e^{-\mu\tau} - \frac{\Lambda}{S^o} + (\beta_1 I^o + \beta_2 E^o)e^{-\mu\tau}\right] + (\beta_1 + \beta_2 E) Se^{-\mu\tau} - \mu E - (\mu + d_1)I - (\mu + d_2)Q - \mu R.$$

$$\frac{dV}{dt} = -\frac{\Lambda(S - S^o)^2}{(SS^o)} - \beta_1 e^{-\mu\tau}(S - S^o)(I - I^o) - \beta_2 e^{-\mu\tau}(S - S^o)(E - E^o) - \mu E\left(1 - \frac{\beta_2 Se^{-\mu\tau}}{\mu}\right) - \mu I\left(1 - \frac{\beta_1 Se^{-\mu\tau}}{\mu}\right) - dI - (\mu + d_2)Q - \mu R$$

$\Rightarrow \frac{dV}{dt} \leq 0$ for $R_0 < 1$, and $\frac{dV}{dt} = 0$ only if $S = S^0, E = I = A = R = 0$. At the end, that trajectory of the system (1) to (5) is unique solution on which $\frac{dV}{dt} = 0$ is C_1. Consequently, with the assumption of Lasalle invariance principle (LIP), C_1 is globally asymptotically stable (GAS).

Theorem: The virus incidence equilibrium (VIE), $C_2 = (S^1, E^1, I^1, Q^1, R^1)$ is globally asymptotical stable (GAS) if $R_0 > 1$, forgiven $t \in [-\tau, 0]$ and $\tau \in [0, \infty)$.

Proof: Considering the Volterra Lyapunov function V: Ω→R, as well defined

$$V = \left(S - S^1 - S^1 \log \frac{S}{S^1}\right) + \left(E - E^1 - E^1 \log \frac{E}{E^1}\right) + \left(I - I^1 - I^1 \log \frac{I}{I^1}\right) +$$

$\left(Q - Q^1 - Q^1 \log \frac{Q}{Q^1}\right) + \left(R - R^1 - R^1 \log \frac{R}{R^1}\right), \forall (S, E, I, Q, R) \in \Omega.$

$\frac{dV}{dt} = \left(1 - \frac{S^1}{S}\right) \frac{ds}{dt} + \left(1 - \frac{E^1}{E}\right) \frac{dE}{dt} + \left(1 - \frac{I^1}{I}\right) \frac{dI}{dt} + \left(1 - \frac{Q^1}{Q}\right) \frac{dQ}{dt} + \left(1 - \frac{R^1}{R}\right) \frac{dR}{dt}$

$\frac{dV}{dt} = (S - S^1)\left[\frac{A}{S} - (\beta_1 I + \beta_2 E)e^{-\mu\tau} - \mu\right] + (E - E^1)\left[\frac{\beta_1 ISe^{-\mu\tau}}{E} + \beta_2 Se^{-\mu\tau} - (q_1 + K + \alpha + \mu)\right] + (I - I^1)\left[\frac{\alpha E}{I} - (r + \mu + d_1)\right] + (Q - Q^1)\left[\frac{q_1 E}{Q} - (q + \mu + d_2)\right] + (R - R^1)\left[\frac{KE}{R} + \frac{rI}{R} + \frac{qQ}{R} - \mu\right].$

$\frac{dV}{dt} = (S - S^1)\left[\frac{\Lambda}{S} - (\beta_1 I + \beta_2 E)e^{-\mu\tau} - \frac{\Lambda}{S^1} - (\beta_1 I^1 + \beta_2 E^1)e^{-\mu\tau}\right] + (E - E^1)\left[\frac{\beta_1 ISe^{-\mu\tau}}{E} + \beta_2 Se^{-\mu\tau} - \frac{\beta_1 ISe^{-\mu\tau}}{E} + \beta_2 S^1 e^{-\mu\tau}\right] + (I - I^1)\left[\frac{\alpha E}{I} - \frac{\alpha E}{I^1}\right] + (Q - Q^1)\left[\frac{q_1 E}{Q} - \frac{q_1 E}{Q^1}\right] + (R - R^1)\left[\frac{KE}{R} + \frac{rI}{R} + \frac{qQ}{R} - \frac{KE}{R^1} - \frac{rI}{R^1} - \frac{qQ}{R^1}\right].$

$\frac{dV}{dt} = \frac{-\Lambda (S - S^1)^2}{SS^1} - (S - S^1)(I - I^1)\beta_1 e^{-\mu\tau} - (S - S^1)(E - E^1)\beta_2 e^{-\mu\tau} - \frac{-(E - E^1)^2 ISe^{-\mu\tau}}{EE^1} - \frac{\alpha E (I - I^1)^2}{II^1} - \frac{(Q - Q^1)^2 q_1 E}{QQ^1} - \frac{KE(R - R^1)^2}{RR^1} - \frac{rI(R - R^1)^2}{RR^1} - \frac{qQ(R - R^1)^2}{RR^1}.$

$\Rightarrow \frac{dV}{dt} \leq 0$for $R_0 > 1$, and$\frac{dV}{dt} = 0$ only if if$S = S^1, E = E^1, I = I^1, Q = Q^1$, $R = R^1$. At the end, that trajectory of the system (1) to (5) is unique solution on which $\frac{dV}{dt} = 0$ is C_2. Consequently, with the assumption of Lasalle invariance principle (LIP), C_1 is globally asymptotically stable (GAS).

Table 1: The parameters' source and their numerical values

Parameters	Values	Source
A	0.5	[8]
q_1	0.001	[10]
K	0.00398	[11]
α	0.0854302	[14]
μ	0.5	[14]
r	0.09871	[15]
d_1	0.0047876	[16]
d_2	0.000001231	[18]
q	0.1243	[20]
β_1	1.05	[21]
β_2	0.05(VAE) 1.05(VIE)	[21]

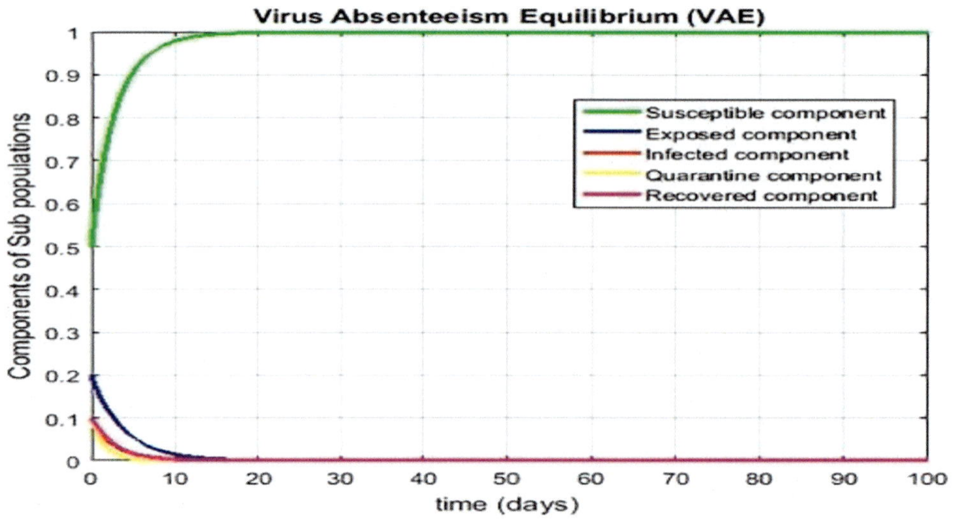

Fig 2: System [1] through [5] graph in the absence of the corona virus

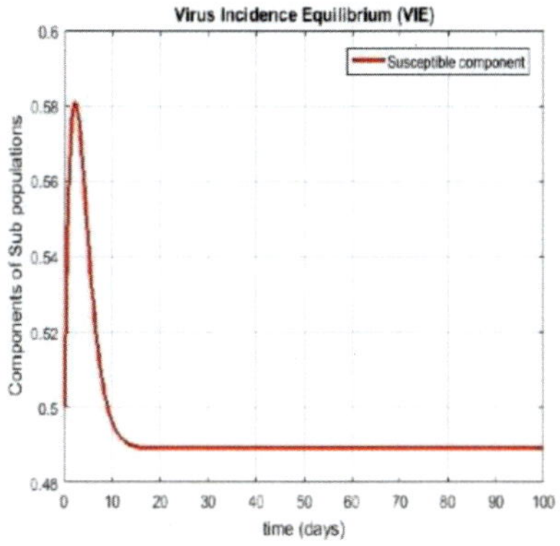

(a)

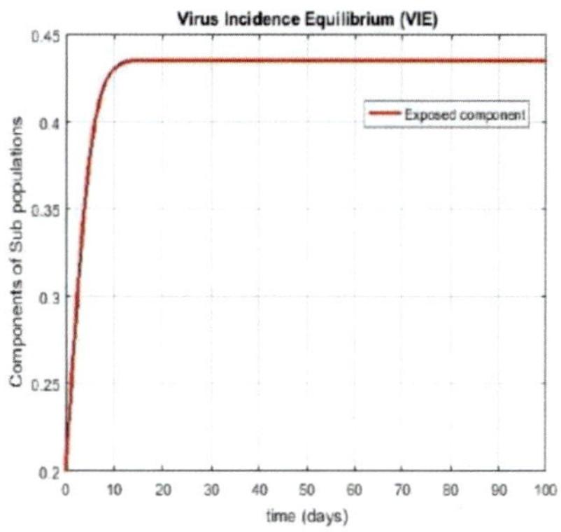

(b)

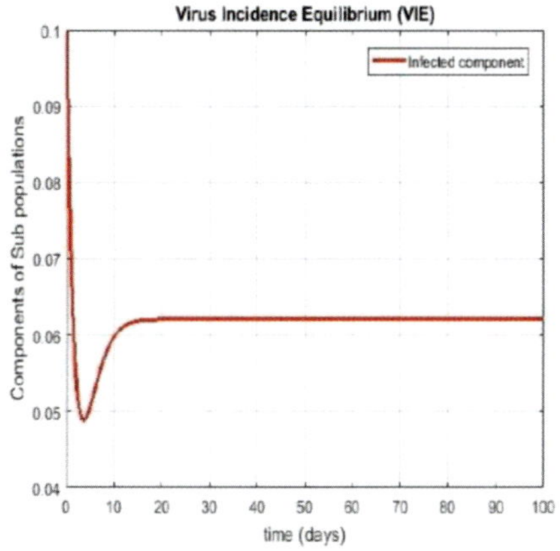

(c)

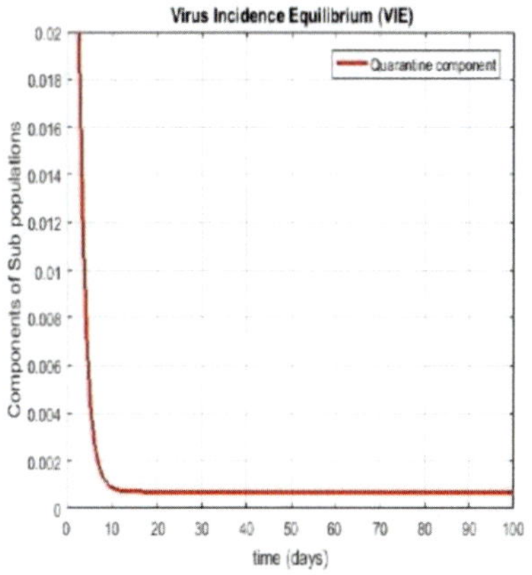

(d)

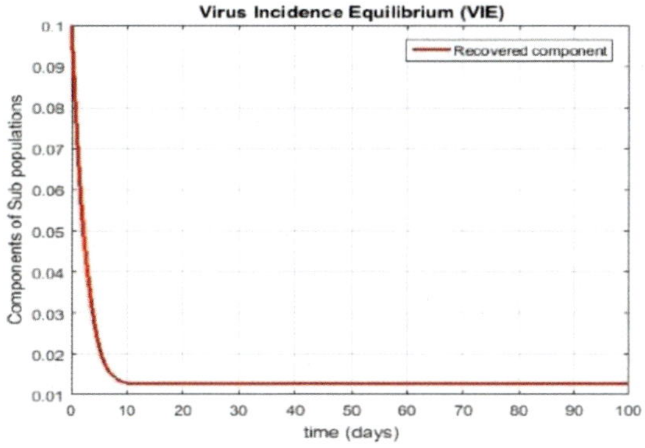

(e)

Fig 3: Graph showing the system from 1 to 5 in the case of a corona virus. (a) VIE-susceptible people (b) Humans exposed at VIE (c) VIE Infected Humans (d) confine humans at the VIE (e)Recovered people at VIE.

Effect of delay term on model reproduction rate

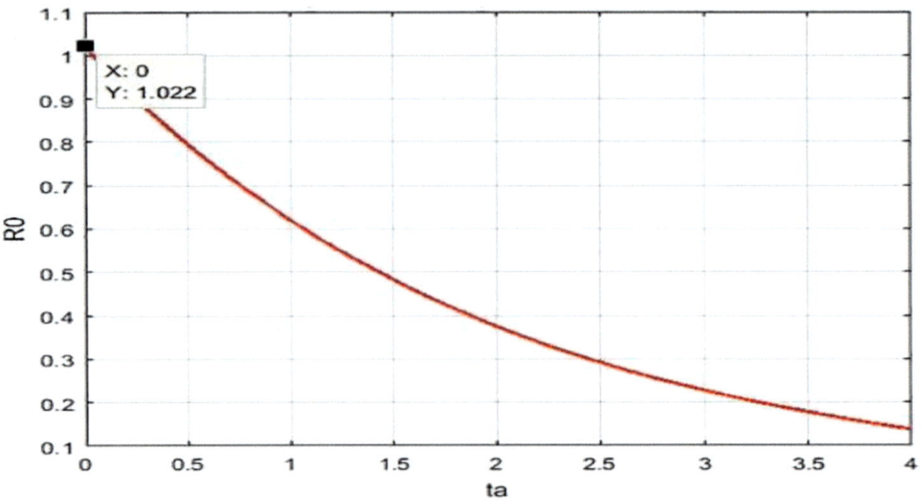

Fig 4: Effect of the delay term on the reproduction time plot

Delay term's impact on the infected component

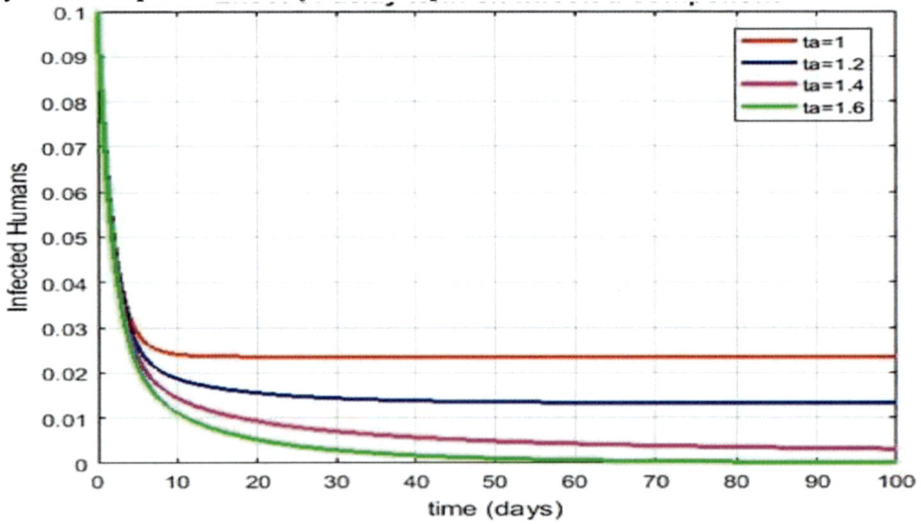

Fig 5: Diagram of an infected person showing the impact of various delay term values at the system's virus incidence equilibrium (VIE).

Using the physical values of the parameters listed in Table 1, we discussed the simulations of Equations (1) to (5) in this section.

Example 1:

Virus absenteeism equilibrium simulation: This section aims to provide the graph of virus absenteeism equilibrium (VAE) using the provided real data, where $R_0 = 0.1702 < 1$ is the value of the threshold/reproduction number. The system eventually reaches $C_1 = (\Lambda/\mu, 0, 0, 0, 0)$. Using the values of the parameters indicated in Table 1 and touching to the required actual equilibria of the model, Fig. 2 illustrates the solution of the system (1) to (5) without delay.

Example 2:

Simulation at virus incidence equilibrium:In this illustration, we show the graph of viral incidence equilibrium (VIE) for the real data presented, where $R_0 = 1.0222 > 1$ is the reproduction number value. The system eventually reaches the C_2 = 0.4891, 0.4353, 0.0621, 0.00069721, and 0.0128). Using the settings of the parameters supplied in Table 1, Fig. 3 shows the solution of the system (1) to (5) without delay and converges to the system's real equilibria as desired.

Example 3:
Simulation of the impact of the delay term on the number of reproductions: Let, $\tau = 1.022$. We can see that, even if the system switches from the viral incidence equilibrium to the virus absenteeism equilibrium, the successful deployment of delay tactics can lower the value of the threshold number. As a result, the corona virus is absent and stable. However, Fig. 4 demonstrates that infection could be managed by the appropriate application of various delay strategies, as required.
Example 4:
Simulation of the delay term's impact on the model's infected component: Let's now assume that has different values (delay term). We may observe that as the infected gradually decreases to zero, infection is under control. Because of this, Fig. 5 demonstrates that the delay strategy or delay tactics, such as vaccination, quarantine, travel restrictions, holidays, and distancing measures, etc. are essential to controlling the present corona virus strain.

Conclusion

In the current work, we used the method of delayed term mathematical modeling to investigate the dynamics of the corona virus model in the human population. The entire population has been divided up into five subpopulations. In order to understand the dynamics of the corona virus in humans, we have analyzed a system of nonlinear delayed differential equations. Using well-known theorems, we have demonstrated its stability both locally and globally. We have investigated the reliability of the delay period with respect to the proportion of infected humans and the rate of reproduction. The use of delay terms affects the studied system's dynamics.

Additionally, delay tactics like social withdrawal, placement of isolation, extension of holidays, and travel restrictions are useful to get beyond the terrible corona virus scenario. Our research can be expanded in the future to include delayed stochastic spatiotemporal and fraction order models.Stochastic differential equations of fractional order and fuzzy differential equations can be used to create numerical algorithms for the simulation of epidemic diseases. We have come to the conclusion that the dynamics of pandemic models are significantly influenced by the analysis of delayed mathematical modeling (DMM).

Chapter 2

Modeling of COVID using machine learning techniques from the B-cell dataset to make predictions[2]

Introduction

B-cells,where B is an acronym for Fabricius' bursa. B cells are the kind of cells that produce antibodies, a Y-shaped protein structure, to fight against viruses and bacteria. These antibodies are particular to certain infections that may surround a cell's surface and prepare it for death by other immune cells. By acquiring various protein epitope areas, B-cells react in vivo by generating a huge number of antigen-specific antibodies. They carry out the function of antibodies in attaching to other antigen proteins. In addition to B-cells, the pandemic coronavirus may infect a person's respiratory system. The family of viruses known as coronaviruses is to blame for this pandemic's existence. The family contains a number of dangerous viruses, including SARS-CoV, SARS-CoV-2, MERS-CoV, and several others divided into classes. The bulk of coronavirus cases among all other family members, notably in kids and the elderly, have been caused by moderate acute respiratory coronavirus syndrome (SARS-CoV) and severe acute respiratory coronavirus syndrome (SARS-CoV-2). SARS-CoV-2 is clearly more deadly than SARS-CoV according to comparisons between the two coronavirus family members. The primary cause of the spread of coronavirus is these two viruses. Therefore, determining which of the two viruses a patient has will assist build an accurate diagnosis. So take into account the COVID-19/SARS B-cell epitope prediction dataset's B-cell dataset.

This dataset was created through analysis of data from the Universal Protein Resource and the Immune Epitope Database (IEDB) (UniProt). Three sub-datasets of the dataset show that SARS-CoV and SARS-CoV-2 could be predicted using the attributes. The patient's health status is fully described in the B-cell dataset, which could be used to train the machine and anticipate test cases. For the implementation, various machine learning models including SVM, KNN, AdaBoost, Gradient Boosting, neural network (NN), etc., are used. The first section of the paper focuses on using a B-cell dataset to predict SARS-CoV after implementing all desired neural networks and machine learning models. In order to predict the presence of the SARS-CoV-2 virus in a human body, the B-cell dataset and the SARS-CoV dataset are combined. As a result, the paper's sole focus is on using various machine learning models and algorithms to predict SARS-CoV and SARS-CoV2.

---

2 *Landmark paper: Nikita Jain, Srishti Jhunthra, Harshit Garg, Vedika Gupta, Senthilkumar Mohan, Ali Ahmadian, Soheil Salahshour, Massimiliano Ferrara, "Prediction modelling of COVID using machine learning methods from B-cell dataset", Results in Physics, Volume 21, 2021, 103813, ISSN 2211-3797, https://doi.org/10.1016/j.rinp.2021.103813.*

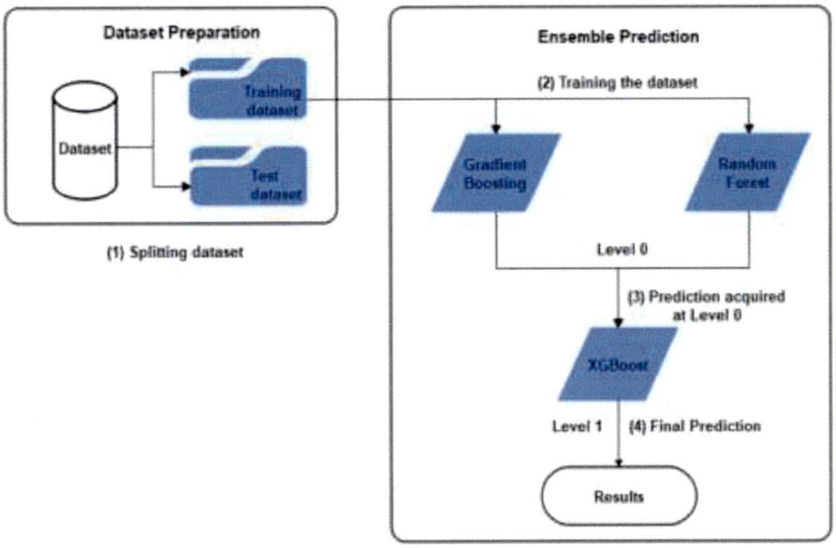

Fig 1: Stacked group

The paper makes a contribution by:
1. Analyzing and predicting the SARS-CoV and SARS-CoV-2 viruses using the B-cells dataset, which contains data on the quantity of proteins and peptides in a human body as well as all of their related information.
2. We suggest a stacked ensemble algorithm that is built using various baseline models and predefined ensembles.

Materials

Algorithm for ensemble learning and planned work

The term "ensembles" describes an approach that combines many machine learning models into a single effective model. By integrating weak predicting models to create a strong predicting model, ensembles are used to increase accuracy. The ensemble utilized in this work is a layered ensemble with XGBoost on the outer layer and random forest with gradient boosting at the inner layer.

Models for supervised learning

A method called supervised learning is used to create a set of decision rules that may aid in the prediction of a known result. Models are the name given to these rules. Therefore, supervised learning models are those that apply a set of decision rules to signal an existing result. Supervised learning models come in a variety of shapes and sizes. The models utilized in this investigation are listed below:

1. Suppor vector machine (SVM)
2. K - the closest neighbors (KNN)
3. Simple Bayes
4. Inference Trees
5. Boosting of gradients
6. The sixth logistic regression
7. XGBoost

8. AdaBoost

All of these supervised learning models were investigated and put into practice in order to train and test the computer on the dataset in order to predict SARS-CoV and SARS-CoV-2, respectively.

Vector support machine (SVM)

A support vector machine (SVM) is a simple yet effective supervised learning method for data prediction. SVM may be used to tackle difficulties with classification and regression. When addressing classification challenges, SVM is helpful in creating high dimensional feature spaces. The model produced effective results when the probability was set to "True" and the regularization value was assumed to be 100.

K-neighbors (KNN)

K-nearest neighbors are also utilized to address classification and regression issues, unlike SVM. KNN, however, stands out from the other algorithms. KNN is a lazy learning method that creates no models. Predictions in this method are made directly from the training dataset. In this investigation, we used 15 as the number of the n closest neighbors.

Naive Bayes

Naive Bayes is a Bayes' Theorem-based classification supervised learning model. It belongs to a family of algorithms where each member is based on the Bayes' Theorem. This indicates that every pair is independent of one another throughout the categorization process. Thus, a "gaussian nb classifier" is used to train the naive bayes model.

Random forest

The random forest requires an estimator (n estimator), or the number of trees, and max (maximum) features, or the maximum features to be chosen as hyperparameters for the tree. To train and test our random forest model in this research, the n estimator is set to 100, and the max features parameter is set to 5.

Gradient boosting

Another supervised learning strategy used to handle classification and regression issues is gradient boosting. It forecasts weak model ensembles and combines them to create a powerful supervised learning model. The estimator, which refers to the number of boosting steps the model needs, is a parameter in the gradient boosting model. When n estimator was set to 100, the model was shown to be more accurate in its prediction of outcomes.

Logistic regression

Binary regression is a kind of logistic regression. A statistical model creates an independent binary variable that is crucial to make predictions using the logistic function technique. The regularization value was set to 100 for training the logistic regression model to predict SARS-CoV and SARS-CoV-2 viruses.

AdaBoost

Adaptive boosting is known as AdaBoost. The first effective boosting method created for binary classification issues was called AdaBoost. This technique may be used as an ensemble and for a variety of tasks, including regression and classification. This technique employs an iterative methodology, which means it continues going back and fixing the flaws in weak classifiers until it creates a strong combined classifier. In this work, AdaBoost employs a decision tree classifier with a maximum depth of 2, where the hyperparameter is the maximum depth of the tree.

Xgboost

The gradient boosting model's optimum solution is called XGBoost. It is portable, adaptable, and very effective. It offers a parallel tree boosting approach and makes use of the gradient boosting architecture to quickly and accurately handle a number of issues. The boosting stage, the maximum depth of the tree, and the learning rate are a few of the hyperparameters of

XGBoost. In this research, the XGBoost model's n estimators are assumed to be 1000, its maximum tree depth to be 4, and its learning rate to be 0.005.

Table 1:Attributes

Attributes.

S. no.	Attributes	Description	Data type
1.	parent_protein_id	Unique parent protein ID	Categorical
2.	protein_seq	Parent protein sequence	Categorical
3.	start_position	Start position of the peptide	Numerical
4.	end_position	End position of the peptide	Numerical
5.	peptide_seq	Peptide sequence	Categorical
6.	chou_fasman	Peptide feature, Beta turn	Numerical
7.	emini	Relative surface accessibility	Numerical
8.	kolaskar_tongaonkar	Antigenicity	Numerical
9.	parker	Hydrophobicity	Numerical
10.	isoelectric_point	Protein feature	Numerical
11.	aromacity	Protein feature	Numerical
12.	hydrophobicity	Protein feature	Numerical
13.	stability	Protein feature	Numerical

Neuronal network techniques

In a neural network, which is a component of learning algorithms, various layer building methods are used to the data in order to predict and evaluate it. A kind of artificial neural networks known as a multilayer perceptron (MLP) has several characteristics and fully linked hidden layers. In this work, the MLP had three hidden layers, each of which was followed by a dropout layer. There were 64, 32, and 16 neurons in each buried layer, correspondingly. The resultant output at the output layer uses sigmoid as its activation function following the sequence of all the hidden and dropout layers.

Methods

The COVID-19/ SARS B-cell epitope prediction dataset was used to accurately predict the viruses SARS-CoV and SARS-CoV-2. As a result, transformation of the dataset was required before implementation. The summary of the dataset's transformation and subsequent division to forecast SARS-CoV and SARS-CoV-2 viruses is provided below:

Description of a dataset

Three sub-datasets make up the COVID-19/SARS B-cell epitope prediction dataset. The predictions for the SARS-CoV and SARS-CoV-2 viruses were made using these sub-datasets in turn. These are the three sub-datasets:

1. B-cell data: Model training largely used the B-cell dataset. It was made up of patient data that will be used to train machine learning algorithms. The total number of 14,362 peptides and 757 proteins in this collection is 14,387 rows. In comparison to SARS-Cov, the prediction outcomes aided in the calculation of the learning models' accuracy and precision dataset. The SARS-CoV dataset was combined with the B-cell dataset after the analysis of the SARS-CoV findings. As a result, the pooled information corroborated the prediction of SARSCoV-2, the main coronavirus cause.

2. Dataset for SARS-CoV: The SARS-CoV dataset was also utilized as a training dataset for predicting SARS-CoV-2, which has been widely distributed over the globe. The resulting dataset is a labeled dataset with 520 rows. This dataset was used to estimate the models' accuracy and precision when applied to the B-cell dataset, which contributed in the prediction of the SARS-CoV virus.

3. COVID dataset: The intended dataset was the COVID dataset. This dataset was used to evaluate SARS-CoV-2. This dataset was not very useful, but it improved the results by testing the model with it, which provided the accuracy and AUC ratings of the models used.The datasets were then studied in Section "Data analysis," and the needed qualities were chosen using feature engineering.

Data Analysis:

There are 13 features shared by all three datasets derived from the COVID-19/SARS B-cell epitope prediction dataset. These characteristics provide data about the patient that may be used to forecast the presence of SARS-CoV and SARSCoV-2. The explanation of each attribute in the dataset is shown in Table 1. The identical characteristics listed in Table 1 are present in all three datasets, which include the B-cell dataset, the SARS-CoV dataset, and the COVID dataset.

Feature selection:

Feature selection is a way for determining the significance of certain qualities. The weighting of qualities grows in accordance with their importance, which helps to provide accurate results. 13 comparable features are shared by all three datasets in this study (ref. to Table 1). The beginning and ending positions of the peptides were represented by two properties with the names start position and end position. Because these two properties display the same functionality, we consolidated them into one property, peptide length. The formula for the peptide length property, which is created by merging the start position and end position attributes, is shown in Eq.

$$\text{peptide length} = \text{start position} - \text{end position} \tag{1}$$

After giving each of the 13 traits a feature priority score. As shown in Fig. 1, the feature importance plot was made, and three attributes—parent protien id, protein seq, and peptide seq—showed null significance.

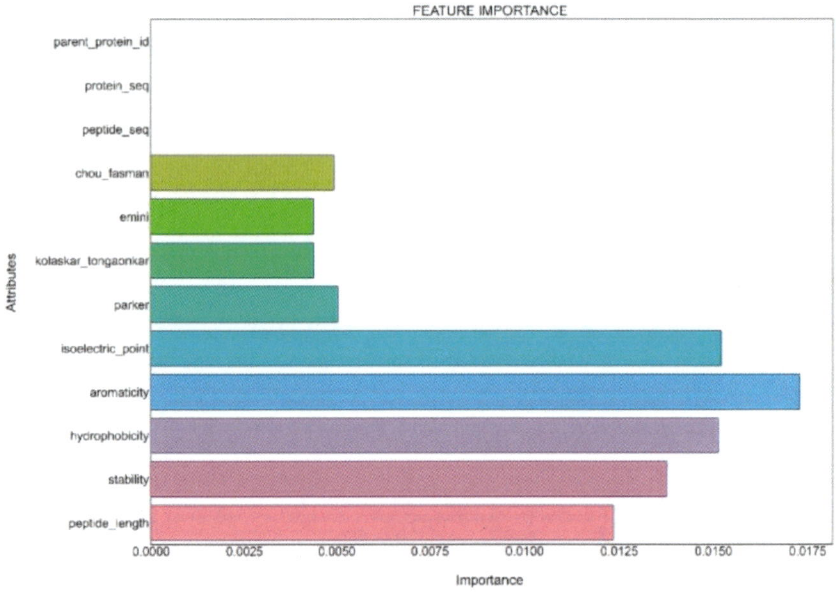

Fig 2: Feature significance

Using the idea of feature engineering, Fig. 2 displays a bar graph of feature significance. The process of picking various characteristics from a raw dataset using data mining methods is known as feature engineering. Choosing characteristics enables the acquisition of more precise and optimum outcomes. As a result, it enhances machine learning models' overall performance. The graphs make it very evident that the characteristics parent protein id, protein seq, and peptide seq are completely unimportant in comparison to each other. Therefore, it is obvious that all of these traits are unnecessary and may be removed. Therefore, after eliminating the three aforementioned characteristics. Nine characteristics that may substantially predict SARS-CoV and SARS-CoV2, respectively, are included in the final dataset. According to the findings, which are shown in Fig. 3, the presented dataset is regularly distributed. There are no missing points in the dataset for any of the attributes considered. This demonstrates that the whole dataset, which includes all nine characteristics, is useful and should be taken into account for the development and evaluation of various machine learning models.

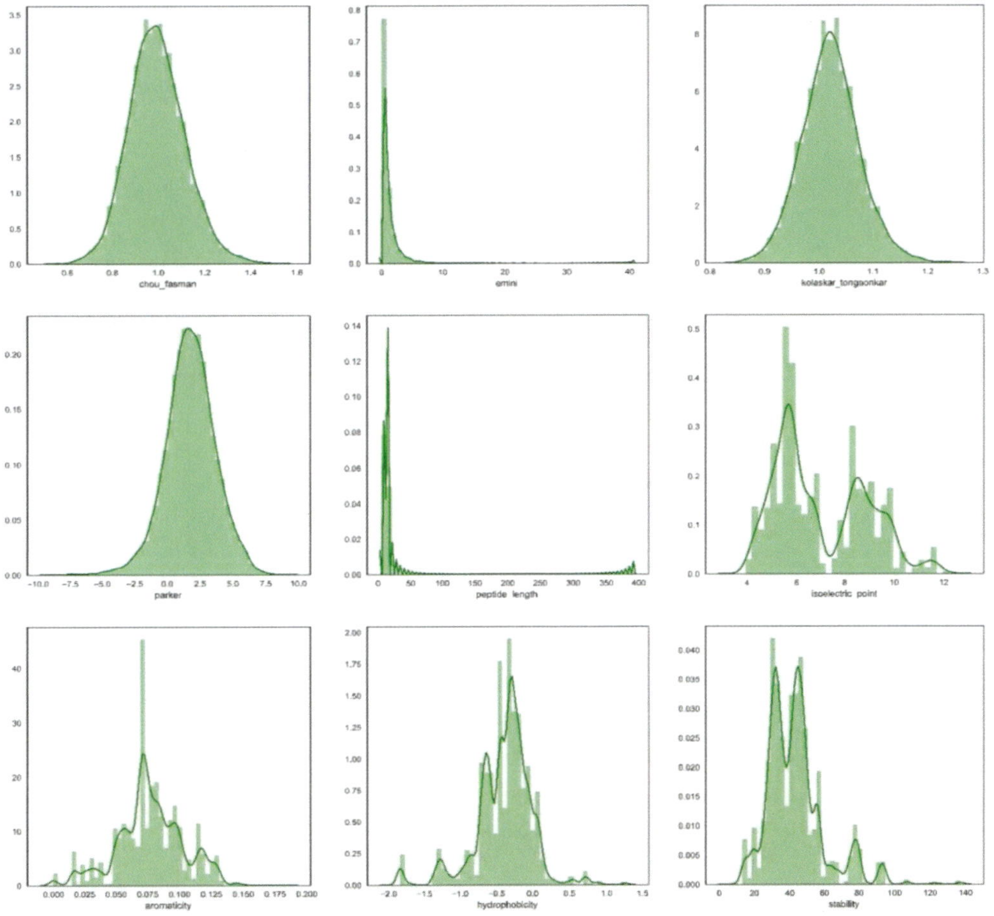

Fig 3: Plots illustrating the data's distribution for certain qualities.

As a result, Fig. 3 clearly demonstrates that the dataset is not well preserved and that all necessary attributes are included in the dataset with no missing points. The training and test datasets were acquired after the final dataset. The dataset was subjected to the application of many machine learning models and algorithms, including SVM, KNN, Naive Bayes, random forest, AdaBoost, gradient boosting, XGBoost, MLP-NN, and the stacked ensemble. The general explanation of the whole process employed in this work is shown in Fig. 4. The graphic shows feature selection, dataset extraction, and several dataset combinations used to forecast SARS-CoV and SARS-CoV-2, respectively. The Figure also displays each model and stacked ensemble that were used to forecast the viruses that cause coronaviruses.

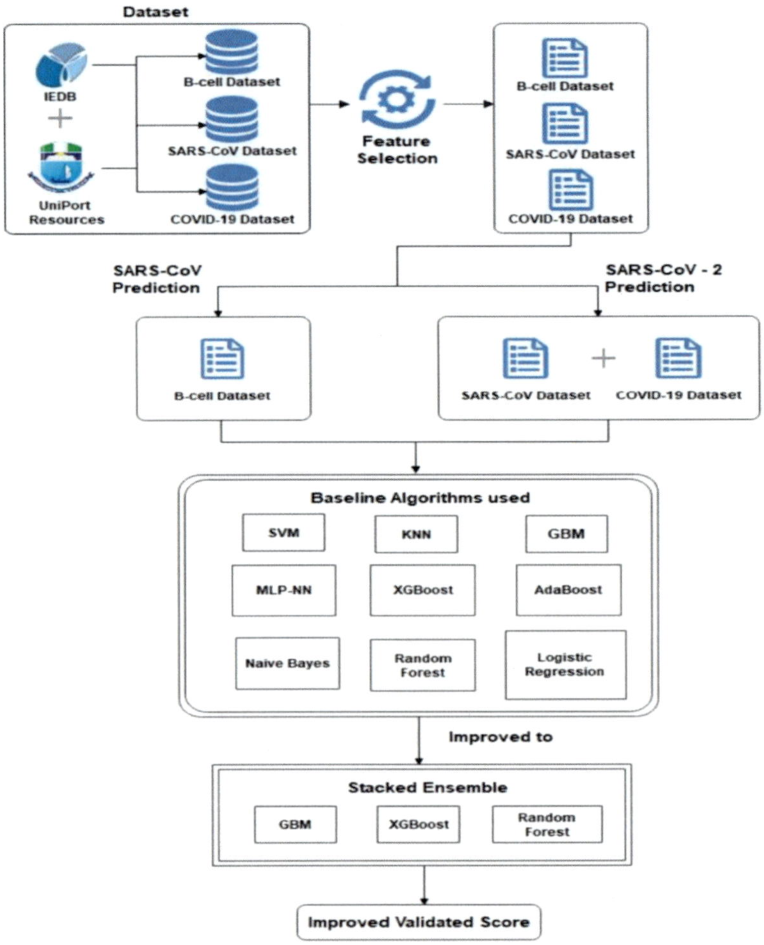

Fig 4: Summary

After gathering the necessary data to accurately forecast the coronavirus diseases caused by SARS-CoV and SARSCoV-2, a variety of machine learning models have been applied to the dataset.

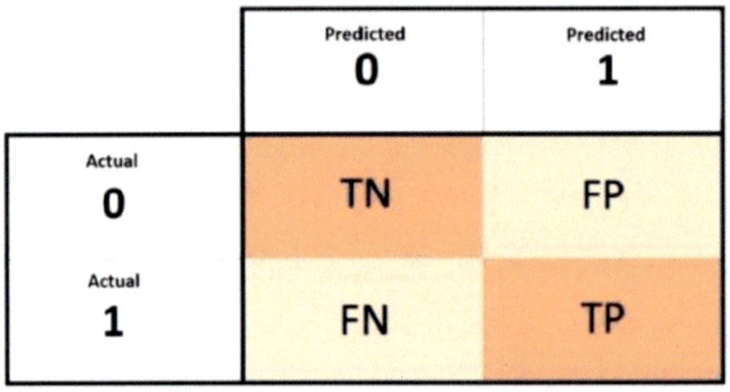

Fig 5: Confusion matrix structure.

The coronavirus family member SARS-CoV was mostly predicted using the B-cell dataset. A validation dataset and a test dataset were created from the B-cell dataset. Several machine learning models were then applied to it after splitting. The confusion matrix and ROC curve of each machine learning model and technique were supplied by the dataset's testing results. The suggested ensemble's training period ranged from 2 to 4 seconds.

The receiver operating characteristic curve is sometimes referred to as the ROC curve. It is a visual depiction of the ratio of false positives to genuine positives. It is used to examine the

AUC score, or the area under the curve, which gauges the overall effectiveness of all potential categorization criteria. The AUC value, as indicated in the Eq., illustrates the accuracy by submitting more true values, increasing the model's accuracy.

$$\text{Accuracy score} = \frac{Correctpredictions}{Allpredictions} = \frac{TP+TN}{TP+FN} \quad (2)$$

True positive and true negative values are denoted by TP and TN, respectively, whereas false negative values are denoted by FN. The confusion matrix, as seen in Fig. 5, made it simple to determine all these values. As a result, the error approximation for all used machine learning models and algorithms could also be studied and estimated. There are three ways to calculate errors: mean average error (MAE), root means square error (RMSE), and mean square error (MSE). Using the formula stated in Eq, mean average error (MAE) emphasizes the average error of the anticipated value vs actual value.

$$\text{MAE}=\frac{1}{n}\sum|y-\hat{y}| \quad (3)$$

The term "root mean square error" describes methods for estimating errors on relatively large scales. It uses the mean square value, which may be computed by calculating the square root of the difference between the predicted and actual values, as shown in the Eq (4).

$$\text{MAE}=\frac{1}{n}\sum|y-\hat{y}| \quad (4)$$

By taking the square root of the MSE value after computing the MSE value, one can easily get the RMSE. MSE and MAE are strongly favored over RMSE because RMSE provides a more accurate and exact inaccuracy of the models used.

$$\text{RMSE}=\sqrt{\frac{1}{n}\sum|y-\hat{y}|} \quad (5)$$

These are the elements that support the conclusions drawn by various machine learning models. It illustrates the models' precision and accuracy, which highlight the model's overall performance. The outcomes of using all machine learning models and algorithms used to forecast SARS-CoV and SARS-CoV-2 virus are shown below. The test and validation findings for identifying the coronavirus that causes the SARS-CoV virus are presented first in the order of the results. Additionally, the validation output is shown, including every ROC curve, confusion matrix, and final table summarizing the validation scores and error approximation.

The outcomes produced by using the B-cell dataset with various machine learning models are fully and in-depth described in the first part of the findings. The SARS-CoV virus's predicted outcomes are all shown in this results section.These models include SVM, KNN, Naive Bayes, Random forest, Gradient boosting, XGBoost, Logistic regression, AdaBoost, MLP-NN, and a stacked ensemble.

After utilizing the B-cell dataset applied to the SVM machine learning model to predict SARS-CoV, the confusion matrix and ROC curve are shown in Figs. 6 and 7. The prediction's real positive and true negative values are represented by the diagonal components (see Fig. 5).

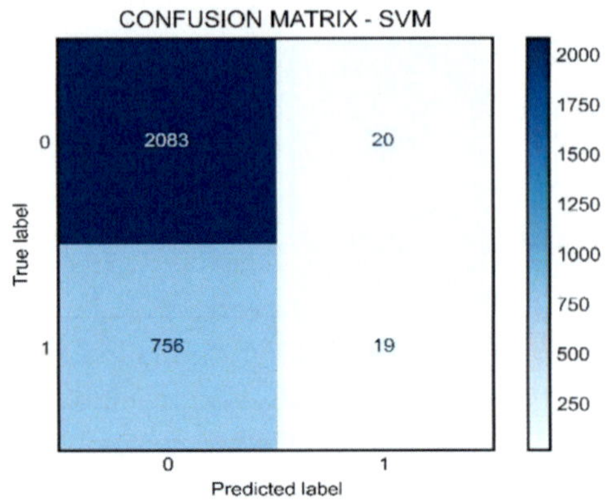

Fig 6: SVM confusion matrix.

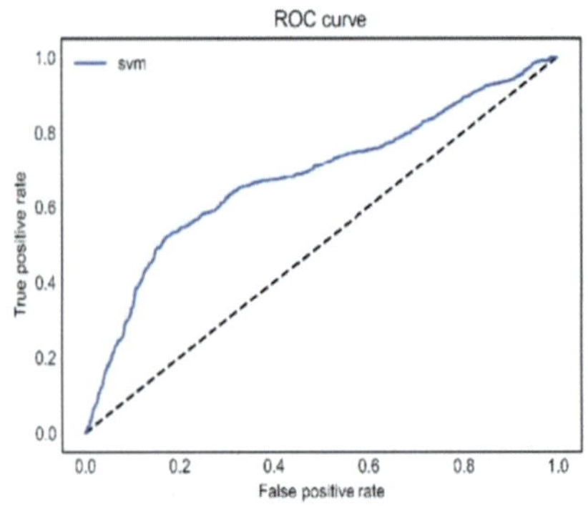

Fig 7: SVM ROC curve

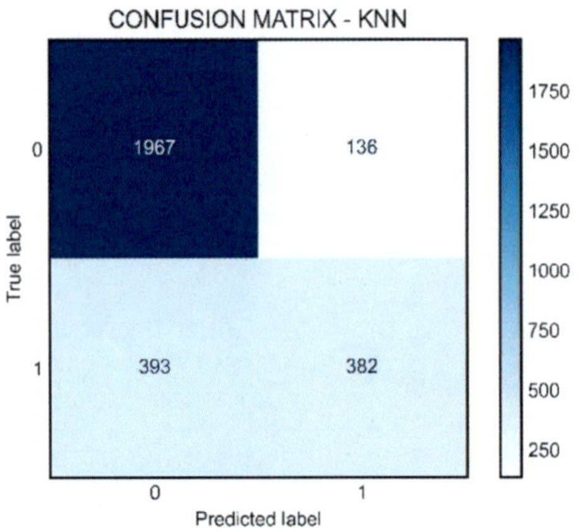

Fig 8: KNN confusion matrix

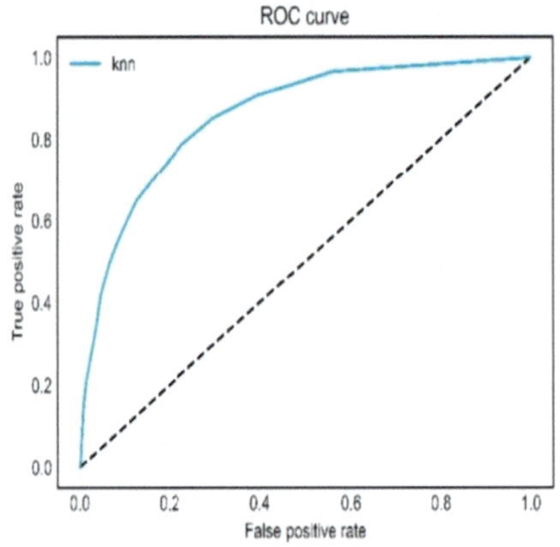

Fig 9: KNN ROC curve

The ROC curve demonstrates that the prediction is acceptable and may get an AUC score of more than 0.5. (ref. to Table 2).The confusion matrix and ROC curve after the application of the KNN model are shown in Figs. 8 and 9.By achieving an AUC score of 0.858, the ROC curve demonstrates that the expected output is effective and has produced an accurate outcome. When the curve shifts to the left top corner, the ROC curve displays correct findings.

The result generated after using the Nave Bayes is shown in Figs. 10 and 11. The ROC curve was influenced by an equal amount of false-negative values that the confusion matrix predicted together with a good number of actual positive values. As a consequence, the ROC curve did not accurately reflect many outcomes. However, because the AUC is more than 0.6, we may infer that the outcomes are just adequate.

Figures 12 and 13 show the outcomes of the random forest model. These images show the ROC and confusion matrix that were produced after utilizing random forest to forecast the SARS-CoV virus. The AUC score of the ROC curve, which is 0.919, is the highest among all the machine learning models used in this work. The ROC curve, which is completely tilted towards the top left corner and indicates that the model used has outperformed all others, clearly demonstrates that it can predict outcomes with the greatest degree of accuracy.

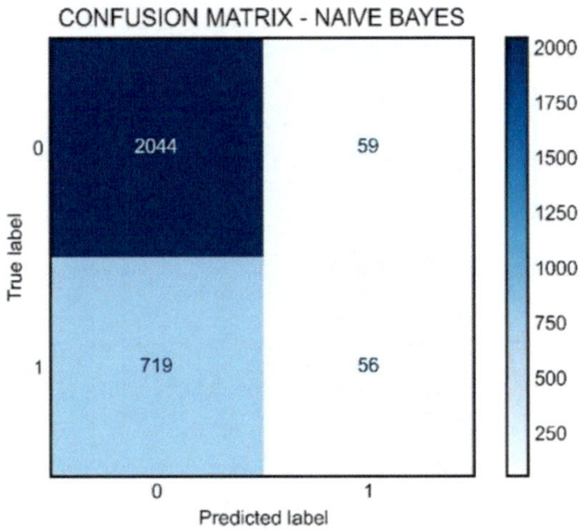

Fig 10: Matrix of confusion for Naive Bayes.

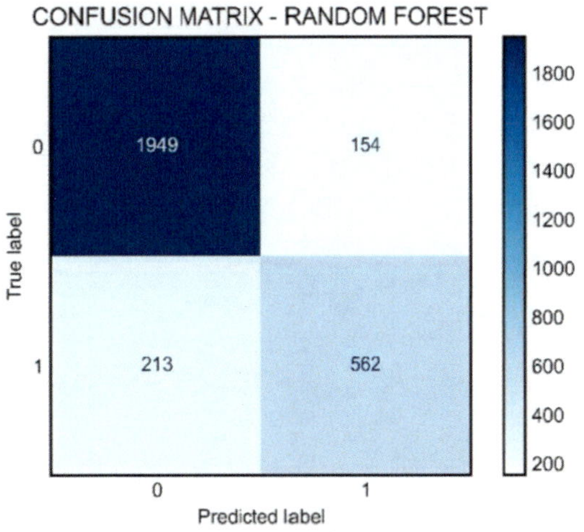

Fig 12: Random forest confusion matrix

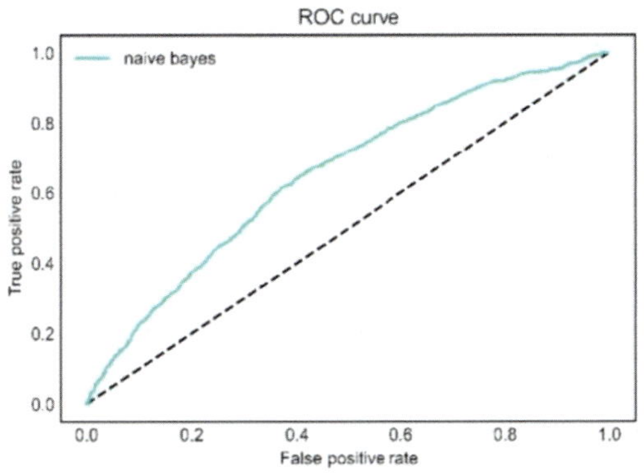

Fig 11: Naive Bayes' ROC curve.

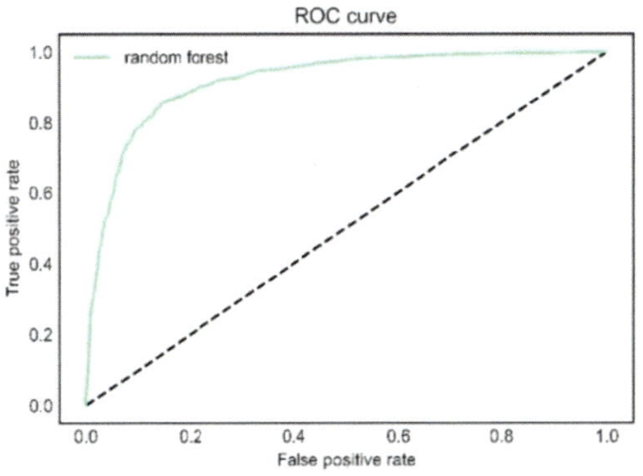

Fig 13: Random forest ROC curve

Table 2: Results of SARS-CoV validation.

Model	Validation AUC	Validation accuracy (%)	MSE	RMSE	MAE
SVM	0.682	73.4190	0.2658	0.5156	0.2658
KNN	0.858	81.6192	0.1838	0.4287	0.1838
Naïve-Bayes	0.652	72.9673	0.2703	0.5199	0.2703
Random Forest	0.909	85.5803	0.2365	0.4863	0.2365
GBM	0.868	81.7582	0.1824	0.4271	0.1824
Logistic	0.652	72.6546	0.2735	0.5229	0.2735
AdaBoost	0.869	82.6963	0.1730	0.4159	0.1730
XGBoost	0.871	81.3065	0.1869	0.4323	0.1869
Ensemble	0.919	87.2481	0.1442	0.3797	0.1442
MLP - NN	0.809	77.4843	0.2252	0.4745	0.2252

After using the random forest model, which is an inherent Ensemble, additional models are utilized to make more accurate predictions and analyze SARSCoV virus-caused coronavirus illness findings. Figs. 14 and 15 illustrate another inbuilt ensemble, gradient boosting, and its outcomes on the dataset. It had numerous false-negative readings, but actual positive values readily overcame them. The ROC curve's AUC value is 0.868.

16 and 17 exhibit logistic regression findings. This model has poor accuracy and AUC. If needed to forecast particular content, it might be employed on a short dataset. The figure's

ROC curve is adequate and might be applied on a small dataset for more accurate findings. AdaBoost is another ensemble used to predict SARS-CoV. Figs. 18 and 19 show the confusion matrix and ROC curve for the B-cell dataset. Better models are ROC curve and confusion matrix. Increasing true positive value in the confusion matrix illustrates the ROC curve's increased sensitivity and cutoff value. The observed cut-off value is the graph point where "sensitivity + specificity 1" is greatest.

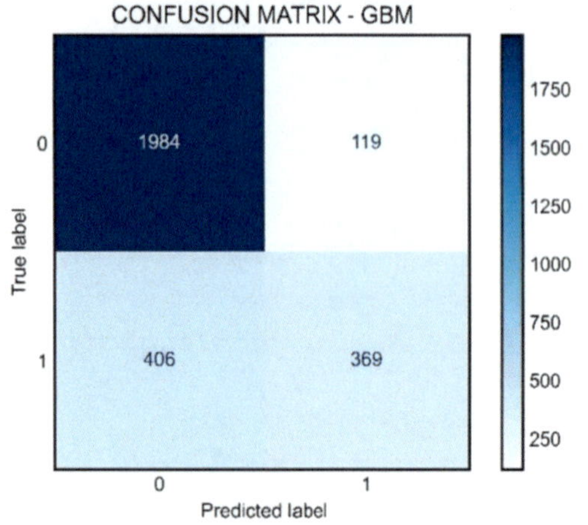

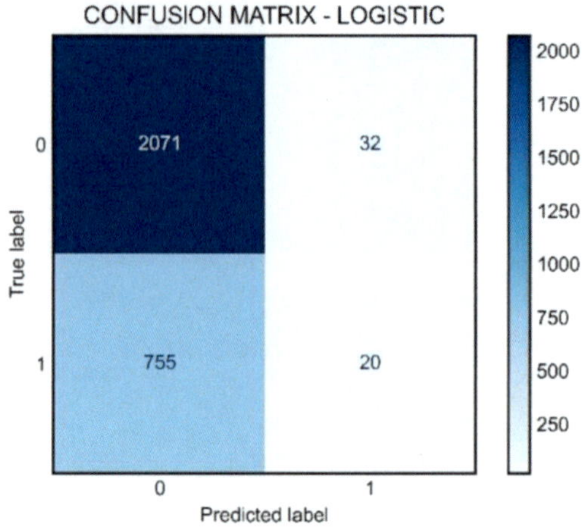

Fig 14: Confusion enhancing gradient matrix. confounding matrix

Fig 16: Logistic regression

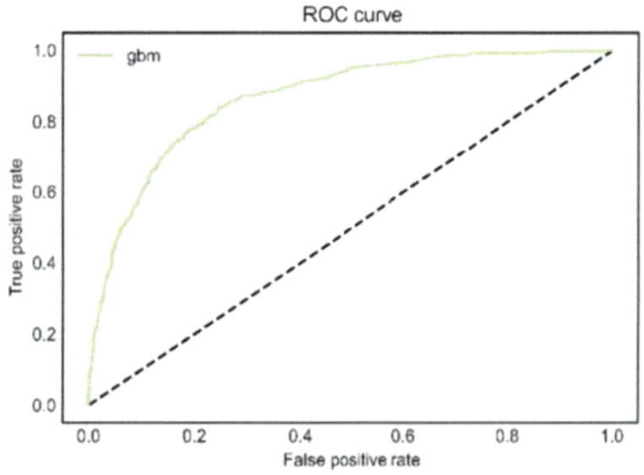

Fig 15: Gradient-boosting ROC curve.

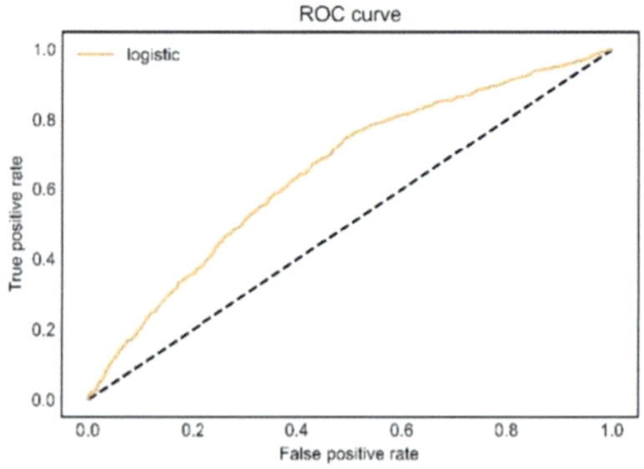

Fig 16: Regression ROC curve.

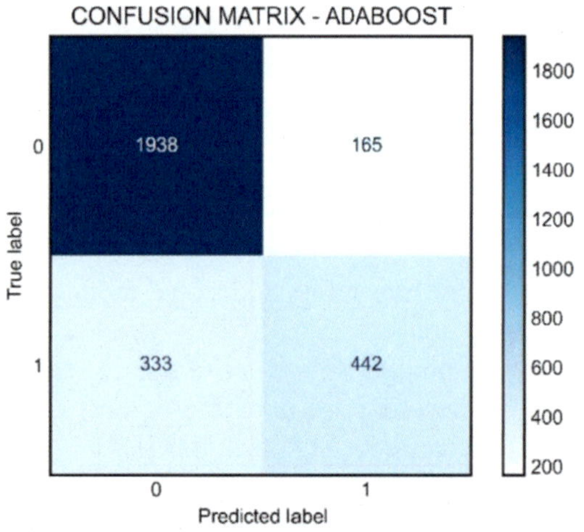

Fig 18: AdaBoost's confusion matrix

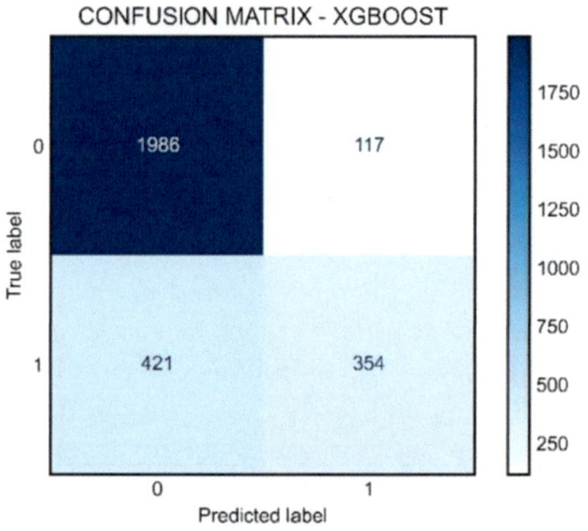

Fig 20: The XGBoost matrix of confusion

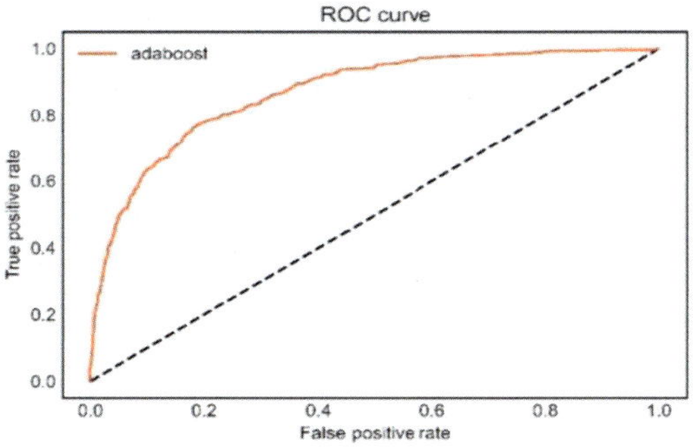

Fig 19: AdaBoost's ROC curve.

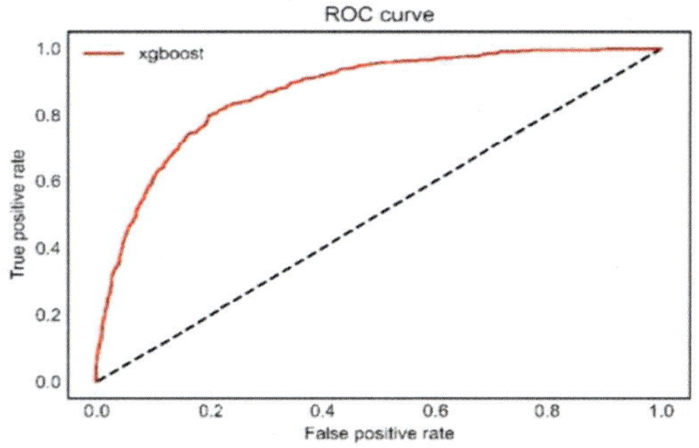

Fig 21:XG's ROC curve

Figs. 20 and 21 show the XGBoost confusion matrix and ROC curve. AdaBoost and XGBoost produce comparable results. Both ROC curves have identical cutoffs. Thus, a better prediction model is obtained. After applying all machine learning models, a correlation matrix was created to compare which model combination gave the best results, as shown in Fig. 22.Best machine learning models include Gradient boosting and Random forest. Gradient boosting and random forest were trained and fitted to XGBoost's outer layer. An ensemble was employed to forecast SARS-CoV more accurately and efficiently. Fig. 22 displays the ensemble correlation matrix.Gradient boosting using random forest and XGBoost achieve the greatest results, 0.92 and 0.99, respectively. The matrix indicates that XGBoost and random forest yield an accurate result of 0.93, indicating that all three models may be integrated to construct a stacked ensemble.

Figs. 23 and 24 show the confusion matrix and ROC curve from combining gradient boosting, random forest, and XGBoost. Good findings from confusion matrix and ROC curve. It's a good model for predicting SARS-CoV coronavirus sickness. After applying all machine learning models, a neural network, MLP-NN, was employed to predict SARS-B-cell CoV's dataset. Figs. 25 and 26 show the confusion matrix and ROC after neural network application. The AUC score and accuracy can be utilized for prediction.

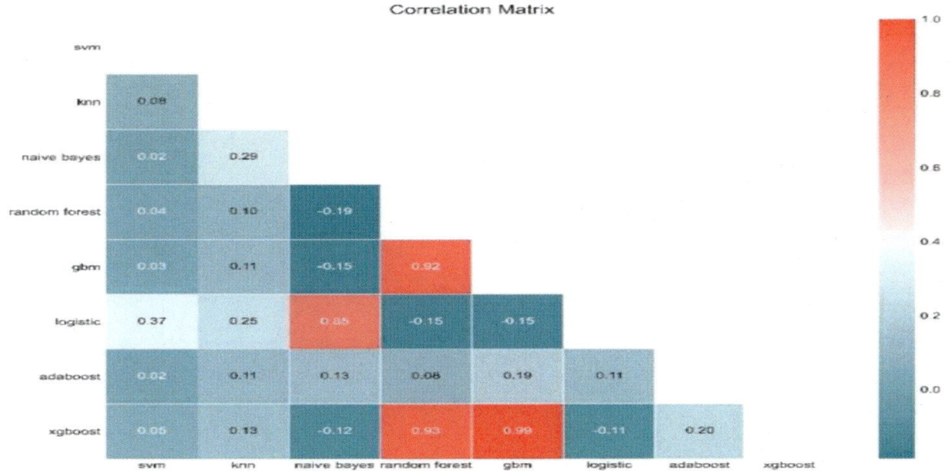

Fig 22: Ensemble correlation matrix.

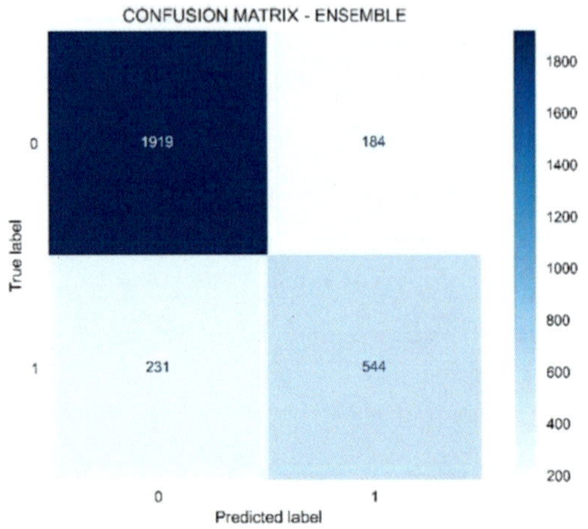

Fig 23: Ensemble confusion matrix.

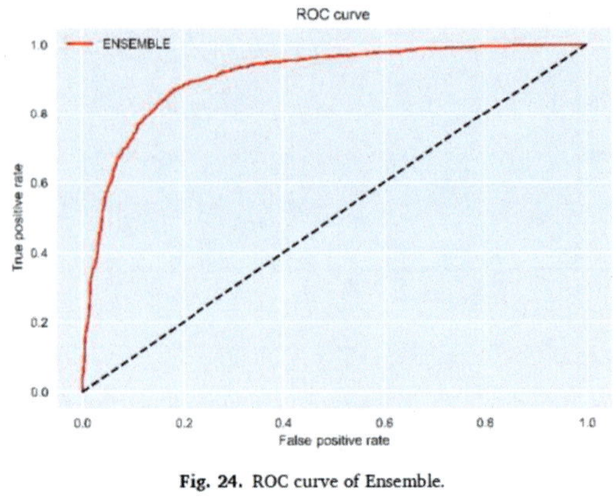

Fig 24: Ensemble ROC curve

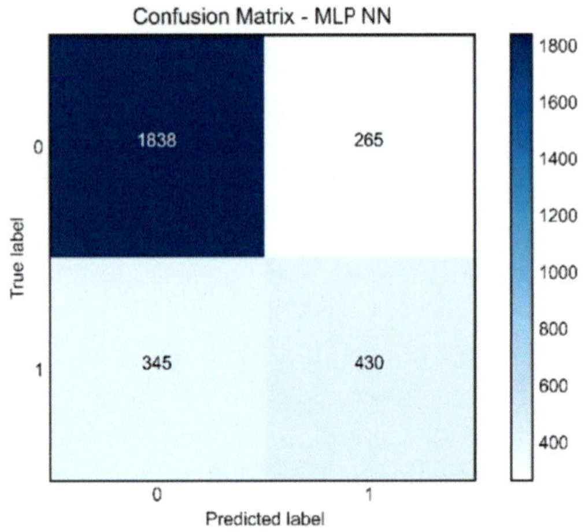

Fig 25: MLP-NN Confusion matrix

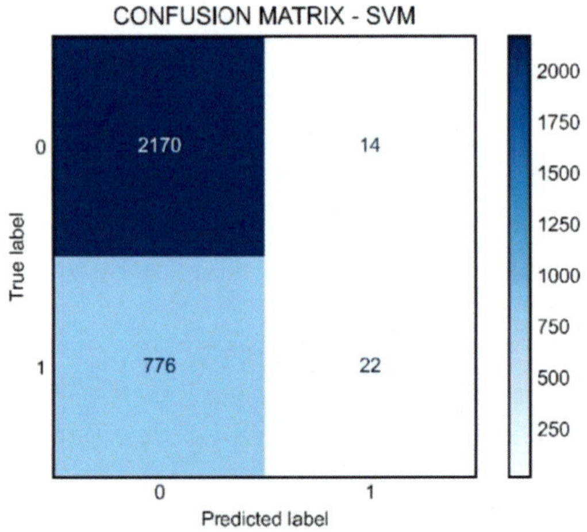

Fig 28: SVM confusion matrix

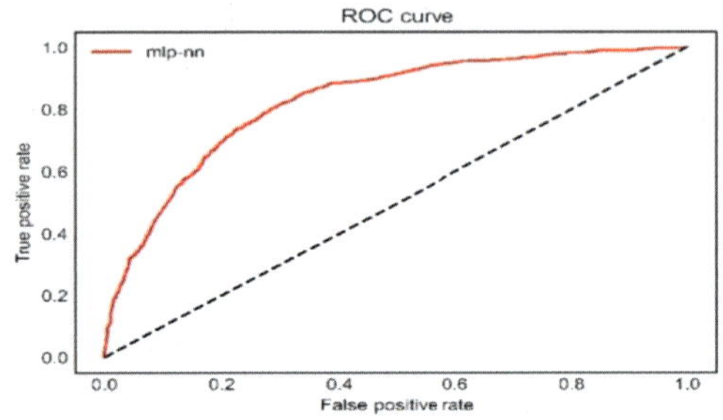

Fig 26:MLP-NN ROC curve

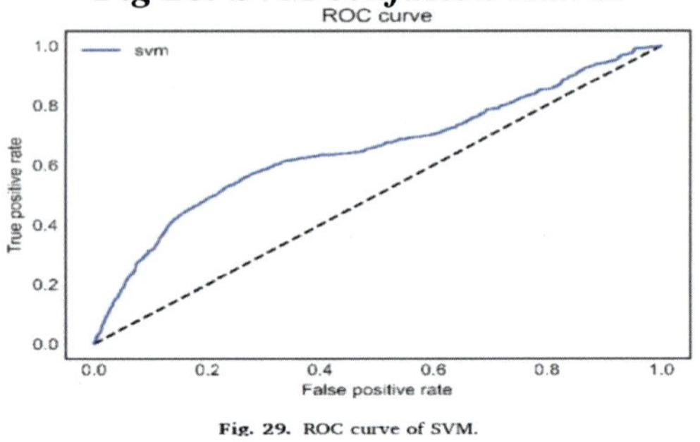

Fig 29:SVM ROC curve

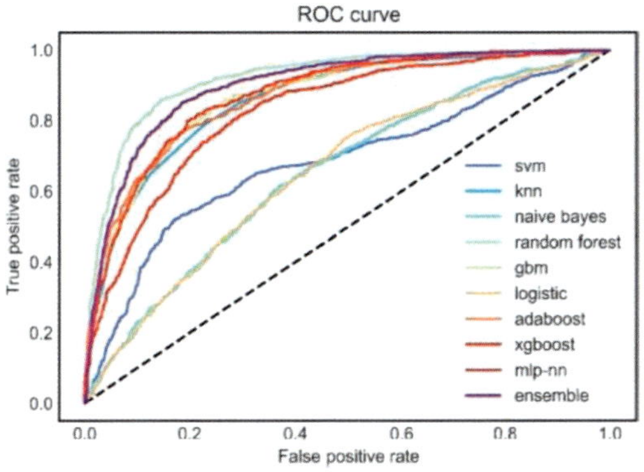

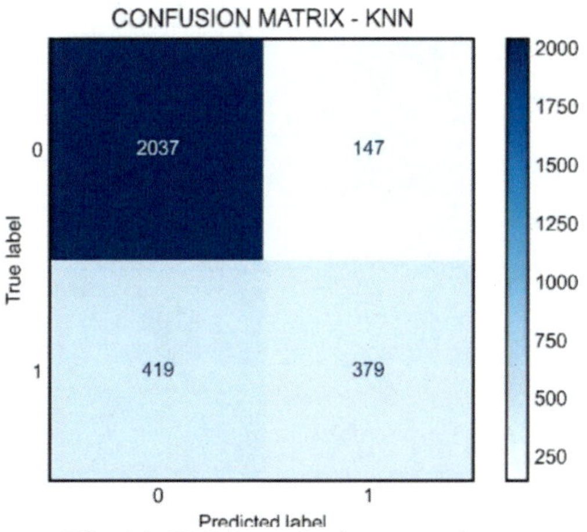

Fig 27:ROC curves comparison

Fig 30:KNN confusion matrix

Fig. 27 shows the combined ROC curve of SARS-CoV prediction models. Random forest has the best ROC curve, followed by ensemble. Fig. 27 compares ROC curves. Table 2 shows the validation accuracy, AUC score, MSE, MAE, and RMSE after applying all models and methods to the B-cell dataset. Tabulated findings of machine learning and algorithms used to the B-cell dataset to forecast SARS-CoV, producing coronavirus sickness. The table demonstrates that the suggested ensemble outperformed all other models and ensembles in this article. It has 87.2481 percent validation accuracy and 0.919 validation AUC, making it efficient. The accuracy is also strong enough for dataset predictions.

The table illustrates that random forests optimize error approximation. Random forest beat all ensembles and machine learning models, as demonstrated in Table 2. The B-cell dataset and SARS-CoV dataset were merged to forecast the SARS-CoV-2 virus producing coronavirus illness. Different machine learning models were used to analyze the processed dataset and predict model validity. Various machine learning models and techniques yielded these results: Figures 28 and 29 exhibit SVM's confusion matrix and ROC curve. ROC curve validation accuracy is 0.652, which is acceptable. True positives outnumber false negatives in the confusion matrix. This signifies that the model can perform pleasing outcomes. Figs. 30 and 31 illustrates the confusion matrix and the ROC curve of KNN models. The ROC curve shows that the model accurately predicts accurate results. KNN can forecast the SARS-CoV-2 virus since the findings reveal an accurate confusion matrix and a strong ROC curve with an AUC of 0.859.

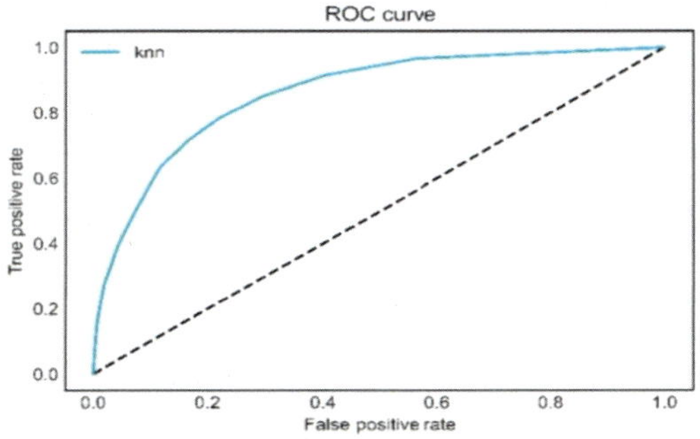

Fig. 31. ROC curve of KNN.

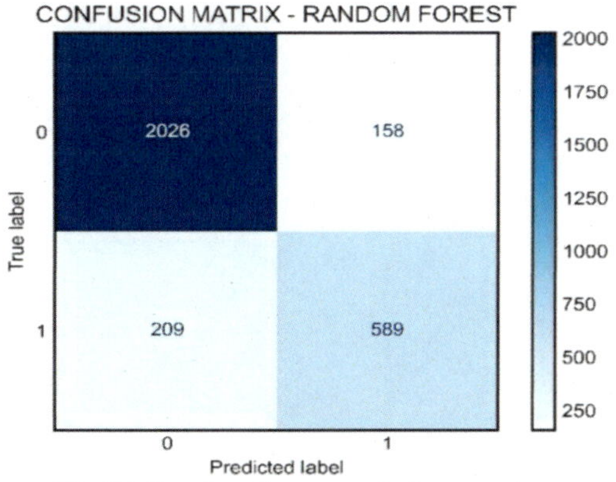

Fig 31: KNN ROC curve

Fig 34:Random forest confusion matrix

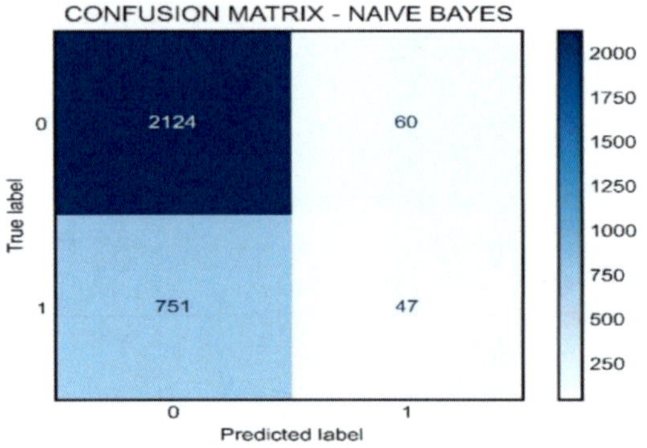

Fig 32: Naïve Bayes confusion matrix

Fig. 32. Confusion matrix of Naive Bayes.

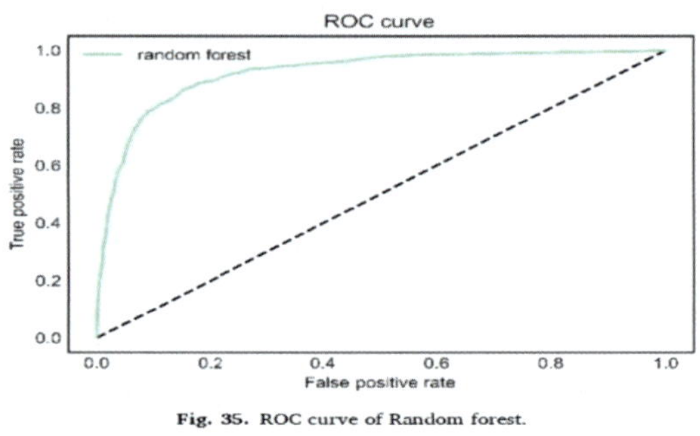

Fig 35:Random forest ROC curve

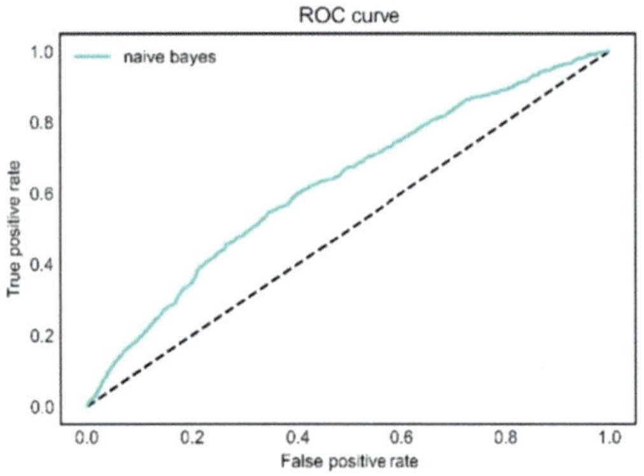

Fig 33: Naïve Bayes ROC curve

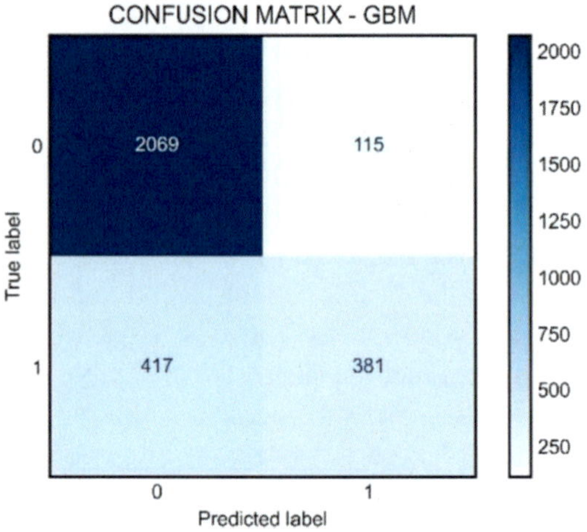

Fig 36: Gradient boosting confusion matrix

Figs. 32 and 33 show another SARS-COV-2 baseline model. AUC = 0.627, same as SVM model. The ROC curve isn't good but can be utilized for limited datasets. After applying baseline models, inbuilt ensembles were used. Figs. 34 and 35 show the confusion matrix and ROC curve for SARS-CoV-2 utilizing random forest, an internal ensemble. The outcome is the best of all applicable models and algorithms. The ROC slanted to the upper left corner indicates its second-highest accuracy and can be used to forecast SARSCoV-2.

Figs. 36 and 37 illustrate gradient boosting's implementation outcomes. It's the confusion matrix and ROC curve after gradient boosting. The model's output is good enough to forecast. The ROC curve's AUC score is 0.873, which is accurate.

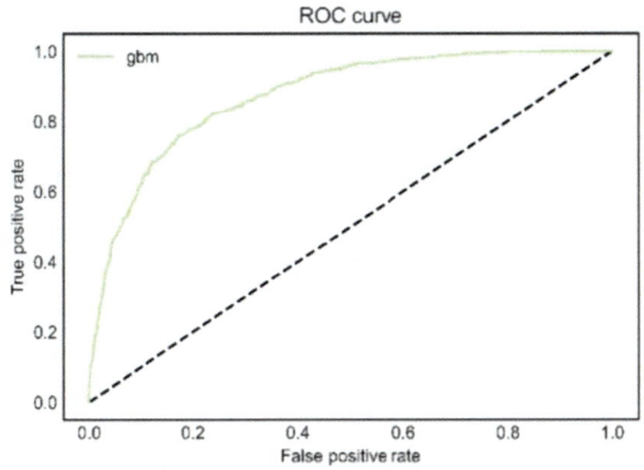

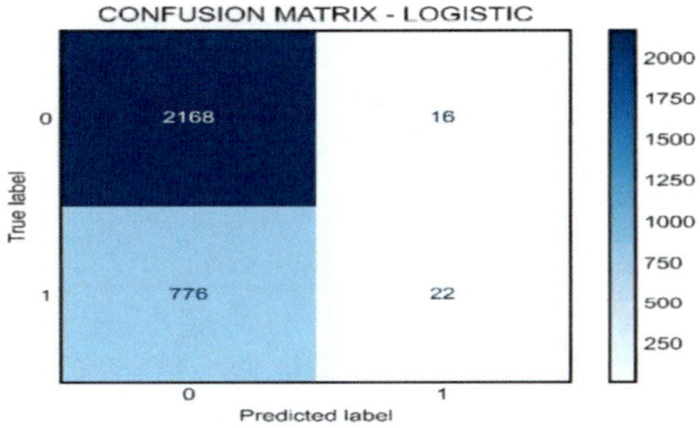

Fig 37: Gradient boosting ROC curve

Fig 38:Logistic regression confusion matrix

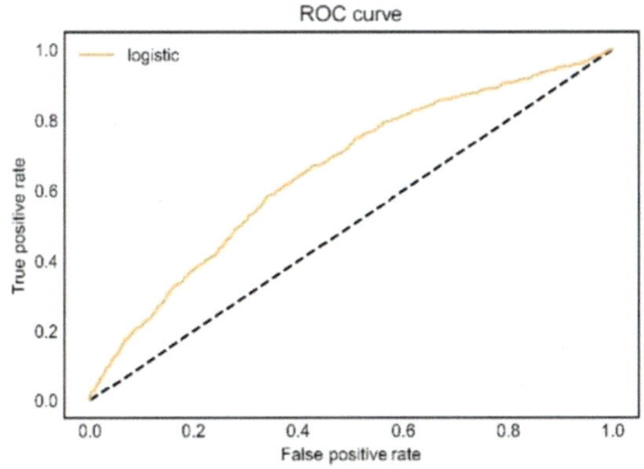

Fig 39: Logistic regression ROC curve

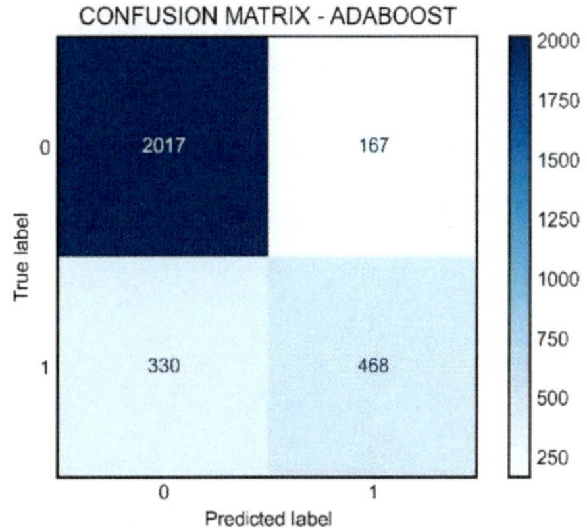

Fig 40:AdaBoost confusion matrix

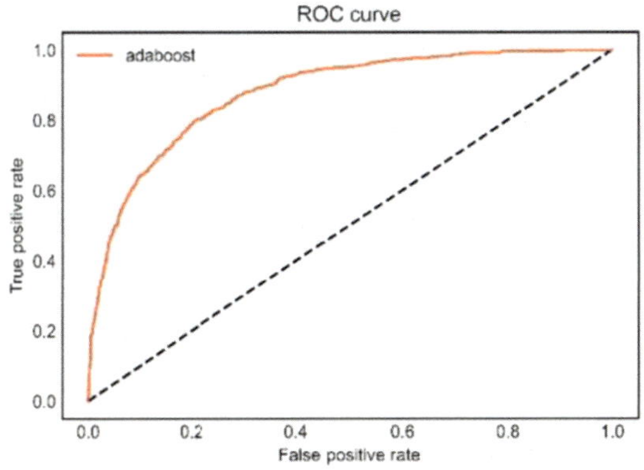

Fig 41: AdaBoost ROC curve

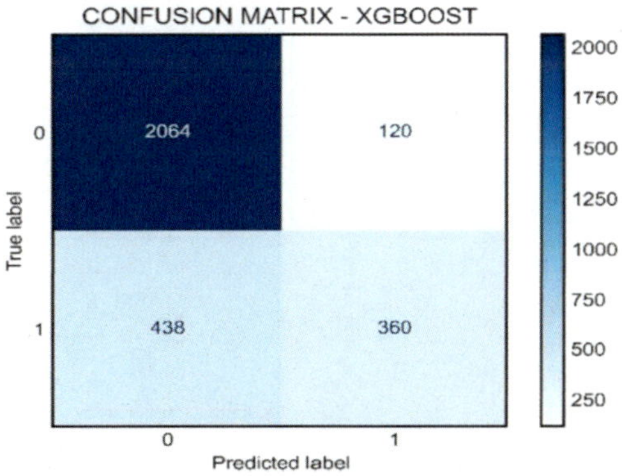

Fig 42: XGBoost confusion matrix

Figs. 38 and 39 illustrate logistic regression's confusion matrix and ROC curve. The model's ROC is adequate. It only worked for tiny datasets. AdaBoost was utilized to create predictions based on baseline models and inbuilt ensemble. Figs. 40 and 41 show AdaBoost's confusion matrix and ROC curve. The ROC curve has a high cut-off and high sensitivity. XGBoost was used to forecast the SARS-CoV-2 coronavirus. XGBoost worked similarly to AdaBoost and produced similar results. Figs. 42 and 43 illustrate AdaBoost's results.

After implementing all the machine learning models and algorithms, a correlation matrix for the models was also produced to test which models worked best together to forecast the coronavirus illness caused by the SARS-CoV-2 virus. The outcomes obtained after plotting the correlation matrix for each model are shown in Fig. 44. In order to create a stacked ensemble using XGBoost on the outer layer and random forest and gradient boosting on the inner layer, three algorithms—XGBoost, random forest, and gradient boosting—must be combined. This is clearly seen in the figure.

Figs. 45 and 46 illustrate the output obtained, i.e., the confusion matrix and ROC curve, after the ensemble was implemented. The ensemble's superior performance to a random forest is supported by the ROC curve. The SARS-CoV-2 virus may be predicted using the model that was created, according to the ROC curve's AUC score of 0.923.

The confusion matrix and ROC curve after using neural networks, namely MLP-NN, on the dataset are shown in Figs. 47 and 48. The ROC curve demonstrates that the model exhibits better results than other models, indicating that it might be utilized as a prediction model. The Confusion matrix shows that the number of accurate positive predictions is large and performing well. following analysis of all outputs from machine learning models and algorithms. The comparison of all the ROC curves is shown in Fig. 49, which amply demonstrates that the ensemble has outperformed all other models for coronavirus illness prediction, with an AUC score of 0.923, followed by the random forest with an AUC of 0.914.

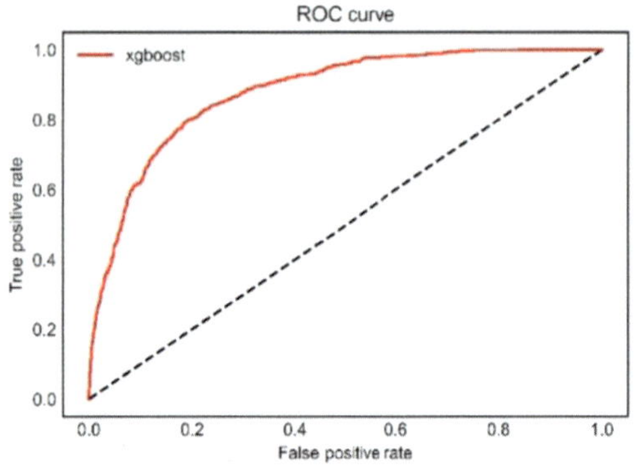

Fig. 43. ROC curve of XGBoost.

Fig 43:XGBoost ROC curve

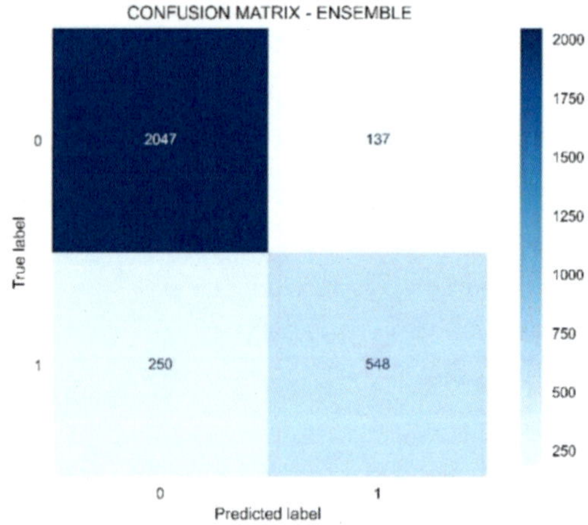

Fig 45:Ensemble confusion matrix

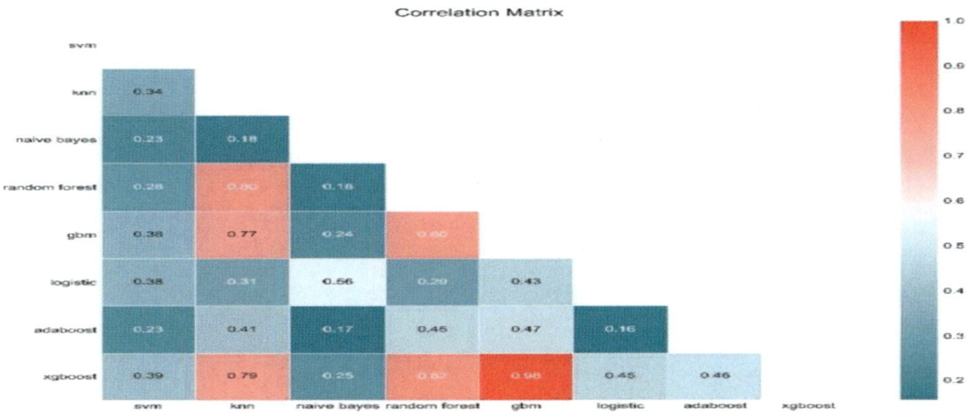

Fig 44: Model-selection correlation matrix

Table 3 shows all the graphs and matrices used to forecast SARS-CoV-2 coronavirus illness. The table shows the validation AUC score, validation accuracy, MAE, MSE, and RMSE of all the models, concluding that the ensemble performs best with 87.7934 validation accuracy and a 0.923 AUC score.

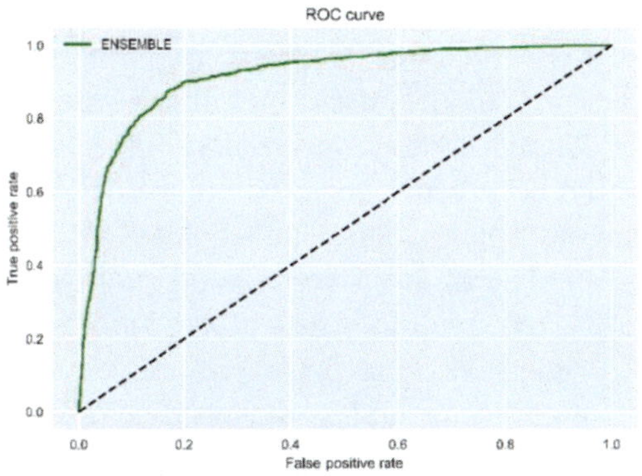

Fig 46:Ensemble ROC curve

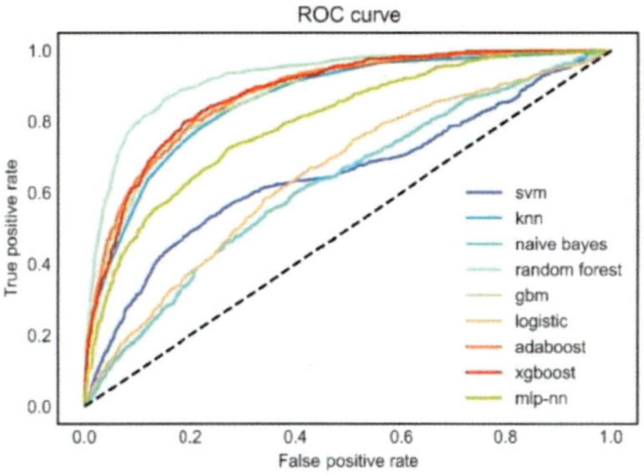

Fig 49:ROC curves comparison

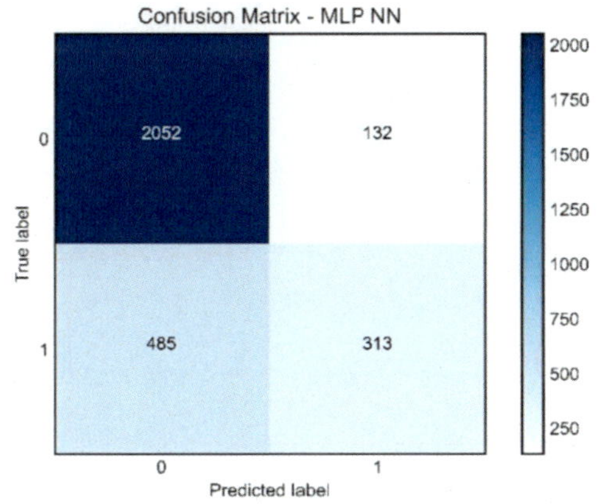

Fig 47: MLP-NN confusion matrix

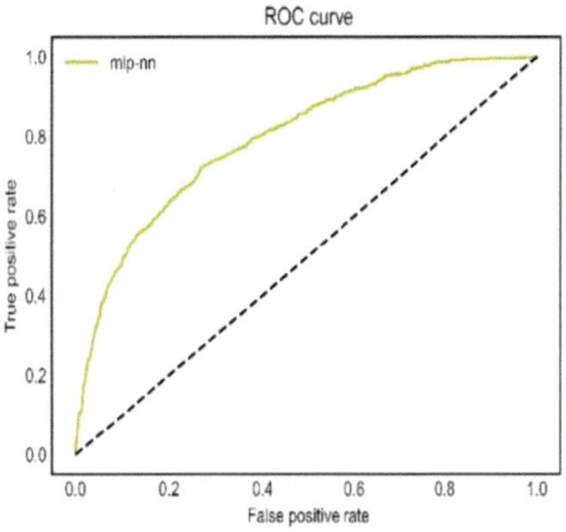

Fig 48: MLP-NN ROC curve

Table 3: Validating SARS-CoV-2.

Model	Validation AUC	Validation accuracy (%)	MSE	RMSE	MAE
SVM	0.652	73.7425	0.2626	0.5124	0.2626
KNN	0.859	81.0195	0.1898	0.4357	0.1898
Naive-Bayes	0.627	72.8035	0.2719	0.5215	0.2719
Random Forest	0.914	87.0221	0.1220	0.3494	0.1220
GBM	0.873	82.1596	0.1784	0.4224	0.1784
Logistic	0.654	73.4406	0.2656	0.5135	0.2656
AdaBoost	0.877	83.3333	0.1667	0.4082	0.1667
XGBoost	0.880	81.2877	0.1871	0.4326	0.1871
Ensemble	0.923	87.7934	0.1298	0.3602	0.1298
MLP-NN	0.810	79.1412	0.2086	0.4567	0.2086

Conclusion

Coronavirus spreads globally. In a pandemic, anticipating and assessing if a patient has SARS-CoV and SARS-CoV-2 would reduce testing and gatherings. Thus, forecasting these viruses might be advantageous for researchers by providing a full description and symptoms, allowing coronavirus to build vaccines quickly. The research uses multiple models and methods on B-cell datasets to forecast SARS-CoV and SARS-CoV-2, which cause coronavirus illness. The research describes baseline and intrinsic machine learning models used to predict viruses. The article also implements a stacked ensemble to make dataset predictions. Random forest with an AUC score of 0.919 and ensemble with 0.908 had the best results for predicting SARS-CoV. These are the B-cell dataset validation findings from multiple models. The labeled SARS-CoV dataset was utilized to test the models after validation. The findings aren't good enough since the SARS-CoV dataset has fewer positive values and is too small to justify all the models used. After predicting SARS-CoV, B-cell and SARS-CoV datasets were pooled to predict SARS-CoV-2. SARS-CoV-2 was predicted using models, algorithms, and a stacked ensemble. The ensemble outperformed a random forest with 0.923 AUC. Thus, viruses and findings are predicted to be accurate. More labeled data and positive values increase the SARS-CoV dataset. This might increase SARS-CoV-2 prediction accuracy and validate SARS-CoV test results. Labeling the COVID dataset would facilitate model and ensemble verification, boosting machine learning models and algorithms.

Chapter 3

Using the detection approach of the hesitant fuzzy multi-criteria decision-making of the primary risk factor linked to the transmission of the Coronavirus[3]

Background:

The first case of Coronavirus infectious disease was discovered in China in Dec 2019 [1]. Since there are still more Corona patients steadily rising, th,e WHO has classified Corona as an outbreak. Situation. There were 1.8 crore cases recorded around the world as 7 Lakh patients perished as a result as of 2020, August 7. Since the beginning of the outbreak, the World Health Organization has been responsible ever since position to raise consciousness and informed the nations about taking the immediate required action. The citizens and administrations of many nations have implemented several defensive measures. No one is susceptible to this illness. Therefore, World Health Organization issued sobering warnings about its seriousness and advised people will do it properly in light of their vulnerability.

The Coronavirus infection induced a severe respiratory disease syndrome that necessitated the declaration of patients in need primarily to the Intensive care units and resulted in actual fatality rates among those with concurrent circumstances. Medical experts that have made unrecognized sacrifices and shown the world when comes their magnificence to humanity provided the data that was gathered for the sufferers [2]. when an affected individual speaks, coughs, or sneezes, it might spread to someone else. In their research, according to writers [3-5], a person may get an illness if they touch a virus-infected façade before touching his nose, eyes, or mouth. Since December of 2019. the illness has been spread through human interaction based on the source [6]; the typical gestational period was calculated to follow exposure by 5.3 days. Coronavirus infection is closely related to Severe acute pulmonary illness, but this condition is milder and less death rate than earlier. The primary means by which the Coronavirus spreads is to affect senior citizens. Based on the writers of [7], men are more significant about the mask use because of the Coronavirus outbreak is now required for everyone in order to stop the illness. Choosing the appropriate masks in this circumstance is crucial. The writers of [8] used a multi-criteria approach. Decision analysis approaches in addition to the spherical algorithm typical fuzzy environment for choosing a mask. They initiated and used mathematical models. Forth the writers of [9–13] forecast the disease's

---

3 *Landmark paper: Neha Ghorui, Arijit Ghosh, Sankar Prasad Mondal, Mohd Yazid Bajuri, Ali Ahmadian, Soheil Salahshour, Massimiliano Ferrara, "Identification of dominant risk factor involved in spread of COVID-19 using hesitant fuzzy MCDM methodology", Results in Physics, Volume 21, 2021, 103811, ISSN 2211-3797,* https://doi.org/10.1016/j.rinp.2020.103811.

adaptive measures. The model was also evaluated for the spread of diseases to dead people from living beings. It also looked at how well the shutdown worked. in terms of preserving life. [14]'s authors research of the use of facemasks to determine which masks could stop the unique Corona disease spread. The authors used a mathematical analysis model. Reference utilized mathematical tools [15–16] according to [17–18], the writers, this sickness will teach us how to eliminate epidemics. People have been seriously affected by the coronavirus around the globe. To stop the global horror and trauma, every country is making every effort to develop an appropriate vaccination or other long-term medical cure.

To determine which risk factor is the most important for the spread, we attempted in order to use a mathematical system of the sickness in this study with the help of literary medical evaluations, experts, and media polls. Regarding this, cautious fuzzy sets using the Technique for Order The most crucial risk factor is examined using TOPSIS (Preference by Similarity to Ideal Response). Multi-criteria decision-ANALYSIS is another thing that has been applied.

Study of the literature:

Humans are typically unsure of the choices they make from the available options offered by the system while making selections for any circumstance. When two decision-makers disagree, for instance, on how much of an element's membership degree to put in set X. While one desires to give 0.1, the other aims to give 0.3 information, which is being neither established nor having a usual membership in accordance with the source [19], the fault line intuitive fuzzy set does not exist because there is a collection of as is the case with fuzzy type-2 sets [20,21], possible values. Instead, it exists since there are a number of distribution values that might be true. The writers of [22,23] produced a tentative fuzzy set, a hypothesis of the fuzzy in accordance with account for such circumstances, the source [24]. The scope of applications for the cautious fuzzy sets has increased qualitatively and quantitatively. Due to the possibility of reluctance while simulating the uncertainty from both a qualitative and a quantitative [25, 26–29] perspective. The writers of [30–40] used fuzzy hesitating sets in MCDM issues, and [41] adopted a multi-expert, multi-criteria approach. Making decisions, using evaluation procedures, and grouping methods created by [43–47]'s authors.

From a tentative, the writers of [48] used aggregate operators in their fuzzy collection to select the optimum production schedule. The [49] authors used the fuzzy TOPSIS for the supplier's application selection difficulty. The author created a massive scale of doubtful operators of power aggregation for fuzzy sets ideology [50]. The creators of [51] created the first fuzzy AHP formula. Triangle-shaped fuzzy membership algorithms are used, and Lootsma's logarithmic least squares move in. [52]'s author proposed utilizing the geometric mean to obtain the pairwise fuzzy weights comparisons; additionally, the approach was enhanced with Uncertain trapezoidal numbers. The author of [53] also made a degree suggestion. Analysis technique for the pairwise comparisons' synthetic extent metrics. According to the writers of [54], a method pertaining to interval AHP fuzzy type-2 was eventuated. [55]'s author suggested as a solution, the TOPSIS approach may be expanded to include fuzzy sets. Suggestions are listed in the reference for [56] and likewise made to expand a version of the fuzzy TOPSIS approach to the field of issues with choosing energies [38]. Table 1 provides an overview of the literature assessment of Coronavirus risk variables and our suggested model.

Error 1: FAHP and HFS-TOPSIS are used in the suggested TFN, which are essential for communicating imprecision, were used by FAHP [60]. HFS illustrates the reluctance to assign a specific value in the face of a hazy outbreak circumstance like the coronavirus. When the decision-maker must make a quick choice, HFS may disagree with the membership benefit of an element and debate whether it ought to be either 0.8, 0.9, or 0.93. Rather than utilizing a single aggregate value in these cases, HFS more accurately depicts the circumstance.

Goals of the current research:

- Selecting the risk factors most crucial to Corona virus dissemination. The data for this study comes from a doctor: viewpoint, a literature analysis, and a media poll.
- To rank various risk factors, the TOPSIS and HFS techniques are used. HFS shows that the substitute is a member degree based on a more flexible standard. As far as we know, there has never been a study combining FAHP, HFS, and TOPSIS to identify significant risk factors in Coronavirus.

The remains preparing the paper in the following manner: Section four states the study's benefits section 5 addresses the research from a scientific perspective. Methodologies. It gives details regarding HFS-TOPSIS, FAHP, and HFS. Section 6 it is detailing how the risk and criteria of the chosen factors. Section 7 presents the empirical research and uses a mathematical model, ranking the risk elements., and mathematical Sensitivity analysis is presented in Section 8. Section 9 deals with the outcomes and the discussion are covered in Section 10.

Scientific advantages of the study:

In this study, the risk elements for the Coronavirus outbreak were figured out and ranked. The federal government can create organizational strategies to reduce the main risk factors with this scientifically achieved outcome. This analysis reveals that the government bodies should adopt measures to limit extended interaction that necessitates strict observance of physical separation. The risk variables in this study for the Coronavirus outbreak were figured out and ranked. The federal government can create organizational strategies to reduce the main risk factors with this scientifically achieved outcome. This analysis reveals that the government bodies should adopt measures to limit extended interaction that necessitates strict observance of physical distance.

Procedures:

In this study, the risk is elements for the Coronavirus outbreak were figured out and ranked. The federal government can create organizational strategies to reduce the main risk factors with the aid of this scientifically achieved outcome. This analysis reveals that the government should put policies in place to limit extended interaction that necessitates strict observance of physical distance.

(Timid) fuzzy sets:

The HFS underlying theory is essential for distance measuring, operating guidelines, and everything else in this part. A certain extension to the fuzzy set's theory is HFS. It was developed by the writer of [22] and is appropriate when determining the degree to which the elements are related there are doubts or trembling. HFS can be used in a variety of ways to express preferences because the concept of decision-analysis incorporates the reluctance or confusion on the part of the decision-makers about the terms of requirements [38]. Creators of the sources [61-65] made use of equations for fuzzy sets delay differential, non-linear fractional delay models, non-linear equations, and using calculus to build balance, a biological model of earth's energy, dynamics of HFS virus, and a stock order issue.

Figure 1 shows the planned study's flowchart.

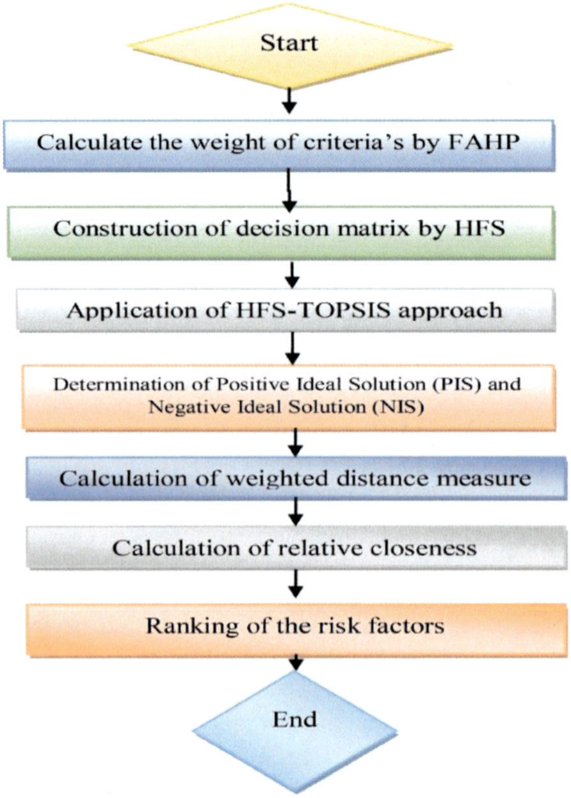

Process of fuzzy analytical hierarchy:

The writer of [67], The logical-based analytical setup employed in the MCDM issue, was produced by the fuzzy analytical method hierarchy method. It is beneficial when using heuristic methods in difficult choices Ranking risk variables demands considerable thought. of the weights of the varied standards. By developing comparison matrices using opinions on qualities, the method of fuzzy analytical hierarchy organization is crucial for ranking. the troublesome echelon. When uncertainty causes issues, FAHP has been employed in this article rather than the processed of fuzz fuzzy analytical hierarchy.

Table 1: Triangular-shaped Fuzzy set Number linguistic terminology used to determine the weight of the criteria

Linguistic Terminology	THFS
Most dominant	{4.5, 5, 5.5}
Dominant	{3.5,4, 4.5}
Quite Significant	{2.5, 3, 3.5}
Low Significant	{1.5, 2, 2.5}
Quite Low Priority	{0.5, 1, 1.5}

Table 2: Creation of a matrix for comparison.

Matrix of Similarities	DM1			DM2		
	Ψ1	Ψ2	Ψ3	Ψ1	Ψ2	Ψ3
Ψ1	1	(3.5, 4, 4.5)	(4.5, 5, 5.5)	1	(0.22, 0.25, 0.286)	(4.5, 5, 5.5)
Ψ2	(0.22, 0.25, 0.286)	1	(3.5, 4, 4.5)	(3.5, 4, 4.5)	1	(4.5, 5, 5.5)
Ψ2	(0.18, 0.2, 0.22)	(0.22, 0.25, 0.286)	1	(0.18, 0.2, 0.22)	(0.18, 0.2, 0.22)	1

Table 3: Weighted representation of the criterion

Criteria's	**Ψ1**	**Ψ2**	**Ψ3**
Weight	0.47	0.45	0.08

Table 4: Creation of a tentative decisionThe infection.

Risk Elements	**Ψ1**	**Ψ2**	**Ψ3**
Verbal Spread Θ1	(0.5,0.7,0.9)	(0.6,0.7)	(0.8)
Long-lasting contact Θ2	(0.9)	(0.6,0.7,0.8,0.9)	(0.7,0.8)
Failing to practice good hygiene Θ3	(0.4,0.5,0.6)	(0.1,0.3,0.5)	(0.5)
Using a substandard mask Θ4	(0.2,0.3,0.4,0.5)	(0.3)	(0.4,0.5)
Not keeping a safe distance in a public location or on a public transportation Θ5	(0.6,0.7)	(0.4,0.5,0.6)	(0.3,0.4,0.5,0.6)
The infection spreading in healthcare facilities Θ6	(0.8,0.9)	(0.6,0.7,0.8)	(0.4,0.5,0.6)

Table 5: The choices' relative similarity.

Risk Factors	D^{+}_{b}	D^{-}_{b}	$RC_b = D^{-}_{b}/ D^{-}_{b} + D^{+}_{b}$
Θ1	0.122	0.5225	0.811
Θ2	0.0715	0.704	0.91
Θ3	0.482	0.357	0.42
Θ4	0.556	0.1725	0.24
Θ5	0.3255	0.3735	0.53
Θ6	0.1375	0.615	0.82

Table 6: Received a different ranking.

Risk \sFactors	FAHP HFS-TOPSIS (M1)	Crisp AHP-TOPSIS (M2)	PIVN AHP-TOPSIS (M3)	FAHP-FTOPSIS (M4)
Θ1(R1)	3	4	5	3
Θ2(R2)	1	5	3	2
Θ3(R3)	5	6	6	6
Θ4(R4)	6	3	4	5
Θ5(R5)	4	2	2	1
Θ6(R6)	2	1	1	4

HFS-TOPSIS method

Introduced by the [69] a research group. Ranking the appropriate choice or stating which alternative the fundamental principle of the TOPSIS approach is to favor most. The effective alternative is farthest from the negative ideal solution and closer to the positive ideal alternative (PIS) (NIS). The selection that is closest in proximity is ultimately the ideal decision. In order to manage MADM in a cautious, the writers of [38] stretched the conventional paradigm to a fuzzy environment TOPSIS methodology. The interval type-2 FAHP was used in this study by authors of [70] to evaluate the weights Using predicted weights and HFS- TOPSIS, the optimum method was chosen.

Empirical study:

Data source: suggestions from medical specialists, journal articles [1, 71, 57], and media surveys.

Figure 2 shows the study's hierarchical structure.

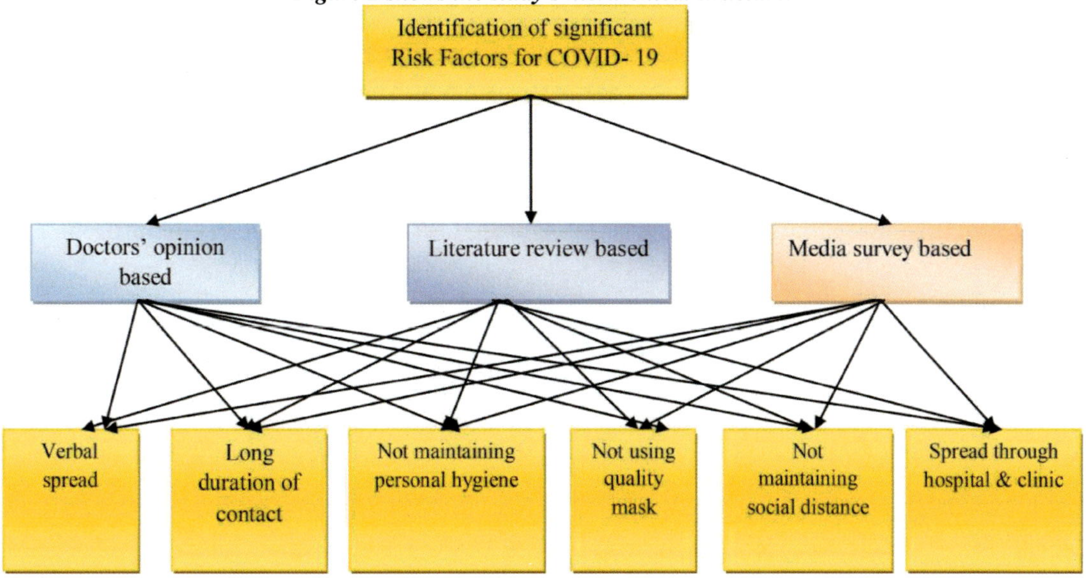

Figure 3: Line chart illustrating the ranking's sensitivity based on various techniques.

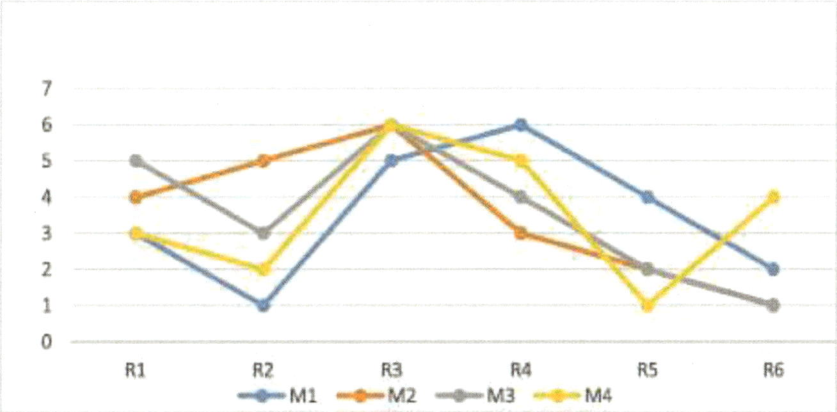

Sensitivity research:

The TOPSIS-HFS approach is the foundation of the paper's focus on finding the most important risk element towards FAHP for weighting criteria. various different ranking algorithms have been used to examine the sensibility of the outcomes. In the Parametric Form of the AHP-TOPSIS of Interval Numbers and the Triangular Fuzzy Number, we applied Crisp values.

Outcomes:

The findings are discussed in this section. the conclusions were reached using HFS-TOPSIS, FAHP, and sensible analysis. The most important risk factor according to the FAHP, HFS-TOPSIS methodology was "long duration of contact with the infected person," which was preceded by "spread via clinics and hospitals," "verbal spread," and "not keeping distance in Public transportation facility," "failing to practice good hygiene," and "not wearing a mask."

Conclusion and projected future:

In this work, we used the FAHP and HFS-TOPSIS approach to examine the most important complication factor for the spread of Coronavirus disease.

The three key factors for the choice of a substantial risk factor are a doctor's judgment, a literature study, and a media poll. The weight of the criteria was established using FAHP. The application HFS-TOPSIS found the biggest risk element. The benefit of employing Hesitant Fuzzy Sets (HFS)TOPSIS Interval is performed a thorough analysis of the risk element. Depending on how Coronavirus spreads globally in the future, further risk variables might be considered. The location of designing for isolation, sanitary facilities, safe homes, secure masks, and epidemic control models for the Coronavirus and bed enhancement models for hospitals to accommodate huge numbers of patients can all be determined scientifically through future studies.

Chapter 4

Prevention of COVID'19 disease outbreak by optimum surveillance: Fractional order compartment model control[4]

Introduction

A fatal coronavirus that essentially originated in Wuhan, China, suddenly imprisoned individuals all over the world. More than 210 nations and territories have been impacted by this variant of the SARS-CoV-2 coronavirus. It has resulted in terrible effects on social and economic activity as well as public health. Worldwide governments spurred monitoring on restricting COVID'19's global spread. The bulk of these drastic actions appear to be successful in slowing the spread of viruses. The most effective ways to stop the spread of this illness are to impose curfews, lock down the cities, and promote social isolation through stay-at-home messages, frequent hand washing, and the use of hand sanitizers in print and digital media. Unquestionably, there will be significant social and financial costs associated with implementing these regulations and involving communities in these initiatives. But these tactics could be crucial until a reliable vaccination or therapy is developed.

An astonishing amount of study has been done quickly to examine the COVID'19 from a variety of angles. Numerous researchers have found epidemiological dynamical systems that can be used to limit the spread of this pandemic by limiting the fundamental reproduction rate. Clinical research to identify therapy options based on this virus's biological characteristics.Opinions of the effects of government prevention measures on other environmental, social, and economic activities. Models for making decisions that take into account a COVID'19 transition management and prevention approach.

High accuracy patient triage using machine learning algorithms to anticipate high risk patients. When examining the dynamical controls of infectious illnesses, mathematical models prove to be useful devices. There are a lot of research articles in the literature that are based on optimum control models. Numerous authors have offered their significant contributions to the current fight against COVID'19 in this regard. In order to study the most cost-effective quarantine procedures, Grigorieva et al. develop two SEIR-type models and numerically assess the best options. The literature may be used to analyze COVID'19 treatments using a transmission model and to identify the best non-pharmaceutical tactics for reducing disease annoyance in

---

4 *Landmark paper: Oyoon Abdul Razzaq, Daniyal Ur Rehman, Najeeb Alam Khan, Ali Ahmadian, Massimiliano Ferrara, "Optimal surveillance mitigation of COVID'19 disease outbreak: Fractional order optimal control of compartment model", Results in Physics, Volume 20, 2021, 103715, ISSN 2211-3797, https://doi.org/10.1016/j.rinp.2020.103715.*

Pakistan. To stop the spread of this fatal epidemic, several initiatives have been made in various contexts of cost-effective approach.

In this effort, we develop a mathematical model that addresses dynamic optimal control and epidemiology, two important fields. First, stability analysis and consideration of the compartmental model with the control variables are made. In order to evaluate the cost-effectiveness of the preventative techniques, optimizing cost functions is also applied to the compartmental model. Although there have been extensive mathematical studies in this area, the innovations that have energized the suggested assessment include:
• This study includes isolation and safety measures in addition to vulnerable, exposed, quarantined, infected, and recovering compartments. SEQIMRP, which stands for susceptible-expose-quarantine-dinfected-isolated-recovered-protected, is the acronym for the model.
• The non-pharmaceutical control factors, the use of masks, promoting social withdrawal, emphasizing frequent hand washing and hand sanitizer usage, and supportive care throughout treatment. • The regulation of fundamental reproduction rate through these programs.
• Including fractional order derivative for the model's dynamical analysis.

The COVID'19 initiatives will surely benefit much from this substantial investment. The proportional fractional SEQIMRP model that has been developed represents a larger use of the fractional definition. The fractional order derivative operator is neatly transformed into integer order by its expansion, allowing the fractional order index to be redistributed linearly in the equations. As a result, memory effects may be used to explain the dynamics of COVID'19, such as the fundamental reproduction number and equilibrium locations. The historical values of these parameters or the compartmental functions will therefore make it possible to design defensive preventative measures that are based on prior experiences. The proportionate fractional derivative further illustrates the impact of memory on the effectiveness of awareness tactics. The devised approach offers a unique addition to the research of epidemic and pandemic illnesses from an epidemiological perspective. It will teach medical researchers a new method of producing data and could be able to look back on earlier data on risk factors or transmission rates for preventative measures. The remainder of the work is divided into parts that examine optimality, analyze equilibrium points' stability, and formulate the dynamical system. Additionally, discussions of numbers are conducted in order to clearly develop an impactful conclusion.

Model development for COVID'19 best control

Susceptible-expose-quarantined-infected-isolated-recovered-protected (SEQIMRP)
The functional behavior of any virus may be studied using mathematical models based on disease dynamics, which therefore helps to prevent or limit its contaminating outbreak. Within a few months, the lethal coronavirus turned into a global epidemic that infected billions of people. Early scientific efforts and laboratory research to develop a medication or vaccination were unsuccessful. In order to calculate the fundamental reproduction rate and forecast the dispersion, recovery, and mortality rates, several epidemiological models also offered major contributions in this regard. Here, a system of differential equations is created with regard to compartmental classes and preventative measures on the basis of the following hypotheses in order to examine the dynamical behavior and impact of the COVID'19 pandemic.
• The model assumes a homogenous mixing of people in the community, regardless of the varied risk rates of COVID'19 for different age groups and pre-existing illness carriers.

• Preventative measures: The ideal method takes into consideration supportive care (sc), regular hand washing (ch), social distance (sd), and the use of medical masks (mm) during treatments as control variables.
• Individuals in any compartment are presumed to be immune to infection and are designated as protected compartments when operational preventative techniques are followed.
• Susceptible is described as logistic growth, which includes the greatest sustainability to survive in an environment's resources.People who have been exposed to the virus are isolated so that they can recover and take precautions to protect themselves afterwards.
• The isolation procedure is used to treat COVID'19 infection in patients, and it is described in the isolation compartment. These compartments may recover and transfer to recovery compartments with the staff's assistance.
As a result, the susceptible expose quarantined infected isolated recovered protected (SEQIMRP) fractional order epidemiological model is mathematically represented as:

$$
\begin{aligned}
{}^{PF}D_t^{\alpha}S(t) &= r_s\,S(t)\left(1-\frac{S(t)}{k_S}\right)-(mm(t)+sd(t)+ch(t))S(t)-\beta S(t)\,I(t)\\
&\quad -d_s\,S(t)\\
{}^{PF}D_t^{\alpha}E(t) &= \beta S(t)I(t)-(mm(t)+sd(t)+ch(t))\,E(t)-\gamma E(t)-d_E\,E(t)\\
{}^{PF}D_t^{\alpha}Q(t) &= \gamma E(t)-(mm(t)+sd(t)+ch(t)+sc(t))\,Q(t)-\eta\,Q(t)\\
&\quad -\psi_Q Q(t)-d_Q Q(t) \qquad (1)\\
{}^{PF}D_t^{\alpha}I(t) &= \eta\,Q(t)-(mm(t)+sd(t)+ch(t)+sc(t))\,I(t)-\sigma I(t)-d_I I(t)\\
{}^{PF}D_t^{\alpha}M(t) &= \sigma I(t)-(mm(t)+sd(t)+ch(t)+sc(t))\,M(t)-\psi_M M(t)\\
&\quad -\rho M(t)\\
{}^{PF}D_t^{\alpha}R(t) &= \psi_Q\,Q(t)+\psi_M\,M(t)-(mm(t)+sd(t)+ch(t))R(t)-d_R R(t)
\end{aligned}
$$

$$
\begin{aligned}
{}^{PF}D_t^{\alpha}P(t) &= (mm(t)+sd(t)+ch(t))(S(t)+E(t)+R(t))+(mm(t)+sd(t)+ch(t)\\
&\quad +sc(t))Q(t)+(mm(t)+sd(t)+ch(t)+sc(t))(I(t)+M(t))-d_P P
\end{aligned}
$$

with initial conditions,

$$
\begin{aligned}
&S(0)=O_1,\quad E(0)=O_2,\quad Q(0)=O_3,\quad I(0)=O_4,\\
&M(0)=O_5,\quad R(0)=O_6,\quad P(0)=O_7. \qquad (2)
\end{aligned}
$$

Table 1
Variables and parameters of the SEQIMRP.

Compartmental functions	Descriptions	Units	Initial values (population = in millions & time = days)	Source
$N(t)$	Total population	Population / day	113	Estimated
$S(t)$	Susceptible	Population / day	111	Estimated
$E(t)$	Exposed	Population / day	0	Estimated
$Q(t)$	Quarantined	Population / day	0	Estimated
$I(t)$	Infected	Population / day	2	Estimated
$M(t)$	Infected isolated	Population / day	0	Estimated
$R(t)$	Recovered	Population / day	0	Estimated
$P(t)$	Protected	Population / day	0	Estimated
α	Order of fractional derivative	Dimensionless	$0 < \alpha \leqslant 1$	Fitted
Parameters	**Descriptions**	**Units**	**Value**	**Source**
ξ	R is taking part in social distancing	Individuals/ (individuals × day)	14.771	Fitted
β	Contact rate of susceptible with infected	Individuals/ (individuals × day)	14.781	Fitted
γ	Rate of exposed individuals quarantined	Individuals/ (individuals × day)	1.887×10^{-7}	Fitted
η	Rate of treated infected and quarantined	Individuals/ (area × day)	0.13266	Fitted
σ	Rate of susceptible exposed to quarantine	Individuals/ (individuals × day)	0.0714	Fitted
r_S	Intrinsic Growth rate of susceptible individuals	Individuals/ (individuals × day)	30	Fitted
k_S	Carrying capacity of susceptible individuals	Individuals/ (individuals × day)	100,000	Fitted
σ	Rate of susceptible exposed to infection	Individuals/ (individuals × day)	0.1259	Fitted
ρ	Death due to COVID'19 disease	Individuals/ (individuals × day)	1.782×10^{-5}	[35]
ψ_Q	Recovery rate of the quarantine individuals	Individuals/ (individuals × day)	0.11624	Fitted
ψ_M	Recovery rate of the isolated infected individuals	Individuals/ (individuals × day)	0.33029	Fitted
d_S	Susceptible death rate	Individuals/ (individuals × day)	0.15	Fitted
d_E	Exposed death rate	Individuals/ (individuals × day)	0.84	Fitted
d_Q	Quarantined death rate	Individuals/ (individuals × day)	0.84	Fitted
d_I	Infected death rate	Individuals/ (individuals × day)	0.9	Fitted

Table 1 (*continued*)

Compartmental functions	Descriptions	Units	Initial values (population = in millions & time = days)	Source
d_R	Recovered death rate	Individuals/ (individuals × day)	0.11	Fitted
d_P	Precautionary death rate	Individuals/ (individuals × day)	0.84	Fitted
mm	Rate of individuals using medical mask	Individuals/ (individuals × day)	0–1	Fitted
sd	Rate of individuals taking part in social distancing	Individuals/ (individuals × day)	0–1	Fitted
ch	Rate of individuals frequently cleaning hand	Individuals/ (individuals × day)	0–1	Fitted
sc	Rate of individuals who follow step of supportive care during treatment.	Individuals/ (individuals × day)	0–1	Fitted

where, $O_i(0) \in \Re_+^7$ for$i = 1, 2, \ldots, 7$. Table 1 further elaborates the dimensions of all the variables and parameters of system (1). Moreover, pictorial demonstration of the compartmental system, representing the flow of the diseases transmission is also given in Fig. 1. Assume$N(t)$ is the total population density of individuals that can be structured as:

$$N(t) = S(t) + E(t) + Q(t) + I(t) + M(t) + R(t) + P(t) \tag{3}$$

Moreover, ${}^{PF}D_t^{\alpha}$ articulates proportional fractional derivative of order$\alpha \in (0, 1]$ [29], which can be expanded as for any continuous function $y(t)$,

$${}^{PF}D_t^{\alpha}y(t) = \ell_0(\alpha, t)\,\frac{dy(t)}{dt} + \ell_1(\alpha, t)y(t), 0 < \alpha \leqslant 1 \tag{4}$$

where, $\ell_0(\alpha, t) \neq 0$ for $\alpha \in (0, 1]$, with $\lim_{\alpha \to 0^+} \ell_0(\alpha, t) = 0$ and $\lim_{\alpha \to 1^-} \ell_0(\alpha,$

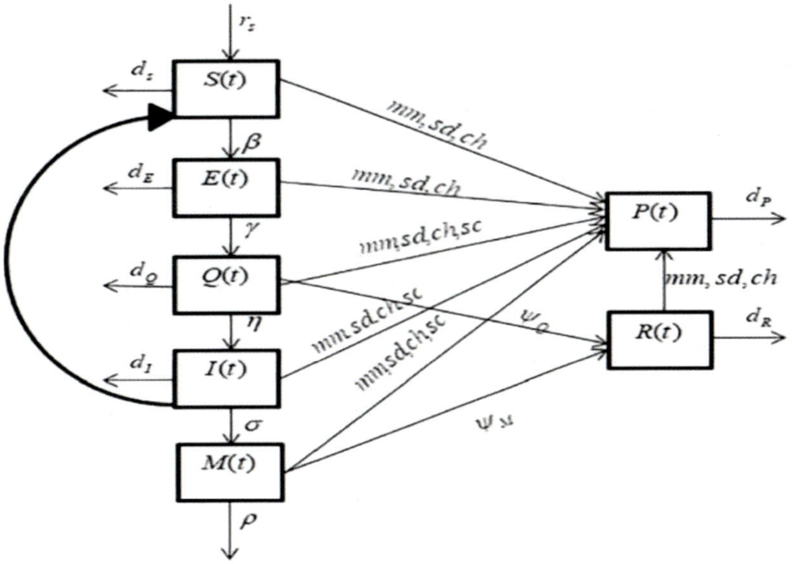

Fig. 1. Pictorial illustration of SEQIMRP model.

$t) = 1$. Additionally, $\ell_1(\alpha, t) \neq 0$ for $\alpha \in [0,1)$, with $\lim_{\alpha \to 0^+} \ell_1(\alpha, t) = 1$ and $\lim_{\alpha \to 1^-} \ell_1(\alpha, t) = 0$. Let, $\ell_0(\alpha, t) = \alpha$ and $\ell_1(\alpha, t) = 1 - \alpha$, so Eq. (4) becomes

$$^{PF}D_t^{\alpha} y(t) = \alpha \frac{dy(t)}{dt} + (1-\alpha) y(t) \tag{5}$$

Assume that all control functions (prevention steps) are constant within time, therefore, by applying expansion (5) on system (1), we get the system as:

$$\dot{S}(t) = \frac{1}{\alpha}\left(r_s S(t)\left(1 - \frac{S(t)}{k_S}\right) - (mm + sd + ch)S(t) - \beta S(t) I(t) - d_s S(t) - (1-\alpha)S(t) \right)$$

$$\dot{E}(t) = \frac{1}{\alpha}(\beta S(t) I(t) - (mm + sd + ch) E(t) - \gamma E(t) - d_E E(t) - (1-\alpha)E(t))$$

$$\dot{Q}(t) = \frac{1}{\alpha}(\gamma E(t) - (mm + sd + ch + sc) Q(t) - \eta Q(t) - \psi_Q Q(t) - d_Q Q(t) - (1-\alpha)Q(t))$$

$$\dot{I}(t) = \frac{1}{\alpha}(\eta Q(t) - (mm + sd + ch + sc) I(t) - \sigma I(t) - d_I I(t) - (1-\alpha)I(t)) \tag{6}$$

$$\dot{M}(t) = \frac{1}{\alpha}(\sigma I(t) - (mm + sd + ch + sc) M(t) - \psi_M M(t) - \rho M(t) - (1-\alpha)M(t))$$

$$\dot{R}(t) = \frac{1}{\alpha}(\psi_Q Q(t) + \psi_M M(t) - (mm + sd + ch) R(t) - d_R R(t) - (1-\alpha)R(t))$$

$$\dot{P}(t) = \frac{1}{\alpha}\left(\begin{array}{c} (mm+sd+ch)(S(t)+E(t)+R(t)) + (mm+sd+ch+sc)Q(t) - d_P P \\ +(mm+sd+ch+sc)(I(t)+M(t)) - (1-\alpha)P(t) \end{array} \right)$$

with the same initial conditions (2). System (6) evidently depicts the lucidity of the proportional fractional derivative, which greatly reduces the manipulation complexities of system (1).

Theorem 1. ((*Boundedness*)) *Let $\Pi \in \Re_+^7$ is the set of all feasible solutions of the system (6), then there exists uniformly bounded subset of $\Re_+^7$ such that:*

$$\Pi = \left\{ (S, E, Q, I, M, R, P) \in \Re_+^7 ;\ \mathrm{N}(t) \leqslant \frac{r_S}{d_N^* k_S} \right\} \tag{7}$$

Proof:. *By applying proportional fractional derivative and its expansion, as defined in the Eqs. (4)-(5), on Eq. (3), we get the expression of the form:*

$$\mathrm{N}(t) = \frac{1}{\alpha}\left(\dot{S}(t) + \dot{E}(t) + \dot{Q}(t) + \dot{I}(t) + \dot{M}(t) + \dot{R}(t) + \dot{P}(t) - (1-\alpha)\mathrm{N}(t) \right) \tag{8}$$

On simplifying by using system (6) and suppose d_N^* be total proportion of deaths in all compartments i.e.

$$d_N^* \mathrm{N}(t) = d_S S(t) + d_E E(t) + d_Q Q(t) + d_I I(t) + d_R R(t) + \rho M(t) + d_P P(t) \tag{9}$$

In addition, since $0 < \alpha \leqslant 1$

$$\dot{\mathrm{N}}(t) \leqslant r_S S(t)\left(1 - \frac{S(t)}{k_S}\right) - d_N^* \mathrm{N}(t) \tag{10}$$

where $0 < \frac{S(t)}{k_S} \leqslant 1$, so the above inequality reduces to

$$\dot{\mathrm{N}}(t) \leqslant \frac{r_S}{k_S} - d_N^* \mathrm{N}(t) \tag{11}$$

On integrating

$$\mathrm{N}(t) \leqslant e^{-t d_N^*} \mathrm{N}(0) + \frac{r_S}{d_N^* k_S} \tag{12}$$

Therefore as $t \to \infty$, we obtained the final statement of boundedness as

$$\mathrm{N}(t) \leqslant \frac{r_S}{d_N^* k_S} \tag{13}$$

Theorem 2. ((*Existence and Uniqueness*)) *Assume the matrix of right hand side of system (6) be the real-valued function $\boldsymbol{\Lambda}(\boldsymbol{F}(t)) : \Re_+^7 \to \Re_+^7$, such that $\boldsymbol{\Lambda}(\boldsymbol{F}(t))$ and $\frac{\partial \boldsymbol{\Lambda}(\boldsymbol{F}(t))}{\partial \boldsymbol{F}(t)}$ are continuous and*

$$\|\boldsymbol{\Lambda}(\boldsymbol{F}(t))\| \leqslant \left(\frac{\mathrm{X}}{|\alpha|} - \nu \right) \|\boldsymbol{F}(t)\|, \quad \forall \boldsymbol{F}(t) \in \Re_+^7 \text{ and } 0 < \alpha \leqslant 1 \tag{14}$$

Then, satisfying the initial conditions (2), there exists a unique, non-negative and bounded solution of the system (6).

Proof:. *Boundedness of system (6) can be followed from Theorem 1, now assume, the system (6) can be expressed as:*

$$\dot{\boldsymbol{F}}(t) = \boldsymbol{\Lambda}(\boldsymbol{F}(t))$$

where,

$$\boldsymbol{F}(t) = [\,S(t) \quad E(t) \quad Q(t) \quad I(t) \quad M(t) \quad R(t) \quad P(t)\,]^T \tag{15}$$

and

$$\boldsymbol{\Lambda}(\boldsymbol{F}(t)) = \frac{1}{\alpha}\begin{bmatrix} r_s S(t)\left(1 - \frac{S(t)}{k_S}\right) - (mm + sd + ch)S(t) - \beta S(t) I(t) - d_s S(t) - (1-\alpha)S(t) \\ \beta S(t) I(t) - (mm + sd + ch) E(t) - \gamma E(t) - d_E E(t) - (1-\alpha)E(t) \\ \gamma E(t) - (mm + sd + ch + sc) Q(t) - \eta Q(t) - \psi_Q Q(t) - d_Q Q(t) - (1-\alpha)Q(t) \\ \eta Q(t) - (mm + sd + ch + sc) I(t) - \sigma I(t) - d_I I(t) - (1-\alpha)I(t) \\ \sigma I(t) - (mm + sd + ch + sc) M(t) - \psi_M M(t) - \rho M(t) - (1-\alpha)M(t) \\ \psi_Q Q(t) + \psi_M M(t) - (mm + sd + ch)R(t) - d_R R(t) - (1-\alpha)R(t) \\ (mm + sd + ch)(S(t) + E(t) + R(t)) + (mm + sd + ch + sc)(Q(t) + I(t) + M(t)) \\ - d_P P - (1-\alpha)P(t) \end{bmatrix} \tag{16}$$

Eq. (16) can be further expanded into:

$$\boldsymbol{\Lambda}(\boldsymbol{F}(t)) = \frac{1}{\alpha}(\Omega_1 \boldsymbol{F}(t) + S(t)\Omega_2 \boldsymbol{F}(t) + I(t)\Omega_3 \boldsymbol{F}(t) - (\alpha - 1)\boldsymbol{F}(t)) \tag{17}$$

such that

$$\Omega_1 = \begin{bmatrix} r_S - M_1 - d_S & 0 & 0 & 0 & 0 & 0 & 0 \\ 0 & -M_1 - \gamma - d_E & 0 & 0 & 0 & 0 & 0 \\ 0 & 0 & -M_2 - \eta - \psi_Q - d_Q & 0 & 0 & 0 & 0 \\ 0 & 0 & \eta & -M_2 - \sigma - d_I & 0 & 0 & 0 \\ 0 & 0 & 0 & \sigma & -M_2 - \psi_M - \rho & 0 & 0 \\ 0 & 0 & \psi_Q & 0 & \psi_M & -M_1 - d_R & 0 \\ M_1 & M_1 & M_2 & M_2 & M_2 & M_1 & -d_P \end{bmatrix}_{7\times 7}$$

$$M_1 = mm + sd + ch$$

$$M_2 = mm + sd + ch + sc$$

$\Omega_2 = [-r_S/k_S \quad \mathbf{0}]_{1\times 7}$ and $\Omega_3 = [-\beta \quad 0 \quad \beta \quad \mathbf{0}]_{1\times 7}$. Then, Eq. (17) can be rewritten as,

$$\|\Lambda(F(t))\| = \left\| \frac{1}{\alpha} (\Omega_1 F(t) + S(t)\Omega_2 F(t) + I(t)\Omega_3 F(t) - (\alpha - 1)F(t)) \right\|$$
$$\leqslant \left|\frac{1}{\alpha}\right| ((\|\Omega_1\| + \|\Omega_2\| + \|\Omega_3\| + |(\alpha - 1)|)\|F(t)\|)$$

Let $X = \|\Omega_1\| + \|\Omega_2\| + \|\Omega_3\|$, so the final statement is achieved as for $0 < \alpha \leqslant 1$,

$$\|\Lambda(F(t))\| \leqslant \left(\frac{X}{|\alpha|} - \nu\right)\|F(t)\|$$

where $\nu = \left|\left(\frac{1}{\alpha} - 1\right)\right|$. Next, we prove the non-negativity of the solutions by using the positivity of initial conditions (2) i.e.,$O_i > 0$ for $i = 1, 2, \ldots, 7$. Considering first equation of system (6), it can be deduced to:

$$\dot{S}(t) = \frac{1}{\alpha}\left(r_s S(t)\left(1 - \frac{S(t)}{k_S}\right) - (mm + sd + ch)S(t) - \beta S(t)I(t) - d_s S(t) - (1-\alpha)S(t)\right)$$
$$\geqslant -\frac{1}{\alpha}(mm + sd + ch + d_S + (1-\alpha))S(t)$$

On manipulating, we get

$$S(t) \geqslant O_1 e^{-((mm+sd+ch+d_S+(1-\alpha))/\alpha)t} \quad (18)$$

Since $0 \leqslant e^{-((mm+sd+ch+d_S+(1-\alpha))/\alpha)t} \leqslant 1$ for $t > 0$, therefore Eq. (18) reduces to,

$$S(t) \geqslant 0$$

Thus, proved the non-negativity of $S(t)$. Analogously, all the remaining equations of system (6) can be proved to have non-negative solutions with the assumption of positive initial conditions.

Optimal control problem

Furthermore, the dynamical model (6) of COVID'19 would be incomplete if the assumption of optimal control of infection and intervention cost is not incorporated. Therefore, we formulate optimal control problem by means of the cost function type of quadratic function as:

$$J(Y_i, U_k) = \int_0^{t_f} \left(\sum_{i=1}^{7} w_i Y_i^2 + \varphi_1 mm^2 + \varphi_2 sd^2 + \varphi_3 ch^2 + \varphi_4 sc^2\right) dt \quad (19)$$

where,$\forall\, Y_i \geqslant 0$ for $i = 1, 2, \ldots 7$are replace by S, E, Q, I, M, R, P,

5

Additionally, the human population cost weights in this example are w_i for $i = 1, 2, \ldots, 7$, whereas the undertaken intervention cost weights for COVID'19 are ψ_K for K = 1, 2, 3, 4. At this point, the expense of intervention comes from government campaigns encouraging the use of masks, social distance, and frequent hand washing. Additionally, when more patients are admitted, the expense of hospitalization for medications, ventilators, and specialized medical staffs for supportive treatment of COVID'19 infected patients also rises. Therefore, if initiatives to enforce the use of masks, social isolation, and regular hand washing are adopted at a higher cost, the COVID'19 transmission will be reduced, which also lowers the cost of supportive care. Thus, for K = 1, 2, 3, 4, we suppose $\psi_K > 0$ Similar to the previous case, the goal of the current one is to stop the spread of COVID'19, which eventually reduces the number of infected people. For this reason, we assume that $w_4 > 0$ and stays equal to zero.

Basic replication code R_0

In this follow-up, we organize the R_0 for the governing model using the next-generation methodology. For this reason, a sub-model of the SEQIMRP that takes into account the four diseased classes—exposed, quarantined, infected, and isolated individuals—is taken into consideration. Consequently, the equation

$$\frac{d\vec{X}}{dt} = F(\vec{X}) - V(\vec{X}) \tag{20}$$

will have $\vec{X}$ as a vector of the$E(t)$,$Q(t)$, $I(t)$, and $M(t)$, which is outlined as,

$$\vec{X} = [E \quad Q \quad I \quad M]'$$

with, $F(\vec{X})$ expressed as,

$$F(\vec{X}) = [\beta S I/\alpha \quad 0 \quad 0 \quad 0]^t$$

On the other hand,$V(\vec{X})$, can be further split down as,

$$V(\vec{X}) = \begin{bmatrix} (mm + sd + ch + \gamma + d_E + (1-\alpha))E(t)/\alpha \\ (mm + sd + ch + sc + \eta + \psi_Q + d_Q + (1-\alpha))Q(t)/\alpha \\ (mm + sd + ch + sc + \sigma + d_I + (1-\alpha))I(t)/\alpha \\ (mm + sd + ch + sc + \psi_M + \rho + (1-\alpha))M(t)/\alpha \end{bmatrix} - \begin{bmatrix} 0 \\ \gamma E(t)/\alpha \\ \eta Q(t)/\alpha \\ \sigma I(t)/\alpha \end{bmatrix}$$

Taking Jacobian matrix of Eq. (20) at disease free equilibrium point,$\Pi_1(-k_S(1 + d_S - r_S + mm + sd + ch - \alpha)/r_S, 0, 0, 0, 0, 0, 0)$, we get,

$$J\left[\frac{d\vec{X}}{dt}\right] = F - V = \begin{pmatrix} 0 & 0 & H_{13} & 0 \\ 0 & 0 & 0 & 0 \\ 0 & 0 & 0 & 0 \\ 0 & 0 & 0 & 0 \end{pmatrix} - \begin{pmatrix} \Delta_{11} & 0 & 0 & 0 \\ \Delta_{21} & \Delta_{22} & 0 & 0 \\ 0 & \Delta_{32} & \Delta_{33} & 0 \\ 0 & 0 & \Delta_{43} & \Delta_{44} \end{pmatrix} \tag{21}$$

where,

$H_{13} = -\beta k_S(1 + d_S - r_S + mm + sd + ch - \alpha)/\alpha r_S$
$\Delta_{11} = (mm + sd + ch + \gamma + d_E + (1-\alpha))/\alpha$
$\Delta_{21} = -\gamma/\alpha, \Delta_{22} = (mm + sd + ch + sc + \eta + \psi_Q + d_Q + (1-\alpha))/\alpha,$
$\Delta_{32} = -\eta/\alpha, \Delta_{33} = (mm + sd + ch + sc + \sigma + d_I + (1-\alpha))/\alpha,$
$\Delta_{43} = -\sigma/\alpha, \Delta_{44} = (mm + sd + ch + sc + \psi_M + \rho + (1-\alpha))/\alpha$

From Eq. (21), we can extract and manipulate,

$$K = FV^{-1}$$

The spectral radius $\Lambda(K)$ is the required basic reproduction number, so after some simplification we get

$$R_0 = -k_S \beta \gamma \eta (1 + d_S - r_S + mm + sd + ch - \alpha)/r_S(1 + d_E + mm + sd + ch - \alpha + \gamma) \quad (1 + d_I + mm + sd + ch + sc - \alpha + \sigma)(1 + d_Q + mm + sd + ch + sc - \alpha + \eta + \psi_Q) \quad (22)$$

Consequently, the generated R_0 contains the fractional derivative index α as well, which advantageously enables to inspect R_0. The health care researchers will be capable to investigate the trajectory of basic reproduction number for the COVID'19 at small change.

$$b_1 = \frac{1}{\alpha^2} \begin{pmatrix} 3 + 2d_Q + 6\,mm + 2\,mm\,d_Q + 3mm^2 + 6sd + 2\,sd\,d_Q + 6\,mm\,sd + 3sd^2 \\ +6\,ch + 2\,ch\,d_Q + 6mm\,ch + 6\,sd\,ch + 3ch^2 + 4\,sc + sc\,d_Q + 4mm\,sc + 4sd\,sc \\ +4\,ch\,sc + sc^2 - \alpha(6 + 2d_Q + 6mm + 6sd + 6ch + 4sc - 3\alpha) \\ +\gamma(2 + d_Q + 2mm + 2sd + 2ch + 2sc - 2\alpha) \\ +\eta(2 + 2mm + 2sd + 2ch + 2sc - 2\alpha + \gamma) \\ +\sigma(2 + d_Q + 2mm + 2sd + 2ch + sc - 2\alpha + \gamma + \eta) \\ +(2 + 2mm + 2sd + 2ch + sc - 2\alpha + \gamma + \sigma)\psi_Q \\ +d_I(2 + d_Q + 2mm + 2sd + 2ch + sc - 2\alpha + \gamma + \eta + \psi_Q) \\ +d_E(2 + d_I + d_Q + 2mm + 2sd + 2ch + 2sc - 2\alpha + \eta + \sigma + \psi_Q) \end{pmatrix},$$

$$b_0 = \frac{Z}{\alpha^3}$$

Dynamical anatomization

In this section, on the strength of proportional fractional derivative, dynamical analysis of equilibrium points and optimality conditions are discussed in fractional environment as follows:

Systematic stability analysis

Theorem 3. (*(Trivial Equilibrium Point)*) *The trivial equilibrium solution, $\Pi_0(0,0,0,0,0,0,0) \in \Re_+^7$, of system (6), is asymptotically unstable, for $0 < \alpha \leqslant 1$.*

Proof:. It can be easily proved by eigenvalues of J at $\Pi_0(0,0,0,0,0,0,0) \in \Re_+^7$, for all $0 < \alpha \leqslant 1$,

$\lambda_1 = \frac{-1-d_P+\alpha}{\alpha}, \lambda_2 = \frac{-1-d_R-mm-sd-ch+\alpha}{\alpha}, \lambda_3 = \frac{-1-d_S+r_S-mm-sd-ch+\alpha}{\alpha},$
$\lambda_4 = \frac{-1-d_E-mm-sd-ch+\alpha-\gamma}{\alpha},$
$\lambda_5 = \frac{-1-d_I-mm-sd-ch-sc+\alpha-\sigma}{\alpha}, \quad \lambda_6 = \frac{-1-mm-sd-ch-sc+\alpha-\rho-\psi_M}{\alpha},$
$\lambda_7 = \frac{-1-d_Q-mm-sd-ch-sc+\alpha-\eta-\psi_Q}{\alpha}.$

Since $r_S > 1 + d_S + mm + sd + ch - \alpha$, it is clear that $\lambda_3 > 0$, for $0 < \alpha \leqslant 1$. Thus, $\Pi_0 \in \Re_+^7$ is unstable.

Theorem 4. (*(Disease Free Equilibrium Point)*) *The disease-free equilibrium of the system (6)*
$\Pi_1(-k_S(1 + d_S - r_S + mm + sd + ch - \alpha)/r_S, 0,0,0,0,0,0) \in \Re_+^7$

For $r_S > 1 + d_S + mm + sd + ch - \alpha$, is locally asymptotically stable if $R_0 < 1$ and unstable when $R_0 > 1$, for $0 \leqslant \alpha < 1$.

Proof:. On manipulating Jacobian at $\Pi_1(-k_S(1 + d_S - r_S + mm + sd + ch - \alpha)/r_S, 0,0,0,0,0,0) \in \Re_+^7$, the negative eigenvalues i.e. $\lambda_i \in \Re_-^7$ for $i = 1,2,3,4$, are attained as:

$\lambda_1 = \frac{1+d_S-r_S+mm+sd+ch-\alpha}{\alpha}, \lambda_2 = \frac{-1-d_P+\alpha}{\alpha}, \lambda_3 = \frac{-1-d_R-mm-sd-ch+\alpha}{\alpha},$
$\lambda_4 = \frac{-1-mm-sd-ch-sc+\alpha-\rho-\psi_M}{\alpha},$

with the equation,

$$P(\lambda) = \lambda^3 + b_2\lambda^2 + b_1\lambda + b_0(1-R_0) = 0 \quad (23)$$

where

$b_2 = \frac{1}{\alpha}(3 + d_E + d_I + d_Q + 3mm + 3sd + 3ch + 2sc - 3\alpha + \gamma + \eta + \sigma + \psi_Q),$

where

$Z = (1 + d_E + mm + sd + ch - \alpha + \gamma)(1 + d_I + mm + sd + ch + sc - \alpha + \sigma)$
$(1 + d_Q + mm + sd + ch + sc - \alpha + \eta + \psi_Q)$

On applying Routh-Hurwitz criteria [31–34] i.e. if $b_2 > 0$, $b_0(1-R_0) > 0$ and $b_1b_2 > b_0(1-R_0)$, then polynomial (23) is greater than zero and thus all the real part of the eigenvalues must be negative. It can be evidently seen that $b_i > 0$ for $i = 0,1,2$, now the thing which left to prove is $(1-R_0) > 0$. Hence, $\Pi_1 \in \Re_-^7$ is locally asymptotically stable if $R_0 < 1$ and if $R_0 > 1$, $(1-R_0) < 0$ implies $P(\lambda) < 0$ that is Eq. (23) must have a nonnegative real part, thus $\Pi_1 \in \Re_+^7$ becomes unstable.

Theorem 5. (*(Endemic Equilibrium Point)*) *The endemic equilibrium $\Pi_2(\hat{S},\hat{E},\hat{Q},\hat{I},\hat{M},\hat{R},\hat{P}) \in \Re_+^7$ is locally asymptotically stable if and only if, $R_0 > 1$, for $0 \leqslant \alpha < 1$.*

Proof:. The Jacobian at $\Pi_2(\hat{S},\hat{E},\hat{Q},\hat{I},\hat{M},\hat{R},\hat{P}) \in \Re_+^7$, generates the negative real eigenvalues,

$\lambda_1 = \frac{-1-d_P+\alpha}{\alpha}, \lambda_2 = \frac{-1-d_R-mm-sd-ch+\alpha}{\alpha}$
$\lambda_3 = \frac{-1-mm-sd-ch-sc+\alpha-\rho-\psi_M}{\alpha}$

with the polynomial equation,

$$D(\lambda) = \lambda^4 + K_3\lambda^3 + K_2\lambda^2 + K_1\lambda + K_0 = 0 \tag{24}$$

where,

$$K_3 = \frac{-(1 + d_S - r_S + mm + sd + ch - \alpha)}{\alpha\, R_0} + b_2$$

$$K_2 = (K_3 - b_2)b_2 + \frac{B}{\alpha^2}$$

$$K_1 = \left(\frac{B(K_3 - b_2)}{\alpha^2}\right)$$

$$K_0 = \frac{(1+d_S-r_S+mm+sd+ch-\alpha)}{\alpha^4 R_0}\left(\frac{k_S(1+d_S-r_S+mm+sd+ch-\alpha)\beta\gamma\eta}{r_S} + A\right)$$

where,

$$\begin{aligned}
A = {} & 1 + d_Q + 3mm + 2d_Qmm + 3mm^2 + d_Qmm^2 + mm^3 + 3sd + 2d_Qsd + 6mm\,sd \\
& + 2d_Qmm\,sd + 3mm^2sd + 3sd^2 + d_Qsd^2 + 3mm\,sd^2 + sd^3 + 3ch + 2d_Qch \\
& + 6mm\,ch + 2d_Qmm\,ch + 3mm^2ch + 6sd\,ch + 2d_Qsd\,ch + 6mm\,sd\,ch \\
& + 3sd^2ch + 3ch^2 + d_Qch^2 + 3mm\,ch^2 + 3sd\,ch^2 + ch^3 + 2sc + d_Qsc \\
& + 4mm\,sc + d_Qmm\,sc + 2mm^2sc + 4sd\,sc + d_Qsd\,sc + 4mm\,sd\,sc + 2sd^2sc \\
& + 4ch\,sc + d_Qch\,sc + 4mm\,ch\,sc + 4sd\,ch\,sc + 24ch^2\,sc + sc^2 + mm\,sc^2 + sd\,sc^2 + ch\,sc^2 \\
& - \alpha\begin{pmatrix} 3 + 2d_Q + 6mm + 2d_Qmm + 3mm^2 + 6sd + 2d_Qsd + 6mm\,sd + 3sd^2 + 6ch + 2d_Qch \\ + 6mm\,ch + 6sd\,ch + 3ch^2 + 4sc + d_Qsc + 4mm\,sc + 4sd\,sc + 4ch\,sc \\ + sc^2 - 3\alpha - d_Q\alpha - 3mm\alpha - 3sd\alpha - 3ch\alpha - 2sc\alpha - \alpha^2 \end{pmatrix} \\
& + \gamma\begin{pmatrix} 1 + d_Q + 2mm + d_Qmm + mm^2 + 2sd + d_Qsd + 2mm\,sd + sd^2 + 2ch \\ + d_Qu_3ch + 2mm\,ch + 2sd\,ch + ch^2 + 2sc + d_Qsc + 2mm\,sc + 2sd\,sc \\ + 2ch\,sc + sc^2 - 2\alpha - 2mm\,\alpha - 2sd\,\alpha - 2ch\,\alpha - 2sc\,\alpha + \alpha^2 \end{pmatrix} \\
& + \eta\begin{pmatrix} 1 + 2mm + mm^2 + 2sd + 2mm\,sd + sd^2 + 2ch + 2mm\,ch + 2sd\,ch + sd^2 + sc \\ + mm\,sc + sd\,sc + ch\,sc - 2\alpha - 2mm\alpha - 2sd\alpha - 2ch\alpha - sc\alpha + \alpha^2 \end{pmatrix} \\
& + \sigma\begin{pmatrix} 1 + d_Q + 2mm + d_Qmm + mm^2 + 2sd + d_Qsd + 2mm\,sd + sd^2 \\ + 2ch + d_Qch + 2mm\,ch + 2sd\,ch + ch^2 + sc + mm\,sc + sd\,sc \\ + ch\,sc - 2\alpha - d_Q\alpha - 2mm\alpha - 2sd\alpha - 2ch\alpha - sc\alpha + a^2 \end{pmatrix} \\
& + \gamma\sigma(1 + d_Q + mm + sd + ch + sc - \alpha) + \eta\sigma(1 + mm + sd + ch - \alpha + \gamma) \\
& + (1 + mm + sd + ch - \alpha + \gamma)(1 + mm + sd + ch + sc - \alpha + \sigma)\psi_Q + \gamma\eta(1 + mm + sd + ch + sc - \alpha - k_S\beta) \\
& + d_I(1 + mm + sd + ch - \alpha + \gamma)(1 + d_Q + mm + sd + ch + sc - \alpha + \eta + \psi_Q) \\
& + d_E(1 + d_I + mm + sd + ch + sc - \alpha + \sigma)(1 + d_Q + mm + sd + ch + sc - \alpha + \eta + \psi_Q)
\end{aligned}$$

and

$$\begin{aligned}
B = {} & 3 + 2d_Q + 6mm + 2d_Qmm + 3mm^2 + 6sd + 2d_Qsd + 6mm\,sd + 3sd^2 \\
& + 6ch + 2d_Qch + 6mm\,ch + 6sd\,ch + 3ch^2 + 4sc + + d_Qsc + 4mm\,sc \\
& + 4sd\,sc + 4sc\,ch + sc^2 - 6\alpha - 2d_Q\alpha - 6mm\alpha - 6sd\alpha - 6ch\alpha - 4sc\alpha \\
& + 3\alpha^2 + 2\gamma + d_Q\gamma + 2mm\gamma + 2sd\gamma + 2ch\gamma + 2sc\gamma - 2\alpha\gamma + 2\eta + 2mm\eta \\
& + 2sd\eta + 2ch\eta + sc\eta - 2\alpha\eta + \gamma\eta + 2\sigma + d_Q\sigma + 2mm\sigma + 2sd\sigma + 2ch\sigma \\
& + sc\sigma - 2\alpha\sigma + \gamma\sigma + \eta\sigma + (2 + 2mm + 2sd + 2ch + sc - 2\alpha + \gamma + \sigma)\psi_Q \\
& + d_I(2 + d_Q + 2mm + 2sd + 2ch + sc - 2\alpha + \gamma + \eta + \psi_Q) + (2 + d_I \\
& + d_Q + 2mm + 2sd + 2ch + 2sc - 2\alpha + \eta + \sigma + \psi_Q)\,.
\end{aligned}$$

The factor $\left(\frac{k_S(1+d_S-r_S+mm+sd+ch-\alpha)\beta\gamma\eta}{r_S} + A\right) < 0$, if the magnitude of $\frac{k_S(1+d_S-r_S+mm+sd+ch-\alpha)\beta\gamma\eta}{r_S} > A$, which implies that K_0 becomes positive if and only if $R_0 > 1$. Thus with reference to Lemma 5.1 of [20], the positive constant of the polynomial $D(\lambda)$ implies $\Pi_2\left(\widehat{S}, \widehat{E}, \widehat{Q}, \widehat{I}, \widehat{M}, \widehat{R}, \widehat{P}\right) \in \Re^7_+$ is locally asymptotically stable if $R_0 > 1$.

Characterization of optimal control

It is evidently clear from Theorem 1 that there exist a unique solution of system (6). Now to optimize the solution, we define the Lagrangian by

$$L(Y_i) = \sum_{i=1}^{7} w_i Y_i^2 + \varphi_1 mm^2 + \varphi_2 sd^2 + \varphi_3 ch^2 + \varphi_4 sc^2 \tag{25}$$

In addition, describing the Hamiltonian Has the inner product of the right hand side of the state system (6) and the adjoint variables $\Omega = (\omega_1, \omega_2, \omega_3, \omega_4, \omega_5, \omega_6, \omega_7)$, we get

$$\begin{aligned}
\mathrm{H}(S, E, Q, I, M, R, P, \Omega, t) = {} & L(Y_i) + \omega_1(t)\dot{S}(t) + \omega_2(t)\dot{E}(t) + \omega_3(t)\dot{Q}(t) \\
& + \omega_4(t)\dot{I}(t) + \omega_5(t)\dot{M}(t) + \omega_6(t)\dot{R}(t) \\
& + \omega_7(t)\dot{P}(t)
\end{aligned} \tag{26}$$

where Ω is to be determined. Now, utilizing the Pontryagin's maximum principle for the Hamiltonian H, following theorem is obtained to determine the adjoint variables.

Theorem 6. ((*Existence of adjoint variable*)) *For the controlling functions mm^*, sd^*, ch^* and sc^* together with the solution $(S^*(t), E^*(t), I^*(t), Q^*(t), M^*(t), R^*(t), P^*(t))$ of the corresponding system (6), there exists adjoint variables $\Omega = (\omega_1, \omega_2, \omega_3, \omega_4, \omega_5, \omega_6, \omega_7)$ that satisfy,*

$$\frac{d\omega_2(t)}{dt} = \frac{-(-1 - d_E - mm - sd - ch + \alpha - \gamma)\omega_2(t)}{\alpha} - \frac{\gamma\,\omega_3(t)}{\alpha} - \frac{(mm + sd + ch)\omega_7(t)}{\alpha}$$

$$\frac{d\omega_1(t)}{dt} = \frac{-\left(-1-d_S-\frac{r_S S^*(t)}{k_S}+r_S\left(1-\frac{S^*(t)}{k_S}\right)-mm-sd-ch+\alpha-I^*(t)\beta\right)\omega_1(t)}{\alpha} - \frac{I^*(t)\beta\omega_2(t)}{\alpha} - \frac{(mm+sd+ch)\omega_7(t)}{\alpha}$$

$$with transversality\ \omega_i(T)=0,\ i=1,2,\ldots,7\ where\ T=t_{final} \tag{28}$$

Furthermore, the optimal control pairs are descripted as:

$$mm^* = max\left(min\left(\frac{B_0}{2\alpha\varphi_1}, mm^{max}\right), 0\right),$$

$$sd^* = max\left(min\left(\frac{B_0}{2\alpha\varphi_2}, sd^{max}\right), 0\right),$$

$$ch^* = max\left(min\left(\frac{B_0}{2\alpha\varphi_3}, ch^{max}\right), 0\right),$$

$$sc^* = max\left(min\left(\frac{Q^*(t)\omega_3(t)+I^*(t)\omega_4(t)+M^*(t)\omega_5(t)-\omega_7(t)(I^*(t)+M^*(t)+Q^*(t))}{2\alpha\varphi_4}, sc^{max}\right), 0\right),$$

$$\frac{d\omega_3(t)}{dt} = \frac{-(-1-d_Q-mm-sd-ch-sc+\alpha-\eta-\psi_Q)\omega_3(t)}{\alpha} - \frac{\eta\omega_4(t)}{\alpha} - \frac{\psi_Q\omega_6(t)}{\alpha} - \frac{(mm+sd+ch+sc)\omega_7(t)}{\alpha}$$

$$B_0 = S^*(t)\omega_1(t)+E^*(t)\omega_2(t)+Q^*(t)\omega_3(t)+I^*(t)\omega_4(t)+M^*(t)\omega_5(t) + R^*(t)\omega_6(t)-\omega_7(t)(E^*(t)+I^*(t)+M^*(t)+Q^*(t)+R^*(t)+S^*(t))$$

Proof:. *By using Pontryagin's maximum principle in state, the adjoint equations with transversality conditions is stated as:*

$$\frac{d\omega_1(t)}{dt} = \frac{-\partial H}{\partial S} = \frac{-\left(-1-d_S-\frac{r_S S^*(t)}{k_S}+r_S\left(1-\frac{S^*(t)}{k_S}\right)-mm-sd-ch+\alpha-I^*(t)\beta\right)\omega_1(t)}{\alpha} - \frac{I^*(t)\beta\omega_2(t)}{\alpha} - \frac{(mm+sd+ch)\omega_7(t)}{\alpha}$$

$$\frac{d\omega_2(t)}{dt} = \frac{-\partial H}{\partial E} = \frac{-(-1-d_E-mm-sd-ch+\alpha-\gamma)\omega_2(t)}{\alpha} - \frac{\gamma\omega_3(t)}{\alpha} - \frac{(mm+sd+ch)\omega_7(t)}{\alpha}$$

$$\frac{d\omega_3(t)}{dt} = \frac{-\partial H}{\partial Q} = \frac{-(-1-d_Q-mm-sd-ch-sc+\alpha-\eta-\psi_Q)\omega_3(t)}{\alpha} - \frac{\eta\omega_4(t)}{\alpha} - \frac{\psi_Q\omega_6(t)}{\alpha} - \frac{(mm+sd+ch+sc)\omega_7(t)}{\alpha}$$

$$\frac{d\omega_4(t)}{dt} = -2I^*(t)w_4 + \frac{S^*(t)\beta\omega_1(t)}{\alpha} - \frac{S^*(t)\beta\omega_2(t)}{\alpha} - \frac{(mm+sd+ch+sc)\omega_7(t)}{\alpha} - \frac{(-1-d_I-mm^*-sd-ch-sc+\alpha-\sigma)\omega_4(t)}{\alpha} - \frac{\sigma\omega_5(t)}{\alpha}$$

$$\frac{d\omega_5(t)}{dt} = \frac{-(-1-mm-sd-ch-sc+\alpha-\rho-\psi_M)\omega_5(t)}{\alpha} - \frac{\psi_M\omega_6(t)}{\alpha} - \frac{(mm+sd+ch+sc)\omega_7(t)}{\alpha}$$

$$\frac{d\omega_6(t)}{dt} = \frac{-(-1-d_R-mm-sd-ch+\alpha)\omega_6(t)}{\alpha} - \frac{(mm+sd+ch)\omega_7(t)}{\alpha}$$

$$\frac{d\omega_7(t)}{dt} = -\frac{(-1-d_P+\alpha)\omega_7(t)}{\alpha} \tag{27}$$

$$\frac{d\omega_4(t)}{dt} = \frac{-\partial H}{\partial I} = -2I^*(t)\,w_4 + \frac{S^*(t)\beta\omega_1(t)}{\alpha} - \frac{S^*(t)\beta\omega_2(t)}{\alpha} - \frac{(mm+sd+ch+sc)\omega_7(t)}{\alpha} - \frac{(-1-d_I-mm^*-sd-ch-sc+\alpha-\sigma)\omega_4(t)}{\alpha} - \frac{\sigma\omega_5(t)}{\alpha}$$

$$\frac{d\omega_5(t)}{dt} = \frac{-\partial H}{\partial M} = \frac{-(-1-mm-sd-ch-sc+\alpha-\rho-\psi_M)\omega_5(t)}{\alpha} - \frac{\psi_M\omega_6(t)}{\alpha} - \frac{(mm+sd+ch+sc)\omega_7(t)}{\alpha}$$

$$\frac{d\omega_6(t)}{dt} = \frac{-\partial H}{\partial R} = \frac{-(-1-d_R-mm-sd-ch+\alpha)\omega_6(t)}{\alpha} - \frac{(mm+sd+ch)\omega_7(t)}{\alpha}$$

$$\frac{d\omega_7(t)}{dt} = \frac{-\partial H}{\partial P} = -\frac{(-1-d_P+\alpha)\omega_7(t)}{\alpha}$$

with transversality $\omega_i(T) = 0, i = 1, 2, \ldots, 7$where $T = t_{final}$. By using optimality condition, we deduce the optimal control pairs as:

$$\frac{\partial H}{\partial mm} = 0 \Rightarrow mm^* = \frac{B_0}{2\alpha\varphi_1}$$

$$\frac{\partial H}{\partial sd} = 0 \Rightarrow sd^* = \frac{B_0}{2\alpha\varphi_2}$$

$$\frac{\partial H}{\partial ch} = 0 \Rightarrow ch^* = \frac{B_0}{2\alpha\varphi_3}$$

$$\frac{\partial H}{\partial sc} = 0 \Rightarrow sc^* = \frac{Q^*(t)\omega_3(t) + I^*(t)\omega_4(t) + M^*(t)\omega_5(t) - \omega_7(t)(I^*(t) + M^*(t) + Q^*(t))}{2\alpha\varphi_4}$$

Further, taking into account the property of the control space, we achieve,

$$mm^*(t) = \begin{cases} 0 & if \quad X_1 \leqslant 0 \\ X_1 & if \quad 0 \leqslant X_1 \leqslant mm^{max} \\ mm^{max} & if \quad X_1 \geqslant mm^{max} \end{cases}, \quad sd^*(t) = \begin{cases} 0 & if \quad X_2 \leqslant 0 \\ X_2 & if \quad 0 \leqslant X_2 \leqslant sd^{max} \\ sd^{max} & if \quad X_2 \geqslant sd^{max} \end{cases}$$

$$ch^*(t) = \begin{cases} 0 & if \quad X_3 \leqslant 0 \\ X_3 & if \quad 0 \leqslant X_3 \leqslant ch^{max} \\ ch^{max} & if \quad X_3 \geqslant ch^{max} \end{cases}, \quad sc^*(t) = \begin{cases} 0 & if \quad X_4 \leqslant 0 \\ X_4 & if \quad 0 \leqslant X_4 \leqslant sc^{max} \\ sc^{max} & if \quad X_4 \geqslant sc^{max} \end{cases}.$$

where,

$$X_1 = \frac{B_0}{2\alpha\varphi_1}$$

$$X_2 = \frac{B_0}{2\alpha\varphi_2}$$

$$X_3 = \frac{B_0}{2\alpha\varphi_3}$$

$$X_4 = \frac{Q^*(t)\omega_3(t) + I^*(t)\omega_4(t) + M^*(t)\omega_5(t) - \omega_7(t)(I^*(t) + M^*(t) + Q^*(t))}{2\alpha\varphi_4}$$

Ultimately, the control pair and state variables are found by using the following composed systems:

$$\dot{S}(t) = \frac{1}{\alpha}\left(r_s S(t)\left(1 - \frac{S(t)}{k_S}\right) - (mm^*(t) + sd^*(t) + ch^*(t))S(t) - \beta S(t)I(t) - d_s S(t) - (1-\alpha)S(t)\right)$$

$$\dot{E}(t) = \frac{1}{\alpha}(\beta S(t)I(t) - (mm^*(t) + sd^*(t) + ch^*(t))E(t) - \gamma E(t) - d_E E(t) - (1-\alpha)E(t))$$

$$\dot{Q}(t) = \frac{1}{\alpha}(\gamma E(t) - (mm^*(t) + sd^*(t) + ch^*(t) + sc^*(t))Q(t) - \eta Q(t) - \psi_Q Q(t) - d_Q Q(t) - (1-\alpha)Q(t))$$

$$\dot{I}(t) = \frac{1}{\alpha}(\eta Q(t) - (mm^*(t) + sd^*(t) + ch^*(t) + sc^*(t))I(t) - \sigma I(t) - d_I I(t) - (1-\alpha)I(t)),$$

$$\dot{M}(t) = \frac{1}{\alpha}(\sigma I(t) - (mm^*(t) + sd^*(t) + ch^*(t) + sc^*(t))M(t) - \psi_M M(t) - \rho M(t) - (1-\alpha)M(t))$$

$$\dot{R}(t) = \frac{1}{\alpha}(\psi_Q Q(t) + \psi_M M(t) - (mm^*(t) + sd^*(t) + ch^*(t))R(t) - d_R R(t) - (1-\alpha)R(t))$$

$$\dot{P}(t) = \frac{1}{\alpha}\left(\begin{array}{c}(mm^*(t) + sd^*(t) + ch^*(t))(S(t) + E(t) + R(t)) + (mm^*(t) + sd^*(t) + ch^*(t) + sc^*(t))Q(t) \\ +(mm^*(t) + sd^*(t) + ch^*(t) + sc^*(t))(I(t) + M(t)) - d_P P - (1-\alpha)P(t)\end{array}\right)$$

and

$$\frac{d\omega_1(t)}{dt} = \frac{-\left(-1 - d_S - \frac{r_S S^*(t)}{k_S} + r_S\left(1 - \frac{S^*(t)}{k_S}\right) - (mm^*(t) + sd^*(t) + ch^*(t)) + \alpha - I^*(t)\beta\right)\omega_1(t)}{\alpha} - \frac{I^*(t)\beta\omega_2(t)}{\alpha} - \frac{(mm^*(t) + sd^*(t) + ch^*(t))\omega_7(t)}{\alpha}$$

$$\frac{d\omega_2(t)}{dt}=\frac{-(-1-d_E-(mm^*(t)+sd^*(t)+ch^*(t))+\alpha-\gamma)\omega_2(t)}{\alpha}-\frac{\gamma\omega_3(t)}{\alpha}-\frac{(mm^*(t)+sd^*(t)+ch^*(t))\omega_7(t)}{\alpha}$$

$$\frac{d\omega_3(t)}{dt}=\frac{-(-1-d_Q-(mm^*(t)+sd^*(t)+ch^*(t)+sc^*(t))+\alpha-\eta-\psi_Q)\omega_3(t)}{\alpha}-\frac{\eta\omega_4(t)}{\alpha}-\frac{\psi_Q\omega_6(t)}{\alpha}-\frac{(mm^*(t)+sd^*(t)+ch^*(t)+sc^*(t))\omega_7(t)}{\alpha}$$

$$\frac{d\omega_4(t)}{dt}=-2I^*(t)\,w_4+\frac{S^*(t)\beta\omega_1(t)}{\alpha}-\frac{S^*(t)\beta\omega_2(t)}{\alpha}\frac{-(-1-d_I-(mm^*(t)+sd^*(t)+ch^*(t)+sc^*(t))+\alpha-\sigma)\omega_4(t)}{\alpha}-\frac{\sigma\omega_5(t)}{\alpha}-\frac{(mm^*(t)+sd^*(t)+ch^*(t)+sc^*(t))\omega_7(t)}{\alpha}$$

$$\frac{d\omega_5(t)}{dt}=\frac{-(-1-(mm^*(t)+sd^*(t)+ch^*(t)+sc^*(t))+\alpha-\rho-\psi_M)\omega_5(t)}{\alpha}-\frac{\psi_M\omega_6(t)}{\alpha}-\frac{(mm^*(t)+sd^*(t)+ch^*(t)+sc^*(t))\omega_7(t)}{\alpha}$$

$$\frac{d\omega_6(t)}{dt}=\frac{-(-1-d_R-(mm^*(t)+sd^*(t)+ch^*(t))+\alpha)\omega_6(t)}{\alpha}-\frac{(mm^*(t)+sd^*(t)+ch^*(t))\omega_7(t)}{\alpha}$$

$$\frac{d\omega_7(t)}{dt}=-\frac{(-1-d_P+\alpha)\omega_7(t)}{\alpha}$$

Deliberation and numerical simulation

In this section, the aforementioned system is subjected to numerical analyses by taking into account some of the numerical values of the parameters, as displayed in Table 1. The topic also includes the graphical predisposition analysis of R0 in relation to the strategies. Additionally, using Mathematica 11.0, simulations of all compartmental class scenarios with and without preventative campaigns are plotted and tabulated.

Table 2: Inspection of R_0's sensitivity and ideal surveillance J based on prevention Weights $w_4 = 200$, $\psi_1 = 100$, $\psi_2 = 20$, $\psi_3 = 150$, $\psi_4 = 300$: Strategies t between [0, 30] and for various values of α.

α	Intervention Strategies	R_0	J
0.8	$mm = 0,\ sd = 0,\ ch = 0, sc = 0$	2.08323	6171.69
	$mm = 0.3, sd = 0.5, ch = 0.65, sc = 0.9$	0.236717	9702.47
	$mm = 0.3, sd = 0.7, ch = 0.5, sc = 0.9$	0.227723	9068.92
	$mm = 0.6, sd = 0.5, ch = 0.3, sc = 0.9$	0.246215	9017.57
0.95	$mm = 0,\ sd = 0,\ ch = 0, sc = 0$	2.83546	9622.94
	$mm = 0.3, sd = 0.5, ch = 0.65, sc = 0.9$	0.266884	9724.52
	$mm = 0.3, sd = 0.7, ch = 0.5, sc = 0.9$	0.252657	9090.57
	$mm = 0.6, sd = 0.5, ch = 0.3, sc = 0.9$	0.278141	9040.02
1	$mm = 0,\ sd = 0,\ ch = 0, sc = 0$	3.17529	10815.9
	$mm = 0.3, sd = 0.5, ch = 0.65, sc = 0.9$	0.278141	9732.32
	$mm = 0.3, sd = 0.7, ch = 0.5, sc = 0.9$	0.266884	9098.23
	$mm = 0.6, sd = 0.5, ch = 0.3, sc = 0.9$	0.290079	9047.98

Parameter sensitivity analysis with optimality

Table 2 and Figures 2-7 show R_0's sensitivity to control variables for the parameters in Table 1 and different values of. These control variables describe COVID'19 prevention efforts. At each value of, the influential strength of each campaign minimizes R_0. The colorized output in these pictures, from bright to dark, represents a reduction in R_0. Table 2 and Figures 2-7 show that R_0 is larger than 1 without any awareness campaign and decreases with increased campaigns. Fig. 2's R_0 lines, obtained by setting ch = 0.1 and sc = 0.1 and altering mm and sd, decline from 1.4 to 0.4. Figs. 3 and 5 show the same pattern of decreasing R_0 for mm = 0.1, sc = 0.1 and mm = 0.1, sd = 0.1. Fig. 4 shows R_0 decreasing from 1.8 to 0.4 for mm = 0.1, sd = 0.1. Figs. 6 and 7 show the same drawings for mm = 0.1, ch = 0.1 and sd = 0.1, ch = 0.1. Table 2 demonstrates the sensitivity of R_0 with different intervention techniques, showing that for mm = 0.3, sd = 0.7,ch = 0.5,sc = 0.9, R_0 declines more quickly than the other combinations at each value of. Table 2's last column shows the least cost function J for each mitigation technique with weights $w_4 = 200$, $\psi_1 = 100$, $\psi_2 = 20$, $\psi_3 = 150$, and $\psi_4 = 300$. The ideal values of J for surveillance cost mitigations, mm = 0.3, sd = 0.7, ch = 0.5, sc = 0.9, which considerably lower R_0 are 9068.92, 9090.57, and 9098.23 for α= 0.8, 0.95, 1, respectively, and tε[0, 30]. Increasing knowledge about social distance and supportive care of affected patients will considerably impact COVID'19 transmission with optimal cost efforts, compared to other mitigation combinations.

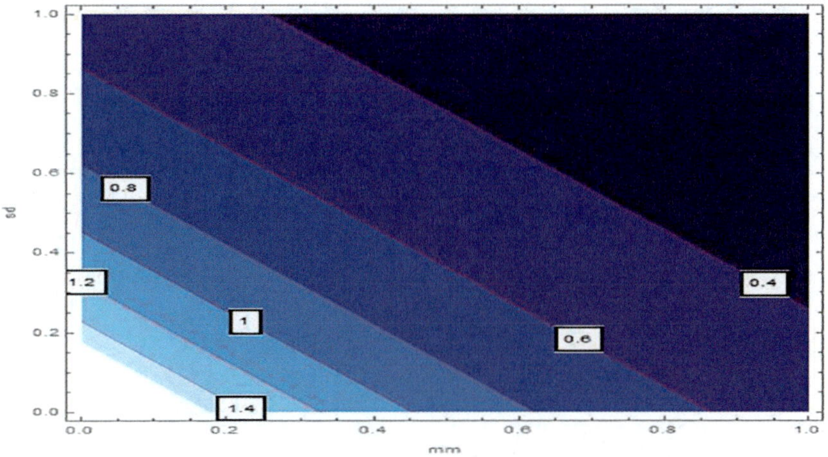

Fig 2: R_0's sensitivity to mm and sd is being examined given the conditions of ch = 0.1, sc = 0.1, and α= 0.95.

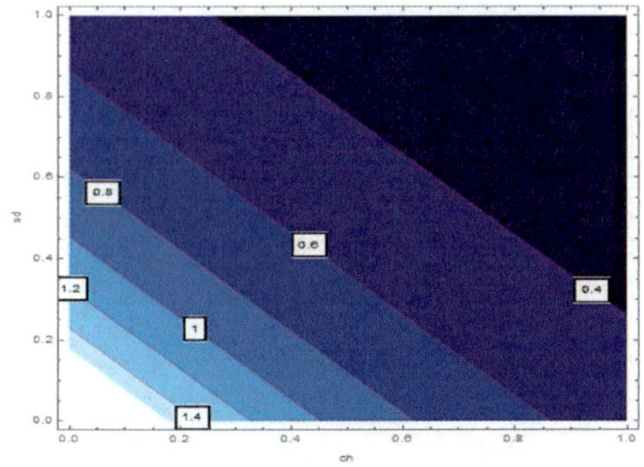

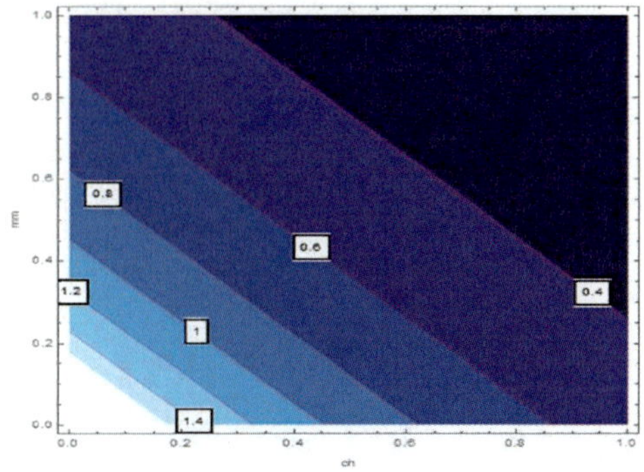

Fig 3: Sensitivity analysis of R_0 for mm = 0.1, sc = 0.1, and at α= 0.95 with regard to ch and sd
Fig 5:Sensitivity analysis of R_0 for sd = 0.1, sc = 0.1, and α= 0.95 with regard to ch and mm.

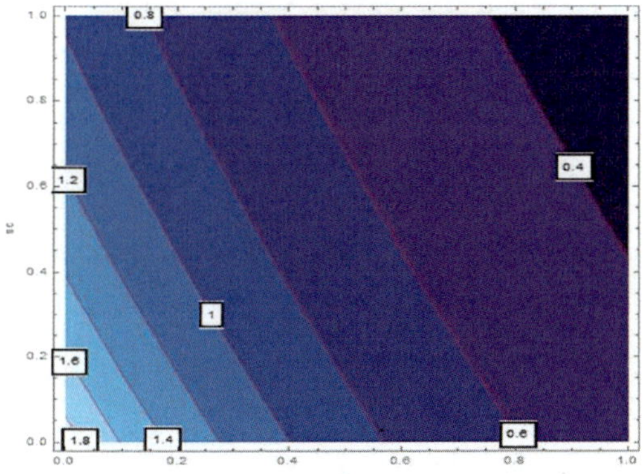

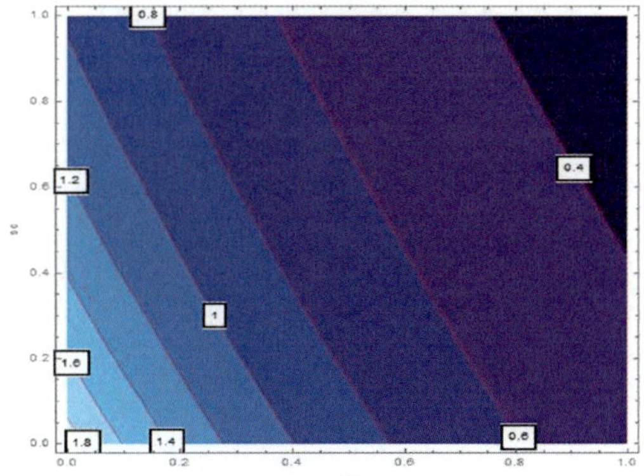

Fig 4: Sensitivity analysis of R0 for mm = 0.1, sd = 0.1, and at α= 0.95 with regard to ch and sc
Fig 6:Sensitivity analysis of R0 for mm = 0.1, ch = 0.1, and at α= 0.95 with regard to sd and sc.

Optimal conditions and equilibrium states

Solving SEQIMRP yields charts defining Π_1 and Π_2 stability. Current equilibrium point estimations are based on preventative initiatives. Table 3 generates mm = 0, sd = 0, ch = 0 and sc = 0 at $\alpha\varepsilon[0, 1]$ and $t\varepsilon[0, 30]$. No preventative actions cause R0 to rise and the pandemic to become endemic.

Figs. 8-14, displayed for mm = 0, sd = 0, ch = 0 and sc = 0, at = 0.8, 0.95, 1 and $t\varepsilon$ [0, 30], show the stability of the lethal endemic condition of COIVD'19 for transmission, recovery, and mortality. Since no preventative measures are implemented during COVID'19's early spread, the protected population curve is a straight line on zero. This explains why the pandemic scenario worsens when everyone is at danger of infection.

Table 4 shows values for mm = 0.2, sd = 0.3, ch = 0.35, and sc = 0.65 at αε(0, 1] and tε [0, 30]. Table 4 shows that when preventative measures are considered, the dynamics are disease-free at all values. Figs. 15-21 illustrate the stability of 1 for mm = 0.2, sd = 0.3, ch = 0.35 and sc = 0.65, at α= 0.8, 0.95, 1 and tε [0, 30]. In disease-free cases, infected cells are zero, but vulnerable and protected persons are not. Awareness efforts concerning masks, social distance, hand washing, and patient support will reduce COVID'19 reproduction and spread.

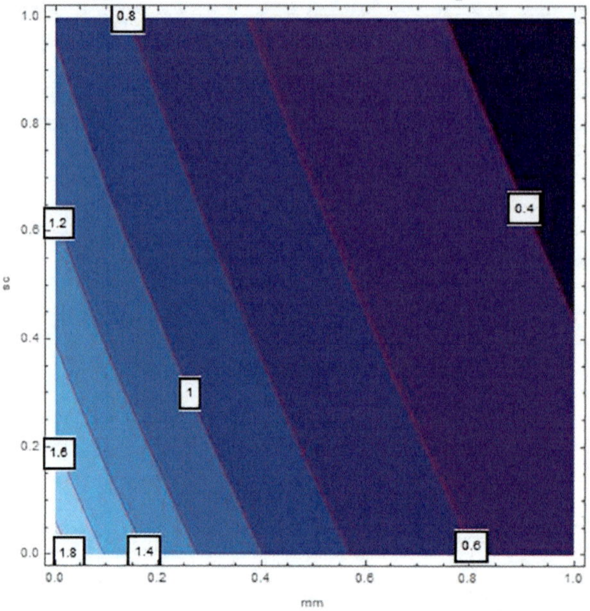

Fig 7: R_0's sensitivity to mm and sc is examined for sd = 0.1, ch = 0.1, and at α= 0.95.

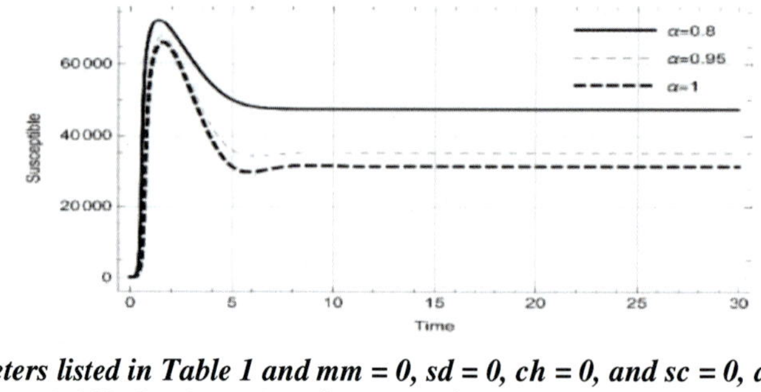

Fig 8: For the parameters listed in Table 1 and mm = 0, sd = 0, ch = 0, and sc = 0, at α= 0.8, 0.95, 1, and t ε[0, 30], the dynamics of $S(t)\varepsilon\Pi_2$ of SEQIMRP are shown.

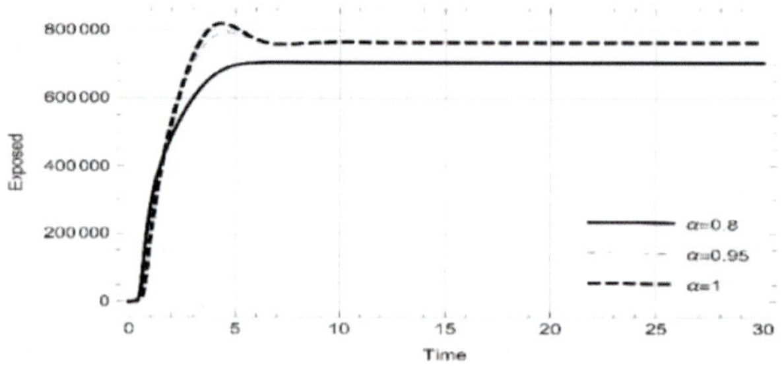

Fig 9: For the values listed in Table 1 and mm = 0, sd = 0, ch = 0, and sc = 0, at α= 0.8, 0.95, 1, and t ε[0, 30], dynamics of $E(t)$ $\varepsilon\Pi_2$ of SEQIMRP.

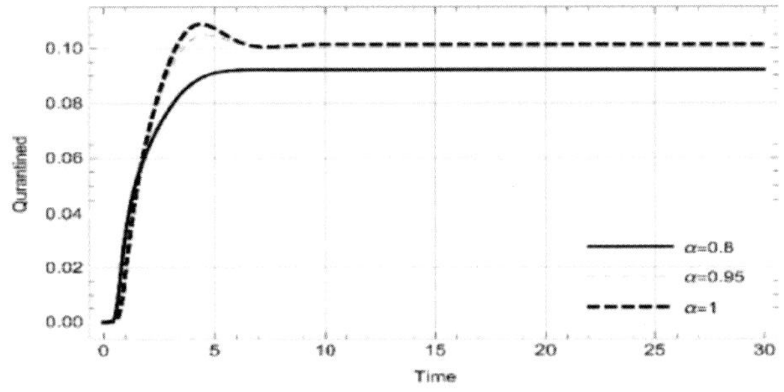

Fig 10: For the parameters listed in Table 1 with mm = 0, sd = 0, ch = 0, and sc = 0, at α= 0.8, 0.95, 1, and t ε[0, 30], the dynamics of Q(t)εΠ2 of SEQIMRP are shown.

Table 3: Basic reproduction number R0 and endemic equilibrium points 2 for mm = 0, sd = 0, ch = 0, and sc = 0, at various values of and tε [0, 30], are parameters described in Table 1.

α	R_0	$S(t)$	$E(t)$	$Q(t)$	$I(t)$	$M(t)$	$R(t)$	$P(t)$
0.4	1.07658	90564.3	130,860	0.0166747	0.14077	0.0108021	0.00775503	0
0.5	1.2482	78379.6	341,367	0.0437936	0.394839	0.0339465	0.0267258	0
0.6	1.46208	67141.9	503,966	0.0650954	0.629689	0.0615493	0.0546976	0
0.7	1.73309	56834.8	623,165	0.0810462	0.84565	0.0957691	0.100128	0
0.8	2.08323	47,442	703,299	0.0921023	1.04305	0.140393	0.184117	0
0.9	2.54613	38947.9	748,529	0.0987099	1.22222	0.202724	0.373485	0
1.	3.17529	31335.7	762,847	0.101305	1.38348	0.298912	1.00458	0

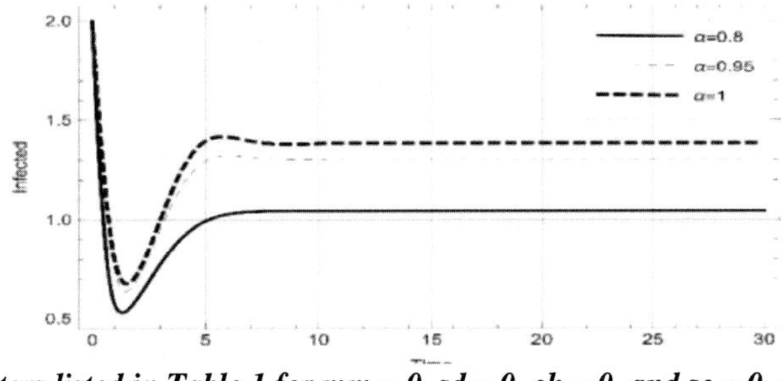

Fig 11: For the parameters listed in Table 1 for mm = 0, sd = 0, ch = 0, and sc = 0, at α= 0.8, 0.95, 1, and t ε[0, 30], determine the dynamics of I(t)εΠ2 of SEQIMRP.

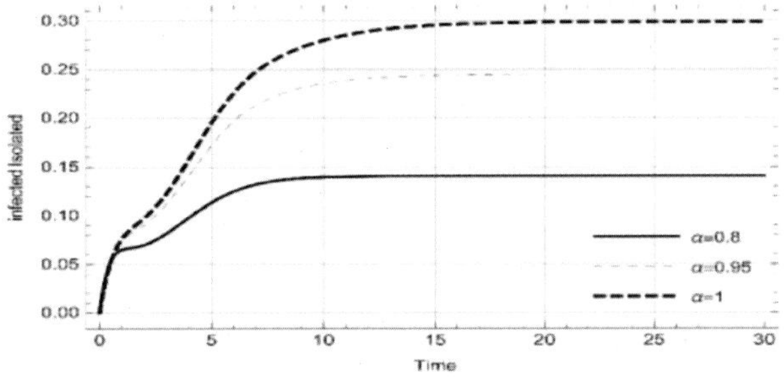

Fig 12: For the parameters listed in Table 1 for mm = 0, sd = 0, ch = 0, and sc = 0, at α= 0.8, 0.95, 1, and t ε[0, 30], determine the dynamics of M(t)εΠ2 of SEQIMRP.

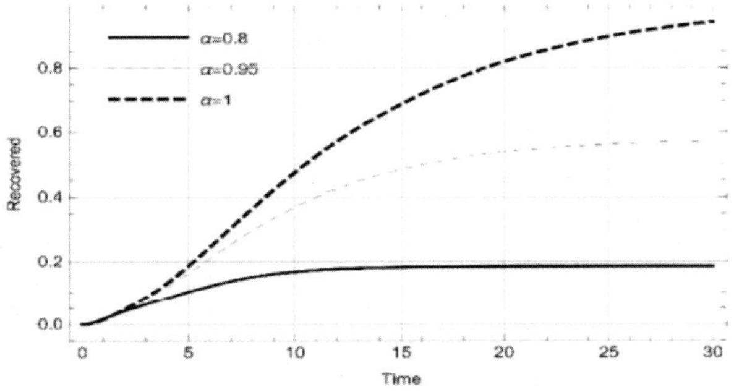

Fig 13: For the parameters listed in Table 1 for mm = 0, sd = 0, ch = 0, and sc = 0, at α= 0.8, 0.95, 1, and t ε[0, 30], determine the dynamics of R(t)εΠ2 of SEQIMRP.

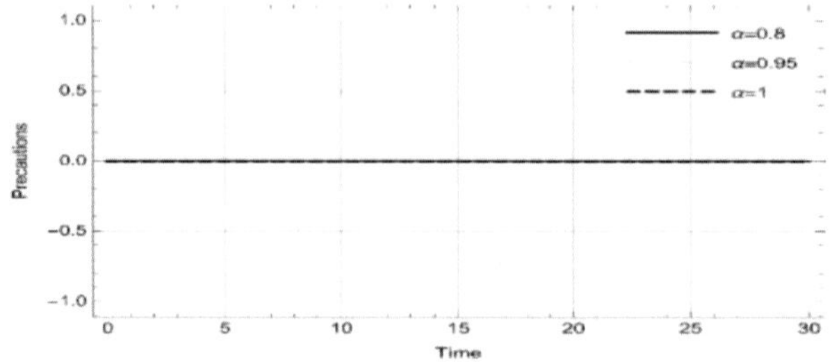

Fig 14: For the parameters listed in Table 1 for mm = 0, sd = 0, ch = 0, and sc = 0, at α= 0.8, 0.95, 1, and t ε[0, 30], determine the dynamics of P(t)εΠ2 of SEQIMRP.

Table 4: For the parameters listed in Table 1 for mm = 0.2, sd = 0.3, ch = 0.35, and sc = 0.65, for various values of α and tε[0, 30], the basic reproduction number R_0 and the disease-free equilibrium points Π_1 are shown.

α	R_0	$S(t)$	$E(t)$	$Q(t)$	$I(t)$	$M(t)$	$R(t)$	$P(t)$
0.4	0.297661	94566.7	0	0	0	0	0	97904.3
0.5	0.324551	94,900	0	0	0	0	0	111,349
0.6	0.354992	95233.3	0	0	0	0	0	128,931
0.7	0.389628	95566.7	0	0	0	0	0	152,907
0.8	0.429253	95,900	0	0	0	0	0	187,538
0.9	0.474857	96233.3	0	0	0	0	0	241,958
1.	0.527691	96566.7	0	0	0	0	0	339,915

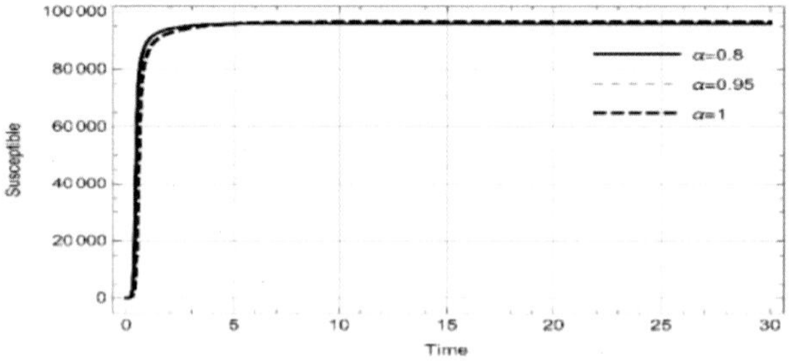

Fig 15: For the parameters listed in Table 1 and mm = 0.2, sd = 0.3, ch = 0.35, and sc = 0.65, at α= 0.8, 0.95, 1, and t ε[0, 30], dynamics of S(t)εΠ1 of SEQIMRP are presented.

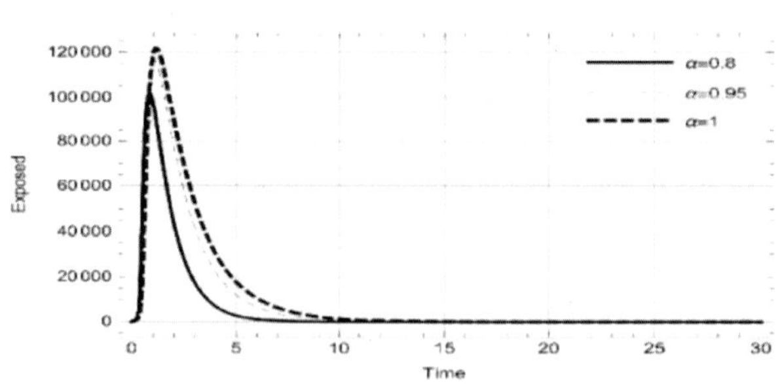

Fig 16: For the parameters listed in Table 1 and mm = 0.2, sd = 0.3, ch = 0.35, and sc = 0.65, at α= 0.8, 0.95, 1, and t ε[0, 30], dynamics of E(t)εΠ1 of SEQIMRP are presented.

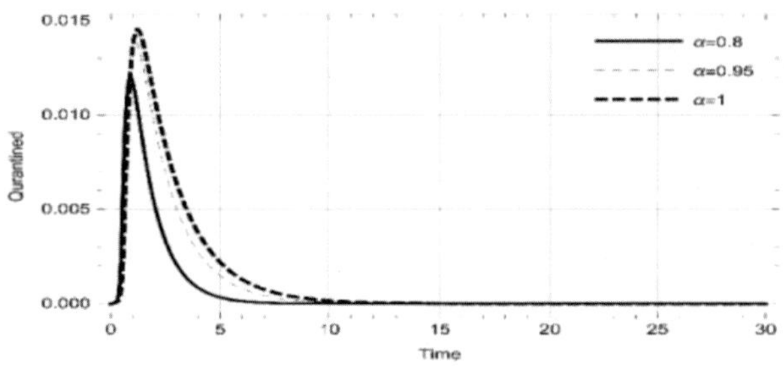

Fig 17: For the parameters listed in Table 1 and mm = 0.2, sd = 0.3, ch = 0.35, and sc = 0.65, at α= 0.8, 0.95, 1, and t ε[0, 30], dynamics of Q(t)εΠ₁ of SEQIMRP are presented.

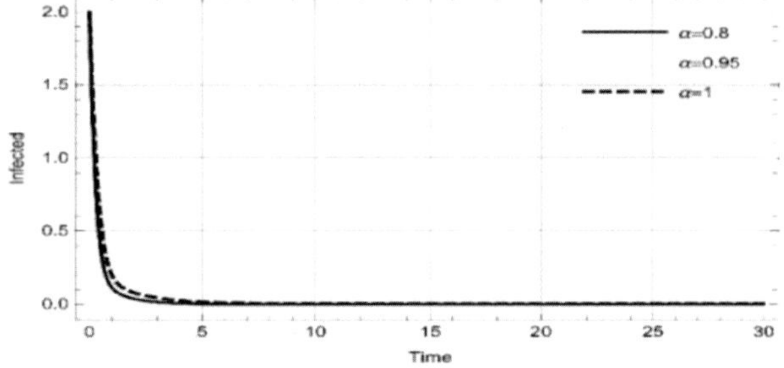

Fig 18: For the parameters listed in Table 1 and mm = 0.2, sd = 0.3, ch = 0.35, and sc = 0.65, at α= 0.8, 0.95, 1, and t ε[0, 30], dynamics of I(t)εΠ₁ of SEQIMRP are presented.

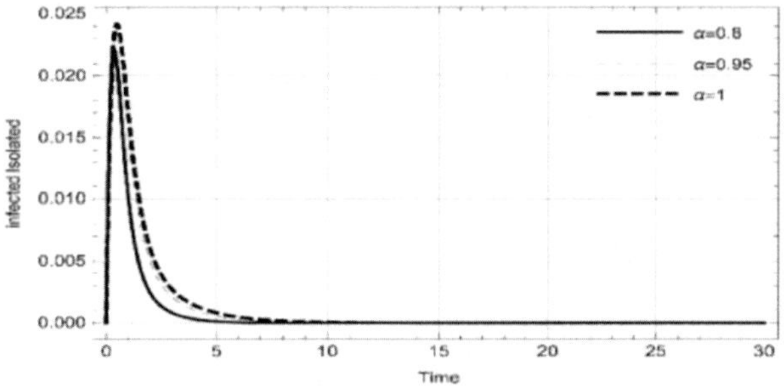

Fig 19: For the parameters listed in Table 1 and mm = 0.2, sd = 0.3, ch = 0.35, and sc = 0.65, at α= 0.8, 0.95, 1, and t ε[0, 30], dynamics of M(t)εΠ₁ of SEQIMRP are presented.

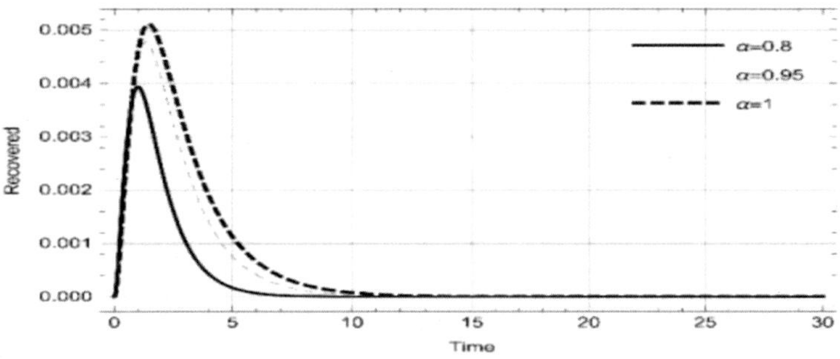

Fig 20: For the parameters listed in Table 1 and mm = 0.2, sd = 0.3, ch = 0.35, and sc = 0.65, at α= 0.8, 0.95, 1, and t ε[0, 30], dynamics of R(t)εΠ₁ of SEQIMRP are presented.

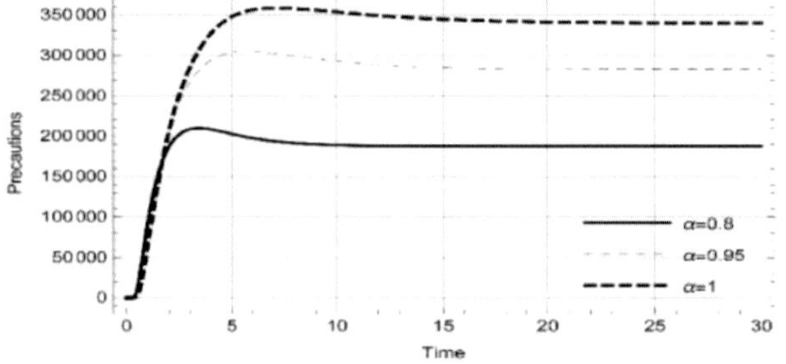

Fig 21: For the parameters listed in Table 1 and mm = 0.2, sd = 0.3, ch = 0.35, and sc = 0.65, at α= 0.8, 0.95, 1, and t ε[0, 30], dynamics of P(t)εΠ₁ of SEQIMRP are presented.

Conclusion

The WHO's PHEIC announcement of the COVID'19 epidemic has alarmed the scientific community and medical professionals worldwide. Adopting non-pharmaceutical limits is the sole practical strategy to slow the spread of COVID'19 after multiple studies on vaccinations were unsuccessful. Different, unprecedented actions, including lockdowns, institution closures, and the launch of various awareness campaigns, are considered for this goal.

Here, we spoke about how much the stakeholders' awareness efforts cost and how well they worked with the general public. These actions include enforcing medical mask usage in public areas, maintaining a 6-foot social distance, often washing hands, using hand sanitizers, and educating medical personnel and officers to provide COVID'19 patients in hospitals with exceptional supportive care. In order to jointly investigate the dynamical stability of the epidemic dynamical system SEQIMRP and the viability of the preventative measures, the optimum control function was developed.

The proportionate fractional derivative was used in the system's formulation so that the basic reproduction number at each chronological change could be examined. Ultimately, the helpful facts that are listed below may be deduced from the aforementioned analytical and numerical illustrations:

- Using medical masks, avoiding social situations, constantly cleaning hands, and providing COVID'19 patients with supportive care are all effective ways to combat this epidemic.
- The understanding and necessity of these lines of action may transform the pandemic situation into a stable environment free of illness.
- By using them, the fundamental reproduction number may be significantly decreased from R0 > 1 to R0 1.
- The best surveillance mitigation strategy in terms of affordability, social isolation, and supportive care may hasten the reduction of COVID'19 spread.
- Illustrations at various fractional derivative indices demonstrate systematic reading in the exposed, confined, infected, recovered, and protected populations.

- If no safeguards are taken, the readings show a step-by-step rise in the population that is vulnerable, exposed, quarantined, infected, isolated, and recovered.
- As the fractional derivative gets closer to the total change, following precautions, the number of people under protection steadily rises, while the numbers for those who are exposed, quarantined, infected, isolated, and recovered stay zero.
- Proficiency in the proportional fractional derivative model for prior identification of the COVID'19 transmission risk.
- Identify the fundamental reproduction number accurately and take preventative action before it turns into a fatal epidemic.

Understanding the epidemiological features is a major point of disagreement for researchers and medical practitioners at the moment. The stakeholders may receive considerable assistance from successful investigations in developing efficient standard operating procedures for interventions. The created model, SEQIMRP, will unquestionably make a significant contribution to dynamically examining and illuminating the best tactic to manage the lethal COVID'19 escalation.

Chapter 5

Modeling the impact of the delay strategy on HIV/AIDS disease transmission dynamics[5]

Literature review

Human immunodeficiency virus is referred to as HIV. In humans, HIV targets and infects the immune system's white blood cells (WBCs). HIV replicates itself in the circulation in the millions, weakening the immune system by destroying WBCs. T-helper cells or CD4 cells are the name for this subset of WBCs. HIV may spread from one person to another through a variety of channels, including unprotected intercourse with an infected person, the use of an infected syringe for injecting drugs, and the use of unsterilized surgical equipment. Therefore, we should raise knowledge about protected sex and the use of sterilized medical equipment in order to stop its transmission. Antiretroviral therapy is necessary for HIV-positive people to combat infections. Although there is no vaccine for HIV currently, there is a treatment called HAART that can be used to stop the spread of the illness. HIV was initially identified by the Centers for Disease Control and Prevention (CDC) in 1981. According to a CDC study from 2011, AIDS has claimed the lives of nearly 34 million individuals. The UNAID study from 2010 estimates that there are presently close to 36 million AIDS patients worldwide. Around 1.8 million individuals worldwide contracted HIV in 2017, and 0.94 million people died as a result.Nearly 25.5 million individuals were reported to have received antiretroviral medication in June 2019. The 21st century has seen an increase in the global impact of AIDS. The analysis of the dynamics of HIV/AIDS transmission relies heavily on mathematical models. The dynamics of time from infection to infectiousness are represented by the delay models, making them more realistic. There are numerous models that depict the dynamics of this illness using a set of nonlinear differential equations that are accessible in the literature. However, including a delay makes the models more realistic. A popular area of study right now is the dynamical behavior of the population model with time delay.

Using compartment models, Ogunlaran et al. presented a successful approach to preventing HIV infection in humans. Duffin and colleagues looked at the dynamics of the immune deficiency virus during the whole infection cycle. Omondi et al. analyzed the effects of HIV testing, treatment, and prevention in Kenya using mathematical modeling. In their HIV etiology and therapy compartment design, Wodarz et al. Ida et al. looked into the deterministic model of HIV infection's nonlinear dynamical analysis. In Cuba, Mastroberardino et al. investigated the dynamics of the virus. In order to examine the dynamics of HIV infection in the human

---

5 *Landmark paper: Raza, A., Ahmadian, A., Rafiq, M. et al. "Modeling the effect of delay strategy on transmission dynamics of HIV/AIDS disease", Adv Differ Equ **2020**, 663 (2020). https://doi.org/10.1186/s13662-020-03116-8*

population, Attaullah et al. used numerical methods. The effect of HIV-I transmission dynamics on host evolution was investigated by Theys et al. Bozkurt et al. looked into the stability study of the HIV pandemic model's nonlinear differential equations. A study of the dynamics of the HIV infection in the human population and the number of risk groups was planned by Nosova et al. Sun et al. explored the calculation of the HIV incidence rate using several mathematical modeling techniques. Sweilam et al. investigated the fractional order derivative's optimum control approach while simulating the HIV/AIDS and malaria diseases. A structure-preserving numerical technique for the delayed simulation of the HIV/AIDS illness was reported by Jawaz et al. The numerical technique maintains the structure-preserving characteristics like positivity, dynamical consistency, and stability in a biological sense. Mathematical modeling was used by Mushanyu et al. to evaluate the effects of HIV diagnosis that occurred too late. This article's major goal is to inspire readers to participate in awareness, treatment, and self-testing initiatives. In 2020, Danane et al. used well-established mathematical presumptions to study the fractional order model for hepatitis B viral infection. Atangana et al. provided a critical examination of Covid-19 in 2020 and discussed the effectiveness of facemasks in containing the pandemic globally. Goufo et al. made significant contributions and looked at the relationship between HIV and Covid-19. Additionally, warnings on the current coronavirus strain were issued for various nations. The dynamics of Ebola hemorrhagic fever in West African nations were studied by Atangana et al. Owusu et al. used modeling using delay techniques of intracellular and interrupts to describe the dynamics of the HIV model of Covid-19 with demographic impacts. In the realm of biomathematics, delayed mathematical modeling is important. The attempt being made right now to simulate HIV/AIDS illness while taking the delay effect into account is given. The implementation of school-based sex education, motivation for voluntary counseling and testing, awareness programs organized at the domestic level, emphasis on condom promotion and social marketing, motivation for sexually transmitted infection (STI) screening and testing, effective use of antiretroviral therapy, and blood donation programs are all part of the delay effect to control the epidemic of HIV/AIDS disease in the human population.

Our paper is organized into the following sections. In Section 2, we talk about the equilibrium points of the HIV/AIDS model with a temporal delay effect. In Section 3, we look at the model's parameter sensitivity and reproduction rate. We introduce well-known theorems for the local and global stability in Section 4. In Section 5, we talk about computer findings to support a fictitious model analysis.

Model formulation

We take into account the HIV/AIDS epidemic's time-delay effect on human population transmission. In our model, N(t) represents the total population which we further categorize into the subpopulations as follows: The uninfected/susceptible people are represented by the letters $H_X(t)$, infectious humans are represented by the letters $H_Y(t)$, and immune humans are represented by the letters $H_Z(t)$. The delay model under consideration's transmission dynamics are depicted in Figure 1.

The following definitions are given for the nonnegative constraints of the delay system: is the rate of natural occurrences of immune humans, μ_1 is the natural mortality rate of susceptible humans, μ_2 is the natural mortality rate of infectious humans,β is the proportionality factor of the virus,α is the contact rate of infectious and immune humans, d is the death rate of humans due to virus which is greater than the natural death rate, and A is the rate of human recruitment. Based on the modeling of HIV/AIDS with delay effect, the following assumptions have been made: The human population is homogenous; the latency time has been disregarded under the law of mass action, which solely takes into account the interaction of vulnerable humans with infected humans. All additional encounters with infected persons have been disregarded without losing generality. The following nonlinear delay differential equations serve as the foundation for the mathematical depiction of the HIV/AIDS disease:

$H'_X = A - Bh_X(t-\tau)H_Y(t-\tau)e^{-\mu\tau} - \mu_1 H_X(t),\ \forall t\ \varepsilon[-\tau,0], \tau\ \varepsilon[0,\infty)$, (2.1)

$H'_Y = \beta H_X(t-\tau)H_Y(t-\tau)e^{-\mu\tau} - \alpha H_Y(t) - \mu_2 H_Y(t),\ \forall t \in [-\tau, 0], \tau \in [0,\infty)72$, (2.2)

$H'_Z = \alpha H_Y(t) - (\mu + d)H_Z(t),\ \forall t \in [-\tau, 0],72$ (2.3)

with the initial conditions $H_X(0) \geq 0$, $H_Y(0) \geq 0$, $H_Z(0) \geq 0$.

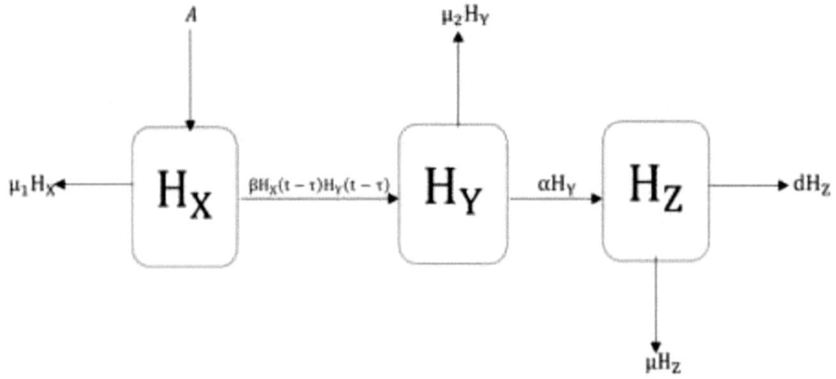

Fig 1: Model for HIV/AIDS stream map

Combining the first three equations yields the system (2.1)-(2.3)'s overall dynamics as follows: $H'_X(t) + H'_Y(t) + H'_Z(t) \leq A - \mu_1 N(t)$ and $H_X(t) + H_Y(t) + H_Z(t) = N(t)$,

$\frac{dN(t)}{dt} \leq A - \mu_1 N(t)$.

The feasible region of model (2.1)–(2.3) is as follows:

$\Gamma = \{H_X(t), H_Y(t), H_Z(t) \in R^3 + N(t) \leq A - \mu_1 N(t)\}$

The solution to the initial value issue, $\Phi'(t) = A - \mu_1(t)$, with $\Phi(0) = N(0)$, is $\Phi(t) = k_1 e^{-\mu 1\tau} - \frac{A}{\mu 1}$ and

$\lim_{t\to\infty}\Phi(t) = \frac{A}{\mu 1}$

As a result, $N(t) < \Phi(t)$, demonstrating that $\lim_{t\to\infty} \sup N(t) \leq \frac{A}{\mu 1}$. As a result, all of the solutions to system (2.1)–(2.3) are in Γ. For system (2.1)-(2.3), the specified area preserves structure as expected. The area Γ is hence nonnegative invariant.

1. Model Equlibria

The system (2.1)-(2.3) will be demonstrated in this part to accept three different forms of equilibrium, including endemic equilibrium (EE), trivial equilibrium (TE), and disease-free equilibrium (DFE), as follows:

A1 = Trivial equilibrium (TE) = $(H^0_X, H^0_Y, H^0_Z) = (0, 0, 0)$;

A2 = Disease-free equilibrium (DFE) = $(H^1_X, H^1_Y, H^1_Z) = (\frac{A}{\mu 1}, 0, 0)$;

A3 = Endemic equilibrium (EE) = (H^*_X, H^*_Y, H^*_Z),

where $H^*_X = \frac{\alpha+\mu 2}{\beta e-\mu\tau}$, $H^*_Y = \frac{A-\mu 1 H*X}{\beta H*Xe-\mu\tau}$, $H_Z^* = \frac{\alpha H*Y}{\mu+d}$

Reproduction number

In this part, we apply the next generation matrix approach to the system (2.1)-(2.3) in order to calculate the transmission and transition matrices in order to determine the reproduction number [21]:

$$\begin{bmatrix} H_Y^* \\ H_Z^* \end{bmatrix} = \begin{bmatrix} \beta X e^{-\mu\tau} & 0 \\ 0 & 0 \end{bmatrix} \begin{bmatrix} H_Y \\ H_Z \end{bmatrix} - \begin{bmatrix} \alpha + \mu_2 & 0 \\ -\alpha & \mu + d \end{bmatrix} \begin{bmatrix} H_Y \\ H_Z \end{bmatrix}.$$

Thus the transmission matrix F and transition matrix V, at the disease-free equilibrium (DFE) A_1, are

$$F = \begin{bmatrix} \frac{\beta A e^{-\mu\tau}}{\mu_1} & 0 \\ 0 & 0 \end{bmatrix} \quad \text{and} \quad V = \begin{bmatrix} \alpha + \mu_2 & 0 \\ -\alpha & \mu + d \end{bmatrix}.$$

Keep in mind that the reproduction number (R_0) is used to define the spectral radius of FV-1.

$$R_0 = \frac{\beta A}{\mu 1(\alpha + \mu 2)} e^{-\mu\tau}$$

We explore the reproduction number's sensitivity to each of the contributing components before wrapping up this section. To that purpose, it is simple to confirm the identity of the following people:

$$S_\beta = \frac{\beta}{R_o} \times \frac{\partial R_o}{\partial \beta} = 1, \qquad S_A = \frac{A}{R_o} \times \frac{\partial R_o}{\partial A} = 1, \qquad S_{\mu_1} = \frac{\mu_1}{R_o} \times \frac{\partial R_o}{\partial \mu_1} = -1,$$

$$S_\alpha = \frac{\alpha}{R_o} \times \frac{\partial R_o}{\partial \alpha} = -\frac{\alpha}{\alpha + \mu_2}, \qquad S_\mu = \frac{\mu_2}{R_o} \times \frac{\partial R_o}{\partial \mu_2} = -\frac{\mu_2}{\alpha + \mu_2}.$$

Keep in mind that S_β and S_A are positive numbers. The remaining figures, however, are negative. We get to the conclusion that β and A are the reproduction number's sensitive parameters.

Local Stability

We propose theorems in this part that give the model's equilibria's properties:

Theorem *The disease-free equilibrium (DFE), $A_2 = (H_X^1, H_Y^1, H_Z^1) = (\frac{A}{\mu_1}, 0, 0)$, is locally asymptotically stable (LAS) if $R_0 < 1$, for any $t \in [-\tau, 0]$ and $\tau \in [0, \infty)$. Otherwise the system (2.1)–(2.3) is unstable if $R_0 > 1$.*

Proof The Jacobian matrix for the system (2.1)–(2.3) at A_2 is evaluated as follows:

$$J(A_2) = \begin{bmatrix} -\mu_1 & -\frac{\beta A}{\mu_1} & 0 \\ 0 & \frac{\beta A}{\mu_1}e^{-\mu\tau} - (\alpha + \mu_2) & 0 \\ 0 & \alpha & -(\mu + d) \end{bmatrix},$$

$$|J(A_2) - \lambda I| = \begin{vmatrix} -\mu_1 - \lambda & -\frac{\beta A}{\mu_1} & 0 \\ 0 & \frac{\beta A}{\mu_1}e^{-\mu\tau} - (\alpha + \mu_2) - \lambda & 0 \\ 0 & \alpha & -(\mu + d) - \lambda \end{vmatrix} = 0.$$

Notice that all eigenvalues of the system are as follows:

$$\lambda_1 = -\mu_1 < 0, \qquad \lambda_2 = -(\mu + d) < 0,$$

but $\lambda_3 = -(1 - R_0) < 0$, if $R_0 < 1$.

Hence, all eigenvalues are negative and, by Routh–Hurwitz criterion, the given equilibrium A_2 is locally asymptotically stable.

If $R_0 > 1$, that is,

$$\frac{\beta A}{\mu_1(\alpha + \mu_2)}e^{-\mu\tau} > 1,$$

$$\beta A e^{-\mu\tau} > \mu_1(\alpha + \mu_2),$$

$$-\mu_1(\alpha + \mu_2) + \beta A e^{-\mu\tau} > 0,$$

then $\lambda_3 > 0$. Hence, A_2 is unstable. □

If $R_0 > 1$, for every $t\varepsilon [-\tau, 0]$ and $\tau\varepsilon[0, \infty]$, the endemic equilibrium (EE), $A_3 = (H^*_X, H^*_Y, H^*_Z)$, is locally asymptotically stable (LAS). Otherwise, if $R_0<1$, the system (2.1)-(2.3) is unstable.

Proof The Jacobian matrix for the system (2.1)–(2.3) at A_3 is evaluated as follows:

$$J(A_3) = \begin{bmatrix} -\beta H_Y^* e^{-\mu\tau} - \mu_1 & -\beta H_X^* e^{-\mu\tau} & 0 \\ \beta H_Y^* e^{-\mu\tau} & \beta H_X^* e^{-\mu\tau} - \alpha - \mu_2 & 0 \\ 0 & \alpha & -(\mu + d) \end{bmatrix}.$$

The eigenvalues of Jacobian matrix $J(A_3)$ are obtained as follows:

$$\lambda_1 = -(\mu + d) < 0,$$

$$|J(A_3) - \lambda I| = \begin{vmatrix} -\beta H_Y^* e^{-\mu\tau} - \mu_1 - \lambda & -\beta H_X^* e^{-\mu\tau} \\ \beta H_Y^* e^{-\mu\tau} & \beta H_X^* e^{-\mu\tau} - \alpha - \mu_2 - \lambda \end{vmatrix} = 0,$$

$$\lambda^2 + \lambda[C_1 + \mu_1 + 2\alpha + \mu_2 - C_2] + [(\alpha + \mu_1)((\alpha + \mu_2) - C_2) + C_1C_2] = 0.$$

Put, $C_1 = \beta H_Y^* e^{-\mu\tau}$, $C_2 = \beta H_X^* e^{-\mu\tau}$.

We check the conditions of the 2nd order Routh–Hurwitz criterion:

$$C_1 + \mu_1 + 2\alpha + \mu_2 - C_2 > 0 \quad \text{and} \quad (\alpha + \mu_1)((\alpha + \mu_2) - C_2) + C_1C_2 > 0, \quad \text{if } R_0 > 1.$$

Hence, A_3 is locally asymptotically stable (LAS).

Global Stability

The global characteristics of the model's equilibria are obtained in this part by using the well-known theorems, as shown in [22].

Definition 1: A function V: $R^n \rightarrow R$ is positive (negative) definite if V(0, 0,..., 0) = 0 and V(x) > 0 (<0) for X ≠ (0, 0,..., 0) in Γ a neighborhood of the equilibria of the model.
Definition 2: If V(0, 0,..., 0) = 0 and V(x)≥ 0 (≤0) for X ≠ (0, 0,..., 0) in Γ, then a function V: $R^n \rightarrow$ R is positive (negative) semidefinite in a neighborhood of the equilibria of the model.

Theorem

Consider the case where X = X($H_X(t)$,$H_Y(t)$,$H_Z(t)$) has equilibria, a feasible area "Γ" of the equilibrium points exists, and a function V is defined in Γ such a way that:

(i) The initial partial derivatives are continuous;
(ii) V is positive definite; and
(iii) V is negative semidefinite.

Consequently, the model's equilibria are globally asymptotically stable (GAS).

Theorem

If R_0<1, for any t ε [-τ, 0] and τε [0,∞], the disease-free equilibrium (DFE), A2 = (H^1_X,H^1_Y, H^1_Z)=($\frac{A}{\mu 1}$, 0, 0), is globally asymptotically stable (GAS). If R_0 > 1, the system (2.1)-(2.3) is unstable.
Proof Consider the Volterra–Lyapunov function V :Γ → R defined as [23]

$$V = (H_X - H^1_X) - H^1_X \log\frac{H1X}{HX} + H_Y + H_Z, \forall(H_X,H_Y ,H_Z) \in \Gamma,$$

$$\frac{dV}{dt} = \left(1 - \frac{H_X^1}{H_X}\right)\frac{dH_X}{dt} + \frac{dH_Y}{dt} + \frac{dH_Z}{dt},$$

$$\frac{dV}{dt} = \left(\frac{H_X - H_X^1}{H_X}\right)(A - \beta H_X H_Y e^{-\mu\tau} - \mu_1 H_X) + \beta H_X H_Y e^{-\mu\tau} - \mu_2 H_Y - (\mu + d)H_Z,$$

$$\frac{dU}{dt} = \frac{-A(H_X - H_X^1)^2}{H_X H_X^1} - \beta(H_X - H_X^1)(H_Y - H_Y^1)e^{-\mu\tau}$$
$$- \mu_2 H_X^1\left[1 - \frac{\beta H_Y e^{-\mu\tau}}{\mu_2}\right] - (\mu + d)H_Z$$

⇒ $\frac{dU}{dt} \leq 0$ for $R_0 < 1$, and $\frac{dU}{dt} = 0$ only if $H_X = H_X^1$, $H_Y^1 = H_Z^1 = 0$. Therefore, the only trajectory of the system (2.1)–(2.3) on which $\frac{dU}{dt} = 0$ is A_2. Hence, A_2 is globally asymptotically stable (GAS) in Γ. □

Theorem *The endemic equilibrium (EE), $A_3 = (H_X^*, H_Y^*, H_Z^*)$, is globally asymptotically stable (GAS) if $R_0 > 1$, for all $t \in [-\tau, 0]$ and $\tau \in [0, \infty)$. Otherwise the system (2.1)–(2.3) is unstable if $R_0 < 1$.*

Proof Consider the Volterra–Lyapunov function $V : \Gamma \to R$ defined as

$$V = K_1\left(H_X - H_X^* - H_X^* \log \frac{H_X}{H_X^*}\right) + K_2\left(H_Y - H_Y^* - H_Y^* \log \frac{H_Y}{H_Y^*}\right) + K_3\left(H_Z - H_Z^* - H_Z^* \log \frac{H_Z}{H_Z^*}\right).$$

where K_i $(i = 1, 2, 3)$ are positive constants to be chosen later. Then

$$\frac{dU}{dt} = K_1\left(1 - \frac{H_X^*}{H_X}\right)\frac{dH_X}{dt} + K_2\left(1 - \frac{H_Y^*}{H_Y}\right)\frac{dH_Y}{dt} + K_3\left(1 - \frac{H_Z^*}{H_Z}\right)\frac{dH_Z}{dt},$$

$$\frac{dV}{dt} = K_1\left(\frac{H_X - H_X^*}{H_X}\right)(A - \beta H_X H_Y e^{-\mu\tau} - \mu_1 H_X) + K_2\left(\frac{H_Y - H_Y^*}{H_Y}\right)(\beta H_X H_Y e^{-\mu\tau} - \alpha H_Y - \mu_2 H_Y) + K_3\left(\frac{H_Z - H_Z^*}{H_Z}\right)(\alpha H_Y - (\mu + d)H_Z).$$

$$\frac{dV}{dt} = -K_1\frac{A(H_X - H_X^*)^2}{H_X H_X^*} - K_1\beta(H_X - H_X^*)(H_Y - H_Y^*)e^{-\mu\tau} - K_2\frac{\beta(H_X - H_X^*)(H_Y - H_Y^*)e^{-\mu\tau}}{H_X H_Y} - K_3\frac{(H_Y - H_Y^*)(H_Z - H_Z^*)\alpha}{H_Z}.$$

For $K_1 = K_2 = K_3 = 1$, we have

$$\frac{dV}{dt} = -\frac{A(H_X - H_X^*)^2}{H_X H_X^*} - \beta(H_X - H_X^*)(H_Y - H_Y^*)e^{-\mu\tau} - \frac{\beta(H_X - H_X^*)(H_Y - H_Y^*)e^{-\mu\tau}}{H_X H_Y} - \frac{(H_Y - H_Y^*)(H_Z - H_Z^*)\alpha}{H_Z} \leq 0$$

Table 1: Parameter values

Parameters	Values
A	0.5
μ	0.5
d	0.03
β	0.5(DFE) 0.7(EE)
α	0.05
μ_1	0.5
μ_1	0.4

For $R_0 > 1$, $\frac{dV}{dT} \leq 0$, and $\frac{dV}{dT} = 0$ only if $H_X = H^*_X$, $H^*_Y = H^*_Y$, and $H_Z = H^*_Z$. Since $\frac{dV}{dT} = 0$ only occurs on A_3, A_3 is the sole trajectory of the system (2.1)-(2.3) that exists. As a result, according to the Lasalle's invariance principle, A_3 is globally asymptotically stable (GAS).

Computer Results

In this part, we examine the simulations of the system (2.1)-(2.3) using various suppositions and values for the parameters shown in Table 1.

Figure 1 (Simulation at equilibria of the model without delay effect) The system (2.1)-(2.3) is solved at the disease-free equilibrium (DFE), $A_2 = (H'_X, H'_Y, H'_z)=(\frac{A}{\mu 1}, 0, 0)$, using the initial conditions $H_X(0) = 0.5$, $H_Y(0) = 0.3$, $H_Z(0) = 0.2$, and the parameter values shown in Table 1. As a result, the system (2.1)-(2.3) converges to A_2, and $R_0 = 0.9091$ 1 represents the reproduction number in the absence of the delay component. Additionally, Figures 2(e)–(h) show the system's solution at endemic equilibrium (EE) $A_3 = (H^*_X, H^*_Y, H^*_Z) = (0.7857, 0.1948, 0.0184)$. As a result, the model converges to A_3, and the reproduction number has the required value of $R_0 = 1.2727 > 1$.

Figure 2 (Simulation at endemic equilibrium of the model with time delay effect) The solution of the systems (2.1)–(2.3) at endemic equilibrium (EE) with time delay effect is shown in Figures 3(a)–(e). We can see that as the delay terms go longer, there are more people who are not infected, and eventually there are less people who are infected. With the employment of delay strategies effectively, the dynamics of the HIV/AIDS model eventually evolve to a disease-free equilibrium as seen in Fig. 3. Additionally, when the use of delay tactics increases, the number of reproductions declines. Furthermore, the reproduction number might be fewer than one in some circumstances. As a result, the dynamics of the reproduction number are unaffected by the parameter values.

Figure 3 (Effect of time delay term on the reproduction number) Let $\tau = 0.47$. It is obvious that when reproduction value declines, the dynamical system shifts from an endemic to a disease-free equilibrium. Therefore, the absence of illness persistence is stable. However, Fig. 4 shows that, when necessary, the HIV/AIDS pandemic may be defeated by increasing the delay tactic. Example 4 (Simulation of the delay term's impact on the model's infected component) It can be shown that the number of infected persons is approaching and even touching zero by letting τ take different values. Finally, the offered real statistics have allowed the specified rate of infected persons to be managed. The delay strategy or tactics, such as vaccine, quarantine, limitations, and distancing measures, etc., are therefore crucial to the intended control of the HIV/AIDS pandemic worldwide, as shown in Fig. 5.

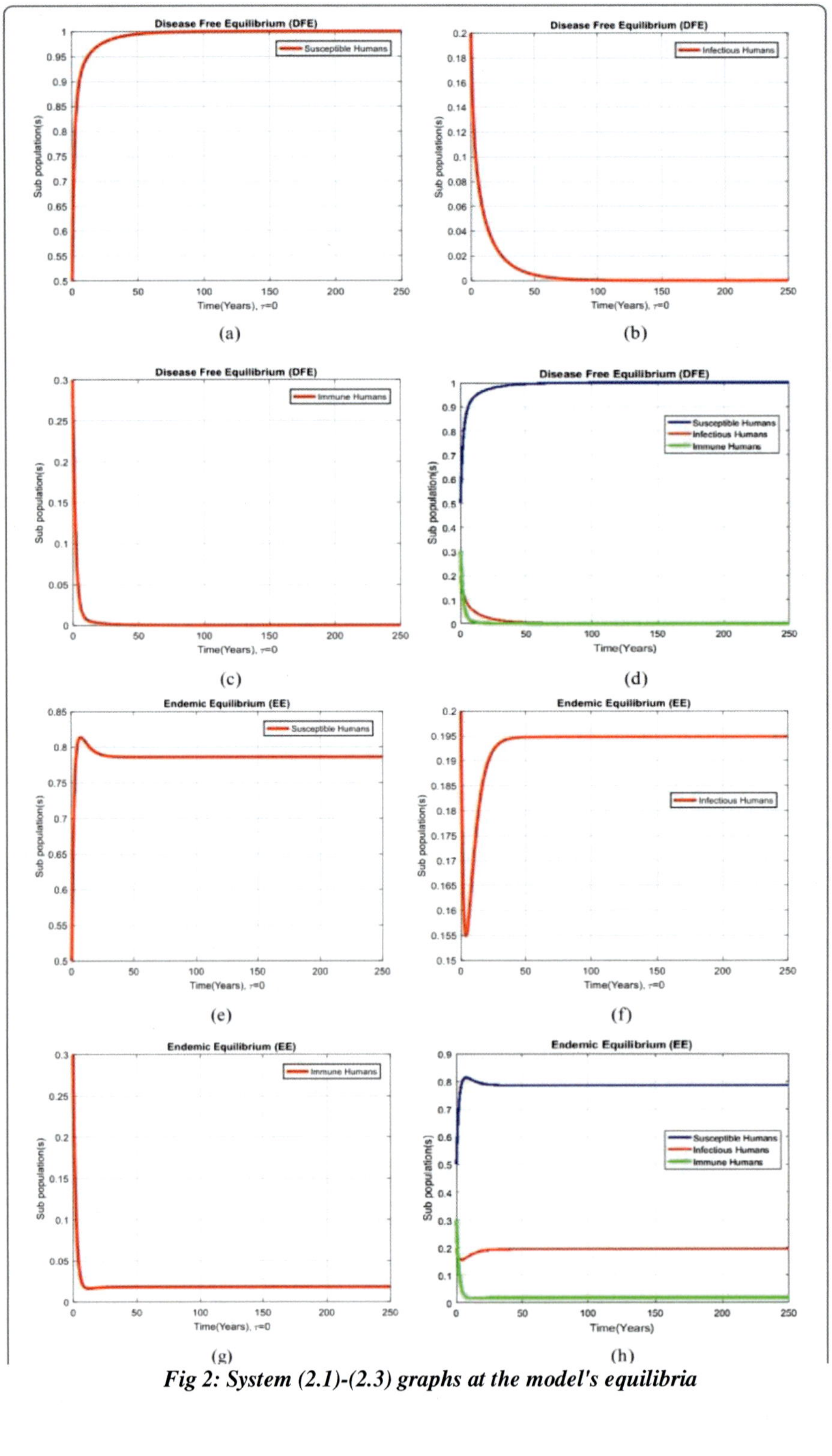

Fig 2: System (2.1)-(2.3) graphs at the model's equilibria

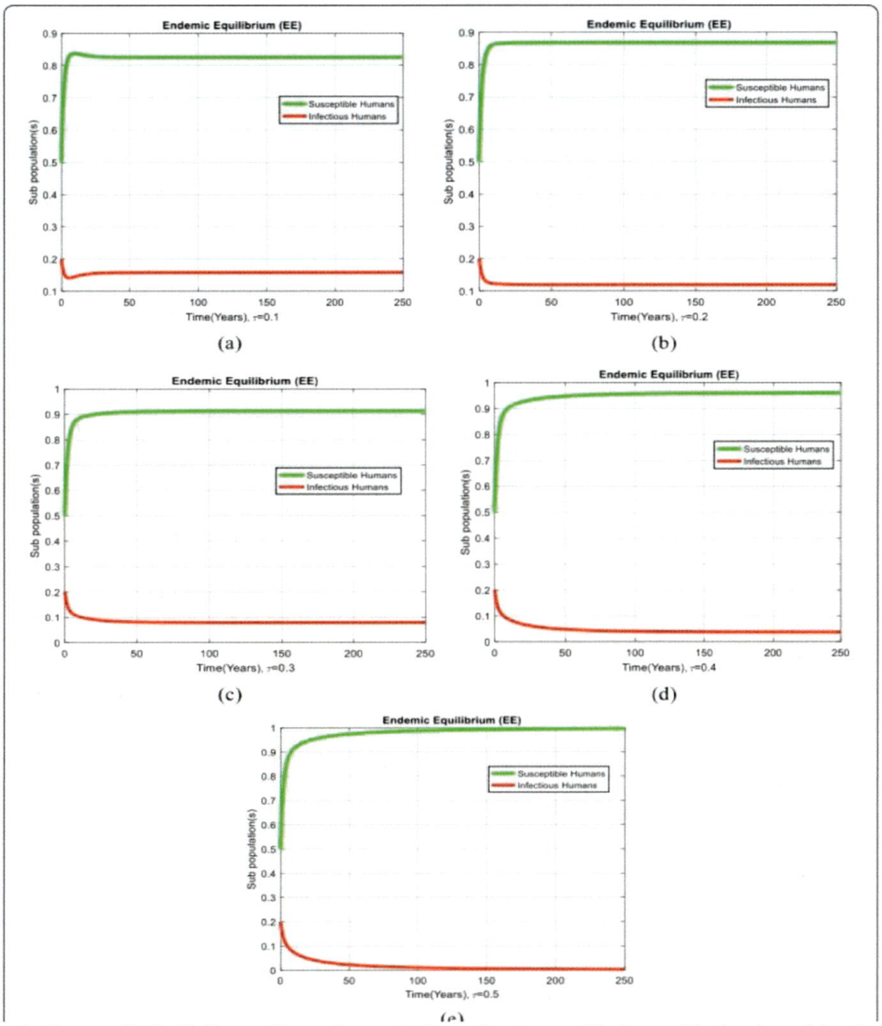

Fig 3: System (2.1)-(2.3) graphs at the model's endemic equilibrium with the time delay impact

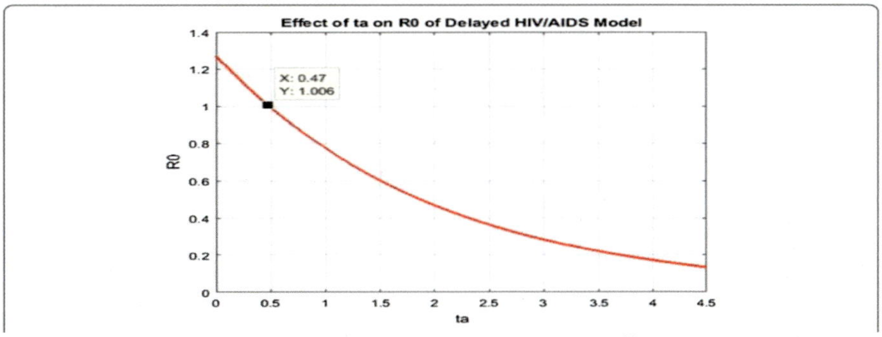

Fig 4: Comparison graph showing how the model's delay term affects the reproduction number

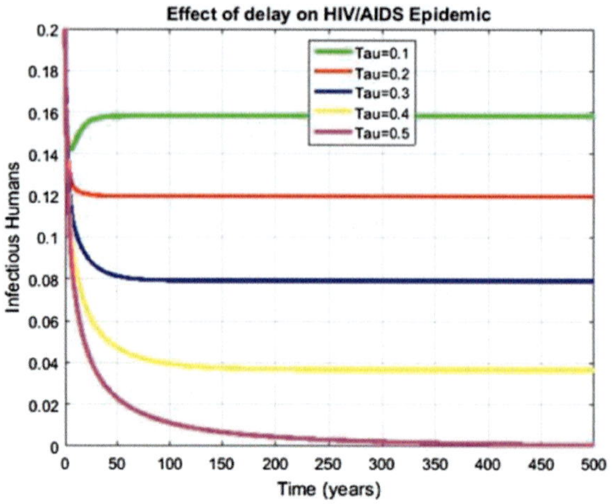

Fig 5: Display showing the delay term's impact on infected people at the model's endemic equilibrium (EE)

Conclusion

In the current work, we used a delayed method approach to analyze the dynamics of HIV/AIDS in people. The three population components susceptible, infectious, and immune have been used to classify the entire population. We have used well-known theorems to confirm the model's stability both locally and globally. In the meanwhile, we have looked at how delay tactics affect the number of reproductions and the infectious component of the human population. Following that, we came to the conclusion that the delay parameters affect all of the model's nonnegative constants. Vaccination, antiretroviral medication (ART), safe sex, and fresh gloves for each patient are further delay methods that have been addressed. Before that part ends, we draw the conclusion that the dynamics of epidemic models are significantly influenced by the examination of delayed mathematical modeling. We'll suggest the delayed fractional order model in the future. For fractal-fractional and fractal-fractional partial differential equation models, this concept might also be expanded.

Chapter 6

Mathematical Fractal-Fractional Model for the Pakistani Corona Virus Situation[6]

Our topic of discussion is COVID-19, which originated in the Chinese city of Wuhan and spread quickly around the world. The COVID-19 illness was called after the corona virus attack that occurred in the Chinese city of Wuhan at the end of 2019. Over 0.616 million people have perished in the first eight months as a result of this sickness. On December 31st, 2019, "Wuhan (Chinese city)" will test for the covid-19 pandemic, a devastating and rapidly spreading virus of recent times. Over the course of the outbreak, 13.5 million people worldwide were impacted. The Crona virus was first identified in "1965" by Tyrrell and Bynoe, who discovered and transmitted a virus known as "B814" that is located in the "embryonic tracheal organ" of humans and spreads through the respiratory system of an elderly person. Such bacteria spreads through the air when sick people congregate with healthy ones and cough or sneeze droplets into the air. It can also spread by keeping hands or fingers on the region or surface of various items that the infected person has touched. Healthy persons can then catch it by touching their nose, mouth, or eyes. This will have an impact on the "respiratory system," and those who are infected will exhibit symptoms including high fever, coughing, and breathing difficulties. The time between infection and the start of symptoms is one to fourteen days. Within five to six days, an infectious person exhibits symptoms. People must practise hand washing every 20 minutes, wear masks, and refrain from congregating in public places to stop the spread of this form of disease.

Politicians and scientists are working to stop the aforementioned infection from spreading and transmitting. The movement of afflicted individuals from one location to another is the primary means by which a pandemic of this kind spreads throughout communities of people in several locations. For this, a number of national and international actions have been taken, with various nations around the world stopping travel and trips on aeroplanes, trains, and buses for predetermined periods of time. Additionally, different economic and business activities have been shut down in cities in order to apply some careful measures to reduce the number of fatalities among the populace. Additionally, every government in the world works to reduce the number of infections and gurnets of individuals within its borders.

Researchers are doing various trials and studies in an effort to contain and stabilise the aforementioned pandemic by developing a vaccine or cure. Understanding how a disease spreads is essential for controlling the pandemic in a community. Another crucial activity to carry out is accepting a right perspective on the spread of the sickness. Engineering in the

---

6 *Landmark paper: Kamal Shah, Muhammad Arfan, Ibrahim Mahariq, Ali Ahmadian, Soheil Salahshour, Massimiliano Ferrara, "Fractal-Fractional Mathematical Model Addressing the Situation of Corona Virus in Pakistan", Results in Physics, Volume 19, 2020, 103560, ISSN 2211-3797, https://doi.org/10.1016/j.rinp.2020.103560.*

medical field educated the public and emphasised the significance of the mathematical modelling method, which is one of the key formulations for managing and comprehending this type of pandemic. In the past, several infections have been treated using mathematical formulations like modelling. The researchers and academics in the physical and medical sciences can learn a lot from mathematical models on how to control certain pandemics and epidemics. These models can also be used to predict the patients that are anticipated by any governing policy in the upcoming days, as well as to determine their goals and objectives. Scholars and scientists have conducted basic research to develop viral infections, and governments have used this information to reduce outbreaks of these diseases. The aforementioned disorders have thus been studied in numerous journals.

Ordinary or partial differential equations (ODEs or PDEs) with numerous equations of integration of natural orders make up the majority of the mathematical formulation models (IDEs). Since 1990, arbitrary order (ODEs) and (PDEs) models of real issues have produced far better and more accurate outcomes. These types of equations can then be used in a variety of sectors, including physics, medicine, engineering, economics, business, and the analysis of various diseases. Arbitrary order differential and integral calculus fall within the category of fractional calculus. Due to well-known aspects of heredity that cannot be found in ODEs and PDEs of integer order, FDEs can be used to create ODEs and PDEs of real-world problems. The FDEs are delocalized and have the past study of historical effects, which is the reason for their superiority to IDEs, which are localised for global challenges. Another factor is that, depending on the circumstances, the future state of the mathematical formulation is influenced not just by the present but also by the past. These characteristics enable FDEs to simulate "non-Markovian behaviour" in real-world challenges. Additionally, no behaviour between any two natural order numbers can be provided by the integer order differential equations (IDEs). To resolve this limit of natural-order derivatives, many fractal dimension types and arbitrary-order derivatives were described in books. Such derivatives can be used in a variety of physical and natural science fields. The study of the epidemiological development of infectious pandemics is the best area for applied research at the moment. More research is being done on the mathematical formulation models to address optimization, existence results, stability theory, and simulation-based predictions.

Due of the current circumstances, numerous analyses have been conducted on the terrifying "COVID-19" pandemic model. Currently, research in the area of mathematical formulation for "COVID-19"-infected disorders is of interest. Due to the significance of this issue, scientists examined a mathematical model of three people: the "healthy or susceptible population" (\$(t), the "infected population"(I(t), and the "recovered class"(R(t)) at time t as having the rate of new born and migrated individuals is denoted by (a), the transmission rate from susceptible to infected is denoted by (b), the contact rate of susceptible with infected by c, μ, the naturally occurring death rate, k is the rate of recovery while λ is the death rate of the affected class from the stated virus, whether there is an infection or not.

$$\begin{cases} \dot{\$}(t) = a - \mu\$ - bc\$\mathbb{I}, \\ \dot{\mathbb{I}}(t) = \mathbb{I}(bc\$ - \mu - k - \lambda), \\ \dot{\mathbb{R}}(t) = k\mathbb{I} - \mu\mathbb{R}, \\ \$(0) = \$_0 \geqslant 0, \quad \mathbb{I}(0) = \mathbb{I}_0 \geqslant 0, \quad \mathbb{R}(0) = \mathbb{R}_0 \geqslant 0, \end{cases} \tag{1}$$

In order to investigate the model provided in (1), we will also take into account retrieved individuals equation for fractal-fractional order derivative with $0<\omega\leq 1$ and $0<r\leq 1$.

$$\begin{cases} {}^{ABC}D_t^{\omega,r}S(t) = a - \mu S - bcSI, \\ {}^{ABC}D_t^{\omega,r}I(t) = I(bcS - \mu - k - \lambda), \\ {}^{ABC}D_t^{\omega,r}R(t) = kI - \mu R, \\ S(0) = S_0 \geqslant 0, \quad I(0) = I_0 \geqslant 0, \quad R(0) = R_0 \geqslant 0, \quad 0 < \omega, r \leqslant 1. \end{cases} \tag{2}$$

Fig. 1 presents the Transfer diagram for (2), which depicts the interaction between the compartments and different rates.

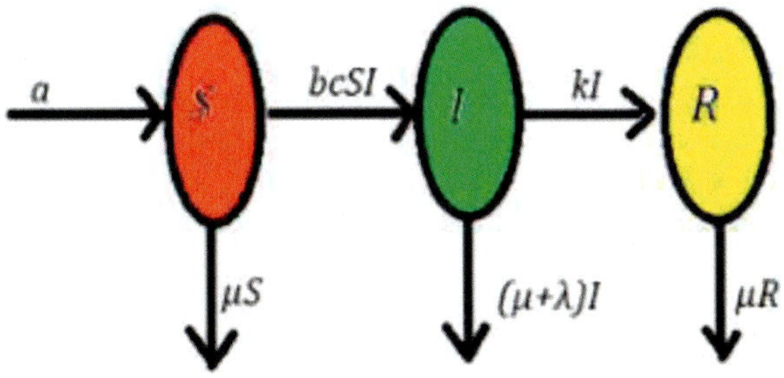

Fig. 1. Dynamical behavior of all the three compartments for the fractal-fractional model (2).

Primary Definitions

Definition 2.1

The fractal-arbitrary order derivative of the continuous and differentiable mapping Ʊ (t) in the form of (a, b) with fractional order 0<ω≤1 and the law of power is provided as follows.

$${}^{ABC}D^{\omega,r}(\mho(t)) = \frac{ABC(\omega)}{1-\omega}\frac{d}{dz^r}\int_0^t \mho(z)\kappa_\omega[\frac{-\sigma}{1-\omega}(t-z\omega)^{\omega}]dz.,$$

We discover that if we replace $\kappa_\omega\left[\frac{-\omega}{1-\omega}(t-z)^{\omega}\right]$ by $\kappa_1 = \exp\left[\frac{-\omega}{1-\omega}(t-z)\right]$, the derivative known as the "Caputo-Fabrizo differential operator" will result. The following is written:

$${}^{ABC}D^{\omega,r}[Constant] = 0.$$

The "normalisation mapping" in this result, ABC(ω), is stated as ABC(0)=ABC(1)=1. Kω The well-known "Mittag-Leffler" mapping, commonly referred to as the generic case of the exponential mapping

Definition 2.2

The fractal-arbitrary order integral of Ʊ(t) in ABC form with arbitrary order 0<ω≤1 and the law of power are provided by": "Let's take the continuous and differentiable mapping Ʊ (t) in (a,b) with 0<r≤1 dimensional order

$${}^{ABC}I_0^{\omega}(\mho(t)) = \frac{1-\omega}{ABC(\omega)}t^{r-1}\mho(t) + \frac{r\omega}{ABC(\omega)\Gamma(\omega)}\int_0^t (t-z)^{\omega-1}z^{r-1}\mho(z)dz. \tag{3}$$

Lemma 2.1. The answer to the given problem for 0 < ω, r≤1

$$
\begin{aligned}
{}^{ABC}D_0^{\omega}\mho(t) &= rt^{r-1}\curlyvee(t,\mho(t)),\ t\in[0,T],\\
\mho(0) &= \mho_0,\ \ 0<\omega, r\leq 1,
\end{aligned}
$$

is supplied by

$$\mho(t)=\mho_0+\frac{(1-\omega)}{ABC(\omega)}t^{r-1}\curlyvee(t,\mho(t))+\frac{r\omega}{\Gamma(\omega)ABC(\omega)}\int_0^t (t-z)^{\omega-1}z^{r-1}\curlyvee(z,\mho(z))dz$$

Note: We use "Banach space" to find existence and uniqueness.

$$Z=Y=F([0,T]\times\mathbb{R}^3,\mathbb{R})$$

where Y=F [0, T] and the space's norm is

$$\|W\|=\|\mho\|=\max_{t\in[0,T]}[|\mathfrak{S}(t)|+|\mathfrak{I}(t)|+|\mathfrak{R}(t)|]$$

Here, we give a fixed point theorem that will be used to support the conclusions of the next sections.

Theorem 2.1

Statement: With the assumption that F1 and F2 are the operators with, let A be a subset that is convoluted in space Zalong.

1. 1. F1(w)+F2(w)∈A for every w∈A.
2. F2 will satisfy the conditions of continuity and compactness; and
3. F1 will satisfy the conditions of contraction;

The functional equations F1w+F2w=w have one or more solutions as a result.

Stability and Possibility

Lemma 3.1

The feasible region has limitations for the roots or zeros of (2), as

$$\mathbb{T}=\left\{(\$,\mathbb{I},\mathbb{R})\in\mathbb{R}_+^3:\ 0\leqslant\mathbb{N}(t)\leqslant\frac{a}{\mu}\right\}.$$

Proof

By combining all of equation (2), we obtain

$$
\begin{aligned}
\frac{d\mathbb{N}}{dt} &= a-\mu\$-bc\$\mathbb{I}+\mathbb{I}(bc\$-\mu-k-\lambda)\\
&\quad +k\mathbb{I}-\mu\mathbb{R},\\
&= a-\mu(\$(t)+\mathbb{I}(t)+\mathbb{R})-\lambda\mathbb{I}(t),\\
&\leqslant a-\mu(\$(t)+\mathbb{I}(t)+\mathbb{R}(t)),\\
&\leqslant a-\mu(\mathbb{N}(t)),
\end{aligned}
\tag{4}
$$

$$\frac{d\mathbb{N}}{dt}+\mu\mathbb{N}\leqslant a.$$

Finding (4), we have

$$\mathbb{N}(t)\leqslant\frac{a}{\mu}+C\exp(-\mu t), \tag{5}$$

The final result demonstrated our desired result if $t\to\infty,\ \mathbb{N}(t)\leqslant\frac{a}{\mu},$. Following that, we will demonstrate some fundamental findings regarding stability analysis. To do this, we must compute the free equilibrium point and pandemic equilibrium point of (2) as

$$
\begin{aligned}
{}^{ABC}D_t^{\omega,r}\$(t) &= 0,\\
{}^{ABC}D_t^{\omega,r}I(t) &= 0,\\
{}^{ABC}D_t^{\omega,r}R(t) &= 0.
\end{aligned}
$$

As previously stated, we shall compute the following two equilibrium points: $E_0 = \left(\frac{a}{\mu}, 0, 0\right)$ is the free equilibrium point of the pandemic in (2), and the pandemic is $E^* = (\$^*, I^*, R^*)$, and

$$
\$^* = \frac{\mu + k + \lambda}{bc},
$$

$$
I^* = \frac{abc - \mu(\mu + k + \lambda)}{bc(\mu + k + \lambda)}
$$

and

$$
R^* = \frac{abck - \mu k(\mu + k + \lambda)}{\mu bc(\mu + k + \lambda)}
$$

Theorem 3.1.

For (2), the fundamental reproductory number is calculated as

$$
R_0 = \frac{bca}{\mu(\mu + k + \lambda)}
$$

Proof

To demonstrate the reproduction number, let's use the second equation in (2), X=I.

$$
\begin{aligned}
{}^{ABC}D_t^{\omega,r}(X) &= {}^{ABC}D_t^{\omega,r}(I) = bcI\$ - I(\mu + k + \lambda),\\
{}^{ABC}D_t^{\omega,r}(X) &= F - V,
\end{aligned}
$$

where F is the infected term of non-linearity and V is the term of linearity, and where F=bcI \$, and V=I(μ+k+ λ). The next generation matrix is FV^{-1} as well.

$$
F = \left[\frac{\partial}{\partial I}(bcI\$)\right] = [bc\$],
$$

and

$$
V = \left[\frac{\partial}{\partial I}(I(\mu + k + \lambda))\right] = [(\mu + k + \lambda)], \quad V^{-1} = \left[\frac{1}{\mu + k + \lambda}\right],
$$

then

$$
FV^{-1} = \left[\frac{bc\$}{(\mu + k + \lambda)}\right].
$$

R_0 is the larger eigenvalue of the matrix FV^{-1} that we are considering $E_0 = \left(\frac{a}{\mu}, 0, 0\right)$, given as follows

$$
\rho(FV^{-1})_{E_0} = \left[\frac{bca}{\mu(\mu + k + \lambda)}\right]. \tag{6}
$$

Consequently, fundamental reproduction number is established and provided by

$$R_0 = \frac{bca}{\mu(\mu + k + \lambda)}.$$

The needed result is displayed in the final result.

Theorem 3.2.
Statement: If $R_0<1$ and $R_0>1$, the pandemic free of disease equilibrium point of (2) is locally asymptotically stable.
Proof
Let's write the Jacobian matrix of (2) as

$$\mathcal{J} = \begin{bmatrix} \frac{\partial}{\partial \$}(\phi_1(t, \$(t), \mathbb{I}(t), \mathbb{R}(t))) & \frac{\partial}{\partial \mathbb{I}}(\phi_1(t, \$(t), \mathbb{I}(t), \mathbb{R}(t))) & \frac{\partial}{\partial \mathbb{R}}(\phi_1(t, \$(t), \mathbb{I}(t), \mathbb{R}(t))) \\ \frac{\partial}{\partial \$}(\phi_2(t, \$(t), \mathbb{I}(t), \mathbb{R}(t))) & \frac{\partial}{\partial \mathbb{I}}(\phi_2(t, \$(t), \mathbb{I}(t), \mathbb{R}(t))) & \frac{\partial}{\partial \mathbb{R}}(\phi_2(t, \$(t), \mathbb{I}(t), \mathbb{R}(t))) \\ \frac{\partial}{\partial \$}(\phi_3(t, \$(t), \mathbb{I}(t), \mathbb{R}(t))) & \frac{\partial}{\partial \mathbb{I}}(\phi_3(t, \$(t), \mathbb{I}(t), \mathbb{R}(t))) & \frac{\partial}{\partial \mathbb{R}}(\phi_3(t, \$(t), \mathbb{I}(t), \mathbb{R}(t))) \end{bmatrix},$$

Or

$$\mathcal{J} = \begin{bmatrix} -\mu - bc\mathbb{I} & -bc\$ & 0 \\ bc\mathbb{I} & bc\$ - (\mu + k + \lambda) & 0 \\ 0 & k & -\mu \end{bmatrix}. \tag{7}$$

Using E_0's values, we obtain

$$\mathcal{J} = \begin{bmatrix} -\mu & \frac{-bca}{\mu} & 0 \\ 0 & \frac{bca}{\mu} - (\mu + k + \lambda) & 0 \\ 0 & k & -\mu \end{bmatrix}.$$

The features equation is now found to be as

$$Det(\mathcal{J} - \Lambda I) = \begin{vmatrix} -\mu - \Lambda & \frac{-bca}{\mu} & 0 \\ 0 & \frac{bca}{\mu} - (\mu + k + \lambda) - \Lambda & 0 \\ 0 & k & -\mu - \Lambda \end{vmatrix} = 0.$$

Therefore, the eigen values are provided by

$$\Lambda_1 = -\mu,$$

$$\Lambda_2 = \frac{bca}{\mu} - (\mu + k + \lambda),$$

$$\Lambda_3 = -\mu$$

Further, Λ_2 can be written as

$$\Lambda_2 = \frac{bca}{\mu(\mu + k + \lambda)} - 1.$$

Last result shows that

"$\Lambda_2 = R_0 - 1$"

and if "$R_0<1$," Λ_2 will not be positive. As a result, (2) is locally asymptotically stable at E_0 and will be unstable elsewhere since all "eigen values" are non-positive.

Theorem 3.3.

Statement

If $R_0>1$ and the minors of the Routh-Hurwitz matrix are positive, the pandemic or equilibrium point $E^* = (\mathfrak{S}^*, \mathfrak{I}^*, \mathfrak{R}^*)$ after infection are locally and globally asymptotically stable, respectively.

Proof

By entering the values of $E^* = (\$^*, \mathbb{I}^*, \mathbb{R}^*)$ in formula (7), we obtain

$$\mathcal{J} = \begin{bmatrix} -\mu - bc\mathbb{I}^* & -bc\$^* & 0 \\ bc\mathbb{I}^* & bc\$^* - (\mu + k + \lambda) & 0 \\ 0 & k & -\mu \end{bmatrix}. \quad (8)$$

After simplifying, we obtain

$$\mathcal{J} = \begin{bmatrix} -\mu - (\frac{abc}{\mu + k + \lambda} - \mu) & -(\mu + k + \lambda) & 0 \\ \frac{abc}{\mu + k + \lambda} - \mu & 0 & 0 \\ 0 & k & -\mu \end{bmatrix}.$$

or

$$\mathcal{J} = \begin{bmatrix} \frac{abc}{\mu + k + \lambda} & -(\mu + k + \lambda) & 0 \\ \frac{abc}{\mu + k + \lambda} - \mu & 0 & 0 \\ 0 & k & -\mu \end{bmatrix}.$$

As a result, the features equation

$$Det(\mathcal{J}-\Lambda I)=\begin{vmatrix} \frac{abc}{\mu+k+\lambda}-\Lambda & -(\mu+k+\lambda) & 0 \\ \frac{abc}{\mu+k+\lambda}-\mu & -\Lambda & 0 \\ 0 & k & -\mu-\Lambda \end{vmatrix}=0,$$

or

$$\Lambda^3+(-\mu+\frac{abc}{\mu+k+\lambda})\Lambda^2+(\frac{\mu abc}{\mu+k+\lambda}+abc-\mu(\mu+k+\lambda))\Lambda+\mu(abc)$$
$$-\mu(\mu+k+\lambda)=0,$$

or

$$a_0\Lambda^3+(a_1)\Lambda^2+(a_2)\Lambda+a_3=0,$$

Constructing the following Hurwitz matrix

$$\begin{bmatrix} a_1 & a_0 & 0 \\ a_3 & a_2 & a_1 \\ 0 & a_4 & a_3 \end{bmatrix}.$$

All of the principle minors meet the Routh-Hurwitz criterion and are higher than those listed below.

$$|a_1|>0,$$

This implies that $a_1=-\mu+\frac{abc}{\mu+k+\lambda}$ or $a_1=-1+R_0$ or $a_1>0$ if $R_0>1.$ Similar reasoning can be used to demonstrate that the subsequent minors must all be favorable.

$$\begin{vmatrix} a_1 & a_0 \\ a_3 & a_2 \end{vmatrix}>0.$$

and

$$\begin{vmatrix} a_1 & a_0 & 0 \\ a_3 & a_2 & a_1 \\ 0 & 0 & a_3 \end{vmatrix}>0.$$

For the system under consideration, local asymptotical and global stability were achieved by $R_0>1$ and positivity of all minors.

Model's existence and distinctiveness (2)

It is crucial to determine whether the dynamical problem we are researching actually exists or not. The theory of fixed points will provide an answer to this fundamental question. In this section of the paper, we assess the relevant necessity for our considered problem (2). Given that the integral is differentiable and the aforementioned need, we may write the right sides of model (2) as

$$\begin{cases} {}^{ABC}D^{\omega}(\$(t)) = rt^{r-1}G_1(\$(t), \mathbb{I}(t), \mathbb{R}(t)), \\ {}^{ABC}D^{\omega}(\mathbb{I}(t)) = rt^{r-1}G_2(\$(t), \mathbb{I}(t), \mathbb{R}(t)), \\ {}^{ABC}D^{\omega}(\mathbb{R}(t)) = rt^{r-1}G_3(\$(t), \mathbb{I}(t), \mathbb{R}(t)), \\ \$(0) = \$_0, \quad \mathbb{I}(0) = \mathbb{I}_0, \quad \mathbb{R}(0) = \mathbb{R}_0. \end{cases} \tag{9}$$

where

$$\begin{cases} G_1(\$(t), \mathbb{I}(t), \mathbb{R}(t)) = a - \mu\$ - bc\$\mathbb{I}, \\ G_2(\$(t), \mathbb{I}(t), \mathbb{R}(t)) = \mathbb{I}(bc\$ - \mu - k - \lambda), \\ G_3(\$(t), \mathbb{I}(t), \mathbb{R}(t)) = k\mathbb{I} - \mu\mathbb{R}. \end{cases} \tag{10}$$

With the help of (9) and for $t \in \mathfrak{g}$, the (10) follows as

$$\begin{aligned} {}^{ABC}D_0^{\omega}\mho(t) = &\ rt^{r-1}\Upsilon(t, \mho(t)), \ t \in [0, T], \\ \mho(0) = &\ \mho_0, \quad 0 < \omega, r \leq 1, \end{aligned} \tag{11}$$

With solution,

$$\begin{aligned} \mho(t) = &\mho_0 + \frac{(1-\omega)}{ABC(\omega)} t^{r-1}\Upsilon(t, \mho(t)) \\ &+ \frac{r\omega}{\Gamma(\omega)ABC(\omega)} \int_0^t (t-z)^{\omega-1} z^{r-1}\Upsilon(z, \mho(z))dz, \end{aligned} \tag{12}$$

Where

$$\mho(t) = \begin{cases} \$(t) \\ \mathbb{I}(t) \\ \mathbb{R}(t) \end{cases} \quad \mho_0(t) = \begin{cases} \$_0 \\ \mathbb{I}_0 \\ \mathbb{R}_0 \end{cases}, \quad \Upsilon(t, \mho(t)) = \begin{cases} G_1(\$(t), \mathbb{I}(t), \mathbb{R}(t)t) \\ G_2(\$(t), \mathbb{I}(t), \mathbb{R}(t), t) \\ G_3(\$(t), \mathbb{I}(t), \mathbb{R}(t), t). \end{cases} \tag{13}$$

Make the (2) into a fixed point problem now. Map T:V→V supplied as follows:

$$T\mho(t) = \mho_0 + \frac{(1-\omega)}{ABC(\omega)} t^{r-1}\Upsilon(t, \mho(t)) + \frac{r\omega}{\Gamma(\omega)ABC(\omega)} \int_0^t (t-z)^{\omega-1} z^{r-1}\Upsilon (z, \mho(z))dz. \tag{14}$$

Assume

$$T = F + G,$$

where

$$\begin{aligned} F(\mho) = &\ \mho_0(t) + \frac{(1-\omega)}{ABC(\omega)} t^{r-1}[\Upsilon(t, \mho(t))], \\ G(\mathbb{Z}) = &\ \frac{r\omega}{ABC(\omega)\Gamma(\omega)} \int_0^t (t-z)^{\omega-1} z^{r-1}\Upsilon(z, \mho(z))dz. \end{aligned} \tag{15}$$

the premise of existence and uniqueness according to Lipschitzian theory and development cognition is:

(C1) There will be a constants $\mathscr{L}_{\curlyvee}, \mathscr{M}_{\curlyvee}$, such that

$$|\curlyvee(t,\mho(t))| \leqslant \mathscr{L}_{\curlyvee}|\mho| + \mathscr{M}_{\curlyvee}.$$

(C2) There exists constants $\mathbb{L}_{\curlyvee} > 0$ such that for each $\mho$, $\bar{\mathfrak{f}} \in \mho$ such that

$$|\curlyvee(t,\mho) - \curlyvee(t,\bar{\mathfrak{f}})| \leqslant \mathbb{L}_{\curlyvee}[|\mho| - \bar{\mathfrak{f}}|];$$

Theorem 4.1

The examined system (2) has the same number of solutions if using hypothesis (C1,C2), as the integral equation (12) has at least one solution.

$\frac{(1-\omega)}{ABC(\omega)} t^{r-1} \mathbb{L}_{\curlyvee} < 1$".

Proof. We prove the theorem in two step as bellow:**Step I:** Let $\bar{\mathfrak{f}} \in \mathbf{A}$, where $\mathbf{A} = \{\mho \in \mho : \|\mho\| \leqslant \phi, \phi > 0\}$ is closed convex set. Then using the definition of F in (15), one has

$$\begin{aligned} \|F(\mho) - F(\bar{\mathfrak{f}})\| &= \frac{(1-\omega)}{ABC(\omega)} t^{r-1} \max_{t\in[0,\tau]} |\curlyvee(t,\mho(t)) - \curlyvee(t,\bar{\mathfrak{f}}(t))| \\ &\leqslant \frac{(1-\omega)}{ABC(\omega)} t^{r-1} \mathbb{L}_{\curlyvee} \|\mho - \bar{\mathfrak{f}}\|. \end{aligned} \tag{16}$$

F will therefore conform to the contraction property. Step-II: We must demonstrate that G is bounded and equicontinuous in order to show that it is relatively compact. Given that G is continuous, Y is similarly continuous, and we have for each ℧∈A

$$\begin{aligned} \|G(\mho)\| &= \max_{t\in[0,\tau]} \| \frac{r\omega}{ABC(\omega)\Gamma(\omega)} \int_0^t (\tau - z)^{\omega-1} z^{r-1} \curlyvee(z,\mho(z))dz| \\ &\leqslant \frac{r\omega}{ABC(\omega)\Gamma(\omega)} \int_0^t (s)^{\omega-1}(1-s)^{r-1} |\curlyvee(s,\mho(s))|ds \\ &\leqslant \frac{r[\mathscr{L}_{\curlyvee}|\mho| + \mathscr{M}_{\curlyvee} T^{\omega+r-1}]}{ABC(s)\Gamma(s)} [B(\omega,r)]. \end{aligned} \tag{17}$$

Thus, (17) demonstrates that G is bounded. Next, if we assume "equi-continuity" and let $t_1 > t_2$ [0, t]

$$\begin{aligned} |G(\mho(t_2)) - G(\mho(t_1))| &= \frac{r\omega}{ABC(\omega)\Gamma(\omega)} | \int_0^{t_2} (t_2 - y)^{\omega-1} y^{r-1} \curlyvee(y,\mho(y))dy - \int_0^{t_1} (t_1 - y)^{\omega-1} y^{r-1} \curlyvee(y,\mho(y))dy| \\ &\leqslant \frac{r[\mathscr{L}_{\curlyvee}|\mho| + \mathscr{M}_{\curlyvee} T^{\omega+r-1}] B(\omega,r)}{ABC(\omega)\Gamma(\omega)} [t_2^{\omega} - t_1^{\omega}]. \end{aligned} \tag{18}$$

At $t_2 \rightarrow t_1$, the right side in (17) becomes zero. Given that G is continuing,

$$|G(\mho(t_2)) - G(\mho(t_1))| \rightarrow 0, \text{ as } t_2 \rightarrow t_1.$$

G is a continuous and bounded operator, thus we have as a result.

$$\|G(\mho(t_2)) - G(\mho(t_1))\| \rightarrow 0, \text{ as } t_2 \rightarrow t_1.$$

G is therefore bounded and uniformly continuous. G is therefore reasonably compact and entirely continuous according to the Arzelá-Ascoli theorem. The equation (12) has one or more solutions, according to Theorem 4.1, and as a result, the equation (2) also has one or more solutions.

We present the following outcome in terms of uniqueness.

Theorem 4.2

Using assumption (C2), (12) has a single solution, indicating that the system (2) also has a single solution $\left[\frac{(1-\omega)t^{r-1}\mathbb{L}_{\Upsilon}}{\mathrm{ABC}(\omega)}+\frac{r[\mathbb{L}_{\Upsilon}T^{\omega+r-1}]\mathrm{B}(\omega,r)}{\mathrm{ABC}(\omega)\Gamma(\omega)}\right]<1$".

Proof

Let's say that the operator T: Ʊ→Ʊ defined by

$$
\begin{aligned}
T\mho(t) = \; & \mho_0(t)+[\Upsilon(t,\mho(t))-\Upsilon_0(t)]\frac{(1-\omega)t^{r-1}}{\mathrm{ABC}(\omega)} \\
& +\frac{r\omega}{\mathrm{ABC}(\omega)\Gamma(\omega)}\int_0^t (t-y)^{\omega-1}t^{r-1}\Upsilon(y,\mho(y))dy,\ t\in[0,\tau].
\end{aligned}
\tag{19}
$$

As $\mho,\bar{\mathfrak{f}}\in\mho$, so we can take

$$
\begin{aligned}
\|T\mho-T\bar{\mathfrak{f}}\|\leqslant\; & \frac{(1-\omega)t^{r-1}}{\mathrm{ABC}(\omega)}\max_{t\in[0,\tau]}|\Upsilon(t,\mho(t))-\Upsilon(t,\bar{\mathfrak{f}}(t))| \\
& +\frac{r\omega}{\mathrm{ABC}(\omega)\Gamma(\omega)}\max_{t\in[0,\tau]}\left|\int_0^t (t-y)^{\omega-1}t^{r-1}\Upsilon(y,\mho(y))dy\right. \\
& \left.-\int_0^t (t-y)^{\omega-1}t^{r-1}\Upsilon(y,\bar{\mathfrak{f}}(y))dy\right| \qquad \leqslant\Theta\|\mho-\bar{\mathfrak{f}}\|,
\end{aligned}
\tag{20}
$$

and

$$
\Theta=\left[\frac{(1-\omega)t^{r-1}\mathbb{L}_{\Upsilon}}{\mathrm{ABC}(\omega)}+\frac{r[\mathbb{L}_{\Upsilon}T^{\omega+r-1}]\mathrm{B}(\omega,r)\mathbb{L}_{\Upsilon}}{\mathrm{ABC}(\omega)\Gamma(\omega)}\right].
\tag{21}
$$

T is hence a contraction of (20). So, there is only one answer to equation (12). Thus, (2) only has one answer.

Ulam-Hyer Constancy

Here, we define and provide well-known stability analysis results for the equation (2). We use the perturbed parameter Φ(t), which depends on the solution having the condition Φ (0)=0 as

- $|\Psi(t)|\leqslant\epsilon$ for $\epsilon>0$;
- ${}^{\mathrm{ABC}}\mathrm{D}_t^{(\omega,r)}\mho(t)=\Upsilon(t,\mho(t))+\Psi(t)$.

Lemma 5.1 The perturbed problem's solution

$$
\begin{aligned}
{}^{\mathrm{ABC}}\mathrm{D}_t^{\omega,r}\mho(t) = \; & \Upsilon(t,\mho(t))+\Phi(t), \\
\mho(0) = \; & \mho_0,
\end{aligned}
\tag{22}
$$

fulfils the specified connection

$$|\mho(t) - \left(\mho_0(t) + [\Upsilon(t,\mho(t)) - \Phi_0(t)]\frac{(1-\omega)}{ABC(\omega)}t^{r-1} + \frac{r\omega}{ABC(\omega)\Gamma(\omega)}\int_0^t (t-y)^{\omega-1}y^{r-1}\Upsilon(y,\mho(y))dy\right)|,$$
$$\leqslant \frac{\Gamma(\omega)t^{r-1} + rT^{\omega+r-1}}{ABC(\omega)\Gamma(\omega)}B(\omega,r)\varepsilon = \omega_{\omega,r}\varepsilon. \tag{23}$$

Theorem 5.1

The analytical results of the system are "Ulam-Hyers" stable if Θ<1, where is given in assumption (C2) and (23), and the solution of the (12) is "Ulam-Hyers" stable as a result (21).

Proof

Consider that f̄ ∈Ʊ is at most the Ʊ∈Ʊsolution to (12) and that is the solution.

$$|\mho(t) - \bar{f}(t)| = |\mho(t) - \left(\mho_0(t) + \left[\Upsilon(t,\bar{f}(t)) - \Upsilon_0(t)\right]\frac{(1-\omega)}{ABC(\omega)}t^{r-1} + \frac{r\omega}{ABC(\omega)\Gamma(\omega)}\int_0^t (t-y)^{\omega-1}y^{r-1}\Upsilon(y,\bar{f}(y))dy\right)|,$$
$$\leqslant |\mho(t) - \left(\mho_0(t) + [\Upsilon(t,\mho(t)) - \Upsilon_0(t)]\frac{(1-\omega)}{ABC(\omega)}t^{r-1} + \frac{r\omega}{ABC(\omega)\Gamma(\omega)}\int_0^t (t-y)^{\omega-1}y^{r-1}\Upsilon(y,\mho(y))dy\right)|,$$
$$+ |\left(\mho_0(t) + [\Upsilon(t,\mho(t)) - \Upsilon_0(t)]\frac{(1-\omega)}{ABC(\omega)}t^{r-1} + \frac{r\omega}{ABC(\omega)\Gamma(\omega)}\int_0^t (t-y)^{\omega-1}y^{r-1}\Upsilon(y,\mho(y))dy\right) \tag{24}$$
$$- \left(\mho_0(t) + \left[(t,\bar{f}(t)) - \Upsilon_0(t)\right]\frac{(1-\omega)}{ABC(\omega)}t^{r-1} + \frac{r\omega}{ABC(\omega)\Gamma(\omega)}\int_0^t (t-y)^{\omega-1}y^{r-1}\Upsilon(y,\bar{f}(y))dy\right)|,$$
$$\leqslant \Omega_{\omega,r} + \frac{(1-\omega)L_\Upsilon}{ABC(\omega)}t^{r-1}\|\mho - \bar{f}\| + \frac{rT^{\omega+r-1}L_\Upsilon}{ABC(\omega)\Gamma(\omega)}B(\omega,r)\|\mho - \bar{f}\|,$$
$$\leqslant \Omega_{\omega,r} + \Theta\|\mho - \bar{f}\|.$$

To write (24), we might do such as

$$\|\mho - \bar{f}\| \leqslant \frac{\Omega_{\omega,r}}{1-\Theta}\|\mho - \bar{f}\|. \tag{25}$$

Consequently, information on the necessary stability is obtained.

Calculated Solution

In this section of the paper, we will use the ABC derivative and the fractal-fractional "Adams-Bashforth approach" to identify numerical solutions to the fractal-arbitrary order model (2). The aforementioned iterative method yields an approximative solution. In order to produce an approximation for the graphing of the system for such an aim, we employ the fractal-fractional AB approaches (2). We continue with (9) so that it may be observed that this serves as an approximation of a technique.

$$\begin{cases} {}^{ABC}D^{\omega}(\$(t)) = rt^{r-1}G_1(\$(t), \mathbb{I}(t), \mathbb{R}(t), t), \\ {}^{ABC}D^{\omega}(\mathbb{I}(t)) = rt^{r-1}G_2(\$(t), \mathbb{I}(t), \mathbb{R}(t), t), \\ {}^{ABC}D^{\omega}(\mathbb{R}(t)) = rt^{r-1}G_3(\$(t), \mathbb{I}(t), \mathbb{R}(t), t), \\ \$(0) = \$_0, \quad \mathbb{I}(0) = \mathbb{I}_0, \quad \mathbb{R}(0) = \mathbb{R}_0. \end{cases} \tag{26}$$

Utilizing ABC form, we apply antiderivative of fractional order and fractal dimension to the first equation of (9) to obtain where G_1, G_2, and G_3 are defined in (10)

$$\$(t) - \$(0) = \frac{(1-\omega)}{ABC(\omega)}t^{r-1}[G_1(\$(t), \mathbb{I}(t), \mathbb{R}(t), t)] + \frac{r\omega}{ABC(\omega)\Gamma(\omega)}$$

$$\int_0^t (t-y)^{\omega-1}y^{r-1}G_1(\$(y), \mathbb{I}(y), y(t), y)dy.$$

Set $t = t_{n+1}$ for $i = 0,1,2\cdots,$

$$\$(t_{n+1}) - \$(0) = \frac{(1-\omega)}{ABC(\omega)}(t_{n+1}^{r-1})[G_1(\$(t_n), I(t_n), R(t_n))]$$

$$+ \frac{r\omega}{ABC(\omega)\Gamma(\omega)} \int_0^{t_{n+1}} (t_{n+1} - y)^{\omega-1} y^{r-1} G_1(\$(y), I(y), R(y))dy.$$

$$= \frac{(1-\omega)}{ABC(\omega)}(t_{n+1}^{r-1})[G_1(\$(t_n), I(t_n), R(t_n))]$$

$$+ \frac{r\omega}{ABC(\omega)\Gamma(\omega)} \sum_{q=0}^{n} \int_q^{t_{q+1}} (t_{n+1} - y)^{\omega-1} y^{r-1} G_1(\$(y), I(y), R(y))dy.$$

Now, using an interpolation polynomial, we approximate the function G1 on the range [tq,tq+1] as follows.

$$G_1 \cong \frac{G_1}{\Delta}(t - t_{q-1}) - \frac{R_1}{\Delta}(t - t_q)$$

it suggests that

$$\$(t_{n+1}) = \$(0) + \frac{(1-\omega)}{ABC(\omega)}(t_{n+1}^{r-1})[G_1(\$(t_n), I(t_n), R(t_n))]$$

$$+ \frac{r\omega}{ABC(\omega)\Gamma(\omega)} \sum_{q=0}^{n} \left(\frac{G_1(\$(t_n), I(t_n), R(t_n))}{\Delta} \int_q^{t_{q+1}} (t - t_{q-1})(t_{q+1} - t)^{\omega-1} t_q^{r-1} \right) dt$$

$$- \frac{G_1(\$(t_n), I(t_n), R(t_n))}{\Delta} \int_q^{t_{q+1}} (t - t_q)(t_{n+1} - t)^{\omega-1} t_q^{r-1} dt \Bigg).$$

$$\$(t_{n+1}) = \$(0) + \frac{(1-\omega)}{ABC(\omega)}(t_{n+1}^{r-1})[G_1(\$(t_n), I(t_n), R(t_n))]$$

$$+ \frac{r\omega}{ABC(\omega)\Gamma(\omega)} \sum_{q=0}^{n} \left(\frac{t_q^{r-1} G_1(\$(t_j), I(t_q), R(t_q))}{\Delta} I_{q-1,\omega} \right. \qquad (27)$$

$$\left. - \frac{t_{q-1}^{r-1} G_1(\$(t_{q-1}), I(t_{q-1}), R(t_{q-1}))}{\Delta} I_{q,\omega} \right).$$

Calculating $I_{q-1,\omega}$ and $I_{q,\omega}$ we get

$$I_{q-1,\omega} = \int_q^{t_{q+1}} (t - t_{q-1})(t_{n+1} - t)^{\omega-1} dt$$

$$= \frac{1}{\omega}[(t_{q+1} - t_{q-1})(t_{n+1} - t_{q+1})^{\sigma} - (t_q - t_{q-1})(t_{n+1} - t_q)^{\sigma}]$$

$$\frac{1}{\omega(\omega-1)}[(t_{n+1} - t_{q+1})^{\omega+1} - (t_{n+1} - t_q)^{\omega+1}],$$

And

$$I_{q,\omega} = \int_{q}^{t_{q+1}} (t - t_q)(t_{n+1} - t)^{\omega - 1} dt$$

$$= \frac{1}{\omega}\left[(t_{q+1} - t_q)(t_{n+1} - t_{q+1})^{\omega}\right]$$

$$\frac{1}{\omega(\omega - 1)}\left[(t_{n+1} - t_{q+1})^{\omega+1} - (t_{n+1} - t_q)^{\sigma+1}\right],$$

put $t_q = q\Delta$, we get

$$I_{q-1,\omega} = \frac{\Delta^{\omega+1}}{\omega}[(q+1-(q-1))(n+1-(q+1))^{\omega} - (q-(q-1))(n+1-q^{\omega}]$$

$$\frac{\Delta^{\omega+1}}{\omega(\omega-1)}[(n+1-(q+1))^{\omega+1}$$

$$-(n+1-q)^{\omega+1}],$$

$$= \frac{\Delta^{\omega+1}}{\omega(\omega-1)}[-2(\omega+1)(n-q)^{\omega} + (\omega+1)(n+1-q)^{\omega} - (n-q)^{\omega+1}$$

$$+(n+1-q)^{\omega+1}],$$

$$= \frac{\Delta^{\omega+1}}{\omega(\omega-1)}[(n-q)^{\omega}(-2(r+1)-(n-q)) + (n+1-q)^{\omega}(\omega+1+n+1-q)],$$

$$= \frac{\Delta^{\omega+1}}{\omega(\omega-1)}[(n+1-q)^{\omega}(n-q+2+\omega) - (n-q)^{\omega}(n-q+2+2\omega)],$$

(28)

And

$$I_{q,\omega} = \frac{\Delta^{\omega+1}}{\omega}[(q+1-q)(n+1-(q+1))^{\omega}] - \frac{\Delta^{\omega+1}}{\omega(\omega-1)}[(n+1-(q+1))^{\omega+1}$$

$$-(n+1-q)^{\omega+1}], = \frac{\Delta^{\omega+1}}{\omega(\omega-1)}[-(\omega+1)(n-q)^{\omega} - (n-q)^{\omega+1}$$

$$+(n+1-q)^{\omega+1}],$$

$$= \frac{\Delta^{\omega+1}}{\omega(\omega-1)}[(n-q)^{\omega}(-(q+1)-(n-q)) + (n+1-q)^{\omega+1}],$$

$$= \frac{\Delta^{\omega+1}}{\omega(\omega-1)}[(n+1-q)^{\omega+1} - (n-q)^{\omega}(n-q+1+\omega)],$$

(29)

When the values of (28), (29) are substituted in (27), we obtain

$$
S(t_{n+1}) = \begin{cases} S(0) + \dfrac{(1-\omega)}{ABC(\omega)}(t_{n+1}^{r-1})[G_1(S(t_n), I(t_n), R(t_n))] \\ + \dfrac{r\omega}{ABC(\omega)\Gamma(\omega)} \displaystyle\sum_{q=0}^{n} \Bigg(\dfrac{t_q^{r-1} G_1(S(t_q), I(t_q), R(t_q))}{\Delta} \\ \times \left[\dfrac{\Delta^{\omega+1}}{\omega(\omega-1)} [(n+1-q)^{\omega}(n-q+2+\omega) - (n-q)^{\omega}(n-q+2+2\omega)] \right] \\ - \dfrac{t_{q-1}^{r-1} G_1(S(t_{q-1}), I(t_{q-1}), R(t_{q-1}))}{\Delta} \left[\dfrac{\Delta^{\omega+1}}{\omega(\omega-1)} [(n+1-q)^{\omega+1} - (n-q)^{\omega}(n-q+1+\omega)] \right] \Bigg). \end{cases} \tag{30}
$$

Similar numerical schemes can be found for the other two compartments, I and R.

$$
I(t_{n+1}) = \begin{cases} I(0) + \dfrac{(1-\omega)}{ABC(\omega)}(t_{n+1}^{r-1})[G_2(S(t_n), I(t_n), R(t_n))] \\ + \dfrac{r\omega}{ABC(\omega)\Gamma(\omega)} \displaystyle\sum_{q=0}^{n} \Bigg(\dfrac{t_q^{r-1} G_2(S(t_q), I(t_q), R(t_q))}{\Delta} \\ \times \left[\dfrac{\Delta^{\omega+1}}{\omega(\omega-1)} [(n+1-q)^{\omega}(n-q+2+\omega) - (n-q)^{\omega}(n-q+2+2\omega)] \right] \\ - \dfrac{t_{q-1}^{r-1} G_1(S(t_{q-1}), I(t_{q-1}), R(t_{q-1}))}{\Delta} \left[\dfrac{\Delta^{\omega+1}}{\omega(\omega-1)} [(n+1-q)^{\omega+1} - (n-q)^{\omega}(n-q+1+\omega)] \right] \Bigg). \end{cases} \tag{31}
$$

$$
R(t_{n+1}) = \begin{cases} R(0) + \dfrac{(1-\omega)}{ABC(\omega)}(t_{n+1}^{r-1})[G_3(S(t_n), I(t_n), R(t_n))] \\ + \dfrac{r\omega}{ABC(\omega)\Gamma(\omega)} \displaystyle\sum_{q=0}^{n} \Bigg(\dfrac{t_q^{r-1} G_3(S(t_q), I(t_q), R(t_q))}{\Delta} \\ \times \left[\dfrac{\Delta^{\omega+1}}{\omega(\omega-1)} [(n+1-q)^{\omega}(n-q+2+\omega) - (n-q)^{\omega}(n-q+2+2\omega)] \right] \\ - \dfrac{t_{q-1}^{r-1} G_1(S(t_{q-1}), I(t_{q-1}), R(t_{q-1}))}{\Delta} \left[\dfrac{\Delta^{\omega+1}}{\omega(\omega-1)} [(n+1-q)^{\omega+1} - (n-q)^{\omega}(n-q+1+\omega)] \right] \Bigg). \end{cases} \tag{32}
$$

Approximate solution using initial conditions and values of several parameters

We now take the numbers from Table 1 for the system (2) under consideration. Data for Pakistan have been collected. There are roughly N=220.0.142 million vulnerable cases in the country in question.

Table 1
Description and numerical values of the parameters.

Parameters	Description	value
S_0	Initial susceptible class	220 millions [68]
I_0	Initial infected class	0.142 million [68]
R_0	Initial value of recovered class	0.0125 million [68]
a	Natural birth rate rate	0.00009
b	Transmission rate	0.001664, 0.001663, 0.0016628
c	Contact rate	0.49
μ	Natural death rate	0.019 [68]
λ	death rate due to virous	0.00134
k	recovery rate	0.001

When b=0.001664 in Case-A,
Using information from 1, we can determine R_0 as

$$R_0 = \frac{bca}{\mu(\mu + k + \lambda)} = \frac{(0.00009)(0.0001664)(0.49)}{0.019(0.019 + 0.001 + 0.00134)} = 8.242 \times 10^{-9} < 1.$$

R01 is the same for the other two cases as it was for case-A. Otherwise, our considered system will be unstable and the infection will be at the top if R0>1, R0=5.7. As a result, our system is stable, and by using the AB approaches described above, we were able to produce the fractional order model 2. (30).

We saw from 2 that the sensitive population will decline at a very high rate, or in a short period of time, over the next 12 weeks. The observed decrease indicates that the susceptible class will initially move toward the infected class and will be quick at smaller non-integer orders and slow at bigger fractional orders and fractal dimensions. If preventative actions are not taken, the infected cases in "Pakistan" will reach their maximum peak value of 0.8 million in the next months, according to the statistics shown in Fig. 3. The rate of infected classes increases rapidly at low arbitrary order with fractal dimensions but decreases steadily as the order increases. Similar to Fig. 3, Fig. 4 depicts recovered cases that may rise due to isolation and precautionary measures, and that increase occurs at lower fractional orders and fractal dimensions. All three figures demonstrate convergence and stability. see Figures 5, 6, and 7.

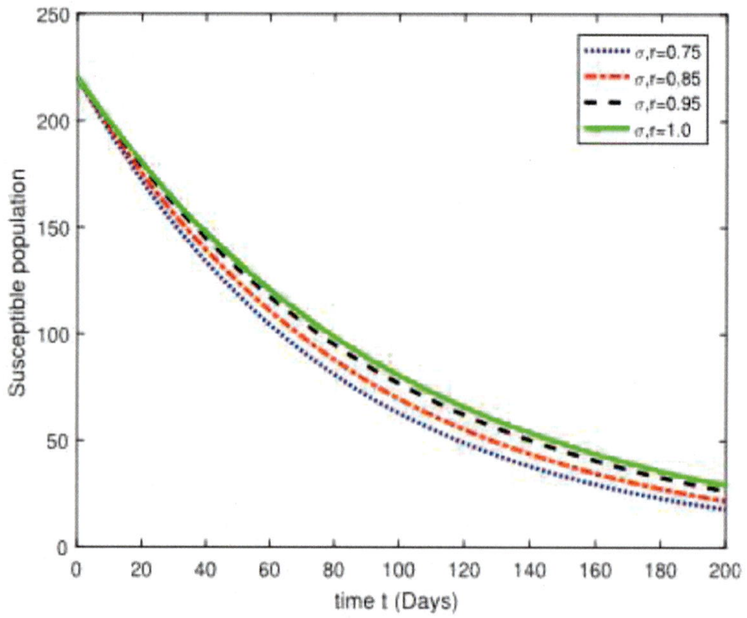

Fig. 2. Dynamics of susceptible population of the fractal-fractional model (2) at various arbitrary order and fractal dimension.

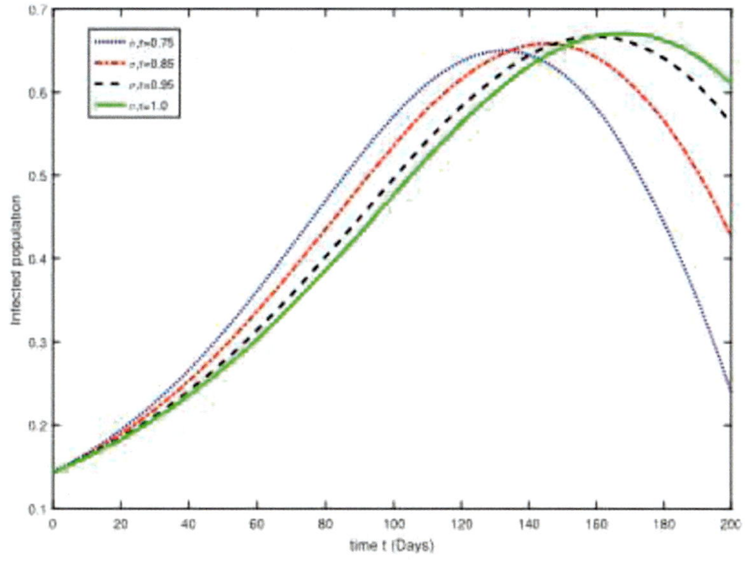

Fig. 3. Dynamics of infected population of the fractal-fractional model (2) at various arbitrary order and fractal dimension.

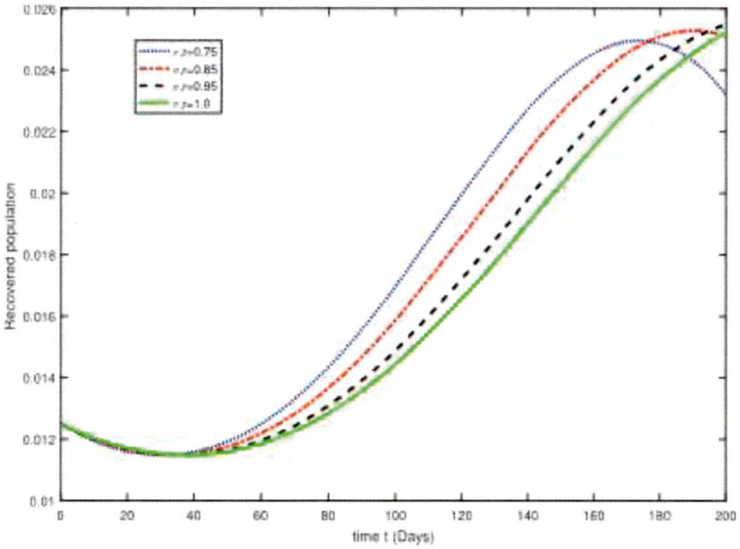

Fig. 4. Dynamics of recovered population of the fractal-fractional model (2) at various arbitrary order and fractal dimension.

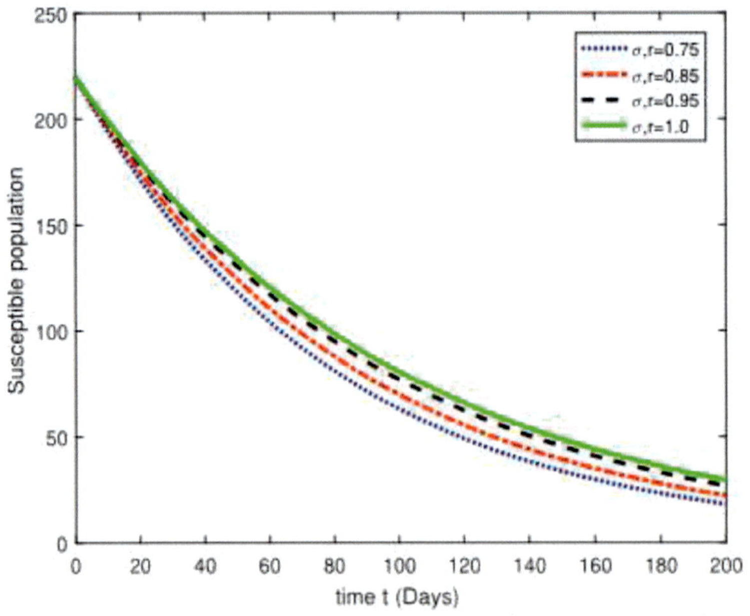

Fig. 5. Dynamics of "susceptible population" of the fractal-fractional model (2) at various arbitrary order and fractal dimension.

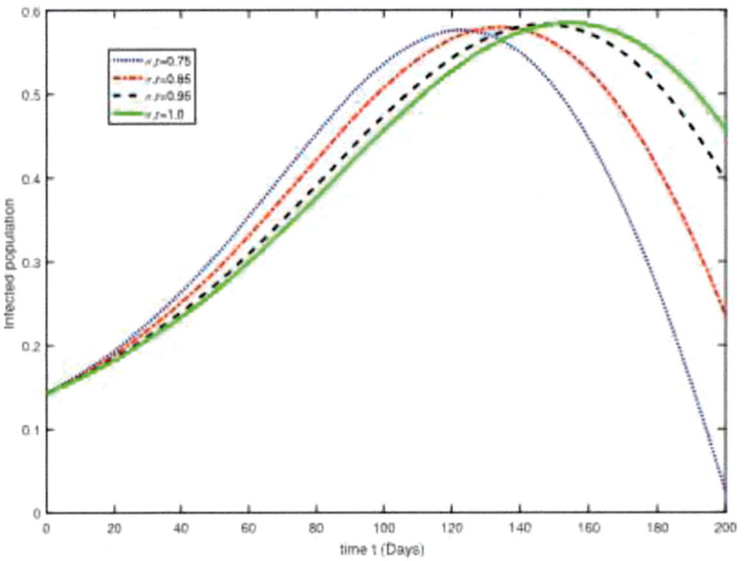

Fig. 6. Dynamics of "Infected population" of the fractal-fractional model (2) at various arbitrary order and fractal dimension.

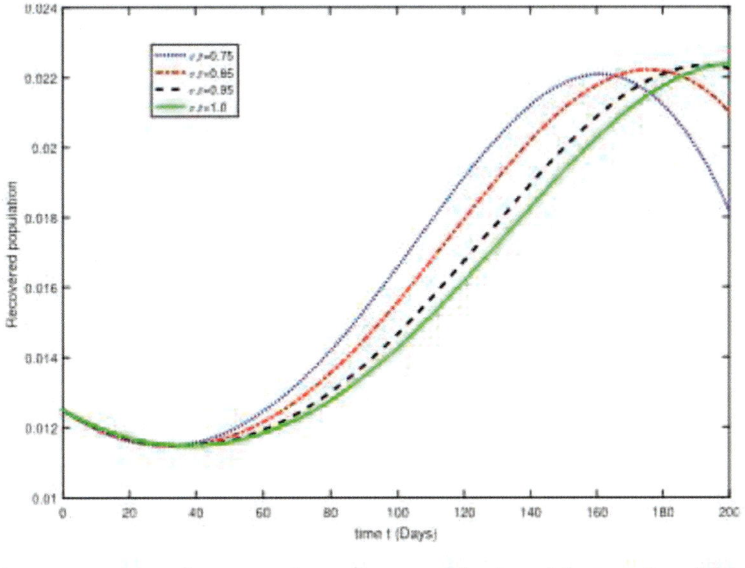

Fig. 7. Dynamics of "recovered population" of the fractal-fractional model (2) at various arbitrary order and fractal dimension.

When b=0.0016630, Case-B

Now, we use the iteration approach mentioned in (5) to get the result while using the transmission rate of 0.0016630. (7). We notice that as the susceptible class declines, the infection population likewise declines as a result of a decline in the rate of transmission through interpersonal contact. The highest value likewise dropped to 0.6 million as the transmission rate fell. When a result, we predict that as the rate of transmission increases over the next four to five months, the total number of infected cases could reach around 0.6 million. The fact that the number is lower in this instance than it was in the one before it illustrates how precautionary measures have an impact on society. The data in instance B likewise suggest stability and convergence, which can be demonstrated using the same values that were plugged into the R0 calculation in case A.

When b=0.0016628, use Case-C

The model performs differently from the prior model in terms of the population of illnesses class, and the peak value lowered obtained it faster. We now notify the same technique for b=0.0016628. This indicates that it will eventually result in fewer COVID-19-infected infections. Our numerical solutions thus offer the most accurate forecast that, with other preventative measures as previously discussed being put in place, a reduction in the transmission rate will result in a reduction in the number of infected cases nationwide. For various compartments, the dynamical system is depicted in Figs. 8, 9, and 10, respectively.

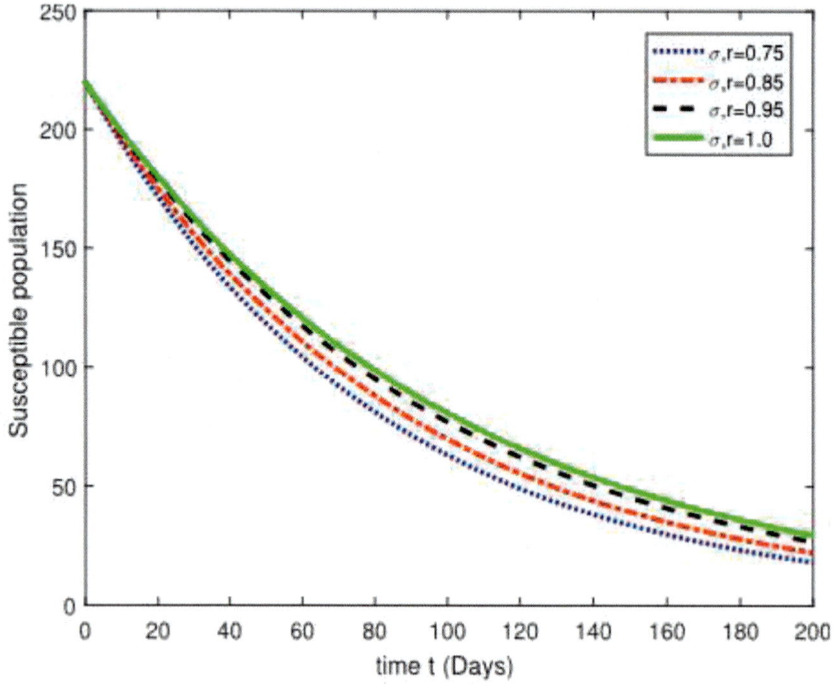

Fig. 8. Dynamics of "susceptible population" of the fractal-fractional model (2) at various arbitrary order and fractal dimension.

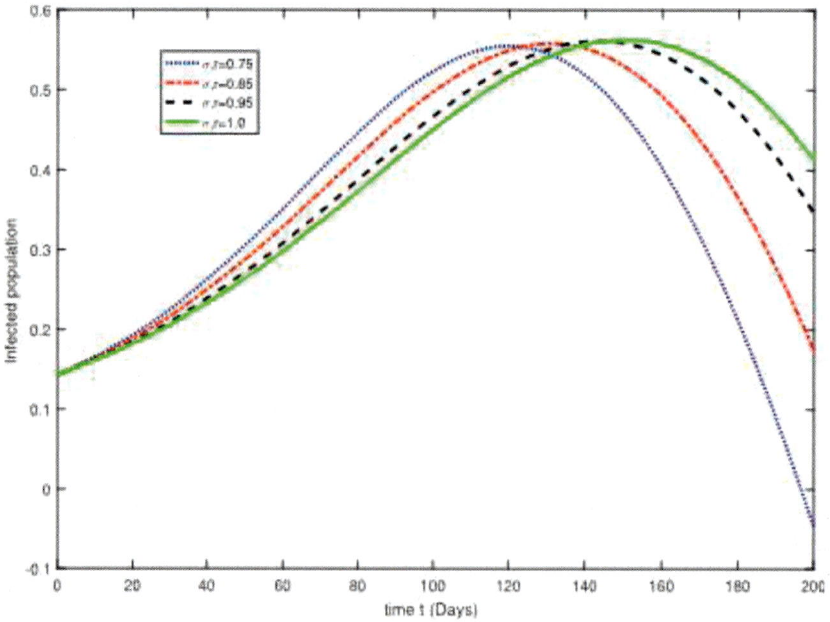

Fig. 9. Dynamics of "infected population" of the fractal-fractional model (2) at various arbitrary order and fractal dimension.

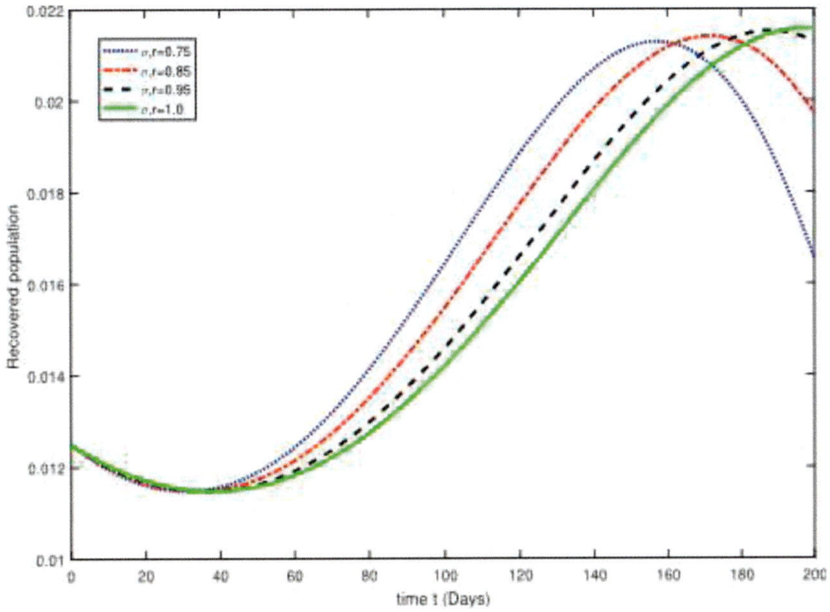

Fig. 10. Dynamics of "recovered population" of the fractal-fractional model (2) at various arbitrary order and fractal dimension.

The Bottom Line

In our talk, we looked into the ABC fractal-arbitrary order derivatives-based SIR fractal-fractional model for the process of COVID-19 prediction in Pakistan. The Routh-Hurwitz criteria, the method of the next generation matrix, and equilibrium point procedures have all been used to determine the global and local stability for the model under consideration. Next, using non-linear approaches, it was demonstrated that positivity and boundedness go hand in hand. There aren't many "fixed point results" for the system's stability and "Hyers-Ulam" stability results for the existence of one or more solutions (2). For the model under consideration, we have offered a rough solution using the "Adams-Bashforth approach." We have graphed the solution and its behaviour under modifying the transmission parameter for various random order and fractal dimension using real data provided for "Pakistan" The biggest beneficial effect on containing or slowing the spread of the Covid-19 will come from reducing the transmission rate and putting precautionary measures in place. It is also evident that the technique adopted produces positive results in battling the nasty virus while minimising interaction with other people.

Chapter 7

Perturbed collage theorem for solving an uncertain inverse issue in Fractional Dynamical Systems[7]

Introduction

In this study, we intend to give an approximation method based on the "Collage technique" to solve a class of inverse problems for differential equations with uncertainty. In the current investigation, we do in fact take three ideas into account concurrently. (1) Inverse issue; (2) Fractional order derivative; (3) Interval uncertainty. By taking into account the aforementioned ideas, we were encouraged to focus on presenting fresh and original findings in this report and for the first time in the literature. In this regard, we describe our involvement and the driving forces behind this study in the questions and answers that follow.

Question 1. Why fractional order derivative?

We opted to use this intriguing operator to model the system due to the significant contributions of fractional calculus to the description of complex dynamics of unsentimental systems, particularly in systems with memory effect on physical structures, such as in signal processing, bioengineering, control processes, economics, and others. In contrast, we use the Caputo-type fractional differentiability of order $\alpha(0<\alpha\leq 1)$ to model the real phenomena because it has advantages over initial conditions that have the same form as those for differential equations of integer-order, which brings the model's behavior closer to that of a typical system. Also included in the category of integer-order systems is the fractional-based system. When a result, we anticipate that the model will become an ordinary case as the order of differentiability approaches a natural number. With smooth behavior or not, but how? This problem's resolution is crucial. Since fractional calculus-based mathematical modeling can only be viewed as a routine generalization of ordinary differential equations systems with prior predictions about the behavior of solutions, it is possible to find some extraordinary situations that are not present in typical dynamical systems!

Question 2: Why is there interval uncertainty?

Considering the uncertainty is inevitable due to the knowledge gap, insufficient data, and many sorts of modeling mistakes that exist. We use the fundamental one, known as "interval uncertainty," in this message. The first reason is because this kind of uncertainty is typically

---

7 *Landmark paper: Soheil Salahshour, Ali Ahmadian, Bruno A. Pansera, Massimiliano Ferrara,*
Uncertain inverse problem for fractional dynamical systems using perturbed collage theorem, Communications in Nonlinear Science and Numerical Simulation, Volume 94, 2021, 105553, ISSN 1007-5704, https://doi.org/10.1016/j.cnsns.2020.105553.

perceived as a generalization of real numbers. Second, because there are numerous real-world applications, calculations based on intervals are generally known. Scientists have just discovered the usefulness of this important idea, which quantifies uncertainties in mathematical models with unknown parameters. As a result, several studies have been conducted to assess the interval-based mathematical systems and investigate the existence and uniqueness of interval solutions to interval differential equations. In reality, when defining a system's states and dynamics, interval arithmetic, a subfield of fuzzy sets, can decrease the complexity and computing challenges compared to fuzzy systems by dealing with the intervals from the first step of modeling or numerical technique. In reality, several research projects have taken into account these types of modeling in terms of theoretical and computational techniques with appropriate applications and interpretation.

Question 3: Why inverse problems?

According to Kunze and Vrscay one intriguing concept involving inverse issues based on the usage of contraction maps in "fractal-based" approximation is as follows: Assume that the metric space (z, d_z) is complete and that Con(z) is the collection of contraction maps on z. If z ε Z serves as a target, then our goal is to come close to it. The query is: If it is possible, how can we locate a mapping $T_\delta \varepsilon \mathrm{Con}(z)$ such that $d_z(z, Z_\delta)$ given a fixed point $\tilde{z}_\delta \varepsilon Z$? The following formulations represent this issue in the fractional dynamical system: We want an appropriate fractional derivative-based system $C_z^{(\alpha)}(t) = f(t, x)$ for a given curve z(t) (as a solution) such that z(t) becomes as near as feasible while the field f should be taken into account within certain predetermined constraints.

We should take into consideration the inverse problem for a class of interval fractional differential equations (IFDEs) and the numerical method by employing Collage theorem for real modeling using dynamical systems under real data (even missing data, lack of information, optimistic/pessimistic situations, sensitivity analysis) in the numerical framework with combination of optimization problem. To best of knowledge of the authors, one publication published concerning inverse problem for solving a class of fractional differential equation and also one research study on interval uncertainty of inverse integral problem. Therefore, the current study is the first attempt for solving inverse issue to manage both uncertainty and fractional differentiability. The work is organized as follows: in Section 2, several fundamental principles of fractional calculus are reviewed, including the definition of a Caputo-type derivative and interval arithmetic properties. The majority of the results, including the inverse issue for IFDEs and the Picard operator, are presented in Section 3. This section further develops the inverse problem utilizing the Collage theorem to solve IFDEs. In Section 4, an example is shown to validate the suggested technique in details. To demonstrate the effectiveness of the proposed method for determining the approximative solution of the IFDEs, different values of fractional-order derivatives are experienced under both types of interval differentiability. In the final part, some final remarks are attracted.

Preliminaries

The following quickly highlights the definitions of the fractional derivative, interval arithmetic, and inverse issues that are necessary and will be referred to in the next portions of the work.

Fractional derivative

Definition 2.1: A continuous and n-time differentiable function in the Caputo sense is required to have a non-integer derivative.

Definition 2.1. *Regarding to [4], the non-integer derivative of a continuous and n-time differentiable function in the Caputo sense is prescribed by*

$$^{C}X^{(\alpha)}(t) = \frac{1}{\Gamma(n-\alpha)} \int_a^t (t-s)^{n-\alpha-1} \left(\frac{d}{ds}\right)^n X(s)ds, \tag{2.1}$$

where $n-1 < \alpha \leq n$.

Definition 2.2. *[4]. The one-parameter Mittag-Leffler function* $E_\alpha(z)$ *is defined by*

$$E_\alpha(z) = \sum_{k=0}^{\infty} \frac{z^k}{\Gamma(\alpha k + 1)}, \quad z, \alpha \in \mathbb{C}.$$

2.2. Interval arithmetic operations

Let $\mathcal{K}_C$ indicate the family of all nonempty, compact and convex intervals of the real line $\mathbb{R}$. The addition and scalar multiplication in $\mathcal{K}_C$, we define as usual, i.e. for $P, Q \in \mathcal{K}_C$, $P = [\underline{p}, \overline{p}]$, $Q = [\underline{q}, \overline{q}]$, $\underline{p} \leq \overline{p}$, $\underline{q} \leq \overline{q}$, and $\varpi \geq 0$ we have

$$P + Q = [\underline{p} + \underline{q}, \overline{p} + \overline{q}], \quad \varpi P = [\varpi\underline{p}, \varpi\overline{p}] \quad (-\varpi)P = [-\varpi\overline{p}, -\varpi\underline{p}].$$

The Hausdorff metric $\mathcal{T}$ in $\mathcal{K}_C$ is defined as follows:

$$\mathcal{T}(P, Q) = \max\{|\underline{p} - \underline{q}|, |\overline{p} - \overline{q}|\},$$

for $P = [\underline{p}, \overline{p}]$, $Q = [\underline{q}, \overline{q}]$. It is known (see e.g. [29]) that $(\mathcal{K}_C, \mathcal{T})$ is a complete, separable and locally compact metric space.

Proposition 2.1. *Given* Ω *a compact topological space, we will denote by* $C(\Omega)$ *the Banach space of all continuous real valued functions, prescribed on* Ω *wit its usual max norm,* $\|.\|_\infty$ *and by* $C(\Omega, \mathcal{K}_C)$*, the set of all continuous functions from* Ω *into* $\mathcal{K}_C$ *endowed with the distance:*

$$H(p, q) := \sup_{\sigma \in \Omega} \max\{|\underline{p}(\sigma) - \underline{q}(\sigma)|, |\overline{p}(\sigma) - \overline{q}(\sigma)|\},$$

with $p(\sigma) = [\underline{p}(\sigma), \overline{p}(\sigma)]$ *and* $q(\sigma) = [\underline{q}(\sigma), \overline{q}(\sigma)]$ *in* $C(\Omega, \mathcal{K}_C)$*. Then,* $(C(\Omega, \mathcal{K}_C), H)$ *is a complete and separable metric space [48].*

Consider the space $C_\alpha(\Omega, \mathcal{K}_C(\mathbb{R}))$, $\alpha \in (0, 1]$ such that $\Omega = [a, b]$, $(. - a)^\alpha X(.) \in C(\Omega, \mathcal{K}_C(\mathbb{R}))$. Note that $C_\alpha(\Omega, \mathcal{K}_C(\mathbb{R}))$ is a complete metric space with respect to the metric:

$$H_\alpha(f, g) := \sup_{t \in \Omega} t^\alpha \mathcal{T}(f, g).$$

Markov originally expanded the idea of Hukuhara-difference (abbreviated H-difference in the new definition) to introduce the idea of generalized Hukuhara-differentiability for the interval-valued functions. The fuzzy Hukuhara-differentiability for the fuzzy-valued functions was later defined by Kaleva using this concept.

Definition 2.3. *(see [49]). Suppose that $p, l \in \mathcal{K}_C$. If there exists $w \in \mathcal{K}_C$ such that $p = l + w$, then w is called the H-difference of p and l, and it is denoted by $p \ominus l$.*

In this paper, the sign "$\ominus$" always stands for H-difference and note that $p \ominus l \neq p + (-l)$.

Definition 2.4. *(see [50]).*

The generalized Hukuhara difference of two intervals, $\mathcal{A}$ and $\mathcal{B}$, (gH-difference for short) is defined as follows

$$\mathcal{A} \ominus_g \mathcal{B} = C \Leftrightarrow \begin{cases} (a), & \mathcal{A} = \mathcal{B} + C, \\ \text{or } (b), & \mathcal{B} = \mathcal{A} + (-1)C. \end{cases}$$

In this report, it is assumed that the H-difference and gH-differentiability are exist.

Definition 2.5. *(see, [51]). Assume that $\mathfrak{p} : (a, b) \to \mathcal{K}_C$ and $\mathbf{z}_0 \in (a, b)$. We say that $\mathfrak{p}$ is strongly gH-differentiable at $\mathbf{z}_0$, if there exists an element $\mathfrak{p}'(\mathbf{z}_0) \in \mathcal{K}_C$, such that*
(i) for all $\hbar > 0$ sufficiently small, $\exists \mathfrak{p}(\mathbf{z}_0 + \hbar) \ominus_g \mathfrak{p}(\mathbf{z}_0)$, $\exists \mathfrak{p}(\mathbf{z}_0) \ominus_g \mathfrak{p}(\mathbf{z}_0 - \hbar)$ and limits (in the metric $\mathfrak{D}$):

$$\lim_{\hbar \searrow 0} \frac{\mathfrak{p}(\mathbf{z}_0 + \hbar) \ominus_g \mathfrak{p}(\mathbf{z}_0)}{\hbar} = \lim_{\hbar \searrow 0} \frac{\mathfrak{p}(\mathbf{z}_0) \ominus_g \mathfrak{p}(\mathbf{z}_0 - \hbar)}{\hbar} = \mathfrak{p}'(\mathbf{z}_0).$$

or
(ii) for all $\hbar > 0$ sufficiently small, $\exists \mathfrak{p}(\mathbf{z}_0) \ominus_g \mathfrak{p}(\mathbf{z}_0 + \hbar)$, $\exists \mathfrak{p}(\mathbf{z}_0 - \hbar) \ominus_g \mathfrak{p}(\mathbf{z}_0)$ and limits (in the metric $\mathfrak{D}$):

$$\lim_{\hbar \searrow 0} \frac{\mathfrak{p}(\mathbf{z}_0) \ominus_g \mathfrak{p}(\mathbf{z}_0 + \hbar)}{-\hbar} = \lim_{\hbar \searrow 0} \frac{\mathfrak{p}(\mathbf{z}_0 - \hbar) \ominus_g \mathfrak{p}(\mathbf{z}_0)}{-\hbar} = \mathfrak{p}'(\mathbf{z}_0).$$

We call that $\mathfrak{p}$ is ((1)-gH)-differentiable on (a, b) if $\mathfrak{p}$ is differentiable under assumption of Case (i), Definition 2.5 and similarly for ((2)-gH)-differentiability with respect to Case (ii), Definition 2.5.

♦ $L_p^{\mathcal{K}_C}(a, b)$, $1 \leq p \leq \infty$ is the set of all interval-valued measurable functions f on $[a, b]$ where $\|f\|_p = \left(\int_0^1 (d(f(t), 0))^p dt\right)^{\frac{1}{p}}$.

♦ $C^{\mathcal{K}_C}[a, b]$ is a space of interval-valued functions which are continuous on $[a, b]$.

Definition 2.6. *(see [52]). Assume that $\mathfrak{p} \in C^{\mathcal{K}_C}[a, b] \cap L^{\mathcal{K}_C}[a, b]$ is an interval-valued function, thus Rieman-Liouville integral of interval -valued function $\mathfrak{p}$ is defined as following:*

$$(I^\alpha f)(x) = \frac{1}{\Gamma(\alpha)} \int_a^x \frac{f(t)dt}{(x - t)^{1-\alpha}}, \quad x > a, \tag{2.2}$$

in which $\alpha \in (0, 1]$.

Definition 2.7. *(see [52]). Assume that $\mathfrak{p} \in C^{\mathcal{K}_C}[a, b] \cap L^{\mathcal{K}_C}[a, b]$ is an interval-valued function, thus $\mathfrak{p}$ is an interval gH-differentiable of Caputo-type at x such that:*

$${}^C\mathfrak{p}^{(\alpha)}(x) = \frac{1}{\Gamma(1 - \alpha)} \int_a^x \frac{\mathfrak{p}'(t)}{(x - t)^\alpha} dt, \tag{2.3}$$

in which $\alpha \in (0, 1]$ and then, we say $\mathfrak{p}$ is ${}^C(1, \alpha)$-differentiable if Eq. (2.3) holds while $\mathfrak{p}$ is ((1)-gH)-differentiable, and $\mathfrak{p}$ is ${}^C(2, \alpha)$-differentiable if Eq. (2.3) holds while $\mathfrak{p}$ is ((2)-gH)-differentiable.

We say that an interval-valued function $F : [a, b] \to \mathcal{I}$ is *w-increasing* (w-decreasing) on $[a, b]$ if the real function $t \to w_F(t) := w(F(t))$ is increasing (decreasing) on $[a, b]$. If F is w-increasing or w-decreasing on $[a, b]$, then we say that F is w-monotone on $[a, b]$ (see, [24]).

Proposition 2.2. *(see, [23]). Let $F : [a,b] \to \mathcal{K}_C$ be such that $F(t) = [f^-(t), f^+(t)], t \in [a,b]$. If F is w-monotone and gH-differentiable on $[a,b]$, then $\frac{d}{dt}f^-(t)$ and $\frac{d}{dt}f^+(t)$ exist for all $t \in [a,b]$. Moreover, we have that:*

(i) $F'(t) = [\frac{d}{dt}f^-(t), \frac{d}{dt}f^+(t)]$ for all $t \in [a,b]$, if F is w-increasing,
(ii) $F'(t) = [\frac{d}{dt}f^+(t), \frac{d}{dt}f^-(t)]$ for all $t \in [a,b]$, if F is w-decreasing.

3. Main results

Suppose that $Con(Y)$ be the set of contraction maps on Y such that

$$Con(Y) = \{T|T : Y \to Y \& \, d_Y(T_{y_1}, T_{y_2}) \le c_T d_Y(y_1, y_2), \ \forall y_1, y_2 \in Y, \ c_T \in [0,1)\},$$

where (Y, d_Y) be complete normed quasi-linear space, $d_Y(a, 0) = \|a\|_I$, as Hausdorff-Pompeiu metric.

Theorem 3.1. *(Banach). Let $T \in Con(Y)$, then there exists a unique $z \in Y$ such that $Tz = z$. Moreover, $d_Y(T^n y, z) \to 0$, as $n \to \infty$ for any $y \in Y$.*

Now, we provide the interval-valued of Collage Theorem.

Theorem 3.2. *Let $y \in Y$ and $T \in Con(Y)$ with contraction factor $c_T \in [0,1)$ and fixed point $z \in Y$, then*

$$d_Y(y, z) \le \frac{1}{1 - c_T} d_y(y, T_y).$$

Proof. See [48]. □

Let $C(\mathcal{I})$ be the Banach space of continuous interval-valued functions $x(t)$ on $\mathcal{I}$ with norm $\|x\|_\infty = \max_{t \in \mathcal{I}} \|x(t)\|_{\mathcal{I}}$.

3.1. Picard operator and inverse problem for IFDEs

Here, we firstly discuss the existence and uniqueness result for the solutions of IFDEs using contraction mappings. Consider the following IFDE:

$$\begin{cases} {}^c x^{(\alpha)}(t) = f(t, x), \\ x(t_0) = x_0, \end{cases} \tag{3.4}$$

where $x \in \mathcal{I}$, $f : \mathbb{R}_+ \times \mathcal{I} \to \mathcal{I}$ and $x_0 \in \mathcal{I}$, and ${}^c x^{(\alpha)}(.)$ stands for Caputo-type of order α, $(0 < \alpha \le 1)$ differentiability. Regarding each type of differentiability, we have the following solutions:
(A) For ${}^c(1, \alpha)$-differentiability, a solution of problem (3.4), satisfies the equivalent interval-valued fractional integral equation:

$$x(t) = x_0 + \frac{1}{\Gamma(\alpha)} \int_{t_0}^{t} (t - s)^{\alpha - 1} f(s, x(s)) ds \tag{3.5}$$

(B) For ${}^c(2, \alpha)$-differentiability, a solution of problem (3.4), satisfies the equivalent interval-valued fractional integral equation:

$$x(t) = x_0 \ominus (-1) \frac{1}{\Gamma(\alpha)} \int_{t_0}^{t} (t - s)^{\alpha - 1} f(s, x(s)) ds \tag{3.6}$$

provided that H-difference exists and f is w-increasing.
The Picard T_1 associated with Eq.(3.5) is defined as

$$T_1 u(t) = x_0 + \frac{1}{\Gamma(\alpha)} \int_{t_0}^{t} (t - s)^{\alpha - 1} f(s, x(s)) ds, \tag{3.7}$$

and the Picard T_2 associated with Eq.(3.6) is defined as

$$T_1 u(t) = x_0 \ominus \frac{(-1)}{\Gamma(\alpha)} \int_{t_0}^{t} (t-s)^{\alpha-1} f(s, x(s)) ds, \tag{3.8}$$

provided that the H-difference exists.

Recently, in [48], the authors obtained some interesting results in combination of inverse problem and interval uncertainty. However, they need to improve for general aspect. On the other hand, we consider the case that the length function $w(f) - w(h)$ can possess different sign over interval (a, b) to apply generalized H-difference. Not that, if always $w(f) \geq w(h)$, then the result only valid for H-difference not the generalized version.

Note that, the type of all the applied H-differences on both sides of the equality are the same.

Proposition 3.1. *Let $f, h : [a, b] \to \mathcal{K}_C^+$ two integrable interval-valued functions and set $\left(h \ominus_g f\right)(t) = h(t) \ominus_g f(t)$, then $h(t) \ominus_g f(t)$ is integrable and*

$$\int_a^b \left(h(t) \ominus_g f(t)\right) dt = \int_a^b h(t) dt \ominus_g \int_a^b f(t) dt.$$

Proof. Since $f, h \in \mathcal{K}_C^+$, then they have the following forms"

$$f(t) = [0, \bar{f}(t)],$$
$$h(t) = [0, \bar{h}(t)].$$

Now, we suppose that

$$\Omega_1 = \{t | \ \bar{f}(t) \leq \bar{h}(t)\},$$
$$\Omega_2 = \{t | \ \bar{f}(t) \geq \bar{h}(t)\}.$$

Then, it is easy to check that

$$h(t) \ominus_g f(t) = \left(h(t) \ominus_g f(t)\right)_{t \in \Omega_1} - \left(f(t) \ominus_g h(t)\right)_{t \in \Omega_2}.$$

Hence,

$$\begin{aligned}
\int_a^b \left(h(t) \ominus_g f(t)\right) dt &= \\
&= \int_{\Omega_1} (h(t) \ominus f(t)) dt - \int_{\Omega_2} (f(t) \ominus h(t)) dt \\
&= \int_{\Omega_1} [0, \left(\bar{h}(t) - \bar{f}(t)\right)] dt - \int_{\Omega_2} [0, \left(\bar{f}(t) - \bar{h}(t)\right)] dt \\
&= [0, \int_{\Omega_1} \left(\bar{h}(t) - \bar{f}(t)\right) dt] - [0, \int_{\Omega_2} \left(\bar{f}(t) - \bar{h}(t)\right) dt] \\
&= \left[\int_{\Omega_2} \left(-\bar{f}(t) + \bar{h}(t)\right) dt, \int_{\Omega_1} \left(\bar{h}(t) - \bar{f}(t)\right) dt\right].
\end{aligned} \tag{3.9}$$

Now, let consider:

$$\begin{aligned}
\int_a^b h(t) dt \ominus_g \int_a^b f(t) dt &= \int_a^b [0, \bar{h}(t)] dt \ominus_g \int_a^b [0, \bar{f}(t)] dt \\
&= [0, \int_a^b \bar{h}(t) dt] \ominus_g [0, \int_a^b \bar{f}(t) dt]
\end{aligned}$$

$$= [0, \int_{\Omega_1} \bar{h}(t)dt + \int_{\Omega_2} \bar{h}(t)dt] \ominus_g [0, \int_{\Omega_1} \bar{f}(t)dt + \int_{\Omega_2} \bar{f}(t)dt]$$

$$= \left([0, \int_{\Omega_1} \bar{h}(t)dt] + [0, \int_{\Omega_2} \bar{h}(t)dt]\right) \ominus_g \left([0, \int_{\Omega_1} \bar{f}(t)dt] \ominus_g [0, \int_{\Omega_2} \bar{f}(t)dt]\right)$$

$$= \left([0, \int_{\Omega_1} \bar{h}(t)dt] \ominus_g [0, \int_{\Omega_1} \bar{f}(t)dt]\right) + \left([0, \int_{\Omega_2} \bar{h}(t)dt] \ominus_g [0, \int_{\Omega_2} \bar{f}(t)dt]\right)$$

$$= \left([0, \int_{\Omega_1} \bar{h}(t)dt] \ominus [0, \int_{\Omega_1} \bar{f}(t)dt]\right) - \left([0, \int_{\Omega_2} \bar{f}(t)dt] \ominus [0, \int_{\Omega_2} \bar{h}(t)dt]\right)$$

$$= [0, \int_{\Omega_1} (\bar{h}(t) - \bar{f}(t))dt] - [0, \int_{\Omega_2} (\bar{f}(t) - \bar{h}(t))dt]$$

$$= [0, \int_{\Omega_1} (\bar{h}(t) - \bar{f}(t))dt] - [0, \int_{\Omega_2} (\bar{f}(t) - \bar{h}(t))dt]$$

$$= [\int_{\Omega_2} (\bar{h}(t) - \bar{f}(t))dt, \int_{\Omega_1} (\bar{h}(t) - \bar{f}(t))dt]. \tag{3.10}$$

By equality of Eq. (3.9) and Eq. (3.10), the proof is complete. □

In [48], the authors introduced an approximation of continuous interval-valued function in the metric space $C(\Omega, \mathcal{K}_C)$ in terms of s Schauder basis in the Banach space $C(\Omega)$. We provide the modification of this interesting result.

Proposition 3.2. *Let Ω be a topological compact space, $\{f_n\}_{n\geq 1}$ be a Schauder basis of $C(\Omega)$ and let $\{\Pi_n\}_{n\geq 1}$ be the associated sequence of projections such that*
(a) If $w \in \Omega$ and $n \geq 1$, then $f_n(w) \geq 0$,
(b) If $g \in C(\Omega)$, $g \geq 0$, and $n \geq 1$, then $\Pi_n(g) \geq 0$.
Then, for a given $f \in C(\Omega, \mathcal{K}_C)$, there exist $n \geq 1$ such that

$$H(f, P_n(f)) < \varepsilon, \ \varepsilon > 0,$$

where

$$P_n(f)(w) = \sum_{k=1}^{n} \alpha_k f_k(w) + \sum_{k\in\Omega_1} (\beta_k - \alpha_k)\Psi_k(w) \ominus_g \left(\sum_{k\in\Omega_2} |\beta_k - \alpha_k| \Psi_k(w)\right),$$

with $\Psi_k(w) = [0, f_k(w)]$, $\alpha_k, \beta_k \in \mathbb{R}_+$, and

$$\Omega_1 = \{k | \beta_k - \alpha_k \geq 0\},$$
$$\Omega_2 = \{k | \beta_k - \alpha_k < 0\}.$$

Proof. Let $f(t) = [\underline{f}(t), \bar{f}(t)]$, $f \in C(\Omega, \mathcal{K}_C)$. Assume that $\underline{f} = \sum_{k=1}^{n} \alpha_k f_k$ and $\bar{f} = \sum_{k=1}^{n} \beta_k f_k$, and also,

$$P_n(f)(w) = \left[\sum_{k=1}^{n} \alpha_k f_k(w), \sum_{k=1}^{n} \beta_k f_k(w)\right], \ n \geq 1, \ w \in \Omega,$$

defines an interval-valued function. Then,

$$P_n(f)(w) = \sum_{k=1}^{n} \alpha_k f_k(w) + \left[0, \sum_{k=1}^{n} (\beta_k - \alpha_k) f_k(w)\right]$$

$$= \sum_{k=1}^{n} \alpha_k f_k(w) + \left[0, \sum_{k\in\Omega_1} (\beta_k - \alpha_k) f_k(w) + \sum_{k\in\Omega_2} (\beta_k - \alpha_k) f_k(w)\right]$$

Case I. Let $\sum_{k\in\Omega_2} |\beta_k - \alpha_k| f_k(w) \leq \sum_{k\in\Omega_2} (\beta_k - \alpha_k) f_k(w)$, then

$$P_n(f)(w) = \sum_{k=1}^{n} \alpha_k f_k(w) + \left[0, \sum_{k\in\Omega_1} (\beta_k - \alpha_k) f_k(w)\right] \ominus \left[0, \sum_{k\in\Omega_2} (\beta_k + \alpha_k) f_k(w)\right]$$

$$= \sum_{k=1}^{n} \alpha_k f_k(w) + \sum_{k\in\Omega_1} (\beta_k - \alpha_k)[0, f_k(w)] \ominus \sum_{k\in\Omega_2} |\beta_k - \alpha_k|[0, f_k(w)]$$

$$= \sum_{k=1}^{n} \alpha_k f_k(w) + \sum_{k\in\Omega_1} (\beta_k - \alpha_k)\Psi_k(w) \ominus \sum_{k\in\Omega_2} |\beta_k - \alpha_k|\Psi_k(w).$$

Case II. Let $\sum_{k\in\Omega_2} |\beta_k - \alpha_k| f_k(w) \geq \sum_{k\in\Omega_2} (\beta_k - \alpha_k) f_k(w)$, then

$$P_n(f)(w) = \sum_{k=1}^{n} \alpha_k f_k(w) - [0, \sum_{k\in\Omega_2} (\alpha_k - \beta_k) f_k(w)] \ominus (-1)[0, \sum_{k\in\Omega_1} (\beta_k - \alpha_k) f_k(w)]$$

$$= \sum_{k=1}^{n} \alpha_k f_k(w) + [\sum_{k\in\Omega_2} (\beta_k - \alpha_k) f_k(w), 0] \ominus [\sum_{k\in\Omega_1} (\alpha_k - \beta_k) f_k(w), 0]$$

$$= \sum_{k=1}^{n} \alpha_k f_k(w) + \sum_{k\in\Omega_2} (\beta_k - \alpha_k)[0, f_k(w)] \ominus \sum_{k\in\Omega_2} (\alpha_k - \beta_k)[0, f_k(w)]$$

$$= \sum_{k=1}^{n} \alpha_k f_k(w) + \sum_{k\in\Omega_2} (\beta_k - \alpha_k)\Psi_k(w) \ominus \sum_{k\in\Omega_1} (\alpha_k - \beta_k)\Psi_k(w),$$

which completes the proof. □

Here, we provide some new results to complete the fractional integral of $P_n(f)$, of order α, $0 < \alpha \leq 1$, in the Riemann-Liouville sense.

Remark 3.1. *Let Ω is a Banach space. a sequence $\{f_n\}_{n\geq 1}$ of elements of Ω is said to be a Schauder basis of Ω if, for every $z \in \Omega$, there is a unique sequence $\{\alpha_n\}_{n\geq 1}$ of scalars such that $z = \sum_{n\geq 1} \alpha_n f_n$. A Schauder basis gives rise to the canonical sequence of (continuous and linear) associated projections $\Pi_m : \Omega \to \Omega$, $\Pi_m(\sum_{n\geq 1} \alpha_n f_n) := \sum_{k=1}^{m} \alpha_n f_n$ [48].*

Proposition 3.3. *Let $I = [a, b]$ and $f \in C(I, \mathcal{K}_C)$, under assumptions of Proposition 3.2, we have*

$$P_n(f)(t) = \sum_{k=1}^{n} \alpha_k I^{\alpha}\Phi_k(t) + \sum_{k\in\Omega_1} (\alpha_k - \beta_k) I^{\alpha}\Psi_k(t) \ominus_g \sum_{k\in\Omega_2} |\beta_k - \alpha_k| I^{\alpha}\Psi_k(t).$$

Proof. Using Propositions 3.1 and 3.2 , the proof is straightforward. □

Remark 3.2. *For $\alpha = 1$, our results coincide with the obtained results in [48].*

3.2. Inverse problem using Collage Theorem

In the classical situation, the concept of Collage result will be as follows:

For a complete metric space (X, d), and self-mapping $\Psi : X \to X$, we have:

$$d(x, x^*) \leq \frac{1}{1-\beta} d(x, \Psi(x)), \quad \beta \in [0, 1),$$

and $x^* \in X$ is a unique fixed point.

Arana-Jimenez et al. [48] discussed the Collage Theorem based on some approximation of $z \in \Psi(x)$, due to its simplification in computing.

In this part, we aim to use a Collage-based method for solving IFDEs with inverse problem.

Lemma 3.1. *Suppose that $\{f_n\}_{n\geq 1}$ be a Schauder basis in $C(I^2)$ with sequence of associated projections $\{\Pi_n\}_{n\geq 1}$ and satisfying the hypothesis Proposition3.2, $X \in C(I,\mathcal{K}_C)$, $\Phi : C(I,\mathcal{K}_C) \to C(I,\mathcal{K}_C)$, as the self-operator defined at X, such that*

$$\Phi(X)(t) := G(t) + \frac{1}{\Gamma(\alpha)} I^\alpha K(t,s,X(s)),\ t \in I,$$

when X is ${}^C(1,\alpha)$-differentiable and

$$\Phi(X)(t) := G(t) \ominus (-1)\frac{1}{\Gamma(\alpha)} I^\alpha K(t,s,X(s)),\ t \in I,$$

when X is ${}^C(2,\alpha)$-differentiable. Then, there exists $n \geq 1$, and $Y : I \to \mathcal{K}_C$ is a continuous interval-valued function such that

$$Y(t) := G(t) + \frac{1}{\Gamma(\alpha)} I^\alpha P_n(K(t,s,X(s))),$$

for the case of ${}^C(1,\alpha)$-differentiability and,

$$Y(t) := G(t) \ominus (-1)\frac{1}{\Gamma(\alpha)} I^\alpha P_n(K(t,s,X(s))),$$

for the case of ${}^C(2,\alpha)$-differentiability. For these cases, we have:

$$H(\Phi(X), Y) < \epsilon.$$

Proof. Let X is ${}^C(1,\alpha)$-differentiable, then over the interval I, we have:

$$H_{1-\alpha}(\phi(X),y) = \sup_{t\in I} t^{1-\alpha}\mathcal{T}\left(G(t) + \frac{1}{\Gamma(\alpha)}\int_0^t (t-s)^{\alpha-1}k(t,s,X(s))ds, G(t) + \frac{1}{\Gamma(\alpha)}\int_0^t (t-s)^{\alpha-1}p_n(t,s,X(s))ds\right)$$

$$\begin{aligned} H_{1-\alpha}(\phi(X),y) &= \sup_{t\in I} t^{1-\alpha}\mathcal{T}\left(\frac{1}{\Gamma(\alpha)}\int_0^t (t-s)^{\alpha-1}k(t,s,X(s))ds, \frac{1}{\Gamma(\alpha)}\int_0^t (t-s)^{\alpha-1}p_n(t,s,X(s))ds\right) \\ &\leq \frac{1}{\Gamma(\alpha)}\left(\sup_{t\in I} t^{1-\alpha}\int_0^t (t-s)^{\alpha-1}s^{\alpha-1}ds\right).H_{1-\alpha}(k(t,s,X(s)), p_n(t,s,X(s))) \\ &\leq \frac{b^\alpha\Gamma(\alpha)}{\Gamma(2\alpha)}.H_{1-\alpha}(k(t,s,X(s)), p_n(t,s,X(s))), \end{aligned}$$

that complete the proof. The proof for the case of ${}^C(2,\alpha)$-differentiability is similar to the previous case, then, we omit it. □

Suppose that Λ as a compact subset of $\mathbb{R}^N$, for $\lambda \in \Lambda, G_\lambda \in C(I,\mathcal{K}_C)$, and $K_\lambda : I^2 \times \mathcal{K}_C \to \mathcal{K}_C$, we consider the problem of finding $X \in C(I,\mathcal{K}_C)$ such that for the case of ${}^C(1,\alpha)$-differentiability,

$$X(t) = G_\lambda(t) + \frac{1}{\Gamma(\alpha)}\int_a^t (t-s)^{\alpha-1}K_\lambda(t,s,X(s))ds$$

and for the case of ${}^C(2,\alpha)$-differentiability,

$$X(t) = G_\lambda(t) \ominus \frac{(-1)}{\Gamma(\alpha)}\int_a^t (t-s)^{\alpha-1}K_\lambda(t,s,X(s))ds.$$

The problem is that:
Starting with target $\tilde{X}$, such that this target is derived as follows:
Let $\lambda_0 \in \Lambda$ and we are going to obtain a numerical approach:

$$X(t) = G_{\lambda_0}(t) + \frac{1}{\Gamma(\alpha)}\int_a^t (t-s)^{\alpha-1}K_{\lambda_0}(t,s,X(s))ds,$$

for the case of ${}^{C}(1,\alpha)$-differentiability and

$$X(t) = G_{\lambda_0}(t) \ominus \frac{(-1)}{\Gamma(\alpha)} \int_a^t (t-s)^{\alpha-1} K_{\lambda_0}(t,s,X(s))ds,$$

for the case of ${}^{C}(2,\alpha)$-differentiability. For this purpose , for $n \in \mathbb{N}$, $X_0 \in C(I, \mathcal{K}_C)$, $j = 1, 2, ...,$ we have obtained $\tilde{X}$ as follows:

$$X_j^n(t) = G_{\lambda_0}(t) + \frac{1}{\Gamma(\alpha)} \int_a^t (t-s)^{\alpha-1} P_n(K_{\lambda_0}(t,s,X_{j-1}^n(s)))ds,$$

for the case of ${}^{C}(1,\alpha)$-differentiability and

$$X_j^n(t) = G_{\lambda_0}(t) \ominus \frac{(-1)}{\Gamma(\alpha)} \int_a^t (t-s)^{\alpha-1} P_n(K_{\lambda_0}(t,s,X_{j-1}^n(s)))ds,$$

for the case of ${}^{C}(2,\alpha)$-differentiability and P_n is defined in Proposition 3.2. Let $\epsilon > 0$ and fixed, also assume that $H(X_m^n, X_{m-1}^n) < \epsilon$, $m \in \mathbb{N}$ and consider $\tilde{X}(t) := X_m^n(t)$ as the target element. Hence, for $\tilde{X} : I \to \mathcal{K}_C$ and fixed $r \in \mathbb{N}$, we have:

$$Y_{\lambda,r}(t) = G_\lambda(t) + \frac{1}{\Gamma(\alpha)} \int_a^t (t-s)^{\alpha-1} P_r(K_\lambda(t,s,X(s)))ds$$

for the case of ${}^{C}(1,\alpha)$-differentiability and

$$Y_{\lambda,r}(t) = G_\lambda(t) \ominus \frac{(-1)}{\Gamma(\alpha)} \int_a^t (t-s)^{\alpha-1} P_r(K_\lambda(t,s,X(s)))ds$$

for the case of ${}^{C}(2,\alpha)$-differentiability. Now, we can obtain the approximation of problem using:

$$H(\tilde{X}, Y_{\lambda_r^*,r}) = \min_{\lambda \in \Lambda} H(\tilde{X}, Y_{\lambda,r}), \tag{3.11}$$

by computing $\lambda_r^* \in \Lambda$.

4. Examples

Example 4.1. *Consider the following IFDE:*

$$\begin{cases} {}^{C}X^{(\alpha)}(t) = \eta t B, \\ X(0) = X_0 = [1,5] \in \mathcal{K}_C, \quad t \in [0,1], \end{cases} \tag{4.12}$$

and $\eta \neq 0$, $\eta \in [-1,1]$, $B = [1,4] \in \mathcal{K}_C$ *and* $W(B) \leq W(X_0)$.

Now, if X is ${}^{C}(1,\alpha)$-differentiability, then we get

$$X(t) = X_0 + \frac{\eta}{\Gamma(\alpha)} \int_0^t (t-s)^{\alpha-1} sBds$$

$$= X_0 + \frac{\eta B t^{\alpha+1}}{\Gamma(\alpha+2)}, \quad for\ \eta \in (0,1].$$

If X is ${}^{C}(2,\alpha)$-differentiability, then we get

$$X(t) = X_0 \ominus \frac{-\eta}{\Gamma(\alpha)} \int_0^t (t-s)^{\alpha-1} sBds$$

Table 1: The best choice for s_1^* under ${}^C(1,\alpha)$-differentiability with $\alpha = 0.9$.

m	n	r	s_1^*	$H(\tilde{X}, Y_{s_1^*,r})$
4	16	16	2.483217	2.01563×10^{-11}
4	64	64	2.487093	4.29717×10^{-11}
4	256	256	2.487093	2.23019×10^{-11}
8	16	16	2.499187	3.78564×10^{-11}
8	64	64	2.499328	3.65193×10^{-11}
8	256	256	2.499917	3.90776×10^{-11}

Table 2: The best choice for s_1^* under ${}^C(1,\alpha)$-differentiability with $\alpha = 0.95$.

m	n	r	s_1^*	$H(\tilde{X}, Y_{s_1^*,r})$
4	16	16	2.487019	4.12731×10^{-11}
4	64	64	2.488325	6.01035×10^{-11}
4	256	256	2.499376	4.38059×10^{-11}
8	16	16	2.499407	5.32805×10^{-11}
8	64	64	2.499578	5.30176×10^{-11}
8	256	256	2.499931	5.43719×10^{-11}

$$= X_0 \ominus \frac{-\eta B t^{\alpha+1}}{\Gamma(\alpha+2)}, \quad for \ \eta \in [-1, 0).$$

Here, consider the family of interval fractional integral equation of Volterra type of order α, $0 < \alpha \leq 1$, as follows:

$$X(t) = Q_\lambda(t) + \frac{1}{\Gamma(\alpha)} \int_0^t (t-s)^{\alpha-1} K_\lambda(t, s, X(s)) ds,$$

when X is ${}^C(1,\alpha)$-differentiability, and

$$X(t) = Q_\lambda(t) \ominus \frac{(-1)}{\Gamma(\alpha)} \int_0^t (t-s)^{\alpha-1} K_\lambda(t, s, X(s)) ds,$$

when X is ${}^C(2,\alpha)$-differentiability, such that

$$Q_\lambda(t) = Q(t),$$
$$= X_0,$$
$$K_\lambda(t, s, X(s)) = \eta s B,$$

in which $\lambda = s_1$, where $s_1 \in [1, 4]$.
By choosing $\lambda_0 = 2$, we derive $\tilde{X} = X_m^n$ and based on this target we compute $Y_{\lambda,r}$.
Now, we are at the step to obtain the approximation of $Y_{\lambda,r}$ using the minimization problem (*).
The otained results for the best choice of $\lambda^* = s_1^*$ are shown in Tables 1, 2 and 3 under ${}^C(1,\alpha)$-differentiability.
Also, under the case of ${}^C(2,\alpha)$-differentiability , and also for the best choice of $\lambda^* = s_1^*$ using the the minimization problem, we obtained the results that are illustrated in Tables 4, 5 and 6. Also, to have a comparative analysis on the best approximation solutions under both types of differentiability, we plotted them for different values of fractional derivative in Fig.1.

Example 4.2. *Let assume the following IFDE:*

$$\begin{cases} {}^C X^{(0.5)}(t) + x(t) = [1,2]t^2 + [2,4]\frac{t^{1.5}}{\Gamma(2.5)}, \\ X(0) = X_0 = 0 \quad t \in [0,1], \end{cases} \tag{4.13}$$

Table 3: The best choice for s_1^* under $^C(1,\alpha)$-differentiability with $\alpha = 0.975$.

m	n	r	s_1^*	$H(\tilde{X}, Y_{s_1^*,r})$
4	16	16	2.488509	2.59371×10^{-11}
4	64	64	2.489227	5.03257×10^{-11}
4	256	256	2.4899716	2.97893×10^{-11}
8	16	16	2.499405	4.98154×10^{-11}
8	64	64	2.499573	4.821776×10^{-11}
8	256	256	2.49954	4.99701×10^{-11}

Table 4: The best choice for s_1^* under $^C(2,\alpha)$-differentiability with $\alpha = 0.9$.

m	n	r	s_1^*	$H(\tilde{X}, Y_{s_1^*,r})$
4	16	16	2.49101	1.76185×10^{-11}
4	64	64	2.49215	3.27709×10^{-11}
4	256	256	2.49273	1.90883×10^{-11}
8	16	16	2.49408	3.01815×10^{-11}
8	64	64	2.49673	3.00562×10^{-11}
8	256	256	2.49781	3.19518×10^{-11}

Table 5: The best choice for s_1^* under $^C(2,\alpha)$-differentiability with $\alpha = 0.95$.

m	n	r	s_1^*	$H(\tilde{X}, Y_{s_1^*,r})$
4	16	16	2.49273	2.03560×10^{-11}
4	64	64	2.49334	3.40191×10^{-11}
4	256	256	2.49418	2.37155×10^{-11}
8	16	16	2.49613	3.21887×10^{-11}
8	64	64	2.49668	3.17501×10^{-11}
8	256	256	2.49801	3.37819×10^{-11}

Table 6: The best choice for s_1^* under $^C(2,\alpha)$-differentiability with $\alpha = 0.975$.

m	n	r	s_1^*	$H(\tilde{X}, Y_{s_1^*,r})$
4	16	16	2.487210	2.487350×10^{-11}
4	64	64	2.490251	4.897650×10^{-11}
4	256	256	2.492875	2.967021×10^{-11}
8	16	16	2.499257	4.781656×10^{-11}
8	64	64	2.499473	4.538254×10^{-11}
8	256	256	2.499938	4.994319×10^{-11}

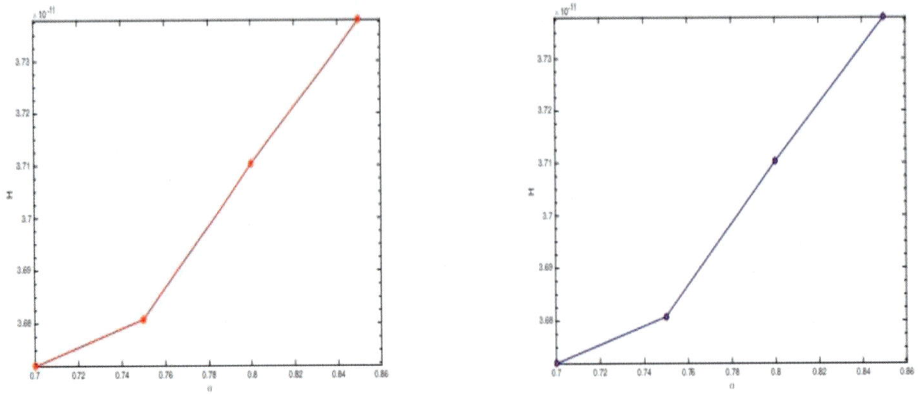

(a) Solution under ${}^{C}(1,\alpha)$-differentiability (b) Solution under ${}^{C}(2,\alpha)$-differentiability

Figure 1: Example 4.1- The best choice for s_1^* under ${}^{C}(1,\alpha)$ and ${}^{C}(2,\alpha)$-differentiability with $m = 8, n = r = 16$ and $\alpha = 0.7, 0.75, 0.8$ and 0.85.

Table 7: The best choice for λ_1^* and λ_2^* under ${}^{C}(1, 1.5)$-differentiability

m	n	r	λ_1^*	λ_2^*	$H(\tilde{X}, Y_{\lambda,r})$
4	16	16	1.482155	2.976114	8.75667×10^{-13}
4	64	64	1.487037	2.981563	9.01256×10^{-13}
4	256	256	1.491731	2.987917	8.97651×10^{-13}
8	16	16	1.493517	2.989163	8.99973×10^{-13}
8	64	64	1.495937	2.992135	8.99807×10^{-13}
8	256	256	1.498763	2.995716	9.00731×10^{-13}

It is easy to verify that the exact solution of the problem under ${}^{C}(1, 1.5)$-differentiability is $X_{exact}(t) = [1, 2]t^2$. Now the equivalent integral form of the problem (4.13) will be as follows:

$$X(t) = X_0 + \frac{1}{\Gamma(0.5)} \int_0^t (t-s)^{-0.5} \left([1,2]s^2 + [2,4]\frac{s^{1.5}}{\Gamma(2.5)} \ominus X(s) \right) ds.$$

Then, the family of fractional integral equations of Volterra-type of order α, $0 < \alpha \leq 1$, is given by:

$$X(t) = Q_\lambda(t) + \frac{1}{\Gamma(0.5)} \int_0^t (t-s)^{-0.5} K_\lambda(t, s, X(s)) ds,$$

where

$$Q_\lambda(t) = Q(t)$$
$$= X_0$$
$$k_\lambda(t, s, x(s)) = \left[s^2 + \frac{2s^{1.5}}{\Gamma(2.5)}, 2s^2 + \frac{4s^{1.5}}{\Gamma(2.5)} \right] \ominus X(s),$$

and $\lambda = (\lambda_1, \lambda_2)$, $\lambda_1 \in [1, 2]$, $\lambda_2 \in [2, 4]$.
By choosing $\lambda_0 = (1.5, 3)$, we obtain $\tilde{X} := X_m^n$ and consequently, we derive the target $Y_{\lambda,r}$. Using the minimization problem (*), we obtained the best choice of $\lambda^* = (\lambda_1^*, \lambda_2^*)$ shown by Table 7.

Conclusion

We have looked at the inverse issue for fractional differential equations under interval uncertainty including Caputo-type of differentiability for the first time in the literature because of the perturbed collage theorem. To achieve this, we have found some approximations of the solutions in the whole metric space using the Schauder basis. In fact, the approximation that was produced as a result of addressing the optimization issue has sufficient precision as indicated by the Hausdorff-Pompeiu distance measure. Future study will focus on the solution of fuzzy uncertain fractional dynamical systems, which will also tackle various fractional operators based on singular and non-singular kernels. We also want to examine this method as a part of our future plan, and it is one of the intriguing areas of research to take into account the inverse problem in order to choose the optimal order of differentiability!

Chapter 8

Prerequisites for a Globally Stable COVID-19-Free State[8]

Introduction

China was the origin of the viral infection that caused the COVID-19 pandemic. The illness COVID-19 is extremely contagious. The virus known as SARS-CoV-2, or severe acute respiratory syndrome coronavirus 2, is the disease's primary cause. In the human population, very quick viral transmission happens wherever there is close contact. When the contact distance is less than two meters, there is a significant likelihood of transmission. When this happens, the virus spreads by respiratory droplets made when an infected person coughs, sneezes, or speaks. These droplets can be immediately ingested or can travel through the air to someone nearby's mouth or nose. However, the virus spreads to neighboring surfaces if a vulnerable person is not there. Although these infected surfaces aid in the viral transmission within the population, this isn't thought to be the primary route of transmission.

A large family of viruses is the coronavirus. There are several infections that this family produces. The severity of the infection can range from the normal cold or flu to MERS, the middle east respiratory syndrome, and more serious infections. In Wuhan, China, in December 2019, severe pneumonia and respiratory issues first surfaced as the unique COVID-19. At that time, it was impossible to determine the exact cause of the illness. The virus was described by WHO as a new coronavirus (2019-nCoV). Coronavirus-2 severe acute respiratory syndrome is the name of the illness (SARS-CoV-2). The virus was initially discovered in one person. In sixteen more cases, the infection was subsequently confirmed. It is anticipated that the virus may have bat origins, and that the illness may have spread from a Chinese seafood market (Huanan Seafood Wholesale Market). As of June 12, 2020, there have been verified 7,597,304 instances of the sickness and 423,844 fatalities worldwide.

About 75% of COVID-19 sufferers healed spontaneously and without showing any signs of the illness. 20% of those who are exposed have symptoms. Tiredness, fever, and a dry cough are COVID-19's three most prevalent symptoms. Aches and pains, runny nose, nasal congestion, muscle aches, chills, loss of taste or smell or both, headache, chest discomfort, and sore throat are among the possible side effects that some individuals may experience. There have also been reports of rash, nausea, vomiting, and diarrhea, which are less typical symptoms. These signs and symptoms normally appear gradually and mildly. About 80% of symptomatic patients recover from the illness without requiring any extra care. COVID-19 is often mild in children and adolescents. However, it can result in significant sickness for certain people. Death might result from this virus's strong onslaught. Sometimes an episode might lead to pneumonia

---

8 *Landmark paper: Muhammad Zamir, Kamal Shah, Fawad Nadeem, Mohd Yazid Bajuri, Ali Ahmadian, Soheil Salahshour, Massimiliano Ferrara, "Threshold conditions for global stability of disease free state of COVID-19", Results in Physics, Volume 21, 2021, 103784, ISSN 2211-3797, https://doi.org/10.1016/j.rinp.2020.103784.*

or SARS (severe acute respiratory syndrome). Within 2 to 14 days, infection symptoms start to manifest. Recovery from moderate instances often takes two weeks, whereas recovery from severe/critical cases might take three to six weeks. The average time to develop dyspnea in patients with severe illness is between 5-8 days. Acute respiratory distress syndrome (ARDS) typically develops between 8 and 12 days. The typical wait for intensive care in the ventilated class is between 10 and 12 days. Long-term data are still sparse, however individuals who have recovered from sickness can have antibodies for at least two weeks.

Although the coronavirus (2019-nCoV) and the coronavirus that caused SARS-2003 share genetic ancestry, the illnesses they produced are genetically quite distinct. Recent reports have discussed the genetic characteristics and various clinical manifestations of the illness. International flight travel helped the illness spread across borders. Regarding its eradication and management, the pathogen has drawn interest on a global scale. The disease's dire future prognosis has raised serious concerns throughout the whole planet. Therefore, the construction of mathematical models is the main focus of scientists and researchers. The model aids in not only forecasting other crucial outcomes but also assessing the dynamics of viral spread. Including recent mathematical modeling. These models mostly concentrated on the coronavirus's transmission/spreading or its fundamental rate of reproduction (R_0). The intrinsic growth rate and the serial intervals were followed by the writers. In their investigation, Wu et al. specifically focused on forecasting and newscasting of the novel coronavirus both domestically and abroad. In their investigation, the authors employed Markov Chain Monte Carlo techniques.

However, these models don't go into detail about the source (bat) and the distribution channel (seafood market). This study was expanded by Chen et al. In their work, the authors produced a thorough model of a new coronavirus. With the use of a sensitivity analysis of the model's parameters, we concentrate our attention in this study on the impact of various interventions on the spread of the disease. We create a strategy by combining several treatments in a certain ratio. To make it easier for organizations battling COVID-19 to choose a strategy, the impact of various disease control measures is visually shown. Finally, we discover a requirement that must be met for the community's disease-free status to be stable on a global scale.

Model construction

Nine subclasses make up the entire human population: the susceptible humans class (S), the quarantine humans class (Q), the exposed humans class (E), the exposed humans class to infection (I_1), the exposed humans class to infection (I_2), the isolated humans class (I_s), the mild humans class (I_M), the critical humans class (I_c), and the recovered humans class (R). Coronavirus-contaminated surfaces, objects, and materials are referred to collectively as WI. The vulnerable human population can become infected at varying rates from sick people (both symptomatic and asymptomatic), exposed people, and objects dyed or contaminated with coronavirus. All those vulnerable people who have touch with an infectious person within the last 14 days are in quarantine. The persons under quarantine are subjected to laboratory examinations and are then moved to the exposed or susceptible classes. After the latency or incubation time has passed, the exposed people transition to infectious classes I_1 or I_2 that are symptomatic or asymptomatic. Individuals with infectious symptoms are kept apart in isolation class I_S. Some people transfer to mild class I_M and the others to critical class I_C after finishing the I_S transition phase. Nearly 49% of infected people in the critical class pass away from the sickness, whereas the majority of people in the moderate class recover.

Table 1: Parameters with their respective descriptions

Notation	Parameter definition	Value	Source
Λ	Humans recruitment rate	0.0015875 day^{-1}	[31]
μ	Humans natural mortality rate	0.00004 day^{-1}	[31]
c_2	Transmission multiple of β_1 with I_2	0.24666	[8]
β_1	Disease transmission probability from I_1	0.65 day^{-1}	[25]
c_4	Transmission multiple of β_1 with E	0.31666	[8]
κ_E	Inverse of disease incubation period	5–14 day	[32]
k_I	Disease clinical detection period	5–10 day	[8]
k_θ	Quarantine period	14 days	[33]
β_2	Disease transmission probability from contaminated stuff	0.165 day^{-1}	[25]
r_n	Transition period in I_2	14–22 days	[34]
r_t	Transition period in I_S	14–21 days	[34]
r_1	The ratio of exposed moving to symptomatic	25%	[8]
ξ_1	Shedding coefficient of I_1	0.5	[25]
ξ_2	Shedding coefficient of I_2	0.5	[25]
D_2	Disease induced death ratio of critical class	0.49%	[35]
ε	The life time of virus on stuff	1–10 days	[25]
ex	Expiry period of contaminated stuff	30 days	assume
k_1	Ratio of quarantine moving to I_S	66%	assume
k_2	Ratio of quarantine moving to S	33%	assume
k_4	Recovery ratio of mild class	99%	[36]
k_5	Recovery rate of critical class	47%	[37]
k_3	Ratio of asymptomatic moving to I_C	4%	[38,39]
δ	Ratio of isolated moving to I_C	15%	[40]
β	Immunity loosing period	15 days	[41]

Both symptomatic and asymptomatic contagious persons pollute their immediate surroundings at a rate known as the shedding coefficient. The term "such things" designates a class. The COVID-19 model is represented by the system (1) of connected nonlinear differential equations as follows:

$$\begin{cases} \dot{S} = \Lambda - \left(\beta_1\left(I_1 + c_2I_2 + c_4E\right) + \beta_2W_I\right)S - \mu S + k_2Q + \beta R \\ \dot{Q} = \left(\beta_1\left(I_1\right)S - \left(k_1 + k_2 + \mu\right)Q \\ \dot{E} = \left(\beta_1\left(c_2I_2 + c_4E\right) + \beta_2W_I\right)S - \left(\kappa_E + \mu\right)E + k_1Q \\ \dot{I}_1 = r_1\kappa_E E - \left(k_I + \mu\right)I_1 \\ \dot{I}_2 = \left(1 - r_1\right)\kappa_E E - \left(r_n + \mu\right)I_2 \\ \dot{I}_S = k_I I_1 - \left(r_t + \mu\right)I_S \\ \dot{I}_M = \delta r_t I_S - \left(k_4 + \mu\right)I_M \\ \dot{I}_C = \left(1 - \delta\right)r_t I_S - \left(k_5 + D_2 + \mu\right)I_C + k_3 r_n I_2 \\ \dot{R} = k_4 I_M + k_5 I_C + \left(1 - k_3\right)r_n I_2 - \left(\mu + \beta\right)R \\ \dot{W}_I = \xi_1 I_1 + \xi_2 I_2 - \left(\varepsilon + e_X\right)W_I \end{cases} \quad (1)$$

Invariant Area

Because the model is concerned with the live population, the state variables and parameters utilized in it are always nonnegative.

Adding together all the human population-related compartments we have:

$$\dot{N} = \Lambda - \mu N - D_2 I_c$$

Using Eq. (2), we obtain

$\dot{N} \leq \Lambda - \mu N$.

Solving the above equation we have:

$N \leq N(0)e^{-\mu t} + \frac{\Lambda}{\mu}(1 - e^{-\mu t}) \Rightarrow N \leq \frac{\Lambda}{\mu} \text{ when } t \to \infty$.

On the basis of above discussion we claim the following result:

Proof. Ω; the region of the proposed model, defined by

$$\Omega = \left[(S, Q, E, I_1, I_2, I_S, I_M, I_C, R, W_I) \in R_+^{10}, N \leq \frac{\Lambda}{\mu} \right]$$

is positively invariant domain, and the model is epidemiologically and mathematically well posed [42] and all the trajectories are forward bounded. □

Reproductive number

The number of secondary infections caused by a single primary infection in completely susceptible population is called reproduction number denoted by R_0. The reproduction number is find by next generation matrix [44,43] as:

$R_0 = \rho(-FV^{-1})$, where ρ is spectral radius, where $F = \mathcal{J}_f$; the jacobian of f and

$$f = \begin{pmatrix} f_1 \\ f_2 \\ f_3 \\ f_4 \\ f_5 \\ f_6 \\ f_7 \end{pmatrix} = \begin{pmatrix} (\beta_1 c_4 E + \beta_2 W_I)S \\ 0 \\ 0 \\ 0 \\ 0 \\ 0 \\ 0 \end{pmatrix}$$

The column in matrix f denotes the individuals who get infected. Similarly.

$V = \mathcal{J}_v$; the jacobian of v and

$$v = \begin{pmatrix} v_1 \\ v_2 \\ v_3 \\ v_4 \\ v_5 \\ v_6 \\ v_7 \end{pmatrix} = \begin{pmatrix} -(\kappa_E + \mu)E + k_1 Q \\ r_1 \kappa_E E - (k_I + \mu)I_1 \\ (1 - r_1)\kappa_E E - (r_n + \mu)I_2 \\ k_I I_1 - (r_t + \mu)I_S \\ \delta r_t I_S - (k_4 + \mu)I_M \\ (1 - \delta)r_t I_S - (k_5 + D_2 + \mu)I_C + k_3 r_n I_2 \\ \xi_1 I_1 + \xi_2 I_2 - (\varepsilon + ex)W_I \end{pmatrix}.$$

The column of matrix V denotes the individuals that enter the infected class or leave the infected class, excluding those coming from susceptible class.

The dominant Eigenvalue of $(-FV^{-1})$ and hence R_0 is:

$$R_0 = \frac{\beta_1 c_4 \Lambda}{\mu(\kappa_E + \mu)} + \frac{\beta_2 \Lambda((r_n + \mu)(1 - r_1)\kappa_E \xi_1 + (k_I + \mu)r_1 \kappa_E \xi_2)}{\mu(\kappa_E + \mu)(k_I + \mu)(r_n + \mu)(\varepsilon + ex)}.$$

Stability analysis

In this part, the threshold condition for global asymptotic stability of *Disease Free State* of the system (1) is studied. The following theorem would be used in the upcoming results, stated here for convenience:

Theorem 3.1. ([45]) *Let the given model be presented as*

$$\begin{cases} \dot{\mathcal{Y}}_1 = \mathcal{B}_1(\mathcal{Y})(\mathcal{Y} - \mathcal{Y}_1^*) + \mathcal{B}_{12}(\mathcal{Y})\mathcal{Y}_2 \\ \dot{\mathcal{Y}}_2 = \mathcal{B}_2(\mathcal{Y})\mathcal{Y}_2. \end{cases}$$

Then the DFS (Disease free state) is GAS (globally asymptotically stable) if the following holds.

(a_1): *All the populations involved in the model are forward bounded and hence the system is mathematically well posed.*

(a_2): *The sub-system of non infected classes* $\dot{\widetilde{\mathscr{Y}}}_1 = \widetilde{\mathscr{B}}_1(\widetilde{\mathscr{Y}}_1, 0)(\widetilde{\mathscr{Y}}_1 - \widetilde{\mathscr{Y}}_1^*)$ *is globally asymptotically stability at the origen.*

(a_3): *The matrix of non infected compartments denoted by* $\widetilde{\mathscr{B}}_2(\widetilde{\mathscr{Y}})$ *is both metzler and irreducible.*

(a_4): *The matrix of infected classes,* $\widetilde{\mathscr{B}}_2$ *is bounded by some matrix* $\overline{\widetilde{\mathscr{B}}_2}$ *and* $\widetilde{\mathscr{N}} = \{\widetilde{\mathscr{B}}_2(\widetilde{\mathscr{Y}}), \widetilde{\mathscr{Y}} \in \Omega\}$. *Then* $\overline{\widetilde{\mathscr{B}}_2}$ *may or may not belong to* $\widetilde{\mathscr{N}}$. *However if* $\overline{\widetilde{\mathscr{B}}_2} \in \widetilde{\mathscr{N}}$ *then for any* $\widetilde{\mathscr{Y}} \in \Omega$ *such that* $\overline{\widetilde{\mathscr{B}}_2} = \widetilde{\mathscr{B}}_2(\overline{\widetilde{\mathscr{Y}}})$, $\overline{\widetilde{\mathscr{Y}}} \in R^{n1} \times \{0\}$

(a_5): *The spectral radius of* $(\overline{\widetilde{\mathscr{B}}_2})$ *is less then or equal to zero.*

To prove the global stability of the disease free equilibrium let $Y=$ (The column vector of all the state variables). Let Y_s be the sub class of Y, containing all noninfected compartments of the total population. Y_I be the sub class of Y containing infected human population. That is

$Y_s =$ (The column vector of all non infected classes of the model)

and

$Y_I =$ (column vector of all infected state variables of the model).

Theorem 3.2. *Given sub system of non-infected population*

$$\begin{cases} \dot{S} = \Lambda - \Big(\beta_1\big(I_1 + c_2 I_2 + c_4 E\big) + \beta_2 W_I\Big)S - \mu S + k_2 Q + \beta R \\ \dot{R} = k_4 I_M + k_5 I_C + \big(1 - k_3\big) r_n I_2 - \big(\mu + \beta\big) R \end{cases} \tag{3}$$

This system of non-infected classes is GAS at the domain G, where

$G = \{\mathscr{Y} \in \Omega; \mathscr{Y}_s \neq 0, \mathscr{Y}_I = 0\}$.

Proof. We re-write the above system as:

$$\dot{\mathscr{Y}}_s = \mathscr{C}_s\big(\mathscr{Y}\big)\big(\mathscr{Y}_s\big) + \mathscr{J}_s$$

At the Domain G, the above system reduces to the form.

$$\begin{cases} \dot{S} = \Lambda - \mu S \\ \dot{R} = -\mu R \end{cases} \tag{4}$$

Here

$$C_S = \begin{pmatrix} -\mu & 0 \\ 0 & -\mu \end{pmatrix} \qquad \Rightarrow \mathscr{J}_s = (\Lambda, 0)^T.$$

All the entries $j_{(i,i)}$ of the matrix C_s are $-ve$, Hence the said system is *GAS* at Disease Free equilibrium (DFE).

The DFE point is $\big(\frac{\Lambda}{\mu}, 0, 0, 0, 0, 0, 0, 0, 0\big)$. □

The sub system of infected population is:

$$\dot{\mathscr{Y}}_1 = \mathscr{B}_I\big(\mathscr{Y}\big)\mathscr{Y}_I,$$

where

$$
\mathscr{Y}_1 = \begin{cases} \dot{E} = \left(\beta_1 c_4 E + \beta_2 W_I\right)S - \left(\kappa_E + \mu\right)E \\ \dot{I}_1 = r_1 \kappa_E E - \left(k_I + \mu\right)I_1 + k_1 Q \\ \dot{I}_2 = \left(1 - r_1\right)\kappa_E E - \left(r_n + \mu\right)I_2 \\ \dot{I}_S = k_I I_1 - \left(r_t + \mu\right)I_S \\ \dot{I}_M = \delta r_t I_S - \left(k_4 + \mu\right)I_M \\ \dot{I}_C = \left(1 - \delta\right)r_t I_S - \left(k_5 + D_2 + \mu\right)I_C + k_3 r_n I_2 \\ \dot{W}_I = \xi_1 I_1 + \xi_2 I_2 - \left(\varepsilon + e_X\right)W_I \end{cases} \tag{5}
$$

Theorem 3.3. *In the system (5), $\mathscr{B}_I$ is irreducible and metzler $\forall\, \mathscr{Y} \in \Omega$. Further more there exist some $\overline{\mathscr{B}_I}$ so as*

$$
\mathscr{B}_I\left(\mathscr{Y}\right) \leqslant \overline{\mathscr{B}_I}\left(\mathscr{Y}\right) \text{for } \mathscr{Y} \in \Omega. \tag{6}
$$

Also

$$
\overline{\mathscr{B}_I} \in \mathscr{N} = \left\{\mathscr{B}_I\left(\mathscr{Y}\right), \mathscr{Y} \in \Omega\right\} \qquad \overline{\mathscr{B}_I} = \mathscr{N}_{max\Omega}. \tag{7}
$$

$$
\varrho\left(\overline{\mathscr{B}_I}\right) \leqslant 0. \tag{8}
$$

ϱ is modulus of stability and denotes the dominant real part of the eigenvalues of $\overline{\mathscr{B}_I}$.

Proof. Let us re-write sub system (5) as:

$$
\dot{\mathscr{Y}}_1 = \mathscr{B}_I\left(\mathscr{Y}\right)\mathscr{Y}_I
$$

$$
\mathscr{B}_I\left(\mathscr{Y}\right) = \begin{pmatrix} E & F \\ G & H \end{pmatrix},
$$

$$
E = \begin{pmatrix} \beta_1 c_4 S - (\kappa_E + \mu) & 0 & 0 \\ r_1 \kappa_E & -(k_I + \mu) & 0 \\ (1 - r_1)\kappa_E & 0 & -(r_n + \mu) \end{pmatrix},
$$

$$
F = \begin{pmatrix} 0 & 0 & 0 & \beta_2 S \\ 0 & 0 & 0 & 0 \\ 0 & 0 & 0 & 0 \end{pmatrix}, G = \begin{pmatrix} 0 & k_I & 0 \\ 0 & 0 & 0 \\ 0 & 0 & k_3 r_n \\ 0 & \xi_1 & \xi_2 \end{pmatrix},
$$

$$
H = \begin{pmatrix} -(r_t + \mu) & 0 & 0 & 0 \\ \delta r_t & -(k_4 + \mu) & 0 & 0 \\ 0 & (1 - \delta)r_t & -(k_5 + D_2 + \mu) & 0 \\ 0 & 0 & 0 & -(\varepsilon + e_X) \end{pmatrix}.
$$

Since the off diagonal entries are non-negative and the diagonal entries are negative. Therefore the matrix $\mathscr{B}_I(\mathscr{Y})$ is irreducible and metzler for all $\mathscr{Y} \in \Omega$. Next let $\overline{\mathscr{B}_I}$ be the upper bond of the matrix $\mathscr{B}_I(\mathscr{Y})$. Then,

$$
\overline{\mathscr{B}_I}\left(\mathscr{Y}\right) = \begin{pmatrix} I & J \\ K & L \end{pmatrix},
$$

$$
I = \begin{pmatrix} \beta_1 c_4 S^0 - (\kappa_E + \mu) & 0 & 0 \\ r_1 \kappa_E & -(k_I + \mu) & 0 \\ (1 - r_1)\kappa_E & 0 & -(r_n + \mu) \end{pmatrix},
$$

$$
J = \begin{pmatrix} 0 & 0 & 0 & \beta_2 S^0 \\ 0 & 0 & 0 & 0 \\ 0 & 0 & 0 & 0 \end{pmatrix}, K = \begin{pmatrix} 0 & k_I & 0 \\ 0 & 0 & 0 \\ 0 & 0 & k_3 r_n \\ 0 & \xi_1 & \xi_2 \end{pmatrix},
$$

$$
L = \begin{pmatrix} -(r_t + \mu) & 0 & 0 & 0 \\ \delta r_t & -(k_4 + \mu) & 0 & 0 \\ 0 & (1 - \delta)r_t & -(k_5 + D_2 + \mu) & 0 \\ 0 & 0 & 0 & -(\varepsilon + e_X) \end{pmatrix}.
$$

Since $S \leqslant S^0$. Therefore $\overline{\mathscr{B}_I}(\mathscr{Y})$ is the upper bond of $\mathscr{B}_I(\mathscr{Y})$. This maximum is uniquely realized in Ω if $S = N = S^0$. This corresponds to the DFE.

Also the matrix $\overline{\mathscr{B}_I}(\mathscr{Y})$ is equal to J_2. Where J_2 represent the Jacobian of the infected sub-system (3) at the DFE. Thus the assumption a_4 of theorem (3.1) holds. This proves (7) and (6). □

Next we prove a_5 or (8).

Theorem 3.4. *The metzler matrix satisfy the axiom a_5 ; $\varrho(\overline{B}_I) \leqslant 0$, if $\xi < 1$, where ξ, is given by:*

$$
\xi = \frac{\beta_1 c_4 \Lambda}{\mu(\kappa_E + \mu)} + \frac{r_1 \kappa_E \xi_1 \beta_2 \Lambda}{\mu(\kappa_E + \mu)(k_I + \mu)(\varepsilon + e_X)} + \frac{(1 - r_1)\kappa_E \xi_2 \beta_2 \Lambda}{\mu(\kappa_E + \mu)(r_n + \mu)(\varepsilon + e_X)},
$$

where

Proof. We use the following decomposition of the matrix $\overline{B_I}$.

$$
\overline{B_I} = \begin{pmatrix} M & N \\ O & P \end{pmatrix}, \text{ where}
$$

$$
M = \begin{pmatrix} n_1 - (\kappa_E + \mu) & 0 & 0 & 0 & 0 \\ r_1 \kappa_E & -(k_I + \mu) & 0 & 0 & 0 \\ (1 - r_1)\kappa_E & 0 & -(r_n + \mu) & 0 & 0 \\ 0 & k_I & 0 & -(r_t + \mu) & 0 \\ 0 & 0 & 0 & \delta r_t & -(k_4 + \mu) \end{pmatrix},
$$

$$
O = \begin{pmatrix} 0 & 0 & k_3 r_n & 0 & (1 - \delta)r_t \\ 0 & \xi_1 & \xi_2 & 0 & 0 \end{pmatrix},
$$

$$
N = \begin{pmatrix} 0 & 0 \\ 0 & n_2 \\ 0 & 0 \\ 0 & 0 \\ 0 & 0 \\ 0 & 0 \end{pmatrix}, P = \begin{pmatrix} -(k_5 + D_2 + \mu) & 0 \\ 0 & -(\varepsilon + e_X) \end{pmatrix}.
$$

$n_1 = \frac{\beta_1 c_4 \Lambda}{\mu}$, $n_2 = \frac{\beta_2 \Lambda}{\mu}$, $p_1 = \left(\kappa_E + \mu\right)$, $p_2 = \left(k_I + \mu\right)$,

$p_3 = (r_n + \mu)$, $p_4 = (r_t + \mu)$, $p_5 = (k_4 + \mu)$ $p_6 = (k_5 + D_2 + \mu)$,

$p_7 = (\varepsilon + e_X)$, $d_1 = r_1 \kappa_E$, $d_2 = (1 - r_1)\kappa_E$.

Table 2: Parametric sensitivity indexes

Parameter	value	index	Parameter	value	index
r_n	0.035714	−0.4869	c_4	0.31666	0.1623
Λ	0.0015875	1	r_1	0.25	0.3707
e_X	0.0333	−0.2093	β_1	0.65	0.1623
β_2	0.165	0.8377	μ	0.00004	−1.0009
k_E	0.142857	−0.1620	k_I	0.1492537	−0.3501
ξ_1	0.5	0.3502	ε	0.1	−0.6284
ξ_2	0.5	0.4875			

The stability of the M and P-OM^{-1}N matrix determines the stability of the B_I matrix. For $I \neq j$, it is evident that all entries $m_{i,j}$ of the M are non-negative, and the eigen values are positive. The matrix M is hence metzler stable. G should be P-OM^{-1}N. The stability of G then determines the stability of BI. According to Routh-Hurwitz, in our situation: $(B_I)\leq 0$ only if

$$\frac{\beta_1 c_4 \Lambda}{\mu(\kappa_E+\mu)}+\frac{r_1\kappa_E\xi_1\beta_2\Lambda}{\mu(\kappa_E+\mu)(k_I+\mu)(\varepsilon+ex)}+\frac{(1-r_1)\kappa_E\xi_2\beta_2\Lambda}{\mu(\kappa_E+\mu)(r_n+\mu)(\varepsilon+ex)}-1>0 \quad (9)$$

$$\frac{\beta_1 c_4 \Lambda}{\mu(\kappa_E+\mu)}+\frac{r_1\kappa_E\xi_1\beta_2\Lambda}{\mu(\kappa_E+\mu)(k_I+\mu)(\varepsilon+ex)}+\frac{(1-r_1)\kappa_E\xi_2\beta_2\Lambda}{\mu(\kappa_E+\mu)(r_n+\mu)(\varepsilon+ex)}>1$$

Let's refer to this equation's R.H.S. as ξ. Then, we have demonstrated that, for 1, the assumption a_5 or (8) is met for $\xi< 1$. We have demonstrated all of the theorem's presumptions in the section above.We assert the following theorem in light of the observations mentioned above:
Theorem 3.5:Given system's DFE would exhibit global asymptotic stability. If the model's input parameters fulfill $\xi<1$, where ξ is as previously specified.

R_0's sensitivity analysis

The model's many input parameters have varying effects on how the illness spreads. The term "sensitivity of Z_t w.r.t. K_t" refers to how the parameter K_t affects the phenomena Z_t and is provided by

$$\Upsilon_{Z_t}^{K_t}=\frac{\partial Z_t}{\partial K_t}\frac{K_t}{Z_t}.$$

Strategies for sensitivity-based control
If the parameter has a positive sensitivity index, as the sensitivity index of the human birth rate, which Λ is +1, it is directly proportional to the initial transmission rate R_0. If the index is negative, it is inversely proportional to R_0. If the parameter's sensitivity index is high, it will play a more significant part in the spread of the disease. However, certain characteristics, although having a high sensitivity index, are uncontrollable by humans, such as the population's natural death rate or the length of a disease's incubation period.

We alter six parameters,k_I: the clinical detection of disease, β_1; the likelihood that a disease will spread from person to person, β_2; the likelihood that a disease will spread from contaminated surfaces, ξ_1; the shedding coefficient of infectious individuals who are symptomatic, ξ_2; the shedding coefficient of infectious individuals who are asymptomatic, and ε the lifetime of the virus on the surface.
Non-pharmaceutical treatments include
Table 2.2:

strategy	k_I	β_1	β_2	ξ_1	ξ_2	ε
strategy 1	0.1492537	0.65	0.165	0.5	0.5	0.1
strategy 2	0.2492537	0.15	0.015	0.3	0.3	0.29
strategy 3	0.8492537	0.015	0.005	0.1	0.001	0.86

- Face mask; This intervention addresses β_1, the human-to-human transmission, and coefficients of shedding ξ_1 and ξ_2.
- Wash your hands. This intervention targets two transmissions: the first β_1, from person to person, and the second β_2, from contaminated surfaces to people.
- Sanitizer; this intervention deals with both ε, the duration of a virus on various surfaces, and $\beta 2$.
- Smart lock down; this intervention takes into account every factor.

The magnitudes of these interventions are shown in the control techniques listed in table 2.2.

Results of the model's simulation

For six sets of values (referred to as a strategy), we create numerical simulations using Matlab and the RK-4 approach. The measurement is daily. The disease's behavior is predicted to last for 3000 days. Some graphics, like Figs., are divided into temporal segments to improve visibility of the behavior of the illness 1-3 illustrates how the quarantine class behaved over the beginning, overall, and final periods of 1500–3000 days, respectively.

Discussion

A mathematical model of COVID-19 was developed in this paper.The study's main concerns are the eradication of the illness and the global stability of the resulting disease-free society. For this, the sensitivity of R0 was computed, and six parameters were chosen for intervention based on the sensitivity analysis, as indicated in the table (2.2). For the six interventions indicated above, three control mechanisms were developed. We advise using method 3 in light of the outcomes from numerical simulations.

According to Fig. 1, approach 3 results in a flattening of the quarantined class's density curve as compared to strategies 1 and 2. To really lessen the load of quarrantina centers, this outcome is sought. Fig. (3) demonstrates that the suggested approach totally defeated the quarantined class in 2600 days.Similar to how the suggested approach flattens the exposed class's density curve and succeeds in eliminating it in 2200 days, as seen in Figs (4). In 1400 days, the density of the symptomatic infectious class will be nil (See Fig. 6).

According to the statistics, the densities of the isolated and moderate classes reach zero after roughly 2200 days. Figures (14), (15), and (16) show the behavior of the crucial class. According to Fig 13., the third proposed technique lowers the density of this class in 2600 days. As illustrated in Figs. (16) and (17), the efficient application of sanitizer lowers the density of contaminated materials in a relatively short amount of time.

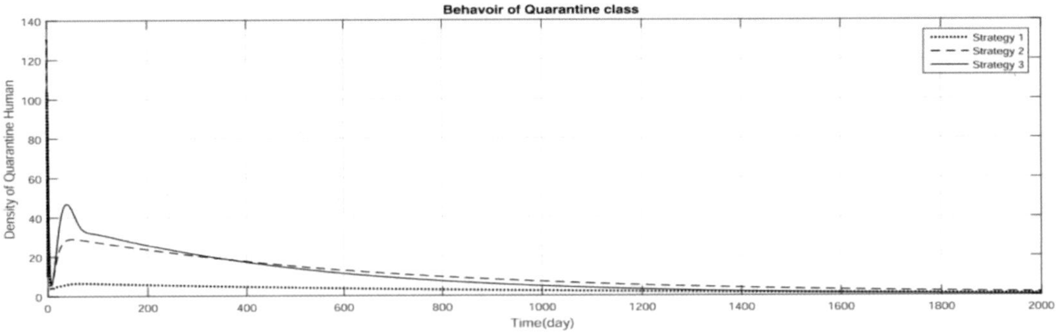

Fig 1: The graph compares several approaches to the early time of human population containment

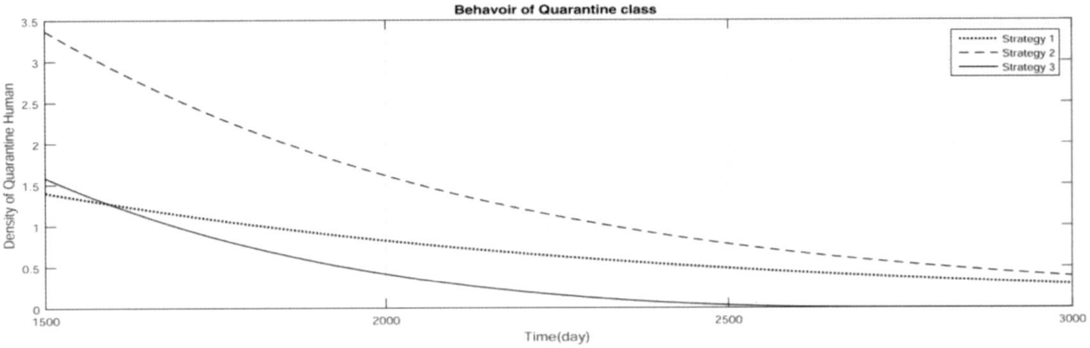

Fig 2: The graph compares several human population quarantine tactics over the course of a full 3000 days.

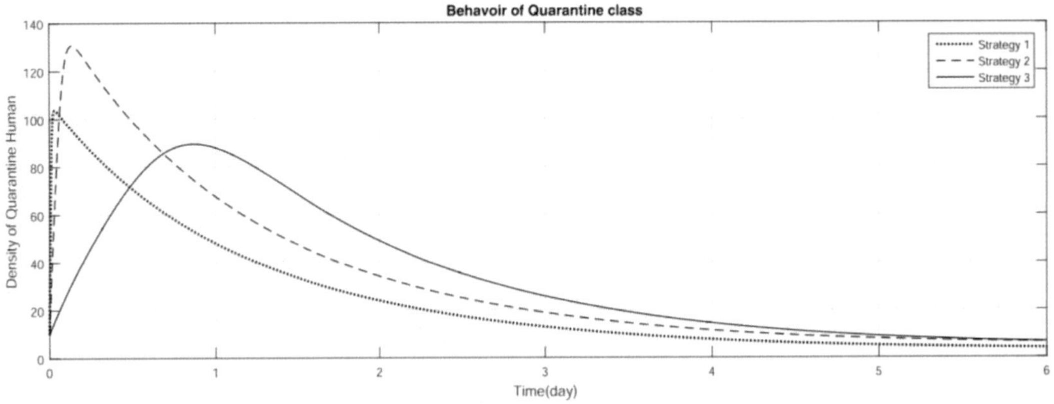

Fig 3: The graph compares several ways for isolating the human population for 1500 to 3000 days.

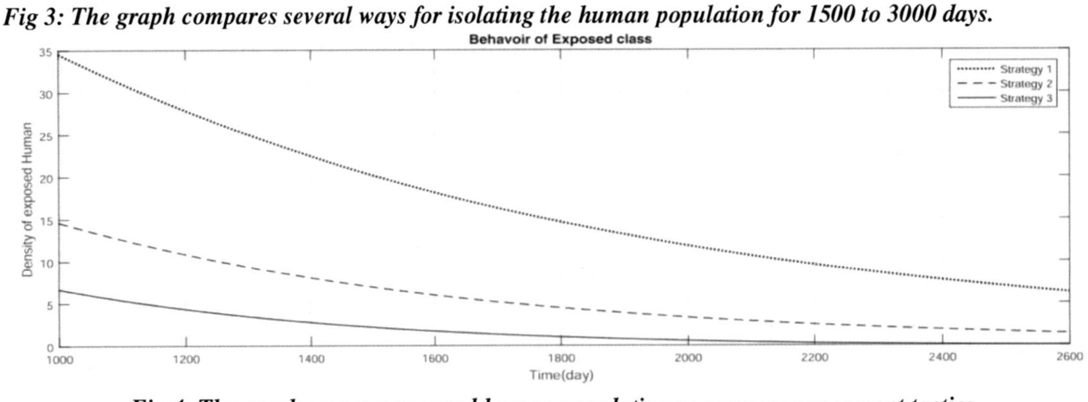

Fig 4: The graph compares several human population exposure management tactics.

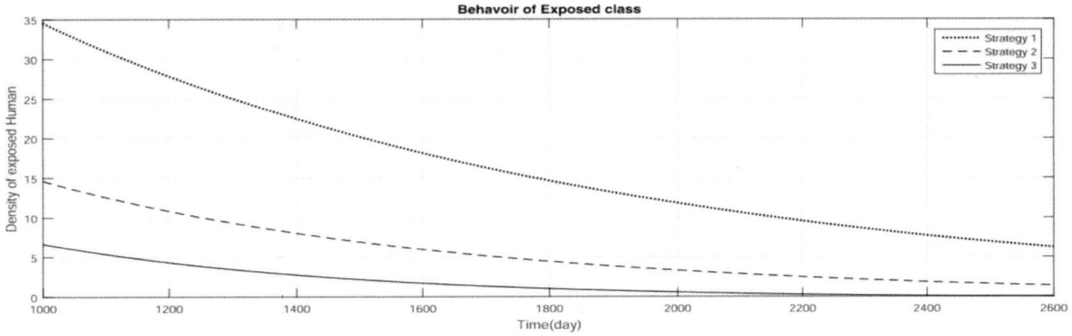

Fig 5: The graph shows a comparison of the first phase methods for the exposed human population.

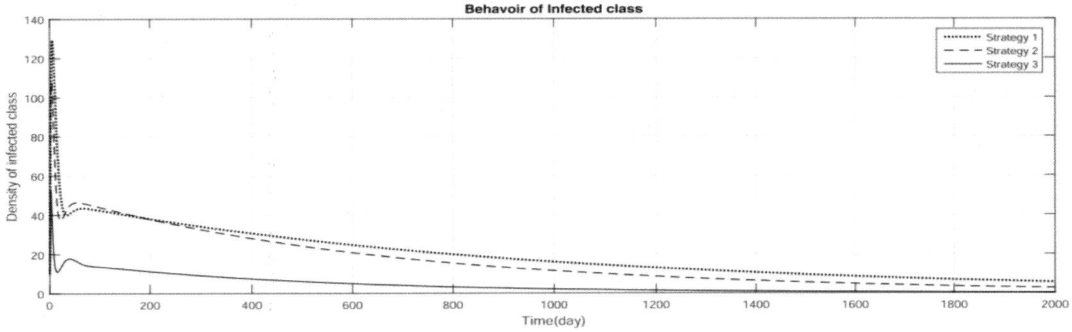

Fig 6: The graph compares several tactics based on the density of the infectious human population between 1000 and 2000 days.

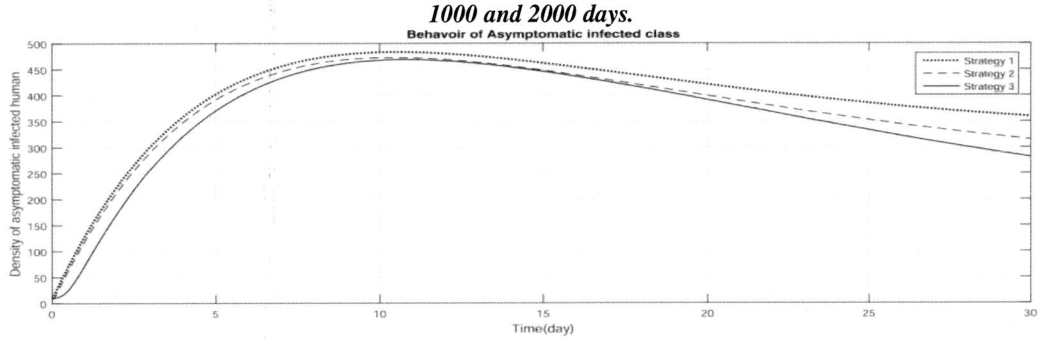

Fig 7: The graph compares various prevention measures for the early period's asymptomatic infected human population.

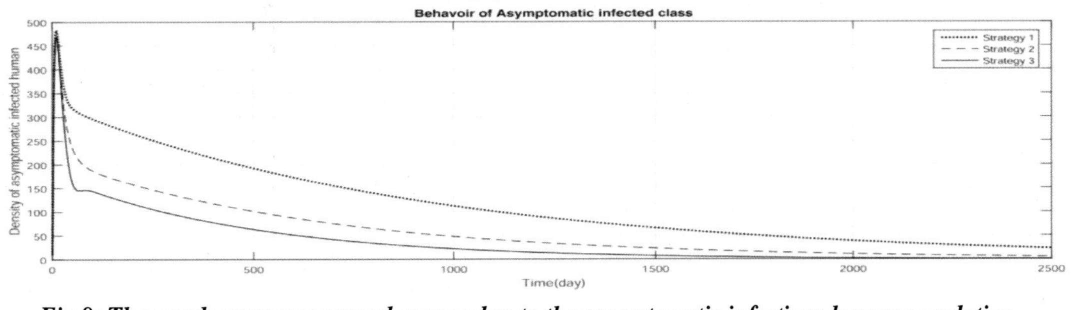

Fig 8: The graph compares several approaches to the asymptomatic infectious human population.

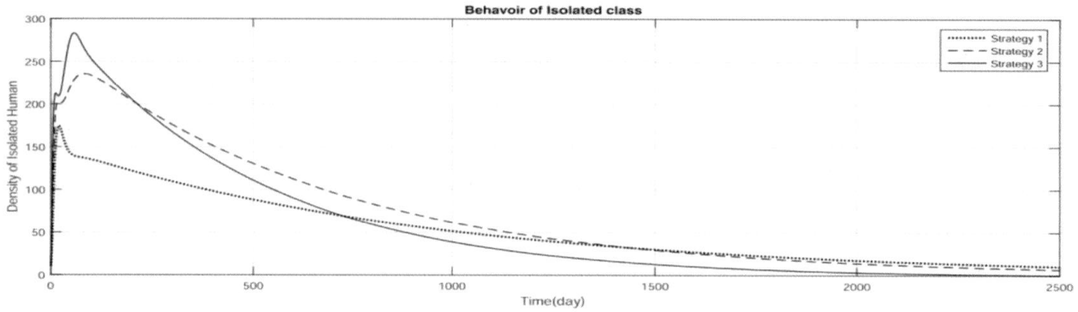

Fig 9: The graph compares several approaches to a certain segment of the population.

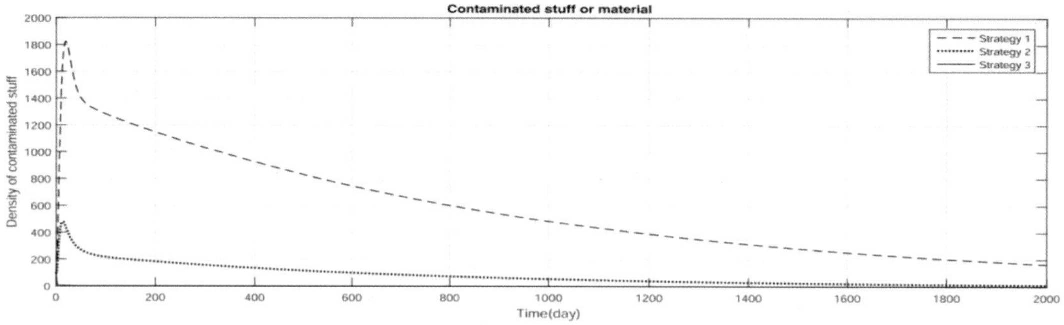

Fig 10: The graph compares several approaches to the density of the moderate class of the human population.

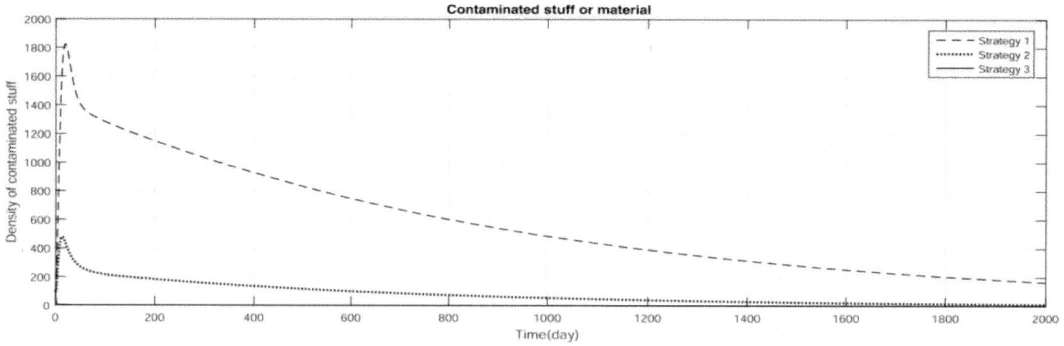

Fig 11: The graph compares several approaches to the first period's density of the most important human class.

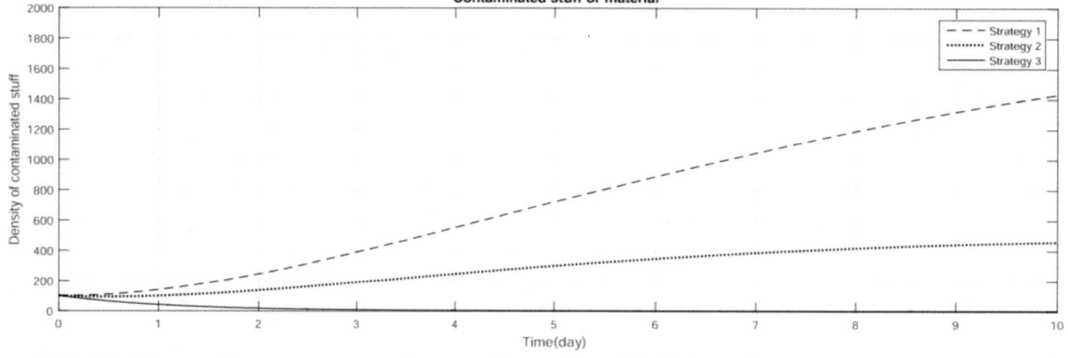

Fig 12: The graph compares several approaches to the critical class of human population's density throughout the course of time.

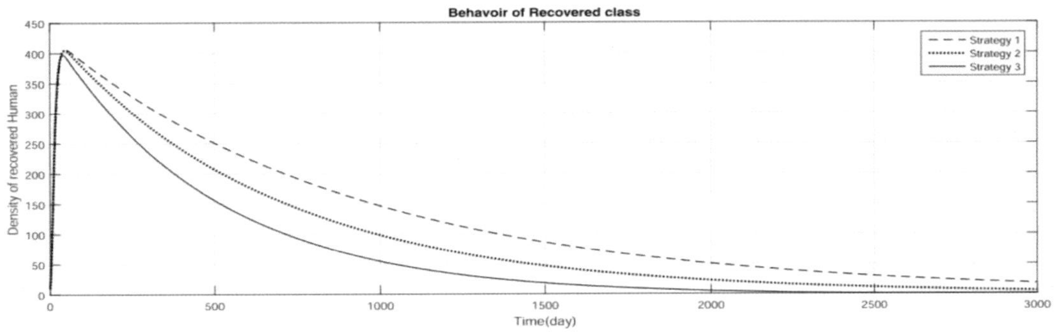

Fig 13: The graph compares several approaches to the density of the most important human group during the most recent time.

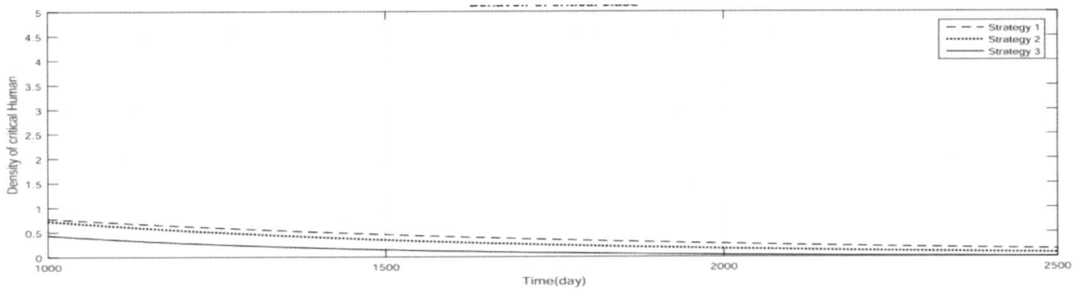

Fig 14: The graph compares several approaches to the density of the population of people who have recovered.

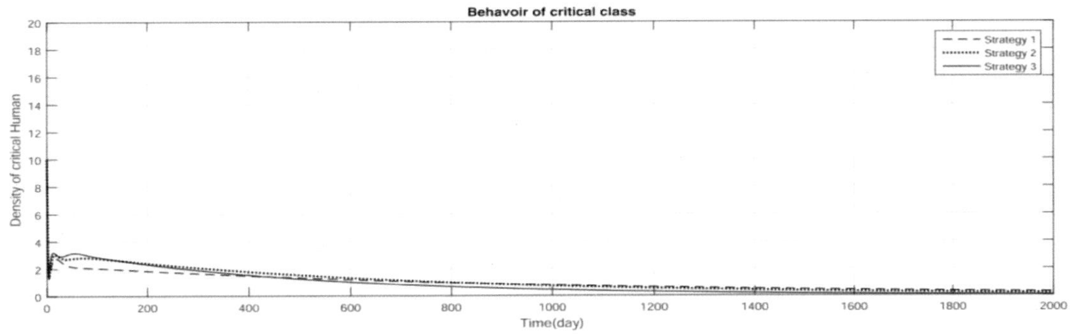

Fig 15: The graph compares several approaches to the initial density of material that has been dyed or shed with the corona virus.

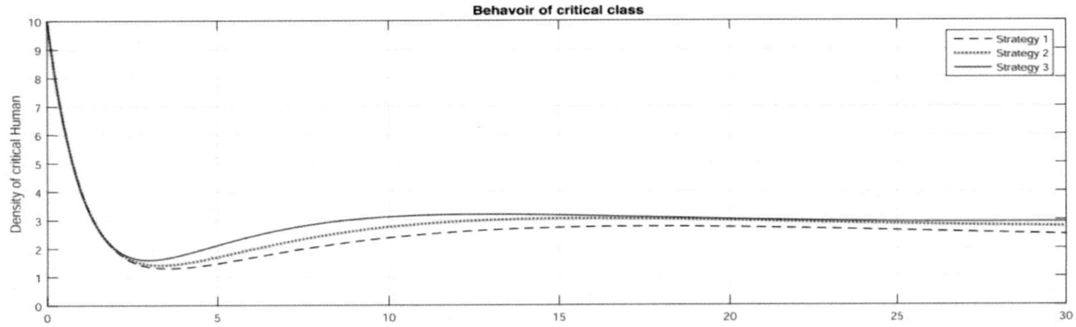

Fig 16: The graph compares several tactics based on how much material was stained or shed with the corona virus over the course of time.

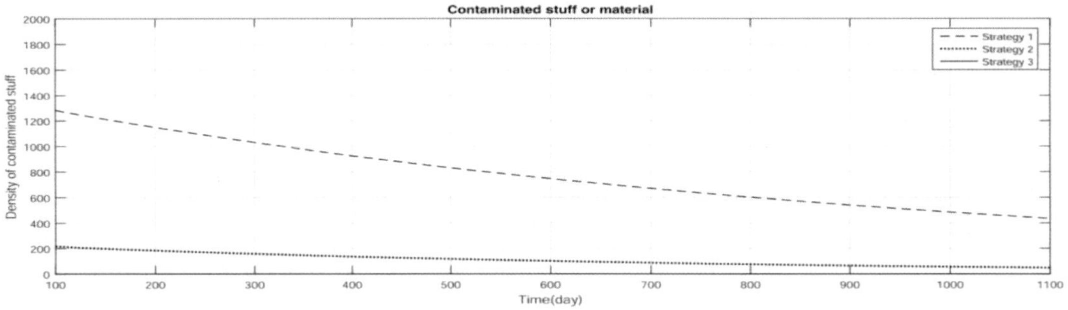

Fig 17: The graph compares several tactics used to determine how much material was stained or shed with the corona virus over time.

Conclusion

The study also derives threshold conditions for global stability of disease free state. It is concluded that the disease can be eradicated with the aid of relaxing non-psychiatric interventions (like Pakistan's smart lock down). However, it may take between six and seven years to completely eradicate the disease. The condition acknowledges that once the illness was eradicated, there would be no outbreak. It is advised, nevertheless, to concentrate on control as well as eradication. Elimination refers to bringing the density of the infection curve to zero whereas control refers to flattening the infection curve. The most effective strategy for reducing the strain on hospitals, isolation units, and quarantine facilities is strategy 3. Additionally, the method works more quickly to clear the virus than the other two.

Part two: ARTIFICIAL INTELLIGENCE AND COVID-19 DETECTION SYSTEMS

Chapter 9

A hybrid meta-heuristic feature selection technique called MRFGRO is used to screen the COVID-19 using deep features[9]

In December 2019, Wuhan, China, witnessed the first case of the COVID-19. Since then, it has spread globally, causing an ongoing pandemic. When a person is in close proximity to an infected person, it spreads through the respiratory system. Since there are now no treatments for this, early detection is crucial. Real-time reverse transcription-polymerase chain reaction (RT-PCR) is the most popular method of COVID-19 detection, but it has a low rate of detection accuracy (around 60–70%), and even after receiving negative results, radiological traces are discovered in the chest computed tomography (CT) scan images. Additionally, it takes nearly a day to deliver the results. The CT scan, on the other hand, uses a spinning X-ray beam and is a non-invasive, painless procedure that enables radiologists to track lung cross-sectional levels. By analysing the CT images using computer-aided methods, several diseases can be diagnosed, including lung cancer, infiltration, hernia, pneumonia, etc. Additionally, CT scan images are preferred over X-ray photos because they provide a more thorough architecture of the lung's air sacs and a precise evaluation of the size, shape, and structure of the lung. X-ray scans are less portable and less ionising. By adopting a minimal computational model and a meta-heuristic technique to reduce the dimension of the feature space, we have employed CT scan pictures to identify COVID-19 in this study.

The coronavirus's true ancestry has not yet been identified. According to scientists, zoonotic animals may be the source of this virus. However, genetic testing has shown that it shares 96% of its genome with bat coronavirus samples (BatCov RaTG13). In Hubei Market in Wuhan, China, the first sick person was discovered, and eventually it spread to other people5. Up until December 21, 2020, 76.9 million people will be afflicted worldwide. Nearly every nation has had some kind of impact. China and a select few other nations have successfully contained this pandemic within their borders. With 17.9 million confirmed cases, the USA is the country most impacted. India follows in second on this list. Unfortunately, COVID-19 caused the deaths of 1.7 million individuals worldwide. The COVID-196 outbreak was most severe in Italy in the middle of March, when there were the most fatalities. Figure 1 depicts an increase in instances in a few nations over the last 10 months.

---

9 *Landmark paper: Dey, A., Chattopadhyay, S., Singh, P.K. et al. MRFGRO: a hybrid meta-heuristic feature selection method for screening COVID-19 using deep features. Sci Rep* ***11****, 24065 (2021). https://doi.org/10.1038/s41598-021-02731-z*

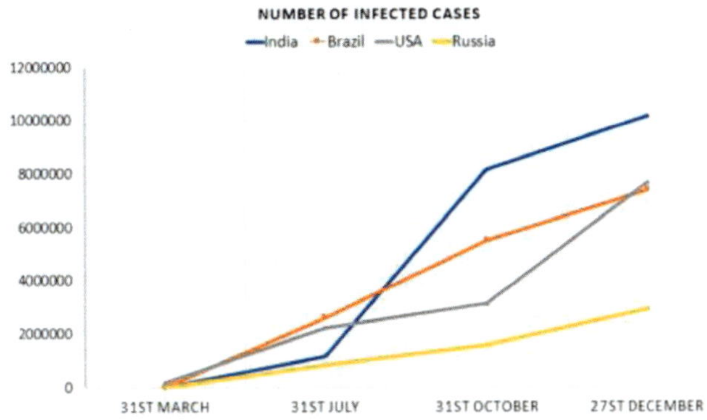

Figure 1. Increasing number of COVID cases in some countries. The data have been collected from the official website of WHO[6].

An infected person's lungs are affected by the virus. According to a study, a condition known as "Ground Glass Opacity" causes the lungs of an infected person to swell up and causes shadowy patches to appear on CT scan pictures. Because the virus is contagious, it spreads far more quickly than it is discovered. As the lungs get inflamed, the symptoms resemble chronic pneumonia quite a bit.

In this study, we provide a strategy that combines machine learning and deep learning to identify COVID-19 in chest CT scans. Deep learning models automatically pick up new features on their own. Machine learning techniques, however, can produce outcomes at a low computational cost. There are numerous standard feature extraction methods for image processing jobs, however in this case we used deep features from five pre-trained convolutional neural networks (CNNs), namely GoogLeNet, ResNet18, ResNet152, VGG19, and VGG16. A high dimensional feature vector is obtained after concatenating all the features. Many redundant features may be present in the concatenated feature vector as we extract features from various CNNs. We have created a hybrid meta-heuristic strategy for feature selection to reduce redundancy and improve the model's accuracy. The question of why we require a hybrid feature selection approach now emerges. It is emphasised by the Nofreelunch11 theorem that there isn't a single method that can handle all kinds of optimization problems. Additionally, the Golden ratio optimizer (GRO) can explore closer to the local minimum, and the Manta ray foraging optimizer (MRFO) has good exploration properties. Good exploration and exploitation are balanced by the MRFO and GRO's hybridization. Golden Ratio Optimizer is the name of the suggested hybrid algorithm, which is based on Manta Ray Foraging (MRFGRO). The following is a list of the paper's contributions.

- In order to find the model that performs best, we have adjusted the settings of CNNs and retrieved features from various pre-trained CNNs (GooGLeNet, ResNet18, ResNet152, VGG19, and VGG16). Out of all the combinations, GoogLeNet and ResNet produce the best results (see "Deep feature extraction" for more information).
- Despite the fact that individual CNN models have fewer redundant features, we have suggested the hybrid meta-heuristic technique MRFGRO to cut down on the total feature dimension and improve the classification accuracy of the model as a whole. In other words, the MRFGRO method focuses on shrinking the dimension of the feature space, which further enables getting better and faster classification outcomes. We have compared the outcomes with those of other optimization algorithms and found that they produce better outcomes (see "Comparison with other optimization algorithms" section for more information).

- On three publicly accessible datasets, COVID-CT, Sars-CoV-2, and MosMed, we assessed our model and obtained accuracy values of 99.15%, 99.42%, and 95.57%, respectively.

Literature review

We've discussed a few strategies for COVID-19 identification that use machine learning and deep learning models in this section. At the end of the 20th century, several computer-aided methods began to diagnose diseases using CT scan images. Deep learning and machine learning based models make it relatively simple to diagnose many chronic diseases.

In order to diagnose various lung disorders, including COVID-19 and chronic pneumonia, many machine learning and deep learning models have been developed. Lack of data is the main obstacle to COVID-19 identification in medical imaging. To help improve the performance of CNNs, Waheed et al. have proposed an Auxiliary Classifier Generative Adversarial Network (ACGAN), which generates more pictures. Horry et al., on the other hand, applied a transfer learning model to various multimodal COVID datasets. To emphasise the temporal aspects, Sabanci et al. added a conjugated system with a pre-trained CNN to a Bidirectional Long Short-Term Memory (BiLSTM). SqueezeNet, a lightweight CNN suggested by Matteo Polsinelli, was used to the dataset created by Zhao et al. and achieved an accuracy of 83.3%. With 13,975 X-ray pictures used to train their deep CNN, Wang et al. reported a 98.9% accuracy rate. In a different study, Ying et al. used chest CT-scan pictures to distinguish COVID and healthy individuals and reached an accuracy of 86%. Additionally, a 17 layer CNN called DarkCovidNet has been proposed by Ozturk et al. For three-class classification, this model has an accuracy of 87.02%, while for two-class classification, it has an accuracy of 98.08%. Additionally, Rajarshi et al. created a model that extracts deep features from several CNNs, and then they used the Harris Hawks optimisation with Simulated Annealing method to select the best feature subset. The proposed technique was tested using the SARS-COV-2 CT-Scan dataset, and the accuracy was found to be 98.85%. The additional research on several models for automated COVID identification using medical image analysis is shown in Table 1.

Work ref.	Method	Dataset	Obtained accuracy
Shibly et al.[19]	Used faster R-CNN	COVIDx dataset	97.65%
Zheng et al.[20]	UNet+3D network	Own dataset	90.8%
Jaiswal et al.[21]	DenseNet 201	SARS-Cov-2 dataset	96.25%
Soares et al.[22]	xDNN	SARS-Cov-2 dataset	97.38%
Panwar et al.[23]	Gradient-weighted class activation mapping (Grad-CAM)	Cohen dataset	97.08%
Kundu et al.[24]	Fuzzy rank-based fusion of VGG-11, Wide ResNet-50-2, and Inception v3	SARS-COV-2 dataset and Harvard Dataverse chest CT dataset	98.93% and 98.80% (respectively on SARS-COV-2 and Harvard Dataverse chest CT datasets)

Table 1. Summarization of previous works reported for COVID-19 detection.

The majority of the researchers have relied on various deep learning models for the detection of COVID-19 from medical pictures, according to the literature review. The feature extraction capabilities of various CNN-based models from the input images can therefore be inferred from the discussion above. Concatenating the feature vectors from those models would result in a high-dimensional feature vector, which would require a lot more storage space and a long training period. An FS model must be able to remove the unnecessary features from the extracted deep feature set in order to fulfil this criteria. Meta-heuristic methods are frequently used to handle this task. Various feature selection techniques have been developed recently. Although in this paper we have discussed various optimization strategies. A single optimization technique might not be able to solve every issue, according to researchers. Cooperative Genetic Algorithm (CGA), Late Acceptance Hill-Climbing (BBA-LAHC), Mayfly algorithm (MA) and

HS named MA-HS algorithm, hybridization of GA with PSO and Ant Colony Optimization (ACO) algorithm, clustering-based equilibrium, and ant colony optimization are some examples of recent hybrid optimization algorithms (EOAS). In the proposed study, we have introduced a hybrid meta-heuristic FS technique called MRFGRO that, when applied to chest CT scan images to detect the COVID-19, decreases the feature dimension of the features generated from the deep learning models.

Components and Procedures

The workflow of the suggested method for COVID-19 detection has been detailed in this section one by one. A dataset description, a deep feature extraction part, and a feature selection portion make up the three main divisions of the complete task.

Description of a dataset

On three publicly accessible datasets—which are succinctly described below—we have used in this work to evaluate our model.

Dataset from COVID-CT

Jhao et al. produced the covid-CT dataset. As the name implies, this dataset includes of 349 verified COVID-19 cases and 397 healthy cases from chest CT-scan pictures. Before being fed to the deep learning frameworks for feature extraction, all photos in this study framework are resized to 224x224x3 and normalised. Because the dataset for deep neural networks is so limited, it is rotated by 50 degrees, tilted by 0.5 degrees, and enabled to be flipped horizontally and vertically throughout the training process.

File SARS-Cov-2

Soares et al. created the SARS-Cov-2 CT-scan dataset. There are 2492 chest CT-scan images in this collection, 1262 of which are COVID-19 positive, and the remaining 1230 photos are of healthy subjects. The photos are enlarged to 224x224x3, same like the previous dataset, and during training, data augmentation techniques are used with a 25 rotation and horizontal flip.

Dataset for MOSMED

This dataset consists of 1110 CT scan images of patients that were separated into five classifications. The following are the classes:

- Normal lung tissue without any indication of viral pneumonia (CT[0]).
- Multiple ground-glass opacities are visible on CT[1], and 25% of the lung parenchyma is affected.
- On a CT[2] scan, many ground glass opacities are visible, and 25–50% of the lung parenchyma is affected.
- On a CT[3] scan, many ground-glass opacities are visible, and 50–75% of the lung parenchyma is affected.
- CT[4] There is diffuse multiple ground-glass opacity, and the lung parenchyma is more than 75% affected.

Extrapolation of deep features

When the underlying dataset is extremely complicated, it can occasionally be challenging to create a competent feature vector using traditional feature engineering techniques. Furthermore, it is discovered that a feature vector created for one dataset may not function well when used with another. As a result, in our research, we have concentrated on extracting deep features using CNN models that have already been trained. We have taken into account five common pre-trained CNNs, including GoogLeNet8, ResNet18, ResNet152, VGG19, and VGG16, for deep feature extraction. The datasets are used to fine-tune all of the pre-trained CNNs throughout the course of 30 training epochs. Adam optimizer has been used to optimise cross-entropy loss for all cases, with learning rate and momentum set to 0.0009 and 0.85, respectively. The model is switched to its evaluation mode after 30 training epochs, and the weights of the epoch that achieves the lowest loss have been loaded. The features from the final layer have been extracted after the model has processed both the training and testing images. Deep feature extraction has been carried out in this investigation in this manner. Table 2 displays the quantity of deep features that were extracted using various CNNs.

Pre-trained CNN	Number of features extracted
ResNet18	512
ResNet152	2048
VGG16	25,088
VGG19	25,088

Table 2. Number of features obtained from different deep learning models when applied over COVID-19 datasets.

Additionally, we tested the combinations of several CNNs by fusing the feature sets, and evaluated by our suggested MRFGRO algorithm for FS. This allowed us to analyse the deep features produced from various CNNs together. The final feature vector is created by concatenating the features from various CNNs throughout the fusing phase. Assume that features f1 and f2 are taken from CNNs 1 and 2 and that f becomes the final feature vector after the fusion function (F(.)). Therefore

$$f = F(f1, f2). \quad (1)$$

The number of features in f would therefore equal the total number of features in each CNN's feature set

$$N_f = \sum_{i=1}^{n} N_{fi}, \quad (2)$$

where N_{fi} represents the number of features in the ith deep feature set and Nf represents the number of features in the fused feature set. Results from various features from various nets are combined to produce the results, which are reported in the "Results and discussion" section. Fig. 2 also provides a graphical diagram of the deep feature extraction method.

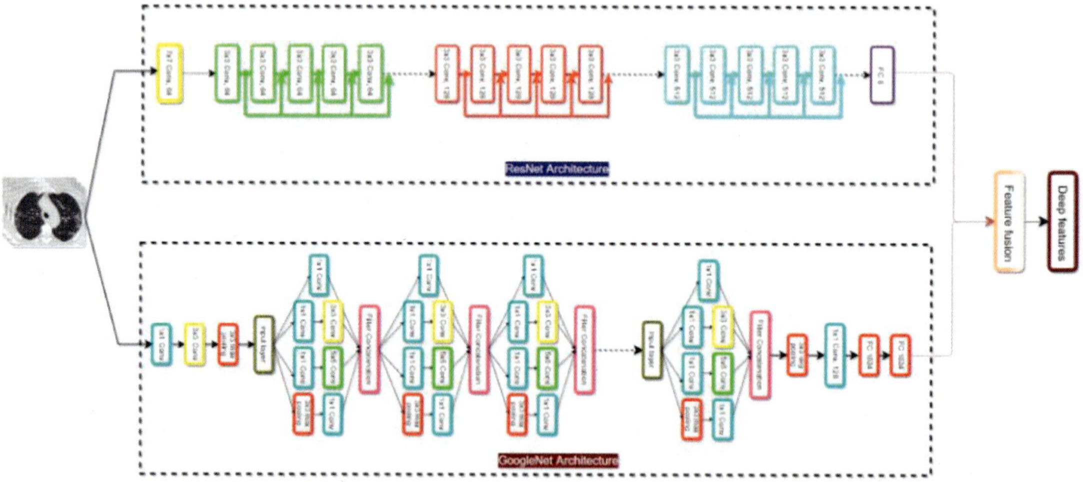

Figure 2. Illustration of the work flow of deep features extraction from GoogLeNet and ResNet18 architectures. The input CT-scan images are taken from CARS-Cov-2 CT-scan dataset[22].

Model for feature selection

We have taken aspects from many CNNs and combined them in different ways. The size of the feature set grows significantly as a result. There is still a potential that a feature vector of this size would overfit the classifiers and contain some redundant features. In order to solve this problem, we develop an FS algorithm that can extract a more abundant feature subset from the full feature collection. As a result, we suggest MRFGRO, a new hybrid meta-heuristic FS method that combines MRFO and GRO. The FS model's premature convergence and tendency to become stuck at the local minimum are two of its key drawbacks. However, a hybrid model can assist in striking a balance between exploration and exploitation, helping to solve the issue of premature convergence. The next subsection discusses each proposed optimization algorithm's mechanism of operation and hybridization process.

Optimizing manta ray foraging

One of the two optimization procedures we selected to create our hybrid FS model is MRFO. Manta rays employ their foraging abilities to haunt their prey, and MRFO is based on these abilities. The algorithm employs three different foraging techniques: chain foraging, cyclone foraging, and somersault foraging. Manta rays use a high level of concentration in the first type of foraging approach to capture their plankton prey. As a result, they establish a chain of foragers, with each manta ray hunting its prey and updating its location across the repetitions. Chain foraging can be expressed mathematically as follows:

$$p_j^{(n+1)} = \begin{cases} p_j^n + d(p_{best}^n - p_j^n) + \beta(p_{best}^n - p_j^n) & j = 1 \\ p_j^n + d(p_{j-1}^n - p_j^n) + \beta(p_{best}^n - p_j^n) & j = 2, \ldots, N \end{cases}, \tag{3}$$

At iteration n, the position of the jth manta ray is provided by the expression $p^n{}_j$, and d, N, and $p^n{}_{best}$ are the best solution, the number of manta rays, and the number of random vectors, respectively. The formula for the weighting coefficient is

$$2 \times d \times \sqrt{|log(d)|}. \tag{4}$$

Manta rays begin to group together in a chain and travel in a spiralling motion in the direction of their food once they are aware of the precise location of the plankton. Each manta ray in cyclone foraging advances one step toward its predecessor in addition to spiralling, creating a cyclonic motion. Two perpendicular components, which are given as follows, can be used to express the cyclonic foraging:

$$X_j^{n+1} = X_{best} + d(X_{j-1}^n - X_j^n) + e^{a\omega} cos(2\pi\omega)(X_{best} - X_j^n), \tag{5}$$

$$Y_j^{n+1} = Y_{best} + d(Y_{j-1}^n - Y_j^n) + e^{a\omega} sin(2\pi\omega)(Y_{best} - Y_j^n), \tag{6}$$

Where ω a random number is used. The position and movement of cyclone foraging towards the minimum can now be expressed similarly to chain foraging as seen below:

$$p_j^{(n+1)} = \begin{cases} p_{best} + d(p_{best}^n - p_j^n) + \gamma(p_{best}^n - p_j^n) & j = 1 \\ p_{best} + d(p_{j-1}^n - p_j^n) + \gamma(p_{best}^n - p_j^n) & j = 2, \ldots., N \end{cases}. \tag{7}$$

Additionally, a weighting factor is used here with the expression.

$$\gamma = 2e^{d_1\left(\frac{I-n+1}{I}\right)} sin(2\pi d_1), \tag{8}$$

where I represents the most iterations and d1 is a random number. Manta rays hunt from their reference places, therefore cyclone foraging has good application in the quest for the best answer. Additionally, the cyclone foraging process forces every manta ray or candidate solution to look for new, superior solutions that are still far superior than the present best. Here, exploitation is made easier in that way. To do this, a random place in the search space is assigned,

$$p_{rand} = lb + d(lb - ub), \tag{9}$$

and

$$p_j^{(n+1)} = \begin{cases} p_{rand} + d(p_{rand}^n - p_j^n) + \gamma(p_{rand}^n - p_j^n) & j = 1 \\ p_{rand} + d(p_{j-1}^n - p_j^n) + \gamma(p_{rand}^n - p_j^n) & j = 2, ..., N \end{cases}, \tag{10}$$

where lb, ub are the lower limit and upper bound of the problem variables, respectively, and P_{rand} is the position that was randomly allocated.

The food is chased like a hinge during the somersault foraging phase of this MRFO. Each manta ray in this sort of foraging tumbles around the hinge in search of a new place. The movement is described as

$$p_j^{(n+1)} = p_j^{(n)} + S \times (d_2 p_{best} - d_3 p_j^{(n)}), \quad j = 1, 2, ..., N, \tag{11}$$

where d_2, d_3, and S are random values, and S is the somersault foraging factor. The disparities between the developing solutions and the global minimum get smaller and converge to the best option during this final phase. Over the repetitions, this foraging eventually decreases adaptively. This is how MRFO goes about finding the best solution: by creating a replica of the manta ray fishes' haunting behaviour.

Golden ratio improvement

The "golden ratio" is a constant ratio formed by a number of physical processes. Fibonacci is credited with coining the phrase "golden ratio." The Fibonacci series, which he defined, is essentially an infinite series in which the kth term is the sum of the (k-1)th and (k-2) th terms. The golden ratio is 1.618, which is the constant ratio between any two consecutive terms in a series. The core concept behind the GRO algorithm is this. The following equation yields the kth Fibonacci number.

$$F(k) = GR \, . \frac{\left(\gamma^k - \left(1 - \gamma^{-k}\right)\right)}{\sqrt{5}} \quad where\ GR = 1.618. \tag{12}$$

Initial population is generated here as well, much like in previous wrapper-based FS algorithms. The candidate solutions in the GRO method are regarded as vectors. These vectors also have certain directions and magnitudes. Over the iterations, these vectors' magnitudes and orientations are updated and moved in the direction of the global minimum. The fitness of each potential solution is first determined using the population's mean value. The population's mean solution is then compared to each candidate solution, and so on. The worst solution is now substituted by the mean solution if the fitness of the mean solution is greater than the fitness of the worst solution. By updating the population after each cycle, this procedure is carried out iteratively. Once more, the worst option in the updated population is determined, and the previous procedures are then carried out. As a result, the population's vectors converge to the minimum.

$$D_{best} > D_{medium} > D_{worst}, \tag{13}$$

$$W_t = W_{medium} - W_{worst}. \tag{14}$$

The solution vectors' absolute position and direction during the search for the global minimum are represented by equations (13) and (14) respectively. In order to improve algorithm exploration, a random movement is now introduced to the population each time the population is upgraded. This makes it easier to find the minimum across the entire solution space rather than just in one area. Eq provides the equation that describes this phenomenon (15).

$$W_{new} = (1 - D_t)W_{best} + rand \cdot W_t \cdot D_t. \tag{15}$$

When the boundary condition is met, the new solutions replace the old ones in the population. This is how solutions are updated.

Proposed method

The suggested MRFGRO method (see Fig. 4) combines MRFO and GRO into one algorithm. This hybridization's primary goal is to fix the problem with the parent algorithms. The extracted feature set is represented by numbers 0 and 1, where 0 denotes the exact opposite of the feature to be picked and 1 the feature to be extracted. Once more, the fundamental aim of FS algorithms is to lower the amount of 1s and, thus, increase accuracy. In contrast to binary search space, continuous search space optimization is considerably different. The binary search space is conceptualised as a hypercube, and the search agents attempt to move bits closer to the hypercube. S-shaped and V-shaped transfer functions are two often used methods for converting a continuous optimization issue into a binary optimization problem. Eq is a representation of an S-shaped function (17). However, we have utilised an S-shaped transfer function in our paper.

$$fitness(x) = \omega \cdot A_{classifier} + (1 - \omega)(1 - |\theta/\theta'|). \tag{16}$$

Function of transfer

The transfer function's job is to turn the feature set into a sequence of 0s and 1s so that the sample can be trained to its final state. We utilised the signoid function for binarization for this purpose. As is well known, the sigmoid function's output falls between 0 and 1. The sigmoid function is discussed in Eq. (17). The graphic depiction of the sigmoid function is shown in Figure 3.

$$t_s(x) = 1/1 + e^{-x}. \tag{17}$$

The steps in our suggested algorithm are as follows:

Step 1: Tweak the MRFO control settings, including population size (Npop), the number of iterations to be performed at a time (Tmax), and the somersault factor (Sf).

Step 2: Initialize the manta rays' randomly generated positions in step two.

Step 3: Using Eq. (16), determine the fitness of each solution in the created population and update the manta rays' current location.

Step 4: If the fitness value is less than the rand, exploitation occurs; otherwise, exploration is carried out. T/Tmax maintains the exploration and exports. The positions of the manta rays are updated using Eq. if rand>0.5 (3). Further, locations are updated using Equation (5) or Equation (2) if the value of t/Tmax is less than rand (6).

Step 5: Identify the fitness value and change the location in step 5. Then compute the average, the best, and the worst iterations of the present solution.

Step 6: The best, worst, and average candidate solutions are then evaluated in comparison to the present candidate solution. If the terminate condition is met, the optimization stops here and produces the best solution; otherwise, it proceeds to step 2.

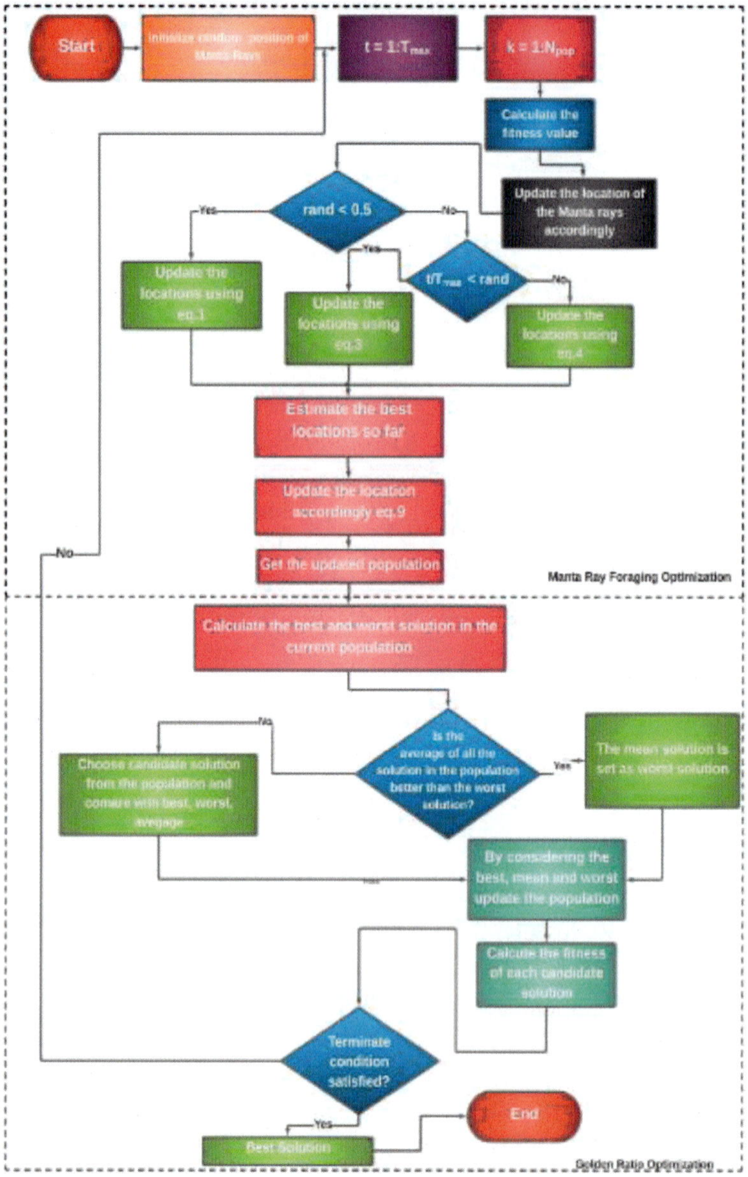

Figure 4. Proposed workflow of our proposed MRFGRO algorithm.

Overview of the used classifiers

We have selected three distinct cutting-edge classifiers, such as SVM, MLP, and ELM, to calculate the fitness function. The hidden layers of the MLP and ELM are fixed at 5 in the proposed approach, and the SVM classifier is assessed using the kernel function "rbf." The value of the SVM's regularisation parameter "C" is 5000.

Statement

All procedures and experiments were completed in accordance with the necessary laws and regulations.

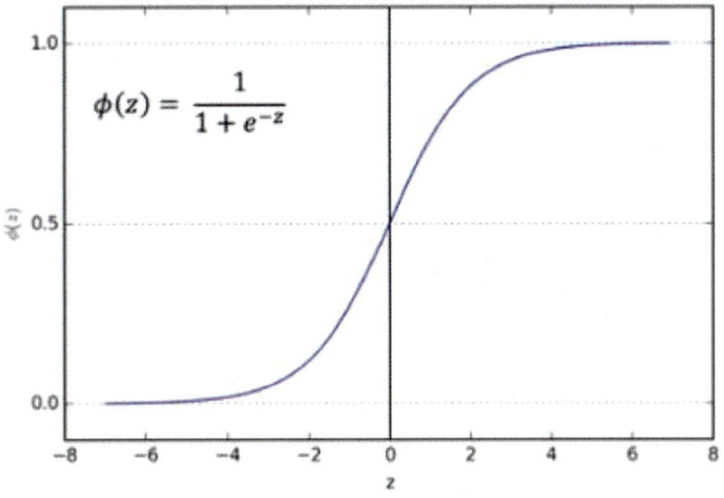

Figure 3. Graphical representation of sigmoid function.

Outcomes and Analysis

In this section, we present the experimental findings from the three COVID-19 detection datasets that were briefly described in the section before. The experiment includes results from various machine learning classifiers used to calculate the MRFGRO algorithm's fitness, as well as loss plots and accuracy plots of various deep learning models, a comparison of the MRFGRO algorithm with other FS algorithms, hyperparameter tuning, and other things. We wrap up this part by comparing the proposed approach of COVID-19 detection with a number of cutting-edge methodologies.

Accuracy, Precision, Recall, and F1 score are the four standard metrics we employed for evaluation. To examine the suggested model more generally and to address the class imbalance issue, all these indicators have been taken into account. These evaluation metrics rely on several basic metrics, including true positive (TP), true negative (TN), false positive (FP), and false negative (FN) (FN). The following equations can be used to calculate the aforementioned metrics based on TP, TN, FP, and FN values:

- Accuracy

$$\frac{TP + TN}{TP + TN + FP + FN}, \quad (18)$$

- Precision

$$\frac{TP}{FP + TP}, \quad (19)$$

- Recall

$$\frac{TP}{TP + FN}, \quad (20)$$

- F1 score

$$\frac{TP}{TP + \frac{1}{2}(FP + FN)}. \quad (21)$$

Broad features

Transfer learning has been applied for deep feature extraction, as was already described. Using the aforementioned deep learning models, we have extracted features from CT scan images and have utilised our suggested MRFGRO technique for feature dimension reduction and classification. Additionally, we tested our model using various concatenations of deep features retrieved using various deep learning models. Table 3 provides the outcomes of several of these models on three COVID-19 detection datasets.

Feature set	SARS-CoV-2 CT-scan dataset		Covid-CT dataset		MOSMED dataset	
	No. of selected features	Accuracy (%)	No. of selected features	Accuracy (%)	No. of selected features	Accuracy (%)
GoogLeNet	780	94.47	680	96.22	811	91.91
ResNet18	445	92.17	328	96.91	378	90.11
ResNet152	1119	90.99	998	94.29	1242	91.49
VGG19	12,400	87.77	9442	85.48	15,987	81.24
VGG16	17,809	85.47	14,899	86.78	12,597	81.24
ResNet18+GoogLeNet	**875**	**99.42**	**756**	**99.15**	**612**	**95.57**
ResNet152+GoogLeNet	1180	97.71	987	96.18	1001	91.23
ResNet18+VGG16	15,489	90.02	14,801	92.24	17,589	92.21
GoogLeNet+VGG19	16,029	91.19	11,549	90.42	18,900	78.48
ResNet152+VGG19	15,014	88.18	17,802	85.44	11,259	80.04
ResNet18+GoogLeNet+VGG16	9002	86.48	15,809	84.48	18,792	79.99
ResNet152+GoogLeNet +VGG19	16,891	87.62	18,722	81.19	11,589	78.48

Table 3. Classification results obtained with different deep feature sets using our proposed MRFGRO algorithm. Best results are given in Bold.

It was noted in the previous part that we retrieved deep features from CT-scan images rather than standard features to enable automatic COVID-19 detection. We used the Adam optimizer and a learning rate of 0.001 to train a few pre-trained networks over a period of 30 epochs. A cross-entropy loss is the loss function that the optimizer seeks to optimise. We employed some data augmentation during training, which is described in the "Dataset description" section, where datasets are summarised. Following training, the refined weights are saved, the photos are then loaded, and the final layer's characteristics are retrieved. Figs. 5 and 6 display the validation loss plots and accuracy plots of each CNN on the SARS-CoV-2 CT-scan dataset. From Figs. 5 and 6, it can be shown that the accuracy and convergence of the GoogLeNet and ResNet18 designs are both superior than those of other CNNs. Since there are more images in the SARS-CoV-2 CT-Scan dataset than in the COVID CT-Dataset, the convergence loss graphs are significantly better. For these two datasets, GoogLeNet and ResNet18's accuracy turns out to be significantly higher than that of the competition, while in the MOSMED dataset, all of the nets produce results that are comparable. ResNet18 achieves 92% and 90% of the maximum findings in the SARS-CoV-2 CT-Scan dataset and COVID CT-Dataset, respectively. On the other hand, GoogLeNet obtains the maximum, or about 88%, for the MOSMED dataset. On the COVID CT-Dataset, ResNet152 performs poorly, however it works well on the SARS-CoV-2 CT-Scan dataset. On the SARS-CoV-2 CT-scan dataset and the COVID-CT dataset, both VGG16 and VGG19 thoroughly produce subpar results, however they show comparable results for the MOSMED dataset.

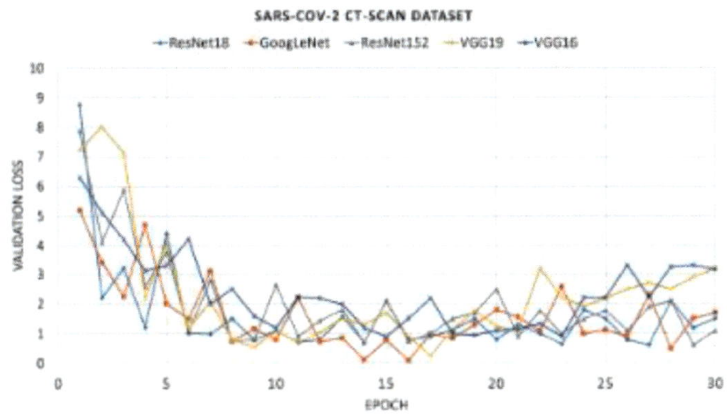

Figure 5. Loss plot of different deep learning models during training process on SARS-CoV-2 dataset.

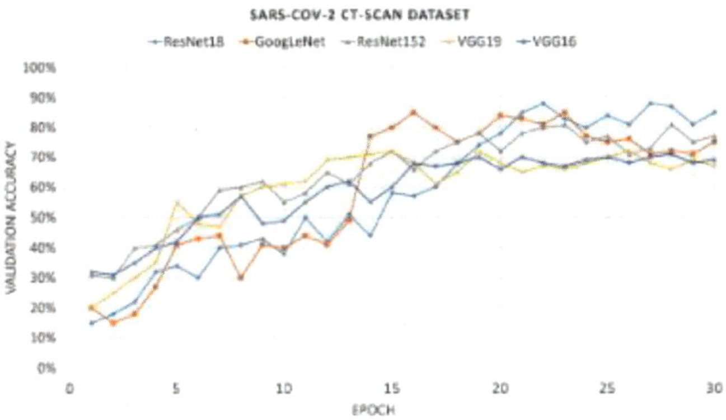

Figure 6. Accuracy plot of different deep learning models during training process on SARS-CoV-2 dataset.

In terms of final classification accuracy for all three datasets, the result produced by integrating the deep features of Google Neural Network with ResNet 18 is superior to all other combinations. While classification accuracy for different combinations varies significantly for the SARS-CoV-2 CT-scan dataset and the MOSMED dataset, the results for the COVID-CT dataset are much more comparable. Due to the sheer quantity of features, both the individual VGG models and their various combinations fall short of expectations. The generation of several unhelpful traits that reduce recognition accuracy overall is one potential explanation. The deep feature sets of the ResNet18 and GoogLeNet models have been integrated in this instance, and this is regarded as our final feature set.

It should be remembered that all findings are analysed after the other parameters have been set to their ideal pairing. These parameters include the machine learning classifier used to determine the fitness function, numerous classifier hyperparameters, and the MRFGRO optimization algorithm's own parameters.

Determining fitness value

The fitness value of the MRFGRO algorithm and the final classification job were calculated using various machine learning classifiers. They are SVM, ELM, and MLP classifiers. The previous section provides a brief summary of these classifiers. It goes without saying that these classifiers' findings differ from one another numerically. Table 4 reports the outcomes of these three classifiers using all three datasets.

Evaluation parameter	SARS-CoV-2 CT-scan dataset SVM (%)	MLP (%)	ELM (%)	COVID-CT dataset SVM (%)	MLP (%)	ELM (%)	MOSMED dataset SVM (%)	MLP (%)	ELM (%)
Accuracy	**99.42**	97.17	98.64	**99.15**	94.44	97.98	**95.57**	90.02	92.29
Precision	97	98	**99**	**98**	92	98	**96**	91	91
Recall	**100**	97	98	**97**	95	97	**95**	91	92
F1 Score	**99**	97	98	**99**	95	97	**95**	90	90

Table 4. Results obtained by the proposed MRFGRO algorithm using different classifiers on all three COVID-19 datasets. Maximum values of accuracy, precision, recall and F1 score for each dataset are made bold.

The SVM classifier performs better than the other two in the majority of Table 4 situations in terms of accuracy and other assessment criteria. While MLP classifier hasn't performed as well, ELM classifier occasionally outperforms SVM classifier in terms of results. For the SARS-CoV-2 CT-scan dataset and the COVID-CT dataset, the ELM classifier's findings and those of the SVM classifier are remarkably similar, while for the MOSMED dataset, the discrepancies are significantly greater. SVM classifier has been picked as a result for both classification and fitness calculation needs.

Tweaking for hyperparameters

This entire framework for applying our suggested MRFGRO algorithm to optimise deep features contains numerous hyperparameters. Some are employed in the proposed FS algorithm, while others are used during deep feature extraction.

The optimizer, learning rate, momentum of the optimizer, batch size, and other parameters are among the key hyperparameters in deep learning models. The optimizer and learning rate for the training method have been set to Adam and $1e^{-3}$ for each of the three datasets. For the SARS-CoV-2 CT-scan dataset, COVID-CT dataset, and MOSMED dataset, the batch sizes are considered to be 50, 25, and 30 accordingly. Fig. 7 illustrates the graphs displaying the final classification accuracy results from utilising various optimizers and learning rates on the three datasets.

The accuracy indicated in the plots was attained using the FS algorithm, not the accuracy produced by the deep learning models, it should be noted. Additional deep learning hyperparameters, like momentum and regularisation constant, have been set to their default values.

The starting population, several kernel functions, and the SVM classifier's regularisation parameters are some of the most crucial hyperparameters of the MRFGRO-based FS technique. Fig. 8 displays the variation in consequent accuracy with regard to the beginning population across all three datasets.

With a population size of 10, the three datasets' maximum accuracy is attained. As a result, in the current investigation, the initial population is set at 10.

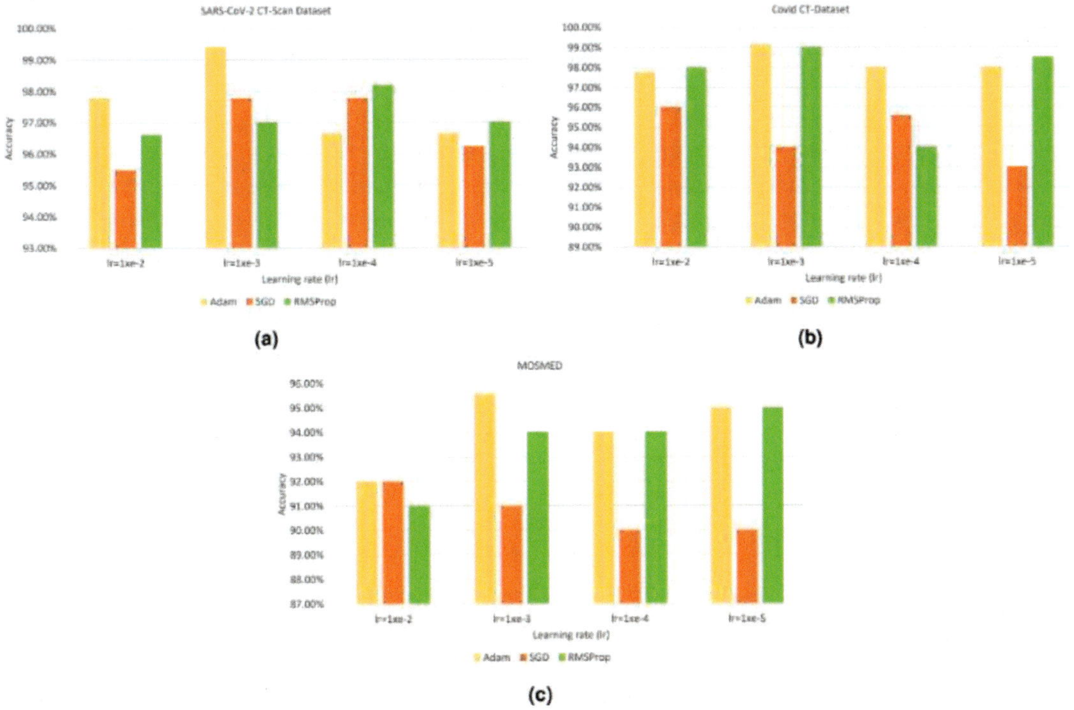

Figure 7. Graph showing the classification accuracies using different combinations of optimizers and learning rates on all three datasets.

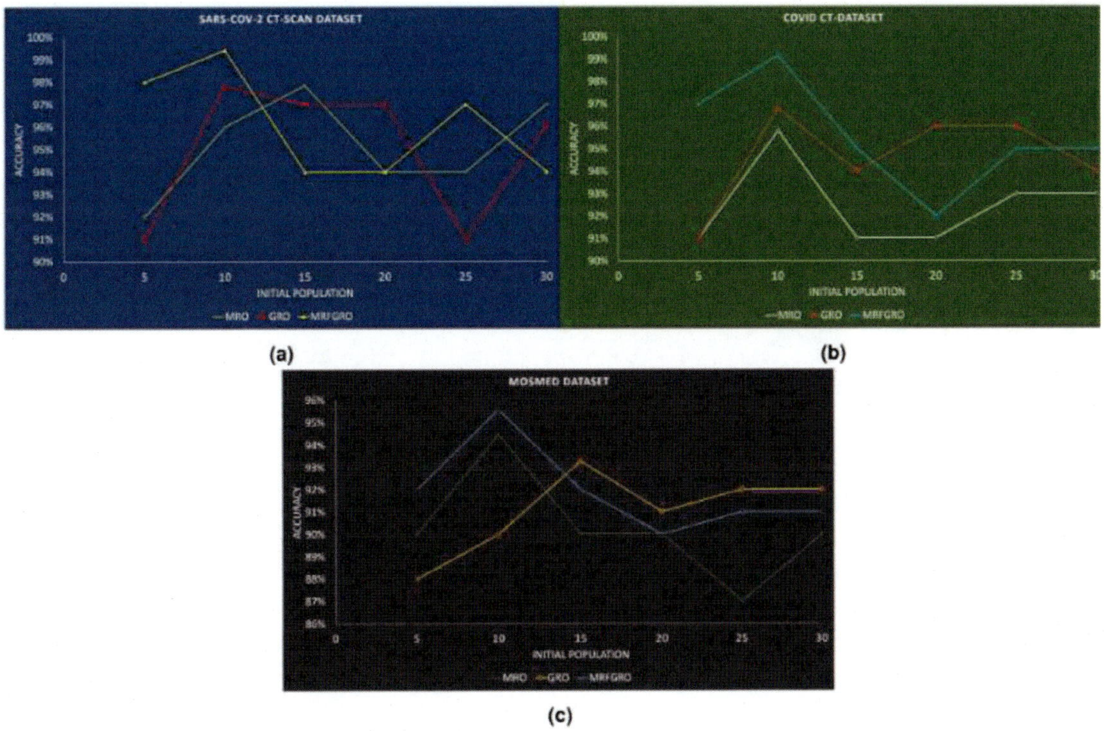

Figure 8. Graph showing the variation of classification accuracies with respect to various hyperparameters of proposed MRFGRO algorithm obtained on: (a) SARS-CoV-2 CT-Scan dataset, (b) Covid CT-dataset and (c) Mosmed dataset.

Evaluation of various optimization techniques

In order to verify the MRFGRO method's superiority, we tested a number of well-known optimization algorithms on all three datasets and compared the outcomes to those attained by the MRFGRO algorithm. These algorithms—Genetic Algorithm (GA), Harmony Search Algorithm (HSA), Particle Swarm Optimizer (PSO), Atom Search Optimizer (ASO), Equilibrium Optimizer (EO), GRO, and MRO—have been selected for comparison. In addition to these, various hybrid algorithms that produced positive results are reported in this article, including GA+EO, PSO+ASO, and HAS+GRO. It should be emphasised that over the past three decades, many optimization methods have been created and are being employed for feature selection. As a result, it is impossible to assess the performances of all potential feature selection algorithm combinations. Therefore, the combinations of the aforementioned algorithms that produced relatively positive and promising outcomes are described here. These optimization techniques using wrappers weren't picked at random. It should be mentioned that while the other three algorithms were invented more recently and have higher efficiency in many competent categories, GA, HSA, and PSO are relatively old algorithms with a successful usage history in many different domains. Table 5 displays the classification accuracy results from several optimization strategies (used for FS in the literature).

	SARS-CoV-2 CT-scan dataset		COVID-CT dataset		MOSMED dataset	
Optimization algorithm	**No. of features**	**Accuracy (%)**	**No. of features**	**Accuracy (%)**	**No. of features**	**Accuracy (%)**
GA	942	92.43	779	91.11	802	91.19
PSO	739	90.15	855	94.49	864	93.29
HAS	1011	94.17	814	92.23	743	92.29
ASO	898	97.57	957	95.59	601	91.11
EO	917	96.69	913	96.28	698	90.19
GRO	868	97.79	809	95.79	713	93.28
MRO	997	97.84	877	96.78	759	94.47
GA+EO	942	95.48	779	95.28	789	94.21
PSO+ASO	1007	97.84	885	92.31	728	91.37
HAS+GRO	941	95.24	855	95.48	738	91.27
MRFGRO	**875**	**99.42**	**756**	**99.15**	**612**	**95.57**

Table 5. Performance comparison of the proposed MRFGRO based FS algorithm with some popular FS algorithms. Best accuracies and number of features selected corresponding to those accuracies are given in bold.

For all three datasets, the proposed MRFGRO algorithm outperforms the old and new FS algorithms by a wide margin in terms of classification accuracy. The MRFGRO method likewise selects extremely few characteristics, which results in outstanding classification accuracy. This shows that the MRFGRO method is quite effective at choosing the best features, increasing the classification accuracy all around.

Comparison with modern techniques

Results from some recent works on the aforementioned datasets have been compared with those from the current one in order to assess the effectiveness of the proposed framework. Tables 6, 7, and 8 present the outcomes of the comparison research. Over all of the aforementioned datasets, the proposed technique produces the best results. Additionally, Shaban et al. achieved outstanding results of 96% in the COVID-CT dataset using conventional machine learning and FS. While H. Aishazly reports 99.4% accuracy on the SARS-CoV-2 CT-scan dataset using transfer learning with ResNet101, which is nearly the same as the accuracy attained by the

MRFGRO model (99.42%). The MOSMED dataset has not yet been extensively studied. Segmentation and classification were performed by Rohila et al., who reported a classification accuracy of 94.9% using their suggested ReCOV-101 net. Overall, we can state that the suggested model of deep feature optimization utilising the MRFGRO algorithm surpasses any model recently published for COVID-19 identification.

Work Ref.	Feature	Method of classification	Obtained accuracy (%)
Loey et al.[49]	Deep features	Data augmentation with classical augmentation technique and CGAN	82.91
Sakagianni et al.[50]	NA	AutoML Cloud Version	88.31
Jhao et al.[32]	Pre-trained CNN learns by itself	TL by DenseNet161 + CSSL	89.1
Alshazly et al.[47]	Transfer learning	DenseNet201	92.2
Shaban et al.[46]	GLCM	HFSM and KNN classifier	96
Saeedi et al.[21]	Deep features of DenseNet121	Nu-SVM	90.61 ± 5
Proposed algorithm	Deep features of ResNet18 and GoogLeNet	MRFGRO based FS algorithm	99.15

Table 6. Comparison of the proposed method with some state-of-the-art methods on COVID-CT dataset.

Work ref.	Feature	Method of classification	Obtained accuracy (%)
Soares et al.[22]	Ensemble learning and classification	Adaboost	95.16
Jaiswal et al.[23]	Deep neural network learns relevant features by itself	DenseNet201	96.25
Alshazly et al.[47]	Transfer learning	ResNet101	99.4
Panwar et al.[51]	Deep neural architecture	Grad-CAM	95.61
Soares et al.[22]	Automated classification with deep xDNN	xDNN	97.38
Proposed algorithm	Deep features of ResNet18 and GoogLeNet	MRFGRO based FS algorithm	99.42

Table 7. Comparison of our proposed work with some state-of-the-art works on SARS-CoV-2 CT-Scan dataset.

Work ref.	Feature	Method of classification	Obtained accuracy (%)
Sharma et al.[52]	No traditional features as it is an end to end learning method	ResNet18 + GradCAM	91
Rohila et al.[48]	Segmentation and classification	ReCOV-101	94.9
Proposed algorithm	Deep features of ResNet18 and GoogLeNet	MRFGRO based FS algorithm	95.57

Table 8. Comparison of our proposed work with some state-of-the-art works on MOSMED dataset.

The Bottom Line

In this study, we suggested a brand-new hybrid FS model termed MRFGRO, which has been tested on three common COVID-19 detection datasets based on CT scans. Because deep features have the previously described advantages over standard features, we computed deep features rather than using typical feature engineering to do this assignment. The "Results and discussion" section covers the cutting-edge findings from all three datasets. In the "Results and discussion" section, it is also explained how effective and superior hybrid MRFGRO is to other FS algorithms. Despite the proposed framework's many benefits, there are some drawbacks as well. Finally, we outline some potential future developments of this study while keeping in mind the MFRGRO algorithm's limitations:

- We have solely used CT-scan datasets to test our model. Chest X-Ray image datasets can also be taken into account to verify the work's robustness.
- For effective learning of the CNN models, hyperparameters of transfer learning such as

optimizer, learning rates, batch size, etc. are crucial. Through much experimentation, we were able to determine the best study parameters. There are, nevertheless, some effective methods to locate them, such as by utilising specific optimization strategies. Deep learning models can have their hyperparameters fixed using Bayesian optimization.

- Squeeze net, Exception net, Capsule net, and more sophisticated neural networks have also been developed recently. Deep feature extraction can also be accomplished with these nets.
- It is also possible to consider the initial population selection of the MRFGRO method, which may aid in boosting the algorithm's rate of convergence.

Chapter 10

CNN models are fused fuzzy rank-based employing the Gompertz algorithm to evaluate COVID-19 CT images[10]

Introduction

One of the most contagious diseases of the twenty-first century, COVID-19 has paralyzed human civilization as a whole. As of January 2021, the novel coronavirus, whose spread began in Wuhan, China, in December 2019, had already resulted in 87 million infections and nearly 2 million fatalities. Due to the paucity of critical care facilities, the epidemic has already had a devastating impact on the global human economy and the health system (ICUs). The unchecked, undetected infection proliferation is the key issue here.

Reverse Transcription Polymerase Chain Reaction (RT-PCR) tests based on swabs and antibody tests based on blood samples make up the majority of the COVID-19 detection tests now available. The lengthy RT-PCR test's time to produce results delays patient prognosis and diagnosis as well as evaluation of the severity of the disease. Additionally, the lack of equipment prevents large-scale RT-PCR testing from being performed in developing nations with overpopulation. As a result, there is a need for some alternate techniques for COVID-19 detection. One such option is to examine chest X-ray or CT scan pictures. Patients from all socioeconomic situations may readily obtain and benefit from this procedure since it is considerably faster. Figure 1 illustrates a lung CT-scan picture of a patient with COVID-19 infection.

Artificial Intelligence, which complements the efforts of the clinicians and has been shown to be a successful alternative in other biomedical applications, is another method to diagnose the infection instead of needing professional radiologists or doctors. In comparison to more conventional techniques, data mining or machine learning is a helpful tool for extracting characteristics from medical pictures, such as Gabor features and Gray-Level Co-occurrence matrix features. Analyzing large-scale, diverse medical picture databases in hospitals is also feasible. There are several data mining techniques that have been used to the COVID-19 identification job, such as KNN and ANN-based classifiers, Support Vector Machine (SVM), the Bayesian approach, decision trees, etc. The practice of combining decision scores from many CNN base models based on Transfer Learning has been quite popular in recent years.

---

10 *Landmark paper: Kundu, R., Basak, H., Singh, P.K. et al. Fuzzy rank-based fusion of CNN models using Gompertz function for screening COVID-19 CT-scans. Sci Rep **11**, 14133 (2021). https://doi.org/10.1038/s41598-021-93658-y*

However, in this study we suggest screening of Covid-19 CT scans by applying a less researched strategy: by producing fuzzy rankings using the Gompertz function, a mathematical model which has been not been investigated previously in this domain, adding to the originality of our research.

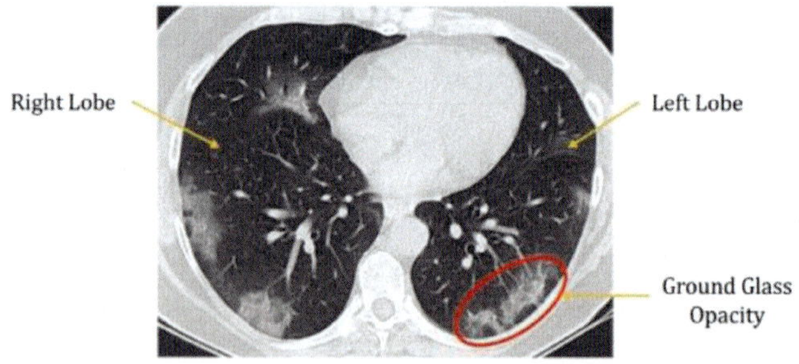

Fig 1: An illustration of a COVID-infected lung CT scan. The SARS-COV-2 dataset served as the source for the CT scan picture. The identifying characteristic of the COVID-19 infection is the ground glass opacity indicated by the red circle in the picture.

In order to improve performance overall and provide more accurate predictions than the individual contributing models, ensemble learning is used to combine the key characteristics of its constituent models. Ensembling lessens the spread or dispersion of the predictions made by the different models, making them resilient. Ensemble methods outperform rival base learner models by reducing the variance of prediction errors and introducing some bias. In this study, we provide the Gompertz function-based Fuzzy Ranking technique. This fusion has the benefit of using adaptive weights based on the confidence ratings of each classifier used to create the ensemble to provide the final prediction for each sample. The Gompertz function was initially developed to transfer a set of data from life tables through a single function, and it was based on the idea that mortality falls exponentially with age until saturating to an asymptote. In a complicated picture classification situation where a classifier's confidence score for a prediction class seldom ever reaches completely zero but instead takes on a modest value, such a function might be helpful for merging the classifiers' confidence ratings. Compared to the conventional RT-PCR approach, CT imaging has been shown to have more discriminating patterns to assure greater sensitivity and specificity. In order to supplement and enhance the early identification of COVID19, artificial intelligence (AI) has been extensively employed to extract patterns from the imaging datasets available. Machine learning and deep learning have many applications in the literature.

On the SARS-COV-2 CT-scan dataset, Jaiswal et al. and Das et al. applied transfer learning with DenseNet-201 for COVID classification. To categorize COVID CT data, Panwar et al. modified the original topology by adding four extra fully connected layers to a pre-trained VGG-19 network. In order to address the issue of the lack of accessible data, Karbhari et al. created Auxiliary Classifer GAN (ACGAN), which synthesizes chest radiograph pictures and employs a classifier to do classification on the synthesized data. In order to extract deep features, Angelov et al. employed the Google Neural Network architecture. However, they trained the model from scratch rather than using pre-trained ImageNet weights. On the dataset of chest CT scans, the deep features that were recovered were utilized to train an MLP classifier for the final classification.

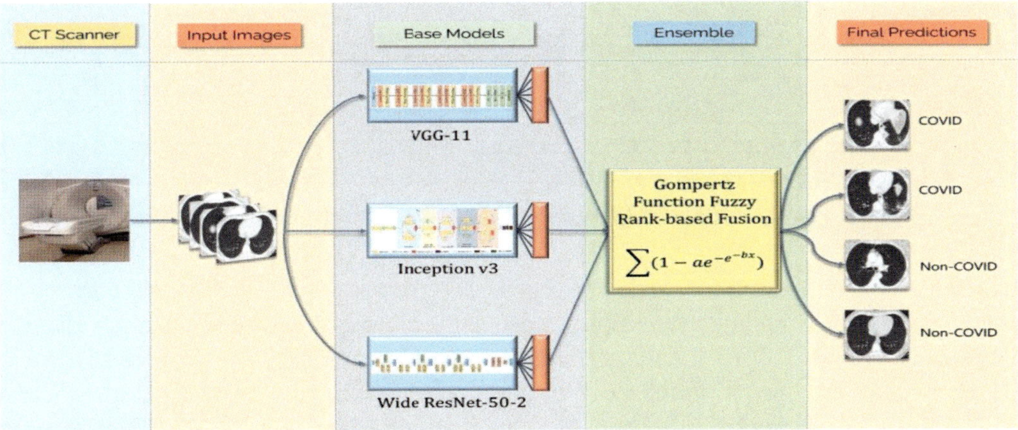

Fig 2: Overall effectiveness of the suggested framework. The chest CT scan pictures utilized in this study were taken from the SARS-COV-2 dataset, and the CT scanner image (open access) was taken from the Progressive Diagnostic Imaging website.

Inspiration and involvement

The global COVID-19 outbreak compelled the medical staff to concentrate of time caring for patients who put their own lives in danger, including COVID patients and those who are contaminated with other diseases. Despite the significant research being done to create a vaccine, it will take longer time to reach every individual; as a result, the transmission of the coronavirus is still crucial, particularly when new strains of the virus appear all over the world. The lengthy, time-consuming, and only 71% sensitive RT-PCR test procedure for COVID-19. A framework for separating COVID-19 patients from non-COVID patients based on chest CT-scan pictures is developed in this research with these facts in mind. By storing the model weights and using the test pictures to create the predictions, the proposed ensemble framework may be utilized as a plug-and-play model. This makes the suggested framework useful for usage in the field and suitable for the Computer-Aided Diagnosis of COVID-19. It enables non-experts to create predictions on fresh pictures with ease.

The following are some of the work's key features:

1. We use transfer learning to produce the first judgment scores using three typical CNN models: VGG-11, Wide ResNet-50-2, and Inception v3. End-to-end classification using a deep learning model requires a huge quantity of data, which is frequently not accessible in the biomedical domain.
2. Since ensembling is a potent method for combining the discriminating features of all the contributing models, it has been utilized to combine the decision scores of the aforementioned models.
3. The constituent classifiers are given fuzzy rankings using the ensemble approach and a re-parameterized Gompertz function. Fuzzy fusion outperforms standard ensemble approaches because it uses adaptive priority depending on the confidence ratings of the classifiers for each sample to be predicted.
4. The Gompertz function, which is important for ensembling the decision scores of the CNN models since the decision score of a class predicted by a classifier seldom approaches genuinely zero, grows exponentially before saturating to an asymptote.
5. Two publicly accessible datasets of chest CT-scan pictures that are both easier to execute and more sensitive to COVID-19 were utilized to assess the efficacy of this approach. The findings achieved significantly outperform the currently used techniques.

Dataset	Category	Total no. of images	No. of images in Train set	No. of images in Test set
SARS-COV-2	COVID	1252	876	376
	Non-COVID	1229	860	369
Harvard Dataverse	COVID	2167	1517	650
	Non-COVID	2005	1404	601

Table 1: Image distribution throughout the two datasets utilized in this experiment.

Results

Datasets

We have utilized two publicly accessible datasets, the Harvard Dataverse chest CT dataset and the Soares et al. SARS-COV-2 dataset, to assess the efficacy of the proposed system. As seen in Table 1, there are uneven numbers of photos in both databases. For this study, the dataset from the Harvard Dataverse has been presented as a 2-class issue with COVID and Non-COVID classes.

Implementation

The VGG-11 model has been used in this study instead of other deeper CNN variations like VGG-13, VGG-16, or VGG-19 since, as Table 2 shows, the deeper models only slightly improve performance while costing more to compute. Table 2 shows that, although having between 1M and 6M more parameters than the VGG-11 variation, VGG-13 and VGG-16 only slightly outperform it in terms of accuracy (0.13% for VGG-13 and 0.4% for VGG-16). On the other hand, the performance of the VGG-19 model, which includes 11 million more parameters than the VGG-11 model, has decreased. The medical domain has a limited amount of data, thus just adding more layers linearly does not improve the model's ability to capture the complicated data pattern. Based on these experimental findings, we combined the other two aforementioned CNN models with the VGG-11 model to extract the supplementary information from the data. WideResNet-50-2 and Inception v3 models with the various VGG models are used in the suggested ensemble technique in order to further support the selection of VGG-11 over its other widely used variations. Table 3 displays the ensemble's findings. The table shows that using the VGG-11 model to execute the ensemble produces the best results, demonstrating that the VGG-11 model obtains supplementary information with regard to the WideResNet-50-2 and Inception v3 models, improving the performance of the individual learners through the ensemble. As a result, in the current study, we formed the ensemble using three CNN models: VGG-11, WideResNet-50-2, and Inception v3.

Table 4 displays the outcomes of the suggested ensemble architecture on two publicly accessible datasets. The table includes both the net results and the results broken down by class. The model has been demonstrated to be trustworthy by achieving high classification accuracies of 98.93% on the SARS-COV-2 dataset and 98.80% on the Harvard Dataverse dataset, as well as high sensitivity values of 98.93% and 98.79% on both datasets, respectively. The Stochastic Gradient Descent optimizer was used to fine-tune the transfer learning-based CNN models for 50 iterations each, starting with an initial learning rate of 0.001. The confusion matrices from the two utilized datasets are displayed in Figure 3. Even if the classification is imperfect, there are relatively few samples in the "COVID-19" and "Non-COVID" groups that were incorrectly classified compared to samples that were correctly classified.

VGG Model Used	Accuracy (%)	Precision (%)	Recall (%)	F1-Score (%)
VGG-11	98.93	98.93	98.93	98.93
VGG-13	98.25	98.26	98.25	98.25
VGG-16	98.12	98.13	98.12	98.12
VGG-19	97.04	97.05	94.04	97.04

Table 2:Performance on the SARS-COV-2 dataset (measured in terms of accuracy) offered by several VGG versions and their parameter count.

VGG Model Used	Accuracy (%)	Precision (%)	Recall (%)	F1-Score (%)
VGG-11	98.93	98.93	98.93	98.93
VGG-13	98.25	98.26	98.25	98.25
VGG-16	98.12	98.13	98.12	98.12
VGG-19	97.04	97.05	94.04	97.04

Table 3: Results from a combination of WideResNet-50-2 and Inception v3 on the SARS-COV-2 dataset using several VGG models.

Dataset	Class	Accuracy (%)	Specificity (%)	Precision (%)	Sensitivity (%)	F1 Score (%)
SARS-COV-2	COVID	99.20	98.92	98.68	99.20	98.94
	Non-COVID	98.65	98.94	99.18	98.64	98.91
	Net Results	98.93	98.93	98.93	98.93	98.93
Harvard Dataverse	COVID	99.08	99.00	98.62	99.08	98.85
	Non-COVID	98.50	98.62	99.00	98.50	98.75
	Net Results	98.80	98.82	98.81	98.79	98.80

Table 4: Results acquired using the suggested ensemble architecture on datasets from the Harvard Dataverse and the SARS-COV-2 test sets.

Discussion

Using the Gompertz function, we propose a Fuzzy rank-based fusion of several CNN base models in this study, utilizing more in-depth data from various CNN modalities. The phenomenon of wrongly identifying a negative number as a positive one is known as the false positive rate (FPR). The high prevalence of false-positive results in medical data analysis can be harmful, particularly in the case of COVID-19 identification, because labeling an infected case as non-infected might lead to the projected non-infected individual becoming a super-spreader, which can lead to additional disease spread.

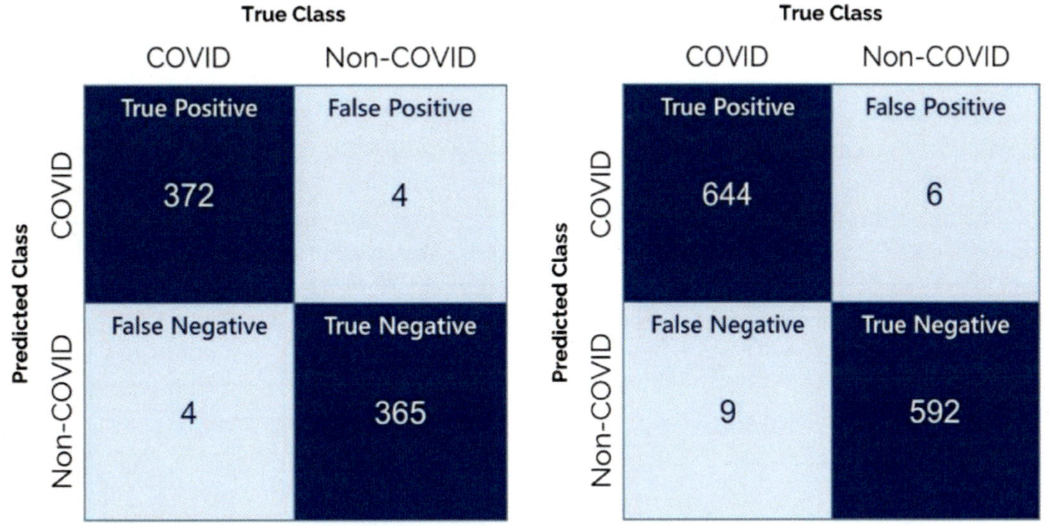

(a) SARS-COV-2 dataset **(b)** Harvard Dataverse dataset

Fig 3: Confusion matrices produced by the ensemble model suggested on the two datasets taken into consideration in the current work.

The ROC curves produced using the suggested method on the two datasets is displayed in Fig. 4. The results demonstrate the excellence of the suggested strategy and highlight its use in the analysis of medical data by demonstrating the significantly low False Positive Rate on both datasets utilized in this study. Also provided are the Area Under the Curve (AUC) values that were determined using the relevant datasets. An AUC value of 98.92% was found on the SARS-COV-2 dataset, whereas 98.78% was found on the Harvard Data verse dataset. A greater value on the X-axis in a ROC curve suggests that there are more false-positive cases than real negative ones. A larger value on the Y-axis, however, indicates that there are more real positive situations than false negatives. Because the point (0, 1) on the ROC graph denotes the point of maximal sensitivity and specificity, the more the ROC curve is tilted toward the top-left corner of the Cartesian plane, the greater the classifier's ability to discriminate between positive and negative class samples. The ROC obtained on the SARS-COV-2 dataset in Fig. 4a is more oriented toward the top-left corner than the ROC obtained on the Harvard Dataverse dataset in Fig. 4b, as can be observed from the figure. To be more precise, we can state that the SARS-COV-2 dataset's ROC is larger than that of the Harvard Dataverse dataset since the classifier is better able to differentiate between samples in that dataset.

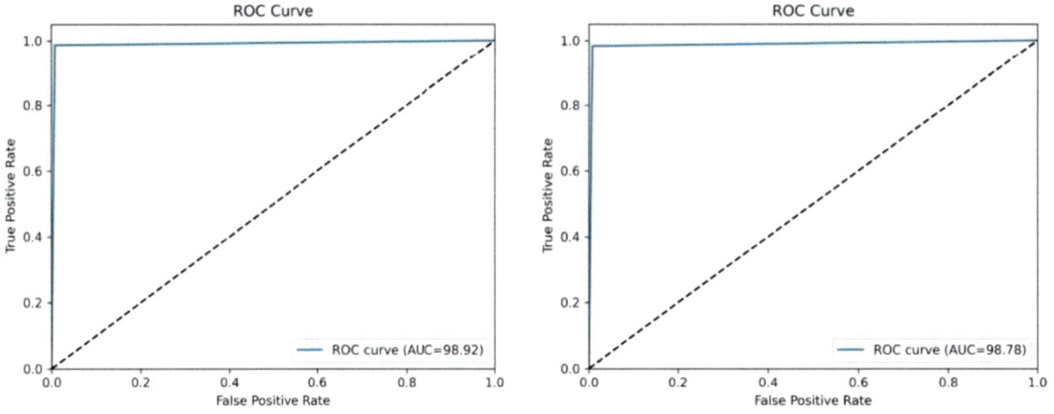

(a) SARS-COV-2 dataset **(b)** Harvard Dataverse dataset

Fig 4: ROC curves from the two datasets using the suggested ensemble model.

Table 4's high sensitivity values for the proposed approach on the datasets show that the ensemble strategy performs well, even outperforming the RT-PCR testing method, which has a sensitivity of just 71%. The robustness of the framework is justified by the great accuracy. Figure 5 displays the loss curves that the base learners on the SARS-COV-2 and Harvard Dataverse datasets utilized in this study. The models only need to be fine-tuned on the COVID dataset since we employ transfer learning models that were previously trained on the ImageNet dataset. We train the models for 50 epochs each to achieve this. As can be observed from the figures, because the majority of the model weights have already been tuned through training on ImageNet, the performance of the models reaches saturation at about 20 epochs. For both datasets, we note that the little overftting of the models in VGG-11 and WideResNet-50-2 is a concern, although the issue is less noticeable in Inception v3.

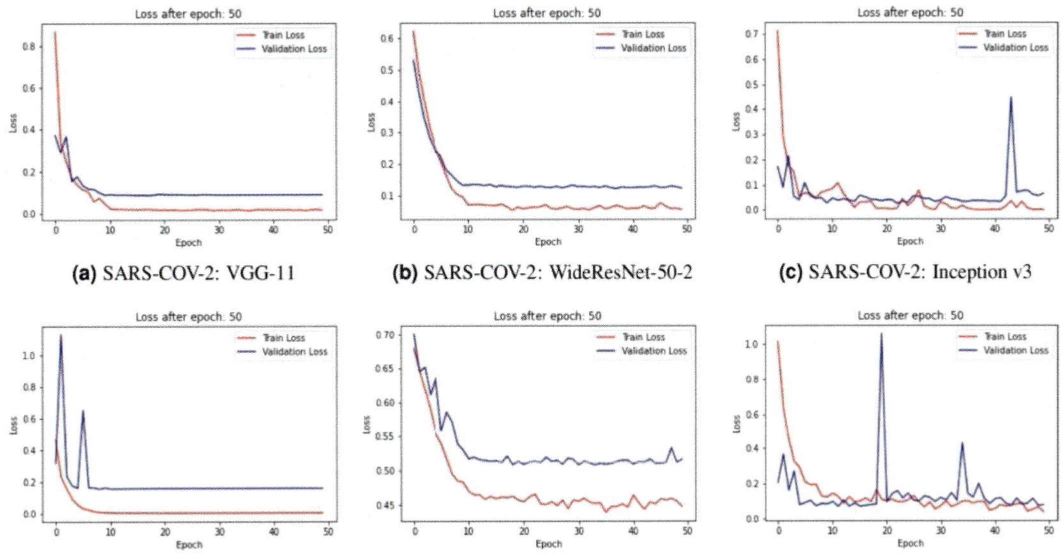

(a) SARS-COV-2: VGG-11 (b) SARS-COV-2: WideResNet-50-2 (c) SARS-COV-2: Inception v3

(d) Harvard Dataverse: VGG-11 (e) Harvard Dataverse: WideResNet-50-2 (f) Harvard Dataverse: Inception v3

Fig 5: Loss curves that the base learners that made up the ensemble in this study's two datasets had obtained. The loss curves for the SARS-COV-2 dataset are shown in (a) through (c), while those for the Harvard Dataverse dataset are shown in (d) through (f).

	Accuracy (%)	
Standard Model	**SARS-COV-2**	**Harvard Dataverse**
VGG-11[37]	96.38	95.92
DenseNet161[38]	96.91	95.38
Wide ResNet-50-2[39]	96.78	92.57
ResNet34[40]	96.11	96.87
ResNet152[40]	95.17	94.33
Inception v3[41]	92.15	97.64
Proposed method	98.93	98.80

Table 5: The suggested framework is put up against several common CNN models.

Evaluation Against Conventional CNN-Based Structures

Since there are frequently insufficient large datasets for building CNNs from scratch, transfer learning is a common solution for issues in the biomedical image classification domain. Transfer Learning facilitates feature learning by allowing a model developed on a large dataset to be fine-tuned by the sparse data in the present challenge. The results of comparing the proposed ensemble-learning based framework to typical CNN Transfer Learning models, including those utilized to create the ensemble, are shown in Table 5. In the current study, the decision scores were fused using the models VGG-1137, Wide ResNet-50-239, and Inception v341, and it is evident that the ensemble of these models performs better than the individual models, demonstrating the validity of the ensemble framework.

Ensemble technique	Accuracy (%)	
	SARS-COV-2	Harvard dataverse
Multiplication Rule	95.82	98.24
Maximum	96.78	98.47
Majority Voting	97.65	97.54
Average	97.83	97.91
Weighted Average	98.12	98.64
Choquet Integral	98.52	98.48
Sugeno Integral	98.52	98.48
Proposed Gompertz function based ensemble	98.93	98.80

Table 6: The proposed Gompertz function-based ensemble method is compared to some well-known ensemble techniques.

Dataset	Method	Accuracy (%)	Precision (%)	Recall (%)	F1-Score	Specificity (%)
SARS-COV-2	Silva et al.[42]	97.89	95.33	97.60	96.45	-
	Horry et al.[43]	97.40	99.10	95.50	97.30	-
	Halder et al.[44]	97.00	95.00	98.00	97.00	95.00
	Jaiswal et al.[28]	96.25	96.29	96.29	96.29	96.21
	Sen et al.[27]	95.32	95.30	95.30	95.30	-
	Panwar et al.[30]	94.04	95.00	94.00	94.50	95.86
	Soares et al.[32]	88.60	89.70	88.60	89.15	-
	Proposed method	98.93	98.93	98.93	98.93	98.93
Harvard Dataverse	Krishevsky et al.[45]	94.72	95.17	94.72	94.94	95.17
	Szegedy et al.[46]	92.64	92.64	93.54	93.09	92.64
	Sandler et al.[47]	89.68	88.12	89.68	88.89	89.68
	Proposed Method	98.80	98.82	98.81	98.79	98.80

Table 7: The suggested ensemble framework is compared to state-of-the-art approaches on the SARSCOV-2 and Harvard Dataverse datasets.

Comparison with various common ensemble methods

Ensemble models outperform individual models because they combine the key traits of all the classifiers that contribute to them. Over time, many well-liked ensemble techniques have developed; some of these techniques have been examined in this study to support the superiority of the proposed ensemble over current techniques. The fuzzy logic-based ensemble performs particularly well because, for each sample, the confidence in a classifier's prediction is taken into account when giving the predictions weights to determine the final classification of an image. Table 6 displays the results obtained using the same three CNN models to create the ensemble. It is clear from this table that the Gompertz function-based decision fusion outperforms the others significantly. The fuzzy integrals-based ensembles (Choquet Integral and Sugeno Integral) perform most closely to the suggested ensemble technique, although the weighted average-based ensemble approach also produces good results. The Weighted Average Ensemble is a static process in which it is not possible to dynamically refactor the weights to the classifiers at the time of prediction. Fuzzy fusion-based techniques, on the other hand, can solve this issue and prioritize the confidence scores, making them a better approach for the ensemble. The proposed Gompertz function-based fuzzy ranking ensemble outperforms the Choquet and Sugeno integrals-based ensembles despite using a similar methodology, demonstrating the effectiveness of the approach.

Compared to modern technology

Since the start of the pandemic, a number of COVID detection techniques have been proposed in the literature, however a large portion of them rely on chest X-ray datasets, which are often less sensitive than chest CT-scan pictures. On the SARS-COV-2 and Harvard Dataverse datasets, which were employed in the current study, some of the most recent state-of-the-art approaches' findings are compared with those of our proposed ensemble model in Table 7. Due to the dearth of publically accessible chest CT data, the majority of approaches rely on transfer learning for classification; nevertheless, end-to-end classification using transfer learning is insufficient. Combining decision scores from many CNN models enhances performance by capturing the complementing information that each model provides. To the best of our knowledge, there are no published papers on the Harvard Dataverse dataset, thus we contrast our findings with several well-known CNN models for transfer learning. The suggested method's excellent classifcation accuracy and sensitivity results in robust performance.

McNemar's Test	*p* value	
Compared with	SARS-COV-2	Harvard Dataverse
VGG-11	4.49E-02	9.50E-03
Wide ResNet-50-2	1.05E-04	1.93E-15
Inception v3	2.88E-02	8.40E-03

Table 8: McNemar's Test results for ensemble models for both datasets: All cases reject null.

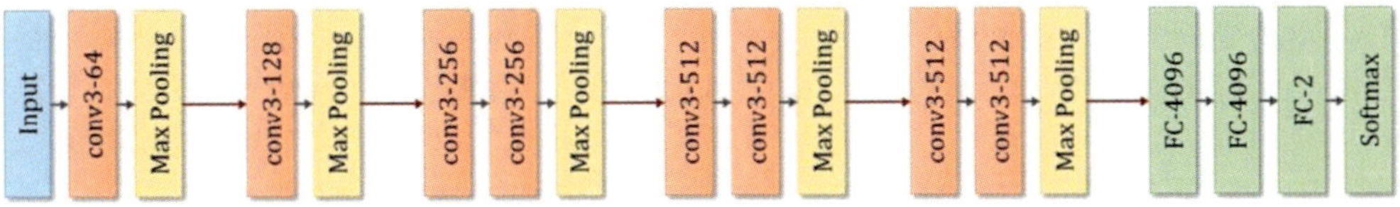

Fig 6: Base model architecture for the VGG-11.

Analysis of data: McNemar's test

In order to statistically evaluate the performance of the proposed ensemble technique to the constituent models whose decision scores were utilized to build the ensemble, we applied the McNemar's test. The results of McNemar's test on the SARS-COV-2 and Harvard Dataverse datasets are displayed in Table 8. McNemar's test's p-value should ideally be less than 5% in order to reject the null hypothesis, and Table 8 clearly shows that this is the case in every scenario when the p value is less than 0.05. But in every instance, the null hypothesis is rejected. This explains why the overall model is different from any of the contributing models since the proposed ensemble framework incorporates the supplementary information provided by the individual classifiers and produces better predictions.

Methods

The two primary steps of the proposed framework for classifying COVID-19 from CT-scan images are the production of confidence scores from various models and the fusing of the decision scores using the Gompertz function and a fuzzy rank-based method. The next sections provide an explanation of these two phases.

Calculation of the confidence score

Three transfer learning-based CNN models, VGG-11, Inception v3, and Wide ResNet-50-2, are first used in the proposed system to calculate the confidence ratings on the sample pictures. The same sets are utilized for all the models, and both datasets are divided into train and test sets at a ratio of 70% to 30%. On top of the ImageNet weights, the networks are fine-tuned using the Stochastic Gradient Descent (SGD) optimizer and Rectified Linear Unit (ReLU) activation functions for 50 epochs each. The following subsections provide a brief description of the three CNN models.

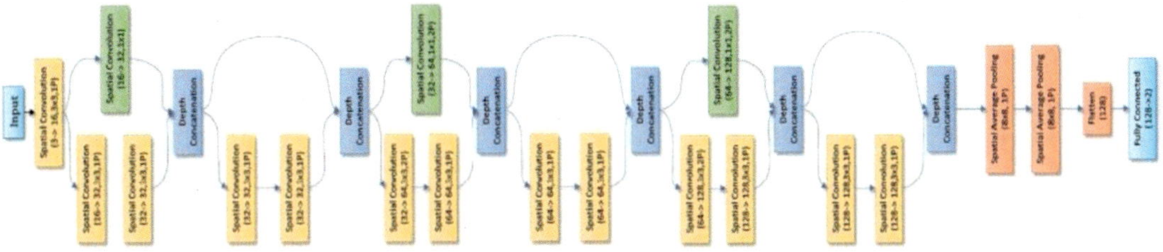

Fig 7: Wide ResNet-50-2 base model architecture.

VGG-11

In 2014, VGG-11 was put out for the International Visual Recognition Challenge (ILSVRC), and it has since been modified and used in a number of picture classification challenges. Several alternative CNN designs were presented in the VGG group to utilize the usage of depth in convolution networks; we selected the VGG-11 for this purpose, which comprises of 8 convolution layers and 3 fully connected (FC) layers, creating 11 layers in total, thus justifying the nomenclature. The network anticipates a 3-channel (i.e., RGB picture) of length 224×224, followed by a number of convolution layers with a very tiny receptive feld of dimension 3 ×3 and stride=1 with the appropriate padding. Then, non-overlapping Max-pooling layers measuring 2×2 are added, with padding of size 2 placed between some of the convolution layers. The VGG-11's hidden layers work as ReLU activators. Figure 6 depicts the architecture of the VGG-11 model.

Wide ResNet-50-2.

Zagoruyko et al. presented the wide ResNet design in 2016. The Broad ResNet model reduces the training time and parameters without sacrificing performance in order to address some of the issues with ResNet by making the network shallow and wide. To enhance the depth, the ResNet developers made the network shallow, which raises the potential that the network won't be able to learn anything during training because there won't be anything to push it to traverse through the residual block weights.

This might result in a feature reuse issue when a small number of blocks contain critical information but the majority of the blocks only make a modest contribution to the final output. Fig. 7 depicts the Wide ResNet-50-2 CNN model's design.

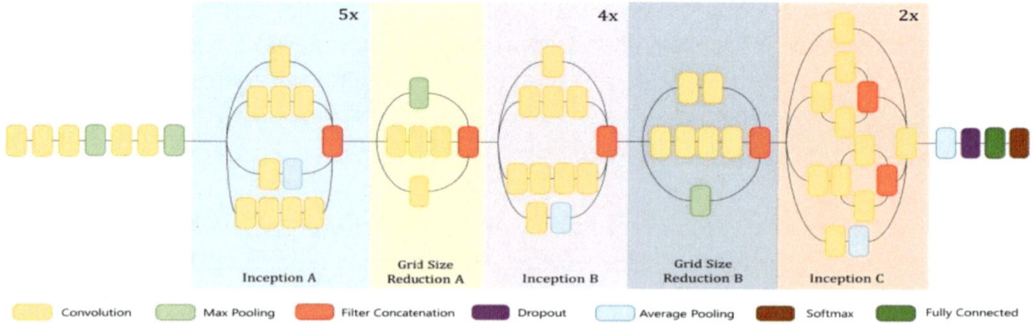

Fig 8: The Inception V3 basic model's architecture

Inception v3

One of the most popular deep learning models is Inception v3, which is a member of the Inception family. To address the shortcomings of the earlier Inception models, Inception v3 makes use of a number of improvements, including an auxiliary classifier, factorized convolutional operations, batch normalization, the RMSProp optimizer, and label smoothing. It creates feature maps with various dimensions in various layers from an input image with dimensions of 299 by 299 by 3. The inception block of Inception v3 gives us the option to use many feature extraction filters from a single feature map. To extract deeper features, these characteristics with various filters are concatenated and sent to the following layer. Figure 8 depicts the architecture of the Inception v3 model utilized in this research.

Gompertz function fuzzy ranking ensemble

The main justification for using a fuzzy rank-based approach is that, unlike traditional ensemble approaches like the average rule, weighted average rule, etc., where classifiers need to be associated with a pre-define fixed weight, this method prioritizes each classifier's confidence in its predictions for each individual test case. In order to detect COVID19 instances from CT scans, we employ the reparameterized Gompertz algorithm to construct the fuzzy rankings for each CNN classifier. We then combine the predictions from three different CNN classifiers, namely VGG-11, Wide ResNet-50-2, and Inception v3.

In terms of biology, the Gompertz model predicts a rise in mortality rate with age, signifying a greater susceptibility to the causes of death experienced by young people. The exponential term of the Gompertz function, where it is believed that becoming older entails a higher likelihood of dying, shows how quickly this vulnerability increases with age. The suggested re-parameterized Gompertz function is depicted in Figure 9, where the independent variable 'x' stands for the classifier's projected confidence score for a test sample. For each picture I, there should be M judgment scores (also known as confidence factors of classifiers) $\{CF^{(1)}, CF^{(2)}, \ldots CF^{(M)}\}$. Since we utilized three CNN models to get the confidence scores on the datasets, M in our case equals 3. Following Eq. (1), the decision scores from the dataset are normalized, where C is the number of classes in the dataset.

$$\sum_{c=1}^{C} CF_c^{(i)} = 1.0;\ \forall i,\ i = 1,2,3,\ldots,M \tag{1}$$

The confidence ratings are used to produce fuzzy ranks for all samples in the dataset that correspond to various classes. The Gompertz function, as shown in Eq., generates the fuzzy rank for a class c based on the confidence ratings of the ith classifier (2).

$$R_c^{(i)} = \left(1 - exp\left[-exp\left[-2.0 \times CF_c^{(i)}\right]\right]\right),\ \forall i, c;\ \ i = 1,2,\ldots,M;\ c = 1,2,\ldots \tag{2}$$

The value of R_c^i falls between [0.127, 0.632]; the smallest value, 0.127, corresponds to rank 1 (best rank), i.e., more confidence results in a lower (better) rank value. The fuzzy rank sum (FRS_c) and complement of confidence factor sum ($CCFS_c$) are now computed as in equations (3) and (4), respectively, assuming $K^{(i)}$ denotes the top k ranks, i.e., ranks 1, 2,..., k, corresponding to class c.

$$FRS_c = \sum_{i=1}^{M} \begin{cases} R_c^{(i)}, & \text{if } R_c^{(i)} \in K^{(i)} \\ P_c^R, & \text{otherwise} \end{cases} \tag{3}$$

$$CCFS_c = \frac{1}{M} \sum_{i=1}^{M} \begin{cases} CF_c^{(i)}, & \text{if } R_c^{(i)} \in K^{(i)} \\ P_c^{CF}, & \text{otherwise} \end{cases} \tag{4}$$

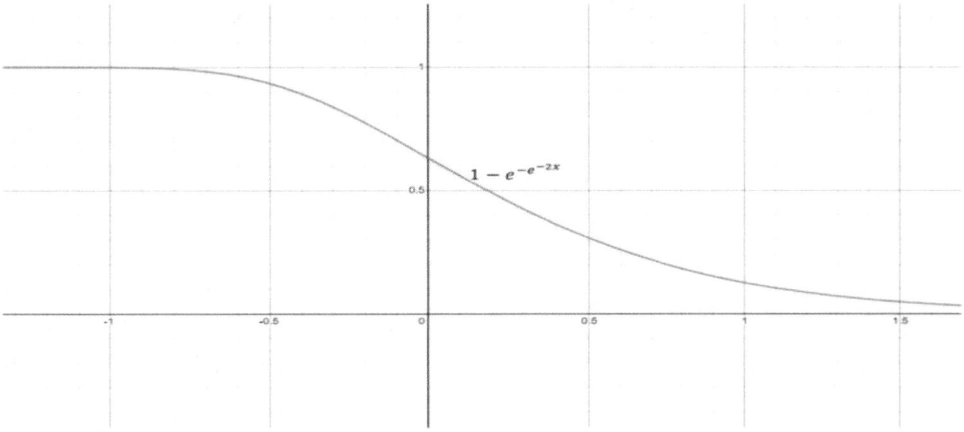

Fig 9: Showing the re-parameterized Gompertz function that was employed in this investigation

If class c is not among the top k class rankings, penalty values P_C^R and P_C^{CF} are applied. By setting CF(i)c = 0 in Eq. (2) and setting the value of PCFc to 0.0, the value of PRc is estimated to be 0.632. Te penalty values prevent class C from emerging as an improbable winner. The combination of FRS_c and $CCFS_c$ yields the final decision score, which is utilized to produce the ensemble model's final predictions. The final decision score (FDS) is determined using Equation. (5).

$$FDS_c = FRS_c \times CCFS_c \tag{5}$$

The final projected class for dataset instance I, which is provided in Eq, is determined by finding the class with the lowest FDS value (6).

$$class(\mathbf{I}) = \underset{c=1,2,\ldots,C}{\arg\min}\{FDS_c\} \tag{6}$$

The suggested ensemble approach's computational complexity is O(n), where n is the number of classes in the dataset.

Conclusion

Because nearly every nation in the world suffers from a lack of medical facilities, early and precise COVID-19 detection is now essential due to the growing threat of new coronaviruses. In order to do this, we have developed a completely automated COVID-19 detection system using deep learning in this research. This framework gets away with the time-consuming RT-PCR testing procedure in favor of classifying chest CT-scan pictures, which are more widely accessible. In order to identify the COVID-19 instances, we have also shown how fuzzy rank-based fusion may be applied to decision scores derived from several CNN models. To the best of our knowledge, the suggested approach is the first of its type to create an ensemble model for COVID-19 detection utilizing the Gompertz function. The significant accomplishments of the proposed technique include its low false-positive rate, high classifcation accuracies of 98.93% and 98.80%, and sensitivities of 98.93% and 98.79% on the SARS-COV-2 and Harvard Dataverse datasets, respectively. The suggested framework has been contrasted with several methodologies from the literature, well-liked ensemble schemes used in various research challenges, and simply transfer learning-based approaches. The suggested fuzzy rank-based fusion system has consistently outperformed the aforementioned techniques, demonstrating its superiority.

Future experiments with various CNN designs and fusion techniques are intended to enhance performance. In order to demonstrate the robustness of the suggested model, we also want to verify the proposed methodology on other datasets. Since an ensemble of many models involves a considerably higher computing cost than a single model architecture, we may strive to create a more computationally efficient model for COVID-19 detection. We may explore methods like snapshot assembly, etc., for this. Additionally, we can observe from the loss curve analysis that certain models have overfitting problems, so we may try to fix that by employing methods like data augmentation or by trying to find bigger datasets to test on. To further improve the CNN models' capacity for recognition, we may partition the lung CT images prior to classification. Since the proposed model can be used as a plug-and-play model where new test images can be passed through the saved model weights and the ensemble prediction can be computed, we anticipate that it will be of great assistance to medical professionals for early detection which may result in an immediate diagnosis of the COVID-19 patients.

Chapter 11

Graph CovidNet: A neural network-based model for identifying COVID19 from chest CT images and X-rays[11]

Introduction

Disease caused by the Coronavirus (COVID-19) has caused a global emergency of unparalleled proportions in recent years. The underlying cause of this illness is the SARS-CoV-2 coronavirus, a new virus with a large single-stranded RNA genomic envelope. Although this virus started in Wuhan, China, in December 2019, it later badly infected America and a number of other nations in Europe in the early days of the year 2020. Recent figures show that compared to other infected nations, both America and India has a greater number of confirmed cases. Given the negative effects of this circumstance, the World Health Organization (WHO) declared COVID-19 a global health emergency on January 30, 2020. It has been shown that both CXRs and CT scans are beneficial for diagnosing the SARS-CoV-2. Medical professionals value CXR pictures higher since they can quickly access them from radiology departments. Radiologists claim that CXR pictures make it easier to grasp the chest pathology. However, CT scans offer great sensitivity; in a case study in Wuhan, for instance, 97% of the positive CT scans were confirmed. It is necessary to build an automated and quick approach that can identify COVID-19 from chest CT-scans or CXR images because to the exponential surge of cases. Examples of these CT-scan and CXR pictures are shown in Figure 1.

SARS-CoV-2 often affects the lungs, and CT scans and CXRs can show murky development of cough surrounding the lungs. The typical COVID-19 symptoms are fatigue, a dry cough, and fever. The symptoms of COVID-19 can range in severity from extremely minor to serious. Some people may only exhibit a few symptoms, and other times there may be no signs at all. In other cases, symptoms begin to deteriorate just a week later and recurrent breathlessness and pneumonia may occur. The risk of developing a severe disease from COVID-19 may be increased in older adults and those with chronic medical problems. Now, CT scans and CXR imaging may not be useful in cases of moderate COVID-19 since the cough clouds may not be obvious. Any other type of pneumonia might also be undetected by CT scan and CXR due to the presence of turbid lungs. Therefore, to accurately categorize these CT-scans and CXR, an advanced classification model is required. Numerous people have become infected due to this epidemic, necessitating urgent testing, medical care, and quarantine. The most popular method to find the virus is a difficult Real Time Reverse Transcription Polymerase Chain Reaction (RT-PCR) test, however it takes 1-2 days to acquire the results. Therefore, an alternate strategy to deal with this pandemic that has a significantly shorter turnaround time can be considered: an automated and accurate classification method that uses CT-scans or CXRs. Even though

---

11 *Landmark paper: Saha, P., Mukherjee, D., Singh, P.K. et al.: GraphCovidNet: A graph neural network based model for detecting COVID-19 from CT scans and X-rays of chest. Sci Rep **11**, 8304 (2021). https://doi.org/10.1038/s41598-021-87523-1*

COVID-19 has just recently begun to spread, scientists have already completed a significant amount of study in this short amount of time. The classification of COVID-19 pictures is the current issue, and several machine learning and deep learning techniques have been suggested. Several works have been briefly mentioned in this section.

On the SARS-CoV-2 CT-scan dataset, Soares et al. obtained 97.31% accuracy in the binary classification of scans between COVID and NonCOVID. They did this by using an explainable deep learning model called xDNN. In this research, Yang et al. introduced the COVID-CT dataset. Since there are over 700 photos in the original dataset, segmentation masks for the lungs and the lesion region were employed to extract more data from the images. The ImageNet pretrained models DenseNet-169 and ResNet-50 have been fine-tuned using an unsupervised learning technique in their research, Contrastive Self-Supervised Learning (CSSL). They have overall gotten the best accuracy, which is 89.1%. Pedro et al. used transfer learning and the EfficientNet model to obtain accuracy rates of 87.60% and 98.99% for the COVID-CT dataset and SARS-CoV-2 CT-scan dataset, respectively. Sharma et al. used ResNet on a database made up of the following datasets, achieving an accuracy of nearly 91%: (i) GitHub COVID-CT dataset; (ii) COVID dataset provided by Italian Society of Medical and Interventional Radiology; (iii) dataset provided by hospitals of Moscow, Russia; and (iv) dataset provided by SAL Hospital, Ahmedabad, India.

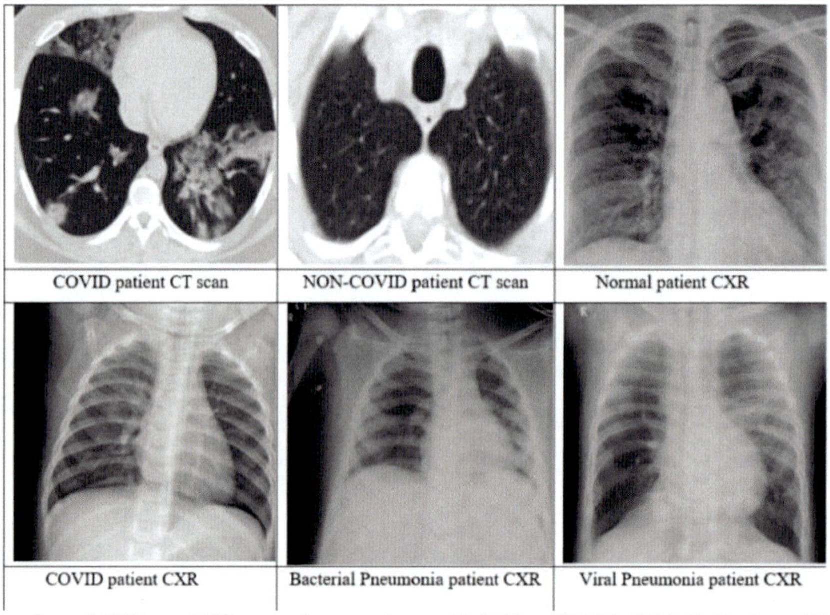

Fig 1: Examples of CXRs and CT scans from patients: (i) CXR—CMSC-678-ML-Project, (ii) CT scan—SARS-COV-2 Ct-Scan Dataset).

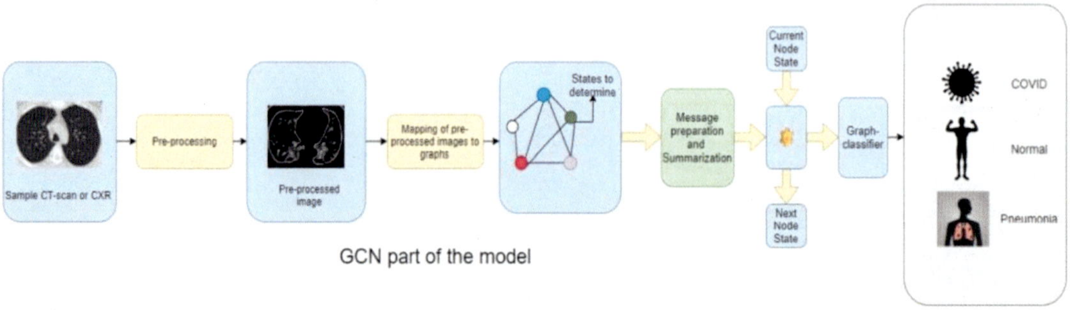

Fig 2: Generic architecture of the GraphCovidNet model that we have developed to identify COVID-19 in CT or CXR images (example CT image source: CT-scan—SARS-COV-2 Ct-Scan Dataset).

Elaziz et al. first selected features using a modified version of Manta-Ray Foraging Optimization (MRFO), and then they classified the data using K-Nearest Neighbor (KNN). They have taken into account two COVID datasets: (i) a merged database of the Chest X-Ray Images (Pneumonia) dataset and the COVID Chest X-Ray Dataset, and (ii) a dataset supplied by Chowdhury et al. On those two datasets, they have obtained accuracy rates of 96.09% and 98.09%, respectively. Transfer learning was used to a pre-trained Convolutional Neural Network (CNN) dubbed AlexNet in Turkoglu et al COVIDetectioNet .'s model. They employed the Relief feature selection technique across the whole architecture, while Support Vector Machines were used for classification (SVM).

The combined dataset from Chowdhury et al., Chest X-Ray Images (Pneumonia), and COVID-19 Radiography Database served as the basis for the researchers' investigations. On the pooled dataset, Teir's suggested model correctly predicted 99.18% of the outcomes. Oh et al. employed ResNet-18 to conduct semantic segmentation on the combined database of the following datasets: (i) JSRT dataset, (ii) SCR dataset, (iii) NLM(MC) dataset, (iv) Covid chest x-ray dataset, and (v) Corona Hack dataset. They have produced 88.9% accurate outcomes in their job.

A four-layer CNN model on the COVID-19 radiology database has been suggested by Nour et al. This dataset is built from many benchmark datasets. Basic machine learning methods KNN, SVM, and Decision Tree (DT) are used to the retrieved data once features from the proposed CNN model have been extracted. SVM produces cutting-edge results with an accuracy rate of 98.97%. On a database made up of three publicly accessible CXR image datasets—the Covid-chest X-ray dataset, the Montgomery dataset, and the NIH Chest X-ray dataset—Chandra et al. employed an ensemble of four classifiers—SVM, KNN, DT, Artificial Neural Network (ANN), and Naive Bayes (NB)—based on majority voting. Eight First Order Statistical Features (FOSF) and eight Grey Level Co-occurrence Matrix (GLCM)-based features make up the total of 8196 features extracted from all of the pre-processed pictures. The remaining 8100 features are Histogram of Oriented Gradients (HOG) features. The suggested classifier ensemble correctly predicted 2 class (normal and abnormal) and 3 class (i.e., normal, COVID-19, and Pneumonia) classification issues with 98.06% and 93.41% accuracy, respectively. On the dataset merged from covid-chest xray-dataset and dataset supplied by Dr. Rosebrock, Hemdam et al. employed seven benchmark image classifier models: VGG19, DenseNet201, InceptionV3, ResNetV2, Inception-ResNetV2, Xception, and MobileNetV2. Results with the highest accuracy were produced by VGG19 and DenseNet201, at 90%. On the CXR pictures gathered from sources like the covid-chest x-ray dataset and the Chest X-Ray Images dataset by Mooney et al., Makris et al. applied a variety of current CNN models as well as transfer learning.

Dataset	Category	Accuracy (%)	Precision (%)	Recall (%)	F1 Score (%)	Training time (s)	Testing time (s)
SARS-COV-2 Ct-Scan Dataset	–	100	100	100	100	342.586	2.328
COVID-CT dataset	–	100	100	100	100	146.365	1.151
covid-chestxray-dataset + Chest X-Ray Images (Pneumonia) dataset	–	99.84	99.84	99.84	99.84	1071.296	7.138
CMSC-678-ML-Project GitHub	3-class	99.11	99.11	99.11	99.11	66.923	0.6
	4-class	99	99	99	99	73.697	0.612

Table 1: For each of the four datasets, specific findings of the proposed GraphCovidNet model in terms of certain common assessment measures.

VGG16 and VGG19 have offered the greatest accuracy at 95% out of all the models used. On the databases consisting of the COVID-19 Chest X-Ray Dataset Initiative dataset, ActualMed

COVID-19 Chest X-Ray Dataset Initiative dataset, Chest X-ray Images (Pneumonia) dataset, and the covid-chest x-ray-dataset, Zhong et al. employed a CNN model based on VGG16 architecture. In the end, they got 87.3% right answers to their questions. On the CT scan database gathered from the Tird Hospital of Jilin University, Ruijin Hospital of Shanghai Jiao Tong University, Tongji Hospital of Huazhong University of Science and Technology, Shanghai Public Health Clinical Center of Fudan University, Hangzhou First People's Hospital of Zhejiang University, and Sichuan University West Ch, Sun et al. have proposed an Adaptive Feature Selection guided Deep Forest (AFS-DF) algorithm and have achieved 91.79% accurate. Chattopadhyay et al. have made two contributions to this field of study. They used a completely new meta-heuristic feature selection technique called Clustering-based Golden Ratio Optimizer after extracting deep features from the original picture dataset (CGRO). On the SARS-COV-2 Ct-Scan Dataset, COVID-CT Dataset, and Chest X-Ray Dataset, the essential experiments have been carried out, and they have obtained the cutting-edge accuracies of 99.31%, 98.65%, and 99.44%, respectively. Sen et al. have suggested using a bi-stage Feature Selection (FS) technique with CNN architecture to extract the most pertinent features from chest CT-scan pictures. In the beginning, they used two filter techniques (i) Mutual Information (MI) and (ii) Relief-F to apply a guided FS approach. The Dragonfy algorithm (DA) was employed in the second step to further identify the most pertinent characteristics. SVM has finally been used to analyze the whole feature collection. The proposed model has been evaluated on two open-access datasets, SARS-CoV-2 CT images and COVID-CT datasets, and has obtained accuracies on the aforementioned datasets of 98.39% and 90.0%, respectively. In addition to the classification of CT scans and CXRs, COVID-19 is a subject of additional study fields. Mask detection is one of these fields. For the final classification, Loey et al. first utilized ResNet50 and then an ensemble of DT and SVM. With 99.64%, 99.49%, and 100% accuracy rates for the three datasets—the Real-World Masked Face Dataset (RMFD), the Simulated Masked Face Dataset (SMFD), and the Labeled Faces in the Wild (LFW)—they have attained the best results for the SVM classifier. Given that this is essentially an image classification problem, it is evident from the aforementioned publications that current or new CNN models are typically utilized as a classifier. However, CNN has several drawbacks. For instance, it might overfit when the dataset contains significant class imbalance. On the other hand, models based on Graph Neural Network (GNN) can solve issues like overfitting and class imbalance. It is clear from the experimental findings in other fields that a GNN-based model often operates quickly. Problems involving graph classification are addressed by GNN, a recent deep learning methodology. GNN thus needs input data that is represented as a graph data structure. While a 2D image matrix may be easily entered into any 2D-CNN model. Therefore, a suitable method for converting an image classification problem to a graph classification problem is required. With the aid of an adequate pre-processing method to transform a picture into graph data, we were able to address this problem. We built our suggested GraphCovidNet, a Graph Isomorphism Network (GIN) based model (a particular category of GNN) named GraphCovidNet, taking into account all the benefits and innovations of the GNN method.

The experimental findings demonstrate that our suggested model works quite well in terms of model time requirements. Due to the injective nature of the aggregation function, our design has also performed well for extremely class-imbalanced datasets. Different graphs can be correctly mapped by the architecture into various representations in the embedding space. As a result, the suggested model accurately identifies the class with less images. Four publicly accessible datasets were used by us: I The SARS-COV-2 Ct-Scan Dataset; (ii) The COVIDCT dataset; (iii) The 3-class and 4-class datasets under the CMSC-678-ML-Project; and (iv) the combination of two datasets: (1) the Covid Chest X-Ray Dataset accessible on GitHub; and (2) the Chest X-Ray Images (Pneumonia) dataset available on Kaggle. Following is a summary of our work's key contributions:

• In our research, we developed GraphCovidNet, a brand-new classification model for analyzing COVID19 CT-scan and CXR pictures.

• The GIN architecture, a subset of the GNN, is employed as the suggested model's backbone architecture. According to the authors' knowledge, no GNN-based architecture has been used to this field before. With the appropriate pre-processing method, we have converted the image classification issue into a graph classification problem.

• By simply taking into account the edges of a picture rather than the entire image, we have also lowered the space complexity of our model, which makes our method computationally simple.

• We have studied both CT-scan and CXR pictures, and we have also worked on the binary to multi-class classification issue, demonstrating that our technique is not restricted to a single type of input.

Results and Discussion

We utilized 5-fold cross-validation in our trials to assess the model. Ten epochs of training are run for each fold. To train our model, we employed the Adam optimizer and the stochastic gradient descent (SGD) method with a learning rate of 0.001. To evaluate the performance of our model, we have employed four common assessment metrics: Accuracy, Precision, Recall, F1 Score, and Receiver Operating Characteristic (ROC) curve. For all four datasets, Table 1 displays the performance results as well as the average amount of time required for training and testing in each fold for our suggested GraphCovidNet model.

Table 1 shows that the GraphCovidNet model has at least 99% accuracy for all datasets, but only 100% accuracy for datasets with two classes. Typically, the prediction performance of our suggested model decreases from 100% to 99% as the number of classes increases. One noteworthy aspect is that the Chest X-Ray Images (Pneumonia) dataset from the combined database of the covid chest x-ray-dataset and our proposed model offers nearly perfect (99.84%) accuracy for the severely class-balanced dataset. According to intuition, a strong GNN can only map two nodes to the same place if the associated nodes have similar sub-trees and properties. Recursively defined sub-tree structures come from node neighbors. To summarize, we may ask if a GNN maps two neighborhoods—that is, two multi-sets—to the same embedding or representation. A GNN with maximum power would never combine two distinct neighborhoods, or several sets of feature vectors, into one representation. Its aggregation strategy must thus be injective. However, it is true that a strong GNN aggregation method may describe injective multi-set functions.

Theorem

Let GNN be A: $G \rightarrow R^d$. If the following criteria are met, A may translate any graphs, such as G1 and G2, to different embeddings with a sufficient number of GNN layers such that the Weisfeiler-Lehman test of isomorphism determines that they are not isomorphic:

- With $h_v^{(k)} = \Phi(h_v^{(k-1)}, f(h_u^{(k-1)}: u \in N(v))$ where the function, *f*, which acts on multi-sets, and Φ are injective, A collects and updates node characteristics repeatedly.

- The graph-level readout of A is injective and acts on a variety of node attributes.

This theorem is adhered to the GIN. This network can translate any two different graphs into any two different embeddings, which aids in resolving the difficult graph isomorphism issue. In other words, although non-isomorphic graphs must be mapped to different representations, isomorphic graphs must be mapped to the same representation. These explanations explain why the suggested model even performs well on datasets with significant class imbalance. It is also noteworthy that our suggested model requires significantly less time during the training (1-18 min) and testing (0.6-7s) phases, according to the data from Table 1. A smaller number of epochs is another factor in the short training period. But once more, training loss gets significantly smaller with time. Therefore, it is unnecessary to take into account a high number of epochs for training purposes. This modest training loss is seen in Fig. 3.

In Fig. 3, it is clear that accuracy is at least 99% at the first epoch while loss is just 0.4 for each dataset. Additionally, training lowers the loss value close to zero while the classification accuracy either stays relatively constant or marginally improves with increasing epoch size. However, as can be seen from Fig. 3, the accuracy seems to be constant since the change in loss is more noticeable than the change in total accuracy. The suggested architecture can correctly interpret the input graphs as a result of suitable pre-processing. However, the loss is quite modest right away, and training is finished in no more than 10 epochs. For each of the datasets depicted in Fig. 4 we created Receiver Operating Characteristic (ROC) curves in order to further assess the accuracy of our classification model. We have also experimented with changing the training to testing ratio from 10% to 90% with a 10% interval. For each of the datasets, we created graphs of training and testing accuracies vs. training to testing ratio, which are displayed in Fig. 5.

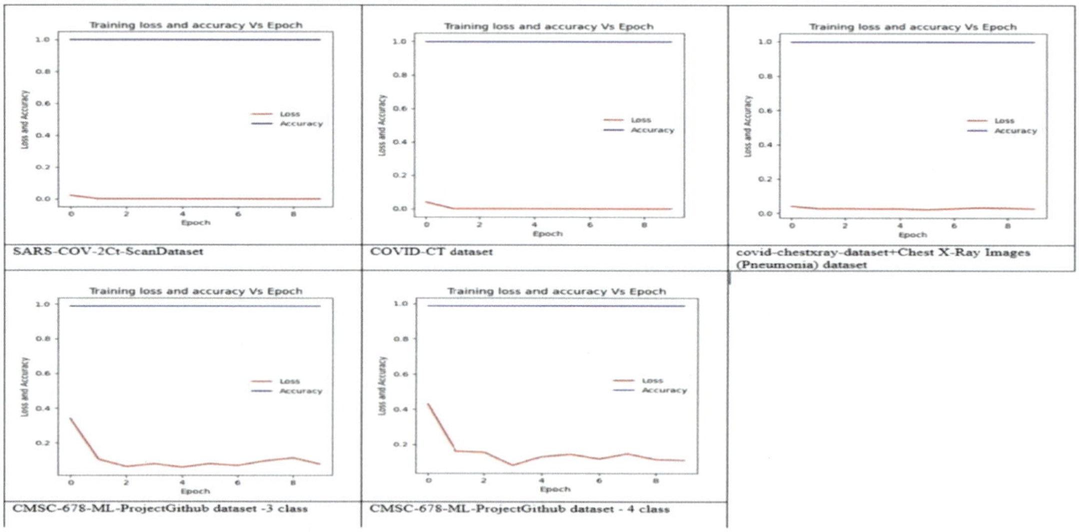

Fig 3: Training accuracy and loss are represented graphically as a function of epoch for each of the selected datasets.

Therefore, it is clear from Fig. 4 that the GraphCovidNet model consistently predicts at least 95% of the samples accurately, which is a testament to its resilience. Because the Area Under the Curve (AUC) for each of the ROC curves is 0.97 units at worst, Figure 5 further demonstrates its effectiveness as a classifier. Both 2-class datasets have AUCs of 1, and the ROC is similarly flawless. In other words, regardless of the training to testing ratio, the GraphCovidNet model can handle both of the 2-class datasets. Additionally, we have performed experiments on several datasets with an equal number of classes for both training and testing. Table 2 lists the outcomes of all such training-testing combinations. Table 2 demonstrates that even when training and testing data come from multiple sources, the proposed model still guarantees accuracy over 98%. Such remarkably exact outcomes support GraphCovidNet's reliability even further. We also assessed our proposed model's performance against other pretrained CNN models, including Inception-ResNet-V2,VGG19, ResNet152, DenseNet201, Xception, and MobileNetV2 for both raw and edge-mapped pictures, to further demonstrate its superiority. The accuracy percentages (%) from all trials using the aforementioned CNN models are shown in Table 3. Comparison of Tables 1 and 3 demonstrates that GraphCovidNet beats each of these traditional CNN models, providing additional evidence of the robustness of the model we propose. We also contrasted the outcomes of our suggested GraphCovidNet model with some earlier analyses carried out on the selected datasets. Table 4 shows these comparable outcomes. Table 4 makes it evident that our suggested method outperforms all of the earlier research included here for comparison in terms of accuracy. The GraphCovidNet model still performs better than those on the same dataset, despite the fact that several of the stated prior efforts were conducted on databases that were different from or even bigger than ours. According to our knowledge, the CMSC-678-ML-Project GitHub dataset has not been the subject of any prior research. Still, there aren't many efforts that have been done on a 4-class database for COVID-19 classification. Therefore, we thought of writing down the findings from the CMSC-678-ML-Project GitHub dataset. Additionally, a deep learning network typically cannot achieve high accuracy for a small number of input samples, such as the CMSC-678-ML-Project GitHub dataset. However, as demonstrated in Table 1, GraphCovidNet can predict with 99% and 99.11% accuracy for its 3-class and 4-class instances, respectively. Therefore, even in datasets with a relatively limited number of samples, our suggested model may still perform quite well.

In a word, we can state that our suggested model is extremely accurate and resilient in comparison to other models already in use.

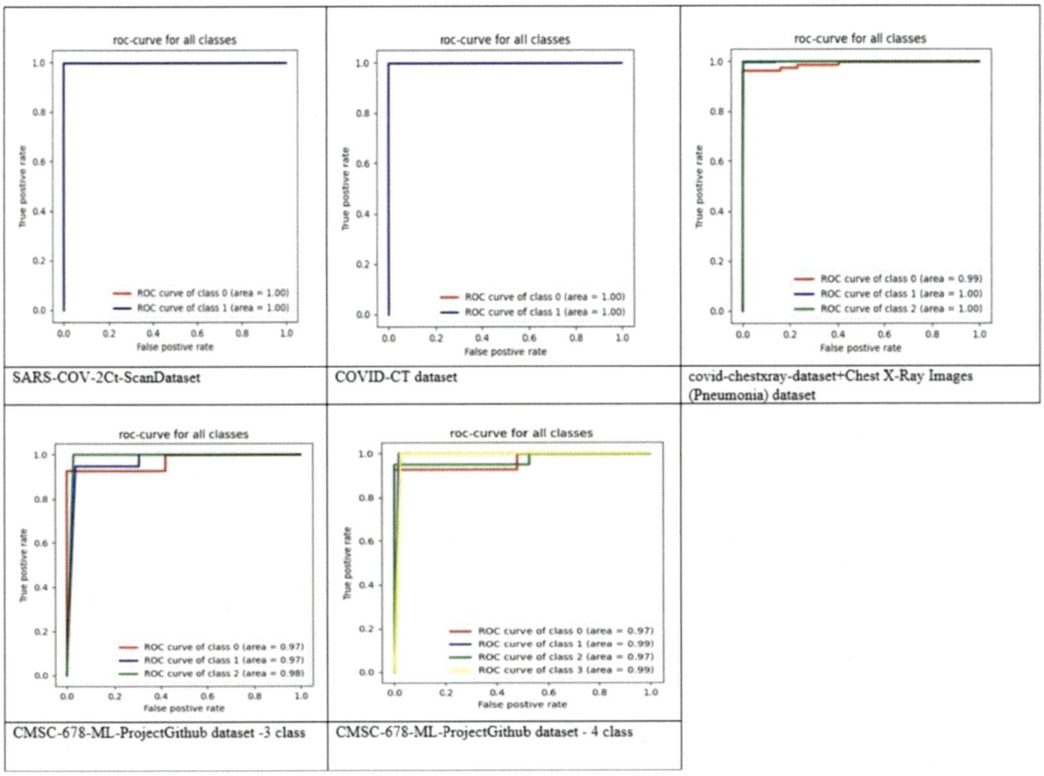

Fig 4: ROC curves produced for each dataset by our suggested GraphCovidNet model.

Methods

We have presented our planned work in this part, along with the appropriate pre-processing necessary for COVID19 picture classification. We've also provided a brief description of the benchmark datasets. There are three subsections in this section: (1) Datasets utilized, (2) Pre-processing, and (3) Proposed model.

Utilized datasets: For our research, we have chosen the following four datasets to run the experiments on their own.
1. The 2-class SARS-COV-2 CT-Scan Dataset, compiled by Plamen et al. and made accessible on Kaggle
2. Yang et al COVID-CT's dataset, a 2-class CT scan dataset that is accessible on GitHub.
3. A 3-class dataset made up of CXR from two sources, including the GitHub-hosted covid-chestxray-dataset compiled by Cohen et al.
• Mooney et al Chest's X-Ray Images (Pneumonia) dataset, which is accessible on Kaggle.

- We used normal, Pneumonia patient scans from the Chest X-Ray Images (Pneumonia) dataset and COVID-19 patient scans from the covidchestxray-dataset to combine these two datasets.

4. The CMSC-678-ML-3-class Project's and 4-class CXR datasets are also accessible on GitHub.

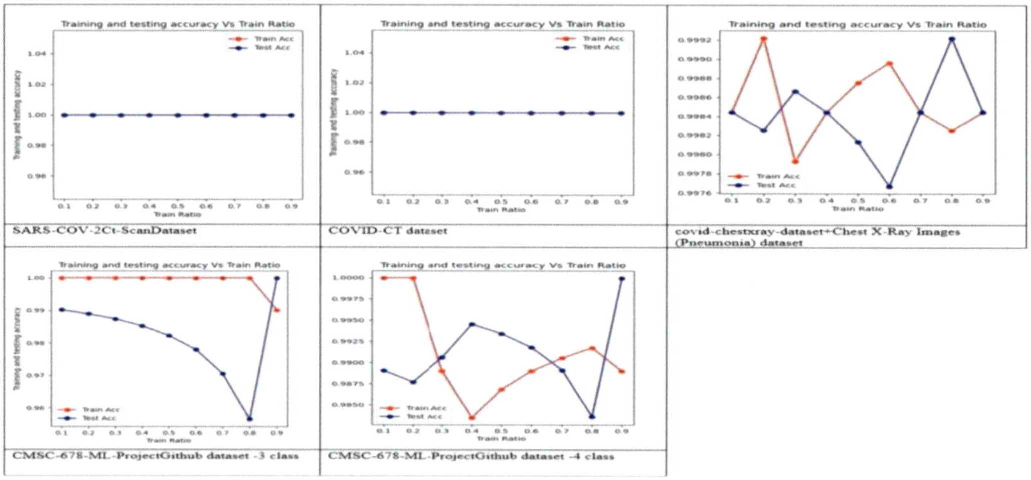

Fig 5: A visual depiction of the correlation between training and testing precisions for each of the selected datasets.

Train data	Test data	Number of classes	Accuracy (%)	Precision (%)	Recall (%)	F1 Score (%)
SARS-COV-2 Ct-Scan Dataset	COVID-CT dataset	2	100	100	100	100
COVID-CT dataset	SARS-COV-2 Ct-Scan Dataset	2	100	100	100	100
covid-chestxray-dataset + Chest X-Ray Images (Pneumonia) dataset	CMSC-678-ML-Project GitHub (3-class)	3	98.78	99.02	97.98	98.54
CMSC-678-ML-Project GitHub (3-class)	covid-chestxray-dataset + Chest X-Ray Images (Pneumonia) dataset	3	99.32	99.23	99.45	99.30

Table 2: Results in great detail for every combination of several train-test datasets with the same number of classes.

Processes Before Hand

In order to use our suggested GraphCovidNet model, the CT scans or CXRs must first undergo pre-processing, as was already indicated. We have thought of two pre-processing phases, which are shown as follows:
1. Edge detection: Prewitt filter is used to estimate the edges of the raw pictures.
2. Graph preparation: These edge maps are then properly transformed into a graph dataset.

Now that these two phases have been discussed, it will be easier to comprehend the entirety of the pre-processing phase.

Model	SARS-COV-2 Ct-Scan Dataset		COVID-CT dataset		covid-chestxray-dataset + Chest X-Ray Images (Pneumonia) dataset		CMSC-678-ML-Project GitHub (3-class)		CMSC-678-ML-Project GitHub (4-class)	
	Raw image	Edge image	Raw image	Edge image	Raw image	Edge image	Raw image	Edge image	Raw image	Edge image
Inception-ResNet-V2	77.85	80.08	74.35	78.95	98.22	98.05	82.61	91.3	77.56	86.45
VGG19	78.27	82.55	79.60	84.27	98.45	96.50	86.96	97.83	79.65	92.2
ResNet152	77.87	84.58	86.65	87.97	98.68	97.82	91.31	91.40	86.13	85.88
DenseNet201	75.86	85.69	89.11	90.21	99.07	97.35	95.65	96.13	88.65	90.44
Xception	83.30	81.79	82.01	87.58	96.74	99.22	82.61	86.96	82.15	83.97
MobileNetV2	77.46	80.48	78.18	76.97	98.76	98.52	93.48	84.74	81.45	82.25

Table 3: Accuracy percentages (%) computed for both raw and edge-mapped pictures using the Inception-ResNet-V2, VGG19, ResNet152, DenseNet201, Xception, and MobileNetV2 models.

Dataset	Authors	Methodology	Accuracy (%)	Precision (%)	Recall (%)	F1-score (%)
SARS-COV-2 Ct-Scan Dataset[8]	Soares et al.[8]	xDNN	97.38	99.16	95.53	97.31
	Pedro et al.[15]	EfficientNet with transfer learning	98.99	99.20	98.80	99
	Proposed	GraphCovidNet	100	100	100	100
COVID-CT dataset[11]	Pedro et al.[15]	EfficientNet with transfer learning	87.68	93.98	79.59	86.19
	Yang et al.[11]	Segmentation masks with CSSL	89.1	-	-	89.6
	Proposed	GraphCovidNet	100	100	100	100
covid-chestxray-dataset[23]+Chest X-Ray Images (Pneumonia) dataset[24]	Makris et al.[33]	VGG16 and VGG19 with transfer learning	95.88	COVID-96 normal-95 Pneumonia-95	COVID-96 normal-100 Pneumonia-91	COVID-98 normal-98 Pneumonia-98
	Elaziz et al.[21]	MRFO + KNN	96.09	98.75	98.75	98.75
	Zhong et al.[34]	VGG16 based CNN model	87.3	89.67	84.4	86.96
	Oh et al.[30]	DenseNet103 for segmentation + ResNet-18	88.9	83.4	85.9	84.4
	Chandra et al.[37]	Majority voting of SVM, KNN, DT, ANN, NB	93.41	-	-	-
	Nour et al.[3]	CNN for feature extraction + SVM	98.97	-	89.39	96.72 (F-score)
	Hemdam et al.[45]	VGG19 or DenseNet201	90	COVID-83 Normal-100	COVID-100 Normal-80	COVID-91 Normal-89
	Turkoglu et al.[26]	AlexNet+ Relief feature selection algorithm and SVM	99.18	99.48	99.13	99.30
	Proposed	GraphCovidNet	99.84	99.84	99.84	99.84

Table 4: Comparing our proposed GraphCovidNet model to some earlier research on all the datasets (Oh et al., Chandra et al., Nour et al., Hemdam et al., and Turkoglu et al. have incorporated other dataset)

Dataset	Number of classes	Scan-type	Total number of images		
			Normal	COVID-19	Pneumonia
SARS-COV-2 Ct-Scan Dataset[8]	2	CT	1229	1252	-
COVID-CT dataset[11]	2	CT	407	349	-
covid-chestxray-dataset[23]+Chest X-Ray Images (Pneumonia) dataset[24]	3	CXR	1592	504	4343
CMSC-678-ML-Project GitHub dataset[9]	3	CXR	79	69	79
	4	CXR	79	69	Bacterial: 79, Viral: 79

Table 5: All the experimental datasets are statistically described.

Edge-detection

In essence, an edge is an area in a picture representing a local change in intensity, meaning that the change in intensity in the edge region will have a local maximum or minimum. The edges may be clearly seen in the original image by using the right filter. For both horizontal and vertical edge detection, which are defined as: in our work, we have convolved the original image matrix with 3*3 Prewitt filter: $\begin{bmatrix} -1 & -1 & -1 \\ 0 & 0 & 0 \\ 1 & 1 & 1 \end{bmatrix}$ and $\begin{bmatrix} -1 & 0 & 1 \\ -1 & 0 & 1 \\ -1 & 0 & 1 \end{bmatrix}$

Prewitt operator was used for this experiment because it is simple to use and effectively recognizes edges. Figure 6 compares the three most common edge filters—Canny, Sobel, and Prewitt—as they are applied to a COVID-CT picture. Figure 6 show that the Canny filter generates the least noisy picture, whereas the Sobel filter creates the highest noise. Prewitt's filter produces a picture that is noisier than Canny's, but unlike Canny, Prewitt's edges have different pixel intensities. Therefore, it would be smarter for Prewitt filter to choose pixel value as a feature. Gradient for each 3*3 sub-matrix has been assessed after convolution has been applied using both the horizontal and vertical filters. Since all of the photos are in grayscale, we assumed that a pixel would be located on an edge if the gradient value is larger than or equal to 128 and the gradient's magnitude crosses halfway. Fig. 7 gives us a clearer picture of the edge-detection stage.

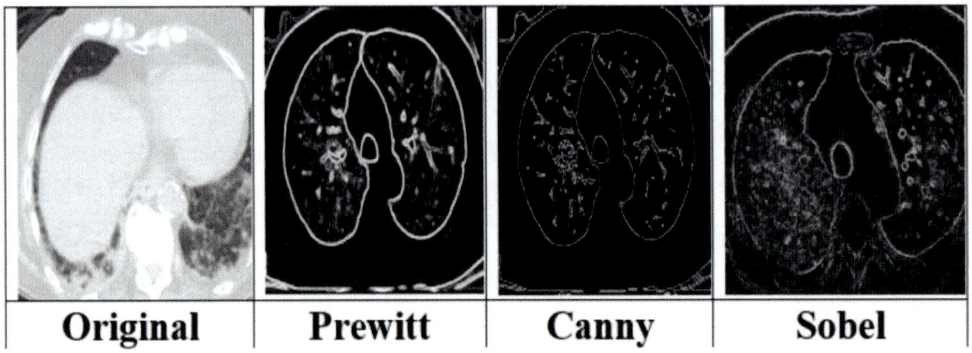

Fig 6: Comparison of the edge picture produced after applying the Prewitt, Canny, and Sobel filters to the original COVID-CT image (raw image source: COVID-CT dataset).

Graph preparation

Each image is transformed into a graph once the Prewitt filter is applied. A three-step process is used to prepare the graph, and it is described below:

1. A node or network vertex is defined as any pixel with a grayscale intensity value higher than or equal to 128. This suggests that nodes are restricted to the edge image's significant edges. The grayscale intensity of the matching pixel makes up a node's feature.
2. The two nodes that correspond to the adjacent pixels in the original picture have an edge between them.
3. A graph is created for each image. This indicates that the whole graph—both the nodes and the edges—was created from a single picture. The graph-wise normalization of the node characteristics, which are only grayscale values. The final step in normalizing is to divide the original value by the standard deviation after taking the mean of all the characteristics beneath the graph out of it.

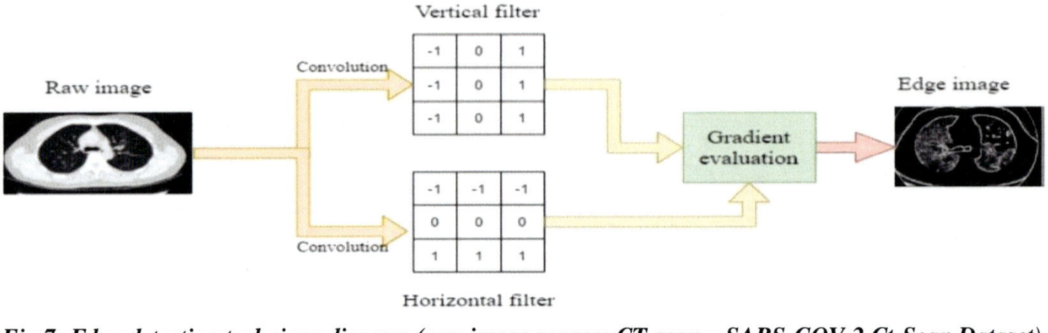

Fig 7: Edge-detection technique diagram (raw image source: CT-scan—SARS-COV-2 Ct-Scan Dataset).

Less memory is required to prepare such data since nodes are created just from edges that are present in a picture rather than the entire image. Since foggy regions for coughs are present in COVID-19 and all other Pneumonia scans, the nature of the graph and the edges that may be recognized will differ. This distinction may be valuable in the future for classification. In all, four different types of datasets are created to capture the graph data from all of the scans, including

1. Node-attribute-dataset: This dataset contains the attribute value of each node, which in this case is the normalized grayscale value.
2. Graph-indicator-dataset: This is where each node's graph ID is kept.

3. Node-label-dataset: This section contains the class labels for each node. Each node inside the same graph would receive the same label, which is really the class-label for the related graph since this is a graph level classification.
4. Graph-label-dataset: This is where each graph's class label is kept.
5. Adjacency-dataset: This is where the sparse adjacency matrices for all the graphs are kept. The entire process of edge preparation is summarized in Figure 8.

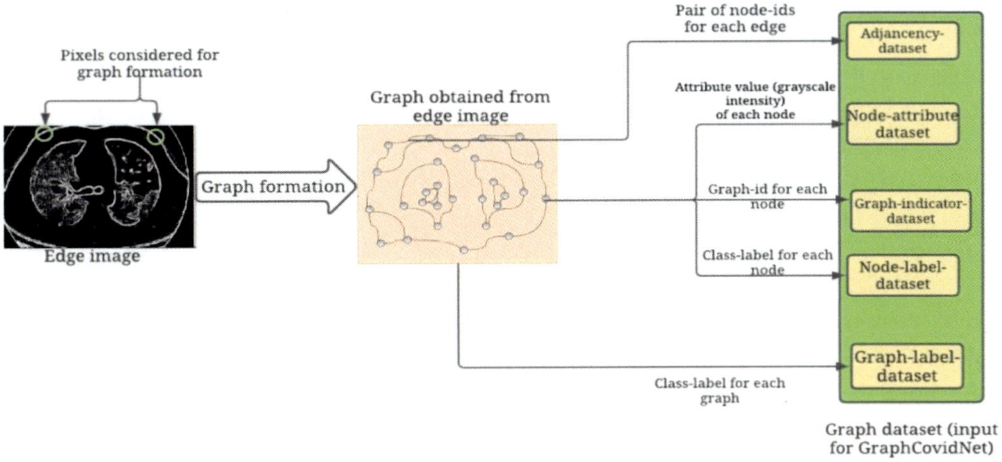

Fig 8: Schematic depicting the process of edge-preparation.

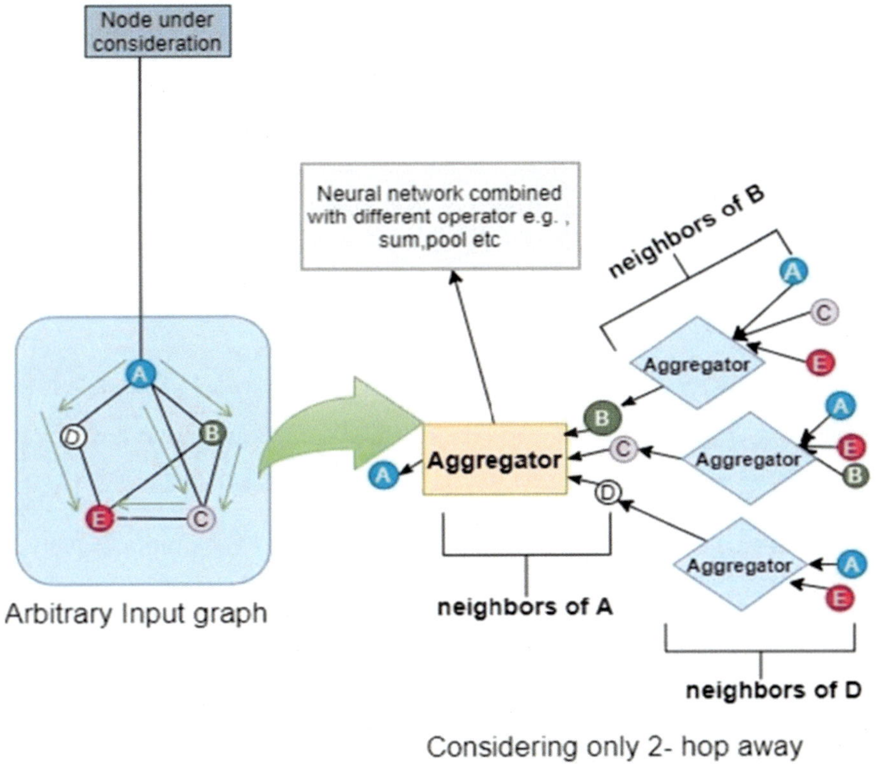

Fig 9: In this diagram, each node represents the computation graph of some other graph.

Proposed model

We have presented GraphCovidNet, an unique technique in which GIN is used for classification and prediction tasks. In order to proceed with the architecture, we must first briefly understand the graphs, GNN, and GIN.

Neural graph network

The collection of nodes (V) and edges (E) that make up a graph g may be used to define it as follows: g = (V, E), where V is the set of vertices and E is the set of edges. In a network where some nodes have labels thanks to supervised learning, GNN may be used to categorize unlabeled nodes. Additionally, it is capable of classifying graphs where each graph has a set of labels. Now that each labeled image has been converted into a single graph, we can apply supervised learning to categorize these graphs.

Graph isomorphism and embeddings

In GNN, graph nodes are embedded in d-dimensional space h_v. These nodes are encoded so that linked or neighboring nodes are close in embedded space and vice versa. Every node utilizes its own feature vector f_v and neighborhood embedding vector h_{nev} to find h_v. GNNs employ graph structure and node features to learn a representation vector of a node, f_v, where each node has feature vectors, f_v ∀ v ϵ V, and each edge contains feature vectors, f_e, ∀ e ϵ E or the complete graph, h_g, where h_g = Readout(h_v,∀ v ϵ V), where h_v is the node's fnal embeddings. V is g's nodes. Every node defines a computation graph depending on its neighborhood, or neural network architecture. Each node's model length is arbitrary. GNN iteratively updates a node's representation by pooling its neighbors'. Each layer has embeddings. After k iterations of aggregation, a node's representation captures structural information inside its k-hop network neighborhood. x_v is the node's feature vector;h_v^0 is the first layer embedding.

Initial layer embeddings are now equivalent to feature vectors since $h_v^0 = x_v$. Formally, a GNN's k-th layer is

a_v^k=$Aggregate^{(k)} h_u^{(k-1)}$:u ϵ N(v)),$Combine^{(k)}$ $(h_v^{(k-1)}, a_v^k)$,

Where, At the k-th layer, node v's feature vector is represented by h_v^k, while its neighborhood-aggregated message is represented by$ha_v^{(k)}$.

A group of nodes near v is known as N(v).

In GNNs, the $Aggregate^{(k)}$ (.) and Combine$^{(k)}$ (.) choices are very important.

Different architectural designs have been put up for the aggregate function. GraphSAGE's pooling variant has computed aggregate as:

a_v^k=$Max(ReLU(b^{(k)} * h_u^{(k-1)})$:uϵN(v)),

Where $b^{(k)}$ is metrics parameter

Max denotes an element-by-element max-pooling.

The Combine step could be made up of the neighborhood aggregation and the embedding of the previous layer.

$h_v^k = w^k *$ Concat(h_v^k, a_v^k)

Instead, element-wise mean pooling is employed in Graph Convolutional Networks (GCN), and the Aggregate and Combine phases are combined as follows:

h_v^k=$(ReLU(W^{(k)} * mean(h_u^{(k-1)})$: ∀uϵN(v)),

Mean and max-pooling aggregators are permutation invariant multi-set functions. Not injectable. Mean(GCN) or max(GraphSage) pooling always returns the same node representation for neighborhood aggregation. Mean and max pooling aggregators fail to capture graph structure. GNNs and the Weisfeiler–Lehman graph isomorphism test are closely related. The WL test has taken the labels of nodes and their neighbors and put them all together. Then, it hashed the combined labels to make new labels that are unique. If at some iteration the labels of the nodes in the two graphs differ, the algorithm determines that the graphs are not isomorphic. Each WL test iteration has been explained as follows:

1.Create a hash of (h_v, h_{v1},..., h_{vn}) for ALL vertices v ϵ g, where h_{vi} are the characteristics of vertex's neighbors.

2. In the following iteration, use v's calculated hash as a vertex property.

When this iteration converges on unique hash-to-vertex mappings, the algorithm ends.
The WL test's injective aggregation update translates node neighborhoods to feature vectors. Our fundamental breakthrough is that a GNN's aggregation technique may represent injective functions and have as much distinguishing power as the WL test. This job required solving graph isomorphism to translate two graphs to different embeddings. We want isomorphic graphs to be represented the same way and non-isomorphic ones differently. The GIN that passes the WL test and generalizes it has the most discriminatory power among GNNs.
The GIN's k-th layer embedding is provided by:

h_v^k = (MLP$^{(k)}$((1+$\epsilon^{(k)}$)*($h_v^{(k)}$): $\Sigma_{u\epsilon N(v)} h_u^{(k-1)}$

where $\epsilon^{(k)}$ is a floating point number and MLP is an acronym for Multi Layer Perception.
The node representation h_v^k of the kth layer is now utilized for prediction in node classification. The Readout function collects node information from the last iteration to derive the embedding h_g of the complete graph, which is provided by the following equation:

h_g=Readout(h_v^k, $\forall v \epsilon V$)

Schematic representation of our GraphCovidNet model

Our design is made up of a block of GINConv layer that employs MLP for neighborhood aggregation in its later layers. A block of successive layers called a Rectangular Linear Unit (ReLU) layer, a linear layer, and then another linear layer are employed in MLP. In Fig. 10, it is depicted.In essence, the GINConv layer accepts two distinct inputs:

1. V is the total number of nodes in the graph and d is an embedded dimension, x is the feature matrix of each node with dimension v*d.
2. The edge index E has a dimension of 2*L and is made up of all the edges in the graph in the form of pairs (v1, v2), where v1 and v2 are the nodes that are connected by an edge, and L is the total number of edges in the graph.

The output of the GINConv layer is routed via a ReLU activation function to induce non-linearity, followed by a 0.5 dropout and a normalization (norm) layer. This layer's output (out1) is sent to another block whose output is out2. Out2 is sent to a block with GINConv-ReLUdropout layers and a global mean pooling layer. After that, a linear layer, a dropout layer with a 0.5 dropout rate, and a linear layer with the problem's class size. The final probability vector, z, is produced using a Log Softmax activation function. Fig. 11 shows the architecture.

$$logsoftmax(z_i) = \log\left(\frac{e^{z_i}}{\sum_{j=1}^{c} e^{z_j}}\right) \quad (1)$$

Where,z_i represents the probability of the *ith* element in the final linear layer vector. The probability values of all the items included in the vector for the number of classes are added together to form $\Sigma_i^c{=}1^{ezj}$.As the objective function for classification, we employed the negative log likelihood (nll) function.

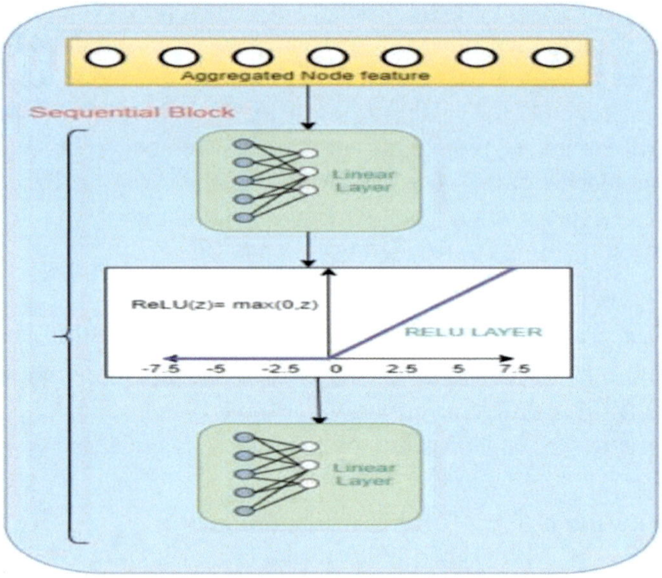

Fig 10: Diagram showing the GINConv Layer's MLP design.

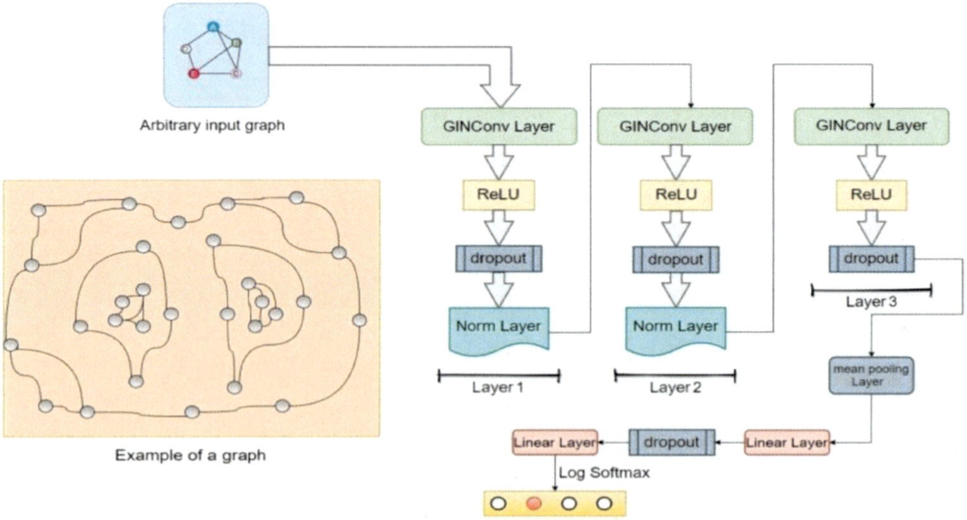

Fig 11: Our suggested GraphCovidNet model's overall structure.

Conclusion

COVID-19 has had a significant impact on our social and economic life over the past year. Researchers in this scenario are concentrating on CT scan and CXR pictures for screening COVID-19 cases of the infected individuals. In this study, we introduce GraphCovidNet, a novel model that focuses on separating COVID-19 or other types of pneumonia patients from healthy individuals. The pre-processing stage, which creates the borders of an image, uses Prewitt flter67. However, compared to conventional CNN-based models, our suggested technique makes better use of memory. The proposed model performs very well on the various datasets taken into consideration in this paper. Its prediction accuracy may sometimes even reach 100%, and it can easily get beyond issues like overfitting and class imbalance. In terms of accuracy, precision, recall, and f1-score, the new model has also fared better than several previous models. In the future, we can use the suggested GraphCovidNet in further COVID-19 datasets or other medical datasets with CT or CXR images. GNN-based models are specifically relevant to all image classification issues. Only 10 epochs were used in the current studies to create the training model. Therefore, in the future, we'll work to make our model faster so that it can be trained quickly even with a high number of examples.

Chapter 12

Predicting COVID-19 infection from chest CT scans using ET-NET, an ensemble of transfer learning models[12]

SARS-CoV-2, the novel coronavirus that triggered the COVID-19 pandemic and killed more than 2 million people between January and October 2020, originated in Wuhan, China and has since infected more than 100 million people globally. Despite a decline in mortality, the epidemic is still ongoing. The real-time Polymerase Chain Reaction and the fast IgM-IgG mixed antibody test are used to detect COVID-19 (RT-PCR). The RT-PCR test has a number of drawbacks, including the following: (1) It takes a while to receive test results; (2) It is an expensive test that requires professionals to conduct it and interpret the data; and (3) They have a high false-negative rate (sensitivity of 71%). Although the IgG and IgM antibodies can be concurrently detected in human blood by the fast antigen test, it may take several days for the human body to create the antibodies, increasing the risk of the virus spreading before it is discovered. As a result, the false-negative rate is extremely high. As an alternative, a quick prediction-based automated diagnosis method that is sensitive and specific to the COVID-19 disease is needed.

At the moment, there are 2.38 million deaths and 108.3 million cases of COVID-19 worldwide. Fig. displays the graphs for the overall cases and daily cases. accordingly, 1a and b. According to Fig., there are 155,000 fatalities and more than 10.8 million total cases in India. Figure 2a displays the daily cases and fatality rates. 2b (All data for the graphics have been collected from the publicly available data by Roser et al) (All data for the graphs have been collected from the publicly available data by Roser et al). Population-wise screening is impossible due to the severe lack of RT-PCR test kits, particularly in developing nations like India. This has allowed the virus to spread unchecked throughout the community. The use of chest CT-scan images for COVID-19 screening may be an appropriate and practical alternative to the laborious and time-consuming RT-PCR test.

The CT-scan, also known as computed tomography, is a test that is rather widespread and that is more easily executed. According to Fang et al., it is significantly more sensitive (98%) than RT-PCR (71%) Figure 3 displays two CT pictures, one of a patient who has COVID-19 and the other of a patient who has not been tested positive. The "ground-glass opacities" dispersed throughout the lungs are the most typical finding from the chest CT scans. As seen by the red circle in Fig., they are microscopic air sacs or alveoli that, as they fill with fluid, change colour in the CT scan from white consolidation to a greyish shade. 3a. The severity of the disease is

---

12 *Landmark paper: Kundu, R., Singh, P.K., Ferrara, M. et al. ET-NET: an ensemble of transfer learning models for prediction of COVID-19 infection through chest CT-scan images. Multimed Tools Appl **81**, 31–50 (2022). https://doi.org/10.1007/s11042-021-11319-8*

inversely correlated with the lung results, which means that on chest CT scans, sicker people exhibit more of these opacities in one or both lobes of the lungs.

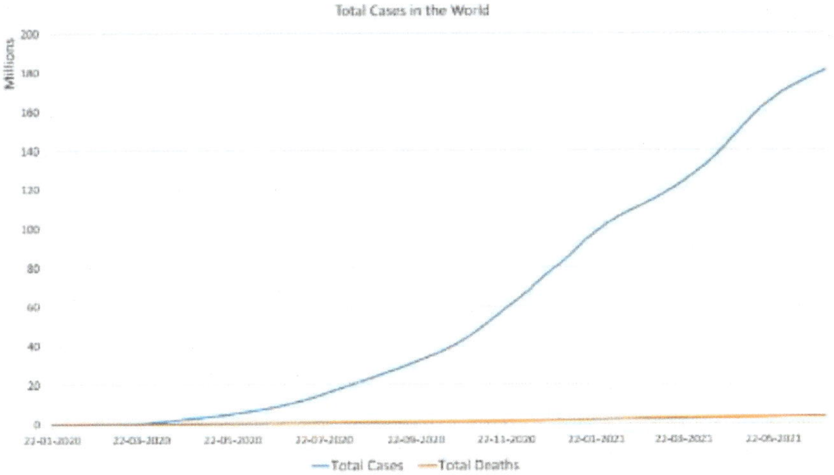

(a) Total Cases and Deaths

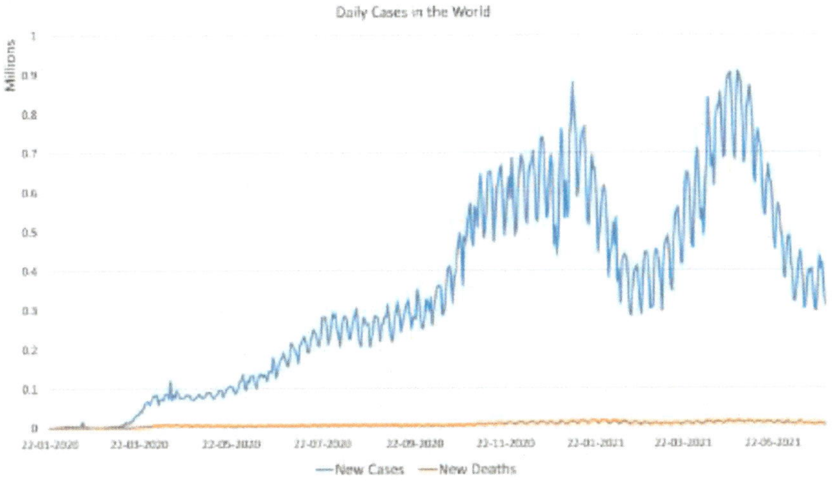

(b) Daily Cases and Deaths

Fig. 1 Current worldwide statistics of COVID-19 **(a)** Total cases and deaths in the world **(b)** Daily new cases and deaths in the world [35]

Additionally, quick and dependable automation-based solutions must be developed to assist doctors in COVID-19 screening. As a result, scientists from all over the world have worked to create computer-aided diagnosis techniques that can identify COVID-19 from chest X-rays or chest CT images. Considering that chest CT pictures provide more information than chest X-rays do, ET-NET uses them to predict patients who are COVID-19 positive. With the aid of a sophisticated decision-making process, deep learning is a potent machine learning technology that employs organised or unstructured data for classification.

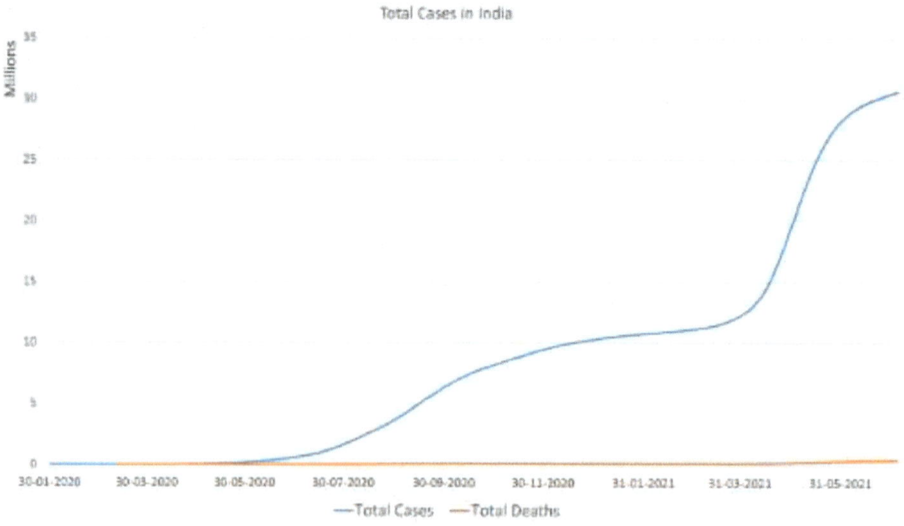

(a) Total cases and deaths due to COVID-19 in India

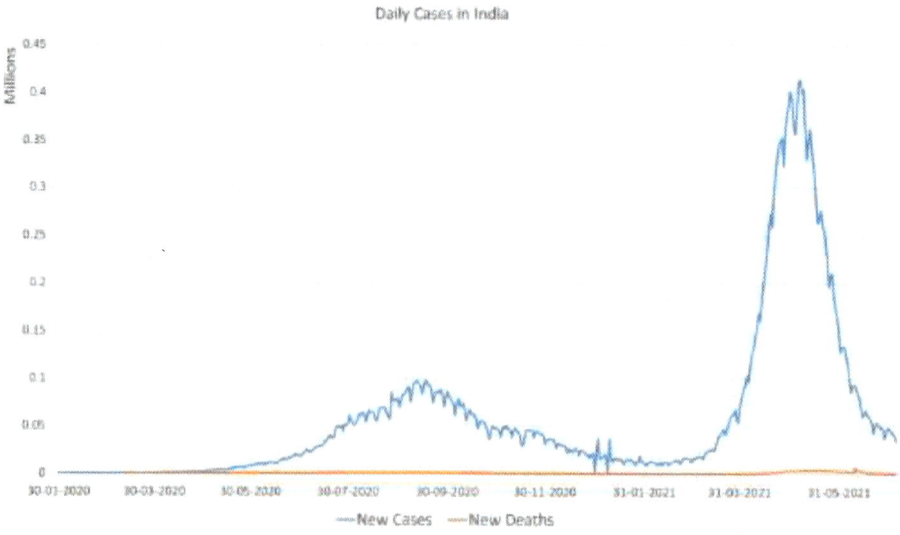

(b) Daily new cases and deaths due to COVID-19 in India

Fig. 2 Current statistics of COVID-19 in India: **(a)** Total cases and deaths **(b)** Daily new cases and deaths [35] (the graph has been formed from the data using Google Sheets)

Fig. 3 Illustration of chest CT image findings of two patients having: **(a)** COVID-19 positive and **(b)** COVID-19 negative. The COVID-19 infection's characteristic "Ground Glass Opacity" has been marked with a red circle in the COVID-19 infected chest CT image

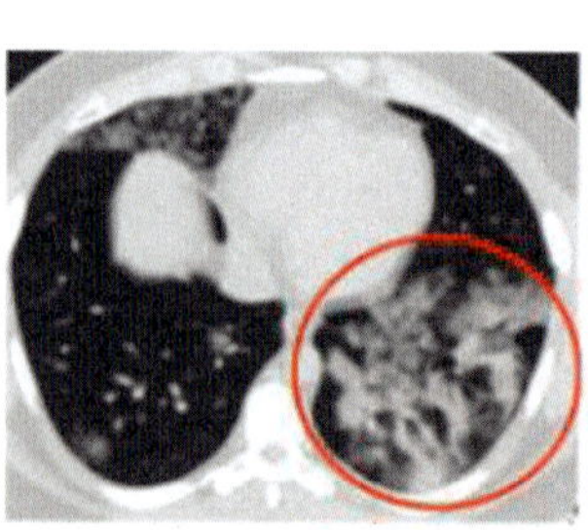

(a) COVID-19 positive patient

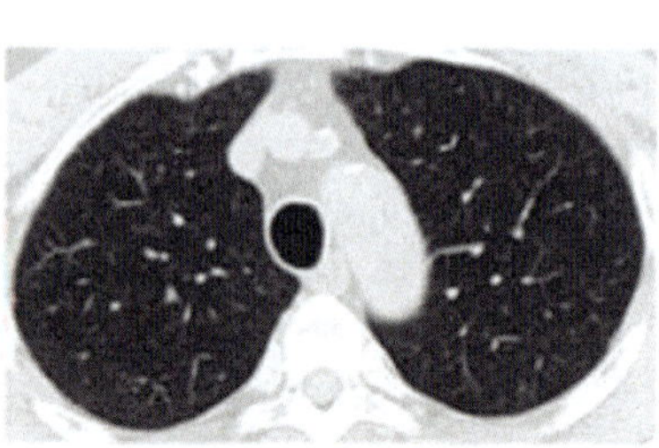

(b) COVID-19 negative patient

This topic of image classification involves supervised learning. When a learning process is referred to as supervised learning, it means that an algorithm is trained on a labelled dataset, which means that the real classes of the samples are already provided so that the model can adjust its parameters based on the training accuracy. Transfer learning is a method where a deep learning model that has been trained for one task is used for a different task entirely. The parameters trained from the previous job are loaded and trained with the new data for fine-tuning, and this method is particularly useful when the task at hand has less data available for training the model.

Ensemble learning enables the integration of key characteristics from various base learners, producing predictions that are more precise than those from individual models. Such a learning strategy is reliable since, after assembly, the variance in the prediction errors decreases. An ensemble model produces better predictions and seeks to capture the supplementary data from the base models. The Bagging technique is employed in the current study as a way to combine the key elements of each transfer learning model that was taken into consideration. Since the dataset supplied has a limited amount of data and the Boosting algorithm could result in considerable overfitting, the Bagging technique is chosen over it in the current study. The bagging method, on the other hand, minimises overfitting and is therefore advantageous for the current issue. The Ensemble Transfer Learning Network, or ET-NET, is therefore suggested in this research.

Literature review

Numerous studies are being carried out to aid in containing the COVID-19 pandemic. The current approaches, however, are more expensive, time-consuming, and less accurate. Chest CT scans have been demonstrated by Yang et al. to be a significant component of the diagnosis of COVID-19. To make comparisons, they employed respiratory samples, such as nose and throat swabs, and bronchoalveolar lavage fluid (BALF). Using sputum samples, the accuracy in COVID-19 detection was only 88.9% for severe patients and 82.2% for moderate cases. Even less accurate results were obtained using nose and throat swabs (accuracies of 73.3% and 60.0%, respectively). The methods for the automated diagnosis of COVID-19 from either CT-scan or chest X-ray images that have recently been suggested in the literature are shown in Table 1.

Since the start of the pandemic, a number of automated frameworks for the screening of COVID-19-infected patients have been suggested; the bulk of these frameworks make use of chest X-ray pictures. Clinicians and medical professionals claim that CT scans are a better input for screening since they are more accurate and sensitive than radiograph (X-ray) pictures.

As a computer-aided detection technique for COVID-19 screening, deep learning has been widely deployed. For the classification of CT images, Gozes et al. combined two subsystems—a 2D slice model and a 3D volumetric model—using deep learning. For the purpose of removing visual characteristics from volumetric chest CT scans, Li et al. developed COVNet. The COVNet they created employed a ResNet50 backbone to extract both 2D local and 3D global features, fuse the features using a max-pooling layer, and use a final fully connected layer to produce the probability scores.

Table 1 Some recent methods for COVID-19 detection

Work Ref.	Approach	Type of Images
Wang et al. [50]	Tailored Covid-Net CNN Model	X-ray
Chattopadhyay et al. [11]	Golden Ratio Optimizer-based feature selection on deep features	X-ray
Zhang et al. [57]	Residual CNN model	X-ray
Karbhari et al. [29]	GAN for synthetic data generation. Classification using deep feature extraction and Harmony Search-based feature selection	X-ray
Sen et al. [42]	Deep feature extraction using VGG-19 and classification using shallow classifiers like KNN, XGB, etc.	X-ray
Zhang et al. [56]	Lung Segmentation using U-Net and classification using a novel 3D-CNN	3D CT-scan
Li et al [31]	Novel COVNet CNN Model	CT-scan
Gozes et al. [23]	Fusion of 2D slice model and 3D volumetric model	CT-scan
Abdel et al. [1]	Few shot semi-supervised lung segmentation using deep learning	CT-scan
Garain et al. [21]	Spiking Neural Network	CT-scan
Angelov and Soares [6]	Feature extraction using non-pretrained GoogLeNet and classification using MLP classifier	CT-scan
Panwar et al. [37]	Modified VGG-19 transfer learning model	CT-scan
Jaiswal et al. [28]	Transfer learning using DenseNet201	CT-scan
Wang et al. [51]	Novel joint learning framework and contrastive learning	CT-scan
Silva et al. [43]	Majority Voting between predictions on different slices of the same patient	CT-scan

An innovative deep learning algorithm was put forth by Zhang et al. to classify sick patients and locate swollen areas in CT scans using 3D chest CT volumes. They segmented the 3D CT scans using a pretrained U-net and sent the 3D segmented chest areas into a deep neural network to predict the likelihood of infection. In their method, the computation time for detecting test images is just 1.93 seconds per image. A semi-supervised meta learning-based lung segmentation model for COVID-19 detection was proposed by Abdel et al. In order to overcome the problem of data scarcity for COVID-19 detection, Karbhari et al. devised a Generative Adversarial Network (GAN) framework and used the generated data to train a classification model. Using a shallow classifier for the final predictions instead of the pre-trained VGG-19 for feature extraction, Das et al. presented a bi-level classification model. To decrease the dimensionality of the feature collection, Sen et al. and Chattopadhyay et al. suggested a framework for deep feature extraction and classification using meta-heuristics. A Spiking Neural Network-based model for COVID-19 detection from CT-scan images was created by Garain et al.

Most of the earlier techniques are represented in Eq. (1) utilise one model for predictions; however, we suggest an ensemble strategy for COVID-19 detection. By lowering the variation in prediction errors, using the complementary data offered by the various base classifiers, based on the confidence ratings, improves overall performance and resilience. The ensemble technique is a type of fusion mechanism that computes the final prediction of the input using the characteristics or outputs from several models. It seeks to improve the framework's performance beyond what the individual models can accomplish. Due to the variety of information taken into account, ensemble learning performs better than individual models. Less noisy forecasts are made when the opinions of many models are taken into account. As a result, this technique has been used in the current work. Two of the most often used ensemble approaches are bagging and boosting, which are among the many ensemble strategies that have been proposed in the literature.

Contributions and inspiration

Due to the pandemic crisis, medical professionals and healthcare workers are working nonstop to combat the illness. The RT-PCR test, which is now the gold standard for COVID-19 screening, is slow and laborious, making it unsuitable for population-wide screening and leading to an uncontrolled number of infected people. The main driving force behind the current publication is the fact that many academics are working to create techniques for quicker and more effective screening of the infected people. Ensemble learning enables the merging of key attributes from the base classifiers, improving performance all around. Since computing the ensemble model reduces the spread (or dispersion) of the predictions of the base models, such models are robust. In other words, prediction error variance is reduced and supplementary information is gathered. A flowchart of the proposed ET-NET model's overall workflow is shown in Figure 4.

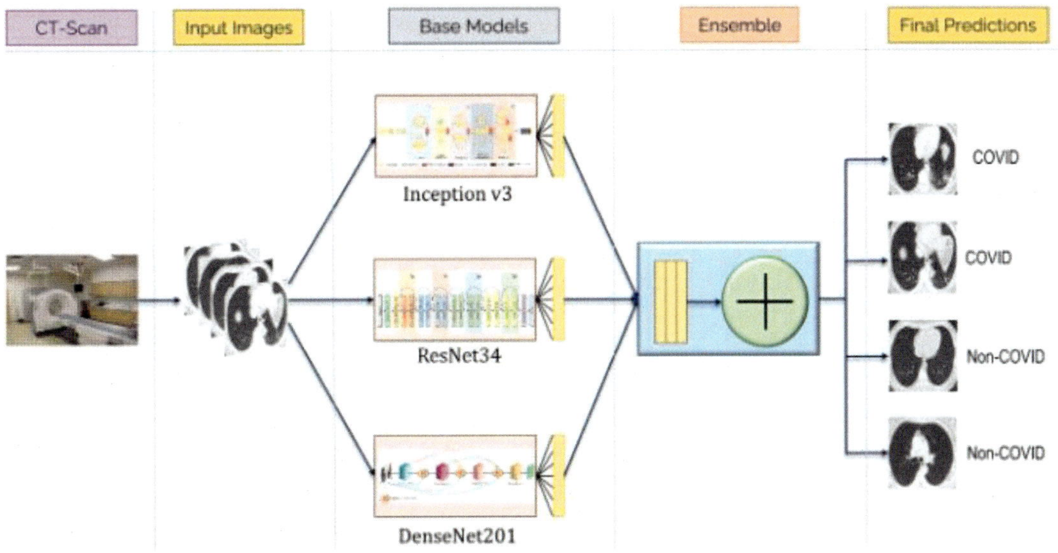

Fig. 4 Overall workflow of the proposed ET-NET ensemble classifier model for COVID-19 detection from chest CT-scan images

Proposed approach

Since an image is a 2D matrix of pixel intensities, convolutional neural networks (CNNs) are chosen for image classification issues. For example, a 300x300 image can be seen in three sections at once for object detection, etc., which is accomplished by the convolution process. Dimensionality reduction is assisted by the pooling operation. CNNs are computationally more efficient even when supporting very deep networks since they are shift-invariant and have fewer parameters than deep fully connected neural networks.

Algorithm 1 Pseudo-Algorithm of ET-NET

Inputs:
D → Dataset
Optimizer → SGD
α → Learning Rate = 0.001
β → Momentum = 0.99
BS → Batch Size = 4
ϵ → Number of epochs = 100
Models → [Inception v3, ResNet34, DenseNet201]
ω → Pretrained Weights
Output:
Predicted Class of image

```
for model in Models do
    Initialize the training and validation sets for model
    Load ω for model

    while epochs ≤ ε do
        Perform forward propagation and compute binary cross-entropy loss on train set
        Perform backward propagation and update SGD optimizer
    end while
    Save prediction probability scores for model on validation set
end for

for image ∈ test set do
    final probability score = average probability scores from the three models
    prediction = class with highest probability
end for
```

Three models, Inception v3, ResNet34, and DenseNet201, have been employed in the proposed study and have been trained on ImageNet before being fine-tuned using the chest CT-scan dataset. Table 2 displays the parameters and layer count for each deep transfer learning model.

Table 2 Number of layers and parameters in each network

CNN	No. of layers	Filter size used in various layers	No. of parameters
Inception v3 [47]	48	(1x1), (3x3), (5x5), (1x7), (7x1)	21.8M
ResNet34 [24]	35	(3,3), (7,7)	21.3M
DenseNet201 [27]	201	(1x1), (3x3) , (7x7)	20.2M

v3 of Inception

The three different types of inception blocks, which have parallel convolutions, are what distinguish the Inception v3 model created by Szegedy et al. in 2016. These modules address the overfitting issue while accounting for more efficient computation in the deep architecture. In Fig., the architecture of the Inception v3 CNN is depicted. 5a.

ResNet34

Residual Networks, or ResNets, were created by He et al. in 2016 and stand out for having skip connections that directly concatenate features from the current layer with information from a previous layer. This preserves features from earlier layers, which may be crucial. One such network, called ResNet34, has 34 layers total (including one fully connected classification layer), and its design is depicted in Fig. 5b.

DenseNet201

Each layer in Huang et alDenseNets .'s from 2017 is made up of the feature maps of all layers that came before it. As a result, these networks are efficient in terms of computation and memory usage, have rich feature representation for the input images, and are compact (i.e., have fewer channels). Fig. depicts the DenseNet201's architectural layout. 5c.

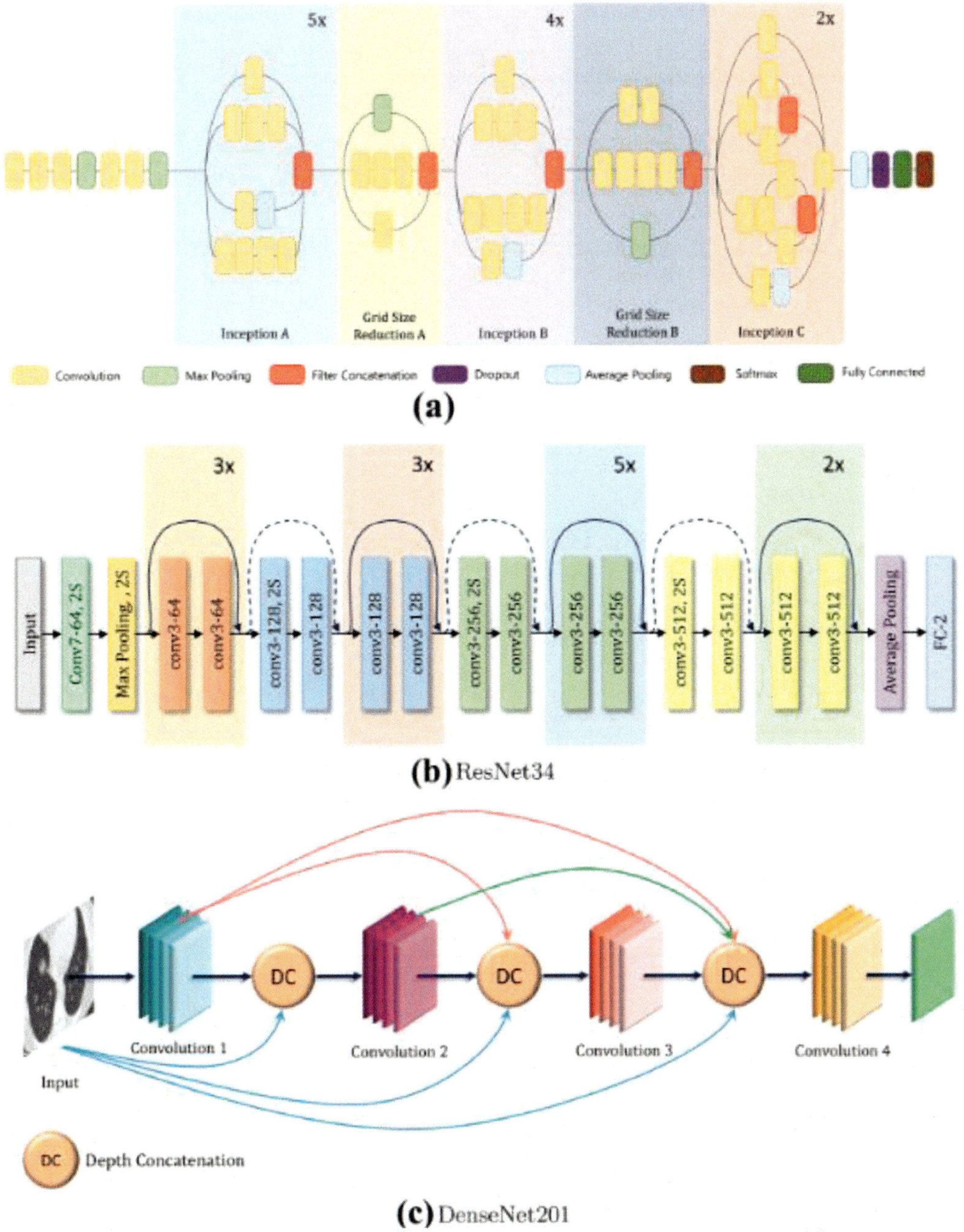

Fig. 5 Architectures of the three CNN base classifiers: **(a)** Inception v3, **(b)** ResNet34, and **(c)** DenseNet201 used to form the proposed ensemble model called ET-NET

Dysfunction loss

A deep learning model's performance is gauged by a loss function. When backward propagation occurs in a neural network, the primary goal of a deep learning model is to reduce the error between the predicted and the original labels.

The cross-entropy loss function is utilised in the current study to assess how well the classifier performs and produces a probabilities matrix (each probability value between 0 and 1). The loss function is known as the Binary Cross-Entropy Loss function since the current classification problem only involves two classes. Because it works well for binary classification issues with a wide decision boundary, the cross-entropy loss function was chosen. Since the use of logarithm cancels out any exponential behaviour brought on by the sigmoid (or softmax) activation function, this loss function also aids in preventing the vanishing gradient descent problem. Large gradients are necessary for making considerable progress during the iterations, hence the logarithm prevents saturation of the gradients at extreme values.

Consider the case where an input x has a true label of y and a predicted label of y from the classifier, which is determined by Eq. 1, where w is the neural network's associated weight matrix and b is its related bias matrix. The neural network's layers' non-linear activation function is denoted by the letter f. The activation function Rectified Linear Unit, or ReLU, has been applied to the current work.

$$\hat{y} = f(w^T x + b) \quad (1)$$

Given as in Eq, the ReLU activation function. 2.

$$ReLU(x) = max(0, x) \quad (2)$$

The loss function L is thus provided by Eq. N indicates the number of classes in the issue, which is 3. N for the current study is 2.

$$L(\hat{y}^{(i)}, y^{(i)}) = -\sum_{i=1}^{N} y^{(i)} \log \hat{y}^{(i)} \quad (3)$$

The cost function for m training samples is provided by Eq. 4

$$J(w, b) = -\frac{1}{m} \sum_{i=1}^{m} L(\hat{y}^{(i)}, y^{(i)}) \quad (4)$$

Using Eq. function, 4. The layers of the neural networks' related weights and biases are adjusted.

Ensemble

The bootstrap aggregating ensemble, often known as a "Bagging" ensemble, is the one used for the current ensemble. This machine learning-based ensemble technique was created to improve the accuracy and stability of machine learning classification algorithms. Because only the incorrectly categorised samples from the previous stage are used as training data in each step of the Boosting algorithm, Bagging ensemble techniques lessen the overfitting problem as opposed to Boosting ensemble techniques, which enhance it.

In the current study, the three pretrained models (Inception v3, ResNet34, and DenseNet201) are trained independently using the same training set. The fine-tuned models then predict the class probabilities of the samples in the test set to calculate the average probability score, giving each classifier the same weight.

Assume that n classes are being classified using m models (classifiers), numbered 1, 2..., m, and that the prediction probability scores are represented by P. The model I prediction scores for a single image can be written as a matrix using the formula in Eq. 5.

$$P^{(i)} = \left[p_1^{(i)} p_2^{(i)} \ldots p_n^{(i)}\right] \quad (5)$$

Therefore, Eq provides the average probability ensemble technique's ultimate prediction score Pensemble. 6.

$$\begin{aligned} P^{ensemble} &= \frac{\sum_{i=1}^{m} P^{(i)}}{m} \\ &= \left[\frac{\sum_{i=1}^{m} p_1^{(i)}}{m} \frac{\sum_{i=1}^{m} p_2^{(i)}}{m} \ldots \frac{\sum_{i=1}^{m} p_n^{(i)}}{m}\right] \\ &= \left[p'_1 p'_2 \ldots p'_n\right] \end{aligned} \quad (6)$$

The class with the highest probability among the values p'1, p'2,..., p'n is now chosen as the predicted class, and accuracy is determined by comparing it to the true labels. The present issue accounts for m=3 and n=2 in Eqs by having 3 models and 2 categories to sort the photos into. 5 and 6.

Outcomes and Analysis

We will briefly summarise the dataset utilised for the current investigation in Sect. in this part. 4.1, which are the evaluation metrics compared to and utilised to validate ET-NET in Sect. 4.2. The use of the created approach and the outcomes resulting from it are detailed in Sect. In Section 4.3, a comparison with the body of existing research and accepted models is made. 4.5.

Description of a dataset

The dataset used to assess the effectiveness of the suggested methodology was created by Soares et al. and is freely accessible on KaggleFootnote 1. As shown in Table 3, the dataset consists of 2481 CT-scan pictures in total, distributed unevenly between COVID and Non-COVID categories. 70% of the images (1736 scans) are used as training data for the proposed framework, and the remaining 30% (745 scans) are used as testing data.

Table 3 Class-wise distribution of images in the Kaggle dataset

Class	Category	Number of Images
1	COVID	1249
2	Non-COVID	1229

Measurement metrics

Parameters like accuracy, precision, recall (or sensitivity), f1 score, and specificity are used to assess how well ET-NET performed on the given binary classification job. To define these words, it is necessary to first define the terms True Positive, True Negative, False Positive, and False Negative.

Assume there are two classes in a binary classification problem: a positive class and a negative class. A sample that has been correctly diagnosed as being in the positive class is said to be true positive (TP). False Positive (FP) samples are those that are labelled as positive even if they belong to the negative category. Similar to this, True Negative (TN) designates a sample that has been accurately identified as falling under the negative category. False Negative (FN) samples are those that belong to the positive class but are mistakenly categorised as negative samples. As of right now, the measurements are as follows:

$$Accuracy = \frac{TP + TN}{TP + FP + TN + FN} \tag{7}$$

$$Precision = \frac{TP}{TP + FP} \tag{8}$$

$$Recall\,(or\,Sensitivity) = \frac{TP}{TP + FN} \tag{9}$$

$$F1Score = \frac{2}{\frac{1}{Precision} + \frac{1}{Recall}} \tag{10}$$

$$Specificity = \frac{TN}{TN + FP} \tag{11}$$

Implementation

The loss curves of the CNN transfer learning models are displayed in Fig. after 100 epochs of training. 6. On the test set photographs, the models' predictions have been saved. Table 4 displays the hyperparameters that were utilised to train the three models.

Table 4 Hyperparameters used for training each model

Hyperparameters	Values Used
Batch size	4
Number of Epochs	100
Optimizer	Stochastic Gradient Descent
Learning Rate	0.001
Momentum	0.99
Input Size	299x299x3 (Inception v3), 224x224x3 (Others)
Loss Criterion	Binary Cross-Entropy Loss

The final prediction scores were calculated by averaging the probability prediction matrices from the three classifiers for each sample, yielding the anticipated outcomes for all the images.

The net result is displayed in Table 6 along with the class-wise metrics that were acquired. Fig. depicts the confusion matrix for the test set. 7 and Fig. 8, which also displays the proposed ET-NET and the Receiver Operating Characteristics (ROC) curves of the various models, respectively.

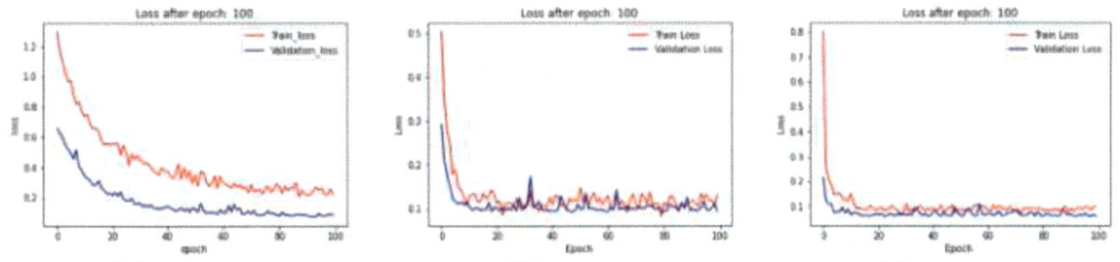

(a) Inception v3 (b) ResNet34 (c) DenseNet201

Fig. 6 Loss curves obtained using the base pre-trained classifiers after 100 epochs of re-training: **(a)** Inception v3 **(b)** ResNet34 and **(c)** DenseNet201

Table 5 Class-wise evaluation metrics generated by the base classifiers and the proposed ET-NET model on Fold-4 (best fold) of 5-fold cross-validation

Class	Metrics	Inception v3	ResNet34	DenseNet201	Proposed ET-NET
COVID	Accuracy(%)	97.59	94.78	97.19	**98.79**
	Precision(%)	97.99	95.16	96.80	**98.38**
	Recall (or Sensitivity)(%)	97.59	94.78	97.19	**98.79**
	F1 Score(%)	97.98	94.97	96.99	**98.39**
	Specificity(%)	97.57	94.72	97.13	**98.78**
Non-COVID	Accuracy(%)	**98.37**	95.10	96.73	97.98
	Precision(%)	97.57	94.72	97.16	**98.78**
	Recall (or Sensitivity)(%)	**98.37**	95.10	96.73	97.98
	F1 Score(%)	97.97	94.91	96.93	**98.37**
	Specificity(%)	97.99	95.16	96.80	**98.38**

Table 6 Evaluation metrics produced by the proposed ET-NET model on 5-fold cross-validation of the dataset

5-Fold cross-validation	Accuracy(%)	Precision(%)	Recall(%)	F1 Score(%)	AUC(%)
Fold-1	98.181	98.18	98.18	98.18	98.18
Fold-2	97.976	97.98	97.98	97.98	97.98
Fold-3	97.608	97.56	97.61	97.57	97.61
Fold-4	98.381	98.38	98.38	98.38	98.38
Fold-5	96.889	96.74	96.89	96.76	96.89
Average ± Std. Dev.	97.81 ± 0.53	97.77 ± 0.58	97.81 ± 0.52	97.77 ± 0.57	97.81 ± 0.53

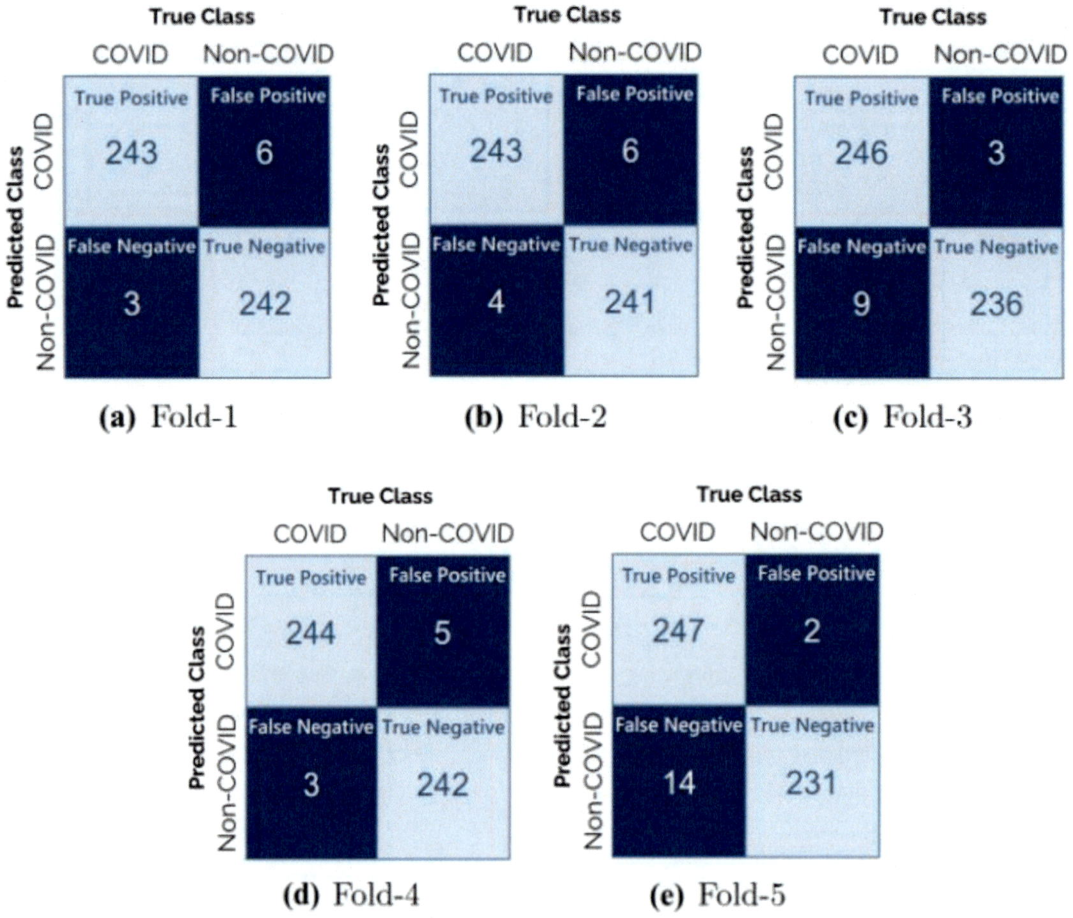

Fig. 7 Confusion matrices of the predictions produced by the proposed ET-NET model on 5-Fold crossvalidation of the dataset: **(a)** Fold-1 **(b)** Fold-2 **(c)** Fold-3 **(d)** Fold-4 and **(e)** Fold-5

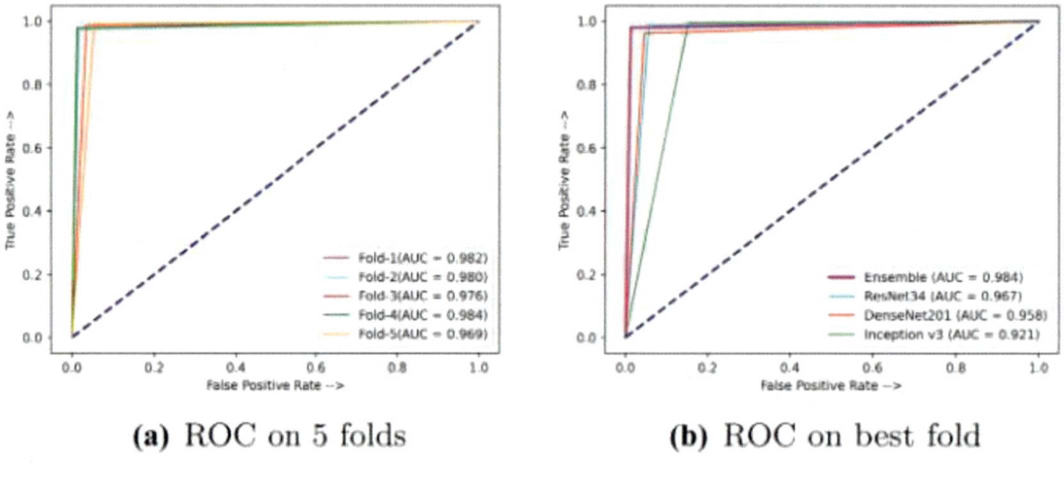

Fig. 8 Receiver Operating Characteristics (ROC) curves obtained on **(a)** 5 folds of cross-validation **(b)** the test set of Fold-4 (best result) and base CNN classifiers

Analysis of errors

With regard to the current classification issue, ET-NET performs remarkably well. Fig. displays examples of photos from each class that were successfully classified. 9. A portion of the lungs in both photos was improperly recorded by the CT scan, resulting in an inaccurate image. The difference for Fig. While Fig. 9a is also too high, the image in 9b is fuzzy. The dataset's photos had all of these restrictions, but ET-NET was still able to categorise them accurately, demonstrating the model's dependability even under problematic imaging conditions. Therefore, ET-performance NET's is unaffected by mildly noisy photos.

Fig. 9 Examples of test cases where the proposed ET-NET model performs correct classification although the images were noisy: **(a)** COVID case and **(b)** Non-COVID case

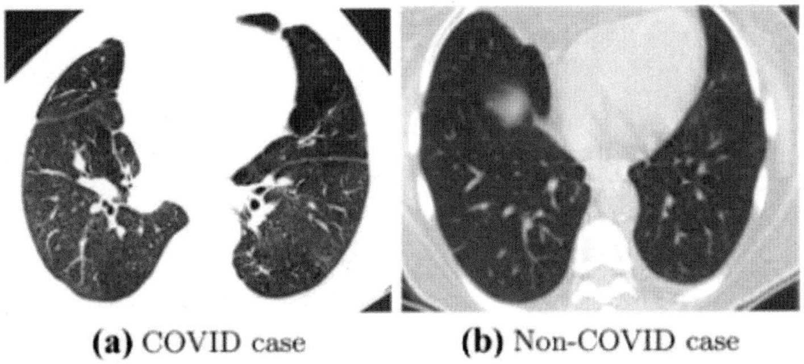

Figure 10 displays one incorrectly categorised image from each dataset class. Figure 10a is part of the dataset's class "COVID," yet ET-NET categorised it as "Non-COVID." The main reason for this is that the lung condition seen on the CT scan is a moderate COVID condition, therefore the lung alveoli do not yet have obvious ground-glass opacity. Therefore, at such an early stage of infection, ET-NET was unable to detect the presence of COVID-19 infection. On the other hand, Figure 10b is a sample from the dataset's "Non-COVID" class, despite ET-prediction NET's that it was a "COVID" condition. One of the causes of this is that the quality of the lung CT-scan is inadequate since the visible lung shape has not been accurately captured. The other potential explanation is that, in contrast to the low level of noise in Fig., the CT-scan is highly foggy. 9b.

Fig. 10 Examples of test set images where the proposed ET-NET model fails to produce correct predictions: **(a)** COVID case and **(b)** Non-COVID case

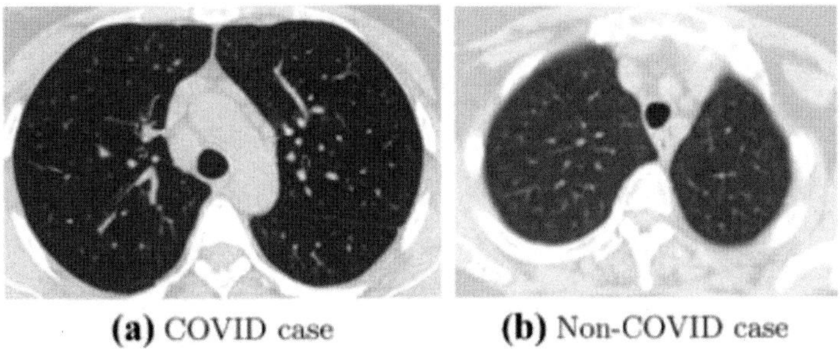

Compared to current models

The effectiveness of the suggested strategy has been compared using a number of transfer learning models, as shown in Table 7. Table 8 compares ET-NET with a few other approaches that are currently in use and use the same dataset.

For the final classification, Angelov and Soares employed a Multi-Layer Perceptron (MLP) after extracting features from untrained GoogleNet. Panwar et al. trained the network using the VGG19 transfer learning algorithm and added five more layers. For feature extraction and classification, Jaiswal et al. used the deep transfer learning technique in conjunction with DenseNet201.

Table 7 Comparison of ET-NET with some standard deep learning models

Model	Accuracy(%)	Precision(%)	Recall(%)	F1 Score(%)	AUC(%)
Inception v3 [47]	96.98	96.98	96.98	96.98	96.98
DenseNet201 [27]	96.96	96.97	96.96	96.96	96.96
VGG19 [44]	96.76	96.85	96.74	96.76	96.74
DenseNet161 [26]	96.36	96.36	96.36	96.36	96.36
ResNet34 [24]	94.94	94.94	94.94	94.94	94.94
ResNet152 [24]	94.74	94.74	94.73	94.74	94.73
Proposed ET-NET	**97.81**	**97.77**	**97.81**	**97.77**	**97.81**

Table 8 Comparison of the proposed ET-NET with some existing models in literature on the Kaggle dataset

Model	Accuracy(%)	Precision(%)	Recall(%)	F1 Score(%)	AUC(%)
Jaiswal et al. [28]	96.25	96.29	96.29	96.29	-
Panwar et al. [37]	94.04	95.00	94.00	94.50	-
Wang et al. [51]	90.83	95.75	85.89	90.87	96.24
Angelov and Soares [6]	88.60	89.70	88.60	89.15	89.20
Silva et al. [43]	87.60	-	-	86.19	90.50
ET-NET	**97.81**	**97.77**	**97.81**	**97.77**	**97.81**

Data analysis

The proposed ET-NET ensemble model's performance is statistically analysed using the McNemar's test in conjunction with the base CNN classifiers that were used to create the ensemble and other common transfer learning classifiers. A non-parametric examination of the distribution of paired nominal data is the McNemar's test. The outcomes of McNemar's test on the Kaggle dataset are shown in Table 9. A lower "p-value" is preferred because it denotes the likelihood that two models are comparable. The p-value must be less than 5% in order to rule out the null hypothesis that the two models are comparable; therefore, if the p-value is less than 0.05, we can safely conclude that the two models are statistically different.

Table 9 Results of the McNemar's test performed between ET-NET and standard CNN models on the Kaggle dataset: Null hypothesis is rejected for all cases

McNemar's Test	p-value
Inception v3 [47]	0.045121
ResNet34 [24]	0.001814
DenseNet201 [27]	0.002199
VGG-19 [44]	0.001456
DenseNet161 [26]	0.042345
ResNet152 [24]	0.0004803

The Bottom Line

Numerous countries' economies have collapsed as a result of COVID-19's spread, and people are still suffering as a result of this pandemic condition. Although RT-PCR is utilized for COVID-19 patient screening, it is a time-consuming procedure with low sensitivity. ET-NET uses Computer-Aided Diagnosis to perform a more accurate CT-scan based detection. For the binary classification task, deep transfer learning and an average probability-based ensemble approach were used to produce results that were superior to those of previously developed CT-scan based screening models, achieving an accuracy of 97.73%, which is remarkable given the small dataset used. Additionally, the suggested ET-NET has superior sensitivity and specificity than RT-PCR, making it a more effective and dependable COVID-19 detection method. Additionally domain-independent, the suggested ET-NET model can be expanded to address issues with gait detection, action recognition, etc.

The main drawback of this approach is that it may be impossible to demonstrate its robustness and generalizability if the data are not available. However, the dataset utilised in this study only contains 2481 photos, but more effective deep learning models need to be trained on larger datasets depending on the complexity of the problem for optimal performance. Deep learning models fundamentally perform best with a very large database. Since ImageNet contains 14 million images, we were forced to employ transfer learning models that were trained on that data before being fine-tuned using the chest CT-scan images from this work. In addition, as contrasted to RT-PCR and IgG-IgM antibody testing, the Middle East respiratory syndrome (MERS) and chronic obstructive pulmonary disease (COPD) are potential biases to the current work. In the future, we want to address the need for segmentation in order to enhance the Non-Covid control group design.

Once more comprehensive datasets of chest CT scans are made accessible, we want to conduct further trials and improve classification models. To overcome the restrictions indicated in Sect., we will attempt to apply picture enhancement techniques. 4.4. To create the ensemble, we might consider adding more pretrained models and using more complex ensemble methods as Dempster-Shafer theory, Choquet fuzzy integral, or rank-based fusions.

PART THREE: PANDEMIC EFFECTS IN THE SOCIETY AND NEW FUTURE CHALLENGES

Chapter 13

A Model of Emotional Care Based on Multimodal Text Analysis of COVID-19[13]

The abrupt outbreak of COVID-19 at the beginning of 2019 and subsequent revelation of the disease's contagious nature brought the world to a standstill. Scientists from all over the world have been drawn to study this unique Coronavirus in an effort to identify its source or explore the possibility of developing a vaccine. In this regard, numerous investigations have also been carried out. The only option left to the governments of various nations was to impose a total lockdown on their respective nations' soils. Businesses, sports, and other forms of entertainment had all stopped in order to respect social distance. Around the world, scientists and doctors are working hard to develop a treatment for the illness and weaken this deadly virus. People all across the world, at all levels of society, are directly or indirectly affected by this crisis and must find solutions to cope with these unprecedented circumstances. However, it is crucial to understand peoples' states of mind, emotions, and concerns before coming up with solutions to combat this infection. It makes sense that such a potent pandemic would have an impact on people's daily life, increasing the use of social media sites. For the sake of this study, India is used as the reference. Given that India has the second-largest population in the world and a larger geographic area, it was intriguing to see different emotional outburst tendencies on the well-known social media network Twitter. Every day, when people connect or communicate with one another, emotion plays a crucial part in their lives. Many factors have prompted people to express their worries. While some people were upset with the nation's declining economy, others were pleased with mother nature.

This analysis of numerous modes about a single category (nature, lockdown, health, education, market, and politics) and the eight emotions circling around those modes is, as far as we can tell, a first of its type. In order to assess the multimodal textual data found in real-time tweets about COVID-19, an unique emotion care scheme has been developed in this research. This study examines eight different emotions, including anger, anticipation, disgust, fear, joy, sadness, surprise, and trust, across a variety of contexts, including the natural world, lockdowns, health, markets, and politics. For the same, a dynamic web application has also been created. There are numerous sectors where the analysis conducted is useful. The views of the people are very important in a democracy. Not only are people being heard, but they are also being heard. Governmental organisations and policy makers must be aware of how their actions affect citizens. Another significant factor is that hearing other people's opinions regarding a topic can help you gain a completely new perspective on its various facets or dimensions. This is crucial because every segment of society is taken into account when formulating policy decisions.

---

13 *Landmark paper: Vedika Gupta, Nikita Jain, Piyush Katariya, Adarsh Kumar, Senthilkumar Mohan, Ali Ahmadian, Massimiliano Ferrara, "An Emotion Care Model using Multimodal Textual Analysis on COVID-19", Chaos, Solitons & Fractals, Volume 144, 2021, 110708, ISSN 0960-0779, https://doi.org/10.1016/j.chaos.2021.110708.*

Relevant work

Multimodal emotion analysis places emphasis on identifying feelings toward various modalities or components of an event. Numerous research projects and studies have been carried out during the COVID-19 epidemic to examine public perceptions of various occurrences. These research assisted the government in developing policies and making calculated choices to stop the spread of contagious diseases. The emotion analysis performed by earlier studies on the COVID-19 is summarised in Table 1.

Table 1
Summarization of Previous work on COVID-19 analysis.

Ref.	Emotion Label	Dataset	Methodology adopted	Lexicon/ Model used	Advantages	Limitations
[32]	Anger, Anxiety, Indignation, Negative emotion, Positive emotion	Wiebo data pool	Online Ecological Recognition (OER)	LIWC2015 Lexicon	For Policy improvement on mental health	Case study on China from a social media platform
[33]	Anger, Anticipation, Disgust, Fear, Joy, Sadness, Surprise, Trust, positive, Negative	Twitter dataset	Lexicon-based approach	NRC Word- Emotion Lexicon	To understand the changing mindsets of people	Only English tweets were collected for the study
[35]	Level of anxiety	Online questionnaires	ML-DL approach	Hybrid Approach	Understand psychological impact of epidemic on college students	Online questionnaire
[39]	Anxiety, Fear, Sadness, Anger	Questionnaire survey	Lexical oriented approach.	NRC Word-Emotion Association Lexicon	To understand the coping strategies of nursing college students	Online questionnaire
[38]	Willingness to self-isolate	Online questionnaires	Unsupervised learning	Automated Model	To help authorities understand public willingness to self-isolate	Online questionnaire is used and study is restricted to U.S. only

Understanding people's emotional states at such trying times as a pandemic attack enables the government to examine outdated regulations, create new standards, and implement policies that will inspire the populace and improve their physical and mental wellbeing. As a result, numerous studies have been carried out to examine how the general population felt about various incidents throughout the pandemic. For the purpose of evaluating public sentiment during the COVID-19 epidemic, various models have been put forth.

A condensed method that examines the emotions of 17865 active Weibo users in China—roughly 25% male and 75% female users—with age ranges of 8 to 56 years has been developed. The majority of users come from Eastern China (about 77%), while a small number also come from Central China (about 9%), and Western China (about 12%). One week before and one week after January 20, 2020, users' moods were examined. Their data showed that mean negative emotions including anger, worry, and indignation had dramatically increased in the population over the previous two weeks. The findings also revealed a large increase in the words "Health," "Family," and "Death," showing that people's concerns about their families and health were growing over time. Another study examined Twitter data to examine the sentiment about e-commerce during the pandemic and the emotions experienced by India during shutdown phases 2 and 3. Their findings demonstrated a shift in feelings over several lockout periods. Comparing lockdowns three and two, there was a considerable decrease in the percentage of these sentiments. An increase in feelings like eagerness, rage, and contempt occurred at the same moment. They also identified how lockdowns two and three affected the e-commerce sales trends. This showed that people's priorities shifted from stockpiling nutrition products, clothing, and domestic goods in lockdown 3 to baby products, beauty products, toys and games, sports, and fitness in lockdown 2.

Additionally, researchers have categorised the attitudes and emotions mentioned in the Coronavirus news headlines. Between 15 January 2020 and 3 June 2020, 1,41,208 news stories with the keyword "CoronaVirus" were subjected to sentiment and emotion analysis from the top 25 English news sources. The findings revealed that only 30% of news headlines elicited favourable thoughts, while 52% of them did. Another 18% of people were neutral. Fear ranked first among the emotions examined in the study, with trust, sadness, anticipation, and anger coming in second and third.

According to studies on the effects of COVID-19 on college students in China, almost 25% of them have felt anxious as a result of the outbreak. The findings showed that the primary causes of rising anxiety were the risk factor and delays in academic work. Living with parents and having a reliable family income, on the other hand, were protective factors against anxiety during the COVID-19 pandemic. As such, Cherish Based on an open-ended questionnaire, Kay L. Pastor et al. examined the opinions of Filipino students regarding the approach of online education. According to their investigation, the majority of students were unprepared for online learning and worried about things like local internet connectivity and other problems.

As the epidemic began, numerous researchers gained insight into the top COVID-19-related tweets, and Alrazaq et al. do the same in their paper. Alrazaq examined the 2.8 million tweets, identifying 12 subjects from 167073 distinct tweets from 160829 distinct people (China, Outbreak of COVID-19, Death causes, Economic losses, Travel bans, and warning.). Their analysis also showed that people's attitudes of 10 issues were generally good, but that attitudes toward two COVID-19-related deaths and rising racism were negative.

By examining the opinions on two different sorts of self-isolating guidelines—those that were either threatening or expressed in persuasive language—Joseph Heffner and colleagues investigated the public's willingness to do so. Their findings demonstrated that even if people reacted negatively to threatening rules, they were willing to isolate themselves.

Components and Procedures

The Twitter streaming API was used to produce the dataset of tweets. The proposed emotional care plan uses real-time tweets to communicate. The multimodal vector list associated to COVID-19 events is then used to identify the various modes that the tweet discusses. It also examines each model's indicated emotion. Each tweet in the curated dataset goes through this process. To achieve a mode-wise analysis, all tweets referencing the six various modes have been compiled into one group. This process is shown in Fig. 1 and covered in sections 3.1 and 3.2.

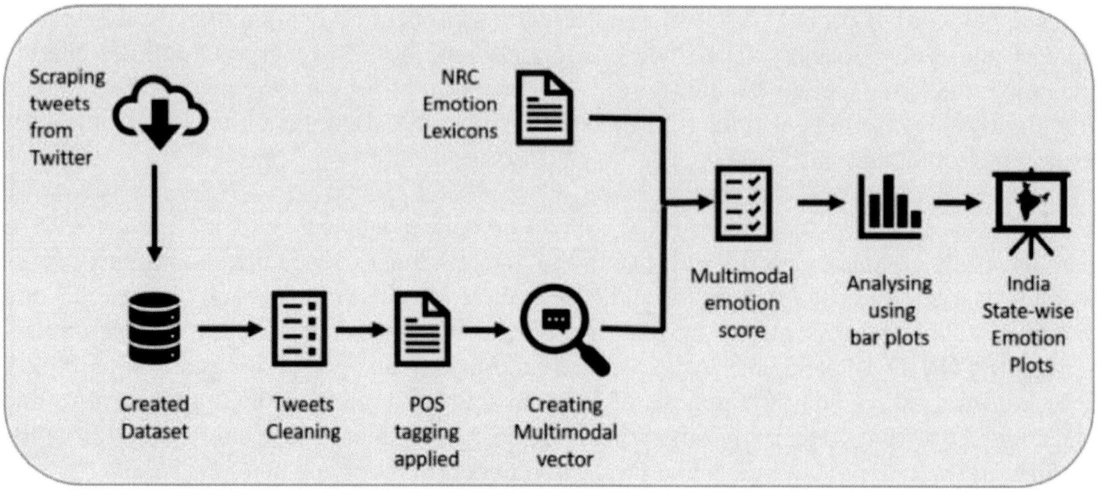

Fig. 1. Emotion-care scheme.

Collection and Pre-processing of Datasets

JavaScript is used to scrape the Twitter tweets from the "scrape-twitter" API. The attributes tweet posted time, location, and India tweets are added to a dataset. All of India's states and union territories are included in the various locations of tweets. The moment the tweet was sent is taken into account for the COVID-19 pandemic lockdown phases in India from March 25, 2020, to June 9, 2020. Only tweets with the hashtags #CoronaVirus, #LockdownDiaries, #Lockdown, and #COVID-19 are taken into account for this study article. Comparing the adjectives and adverbs produced by Stanford POS Tagger's POS tagging of tweets with the terms in the multimodal vector list. Using the frequency of terms appearing in tweets and the emotion score provided by NRC emotion lexicons, the resulting list is then evaluated against the NRC emotion lexicon to calculate its emotion score.

This study makes use of the NRC emotion lexicon. The NRC emotion lexicons are taken into account when determining a tweet's score. Anger, anticipation, trust, sadness, love, contempt, fear, and surprise are among the emotions that each word in the NRC emotion lexicon represents. The most popular phrases used on Twitter during the pandemic are shown in Fig. 2. To obtain multimodal tweets for each emotion group, a sizable dataset of 8,84,111 tweets was separated.

Fig. 2. Word Cloud of tweeted words.

In this section, the cleaning of tweets is carried out using fundamental NLP techniques. Lower case strings are first created from the tweets. The user's mentions, retweets, special characters (a-z, A-Z excepted), links, and punctuation are then quickly and successfully erased. Using stop words imported from the NLTK library, the stop words are eliminated. Tweets that have been cleaned are processed for tokenization, which separates each text into terms that should be regarded as emotional words. Given that the word list contains numerous duplicates, it is condensed into distinct words. NRC emotion lexicons are.csv files that have had any "Nan" values removed by being replaced with zero. Next that, multimodal categories are analysed using the dataset of tweets, as is covered in the following section.

Methodology

The suggested method assesses the emotion score across several modalities. Additionally, the modes were chosen by hand after carefully considering the severity of the circumstance on each of its related dimensions. The most frequently occurring words in the tweet dataset were examined using the term frequency-inverse document frequency to produce a multimodal vector (shown in Table 2). (TF-IDF). Nature, Lockdown, Education, Politics, Health, and Market are among the many modes that are taken into account for emotion analysis.

Table 2
Multimodal Vector.

Multimodal Category	Multimodal Terms
Nature	'environment', 'pollution', 'polluted', 'pollute', 'sky', 'stars', 'nature', 'earth', 'locusts', 'cyclone', 'garden', 'geography', 'greenhouse', 'habitat', 'sun', 'moon', 'peacock', 'bird', 'butterfly', 'weather', 'climate', 'marine', 'snow', 'species', 'natural', 'island', 'sunlight', 'sunny', 'sunrise', 'sunset'
Lockdown	'home','stay','safe','lockdown', 'extended', 'confinement', 'quarantine', 'curfew', 'holiday', 'imposing', 'incurable', 'industry', 'isolate', 'starvation', 'social', 'distancing', 'restriction', 'captive', 'homecare'
Education	academic','online','education','study','student','teach','coach','train','school','college','exam','grade','graduation','university','placement', 'teacher','madam','scholar','homework','master','institute','mentor', 'subject', 'stationary', 'tuition', 'screen', 'professor', 'lecture', 'class', 'lab', 'book'
Politics	'civil','politics','government','govt','rajya','sabha','party','elect','lok','cm','pm','policy','strategy','governor','minister','summit', 'opposition','scheme','majority','serve','manifesto','society','mayor','power', 'affairs', 'diplomacy', 'alliance', 'coalition', 'politician', 'legislation', 'guidelines'
Health	'patient','virus','healthy','test','hospital','medical','vaccine','disease','doctor','nurse','infection', 'transmission','mask','handwash', 'immune','fitness','sanitize','disinfect','medicine','homeopathic','hygiene','ill','cough','breath','lungs','ventilator','oxygen','recovery', 'spread','outbreak','pandemic','epidemic', 'suffocation', 'metabolism'
Market	'essentials','gdp','economy','recession','business','tax','customer','grocery','revenue','stock','gst','sale','salary','mall','share', 'shareholder','shop','manufacture','marketplace','mart','material','income','stake','statistics','store','subscription','merchandise', 'supply','demand','trade','advertisement','wholesale', 'retail', 'exchange'

The collection of tweets (T) retrieved from the Twitter streaming API for each tweet is T = {t1, t2, tn}. Each tweet could express a distinct sentiment about a different mode, and the language of the tweet can use different terms or phrases to describe each mode. In order to do this, we have thought about The set of multimodal words is denoted by Mk = "m1k, m2k,..., myk," while the set of multimodal categories is denoted by Mc = {Mc1, Mc2,..., Mck}. Consider the following scenario: When referring to the health of Indian nationals, a user may use the terms "vaccine," "medication," "doctor," or "treatment." Thus, the concept of "health" can be thought of as a multimodal category, and the terms "vaccine," "medicine," "doctor," and "therapy" are comparable multimodal terms for the concept of health. Finding multimodal emotion intensity is a challenge. By compiling multimodal ratings for each tweet, this can be generated. In a tweet, a multimodal category Mc score is equal to:

E = [Anger,Anticipation, Disgust, Fear, Joy, Sadness, Surprise, Trust]

$$\sum_{i=1}^{6} Mk(i) \cap T = Cw, \qquad (1)$$

Cw stands for Category wise words,

$$POS(CW) = AnA, \qquad (2)$$

If POS denotes POS tweet tagging,

$$\sum_{x=1}^{8} AnA \cap NRC(E(x)) = Emotion\_Score, \qquad (3)$$

where x is a component of E and AnA is a set of adjectives and adverbs.

Using this multimodal vector, a list of common terms is constructed by matching the list of adjectives and adverbs found in processed tweets following POS tagging. To establish each word's emotion score, the common word list is contrasted with the NRC emotion lexicon word list. The resulting list is used to generate a dictionary of words based on multimodal categories, with the keywords and value representing the frequency of occurrence in tweets for each category. Algorithm 1 is used to determine each category's ratings for the following emotions: disgust, fear, joy, sadness, surprise, and trust. Results are examined using bubble plots and based on their emotion score.

Algorithm 1

```
T = List(t)
Ct = List()
w = Set()
At = List(multimodal_terms)
csv = DataFrame()
def clean(T):
for each t∈T do:
t.remove_hyperlinks()
t.remove_punctuation()
Ct.append(t)
end for
return Ct
def category_wise(Ct, w, At):
for each t∈Ct do:
w = Set(t.split())
if w intersection At != NULL do:
csv.append(t)
end if
end for
return csv
def pos_tagging(csv):
for each t∈csv do:
pos_tagged = List(pos_tag(t))
if word_class == adj or word_class == adv
pos_words.append(word)
end if
end for
return pos_words
def lexicon(pos_words):
for word in lexicon_words do:
if word intersection pos_words != 0
do: emotion_words.append(word)
end if
end for
return emotion_words
def count_frequency(emotion_words):
for each emotion_words∈tw do:
word_count += 1
word_dict.add(emotion_word,word_count)
end for
return word_dict
def scoring_system(word_dict):
for row in lexicon_words.itertuples():
if key,value in word_dict.items():
if (row.key ==1):
value += 1
end for
end for
end
```

To determine the score for each multimodal category, this algorithm is employed. In this algorithm, "T" stands for the list of "t" tweets, "Ct" for the list created after cleaning the "t" tweets, "w" for the set of tokenized words from the "t" tweets, "At" for the set of multimodal terms, and "csv" for the two-dimensional data frame that, after processing, creates various category-wise tweets. Tweets can be cleaned up using the clean function. For the purpose of separating tweets based on multimodal phrases, the category wise function is utilised. The POS tagging function is used to identify the adjectives and adverbs in each category of "t" tweets. From POS-tagged words and lexicon terms, the lexicon function creates a list of common words. The count frequency function is used to create dictionaries with words as the keys and their frequency in the tweets listed in the 'tw' list as the values. The emotion score for each multimodal category is determined using the scoring system function.

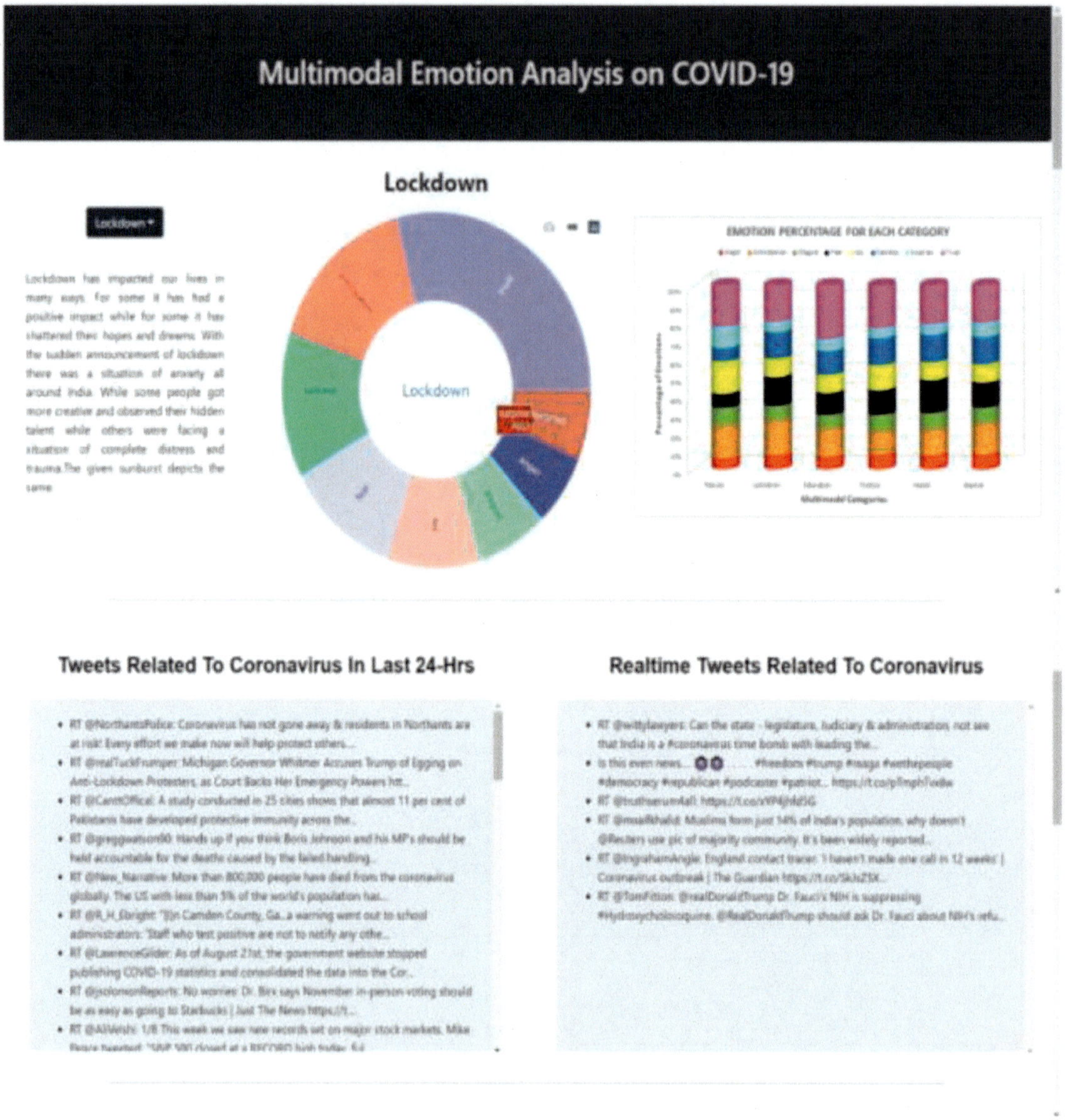

Fig. 3. Web Application https://emotionofindia.herokuapp.com.

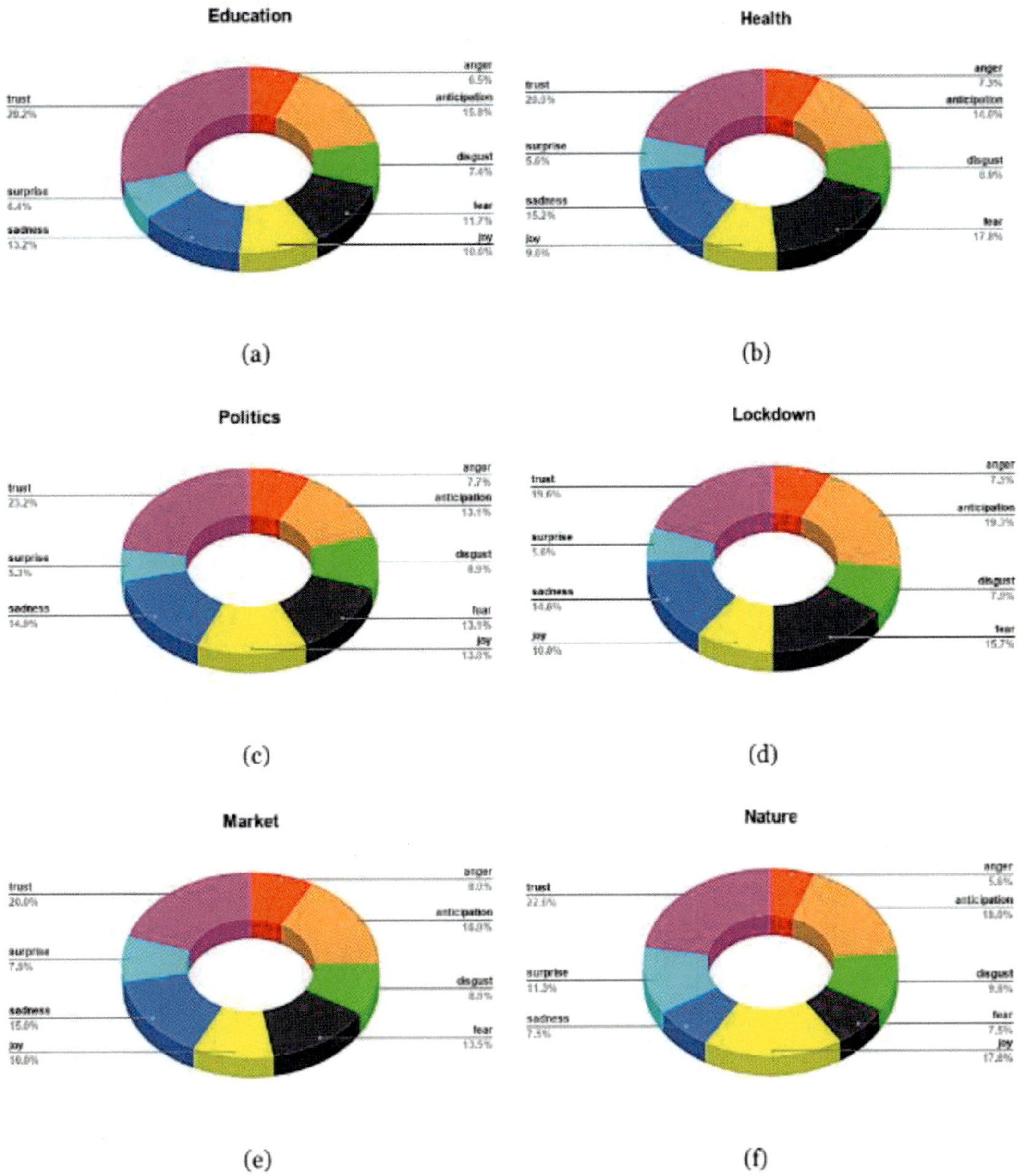

Fig. 5. Multimodal Emotion Analysis: (a) Education; (b) Health; (c) Politics; (d) Lockdown; (e) Market; (f) Nature.

The process utilised to create the subsequent emotion score chart, as illustrated in Fig. 4, was all a result of one function that was run on the dataset. The scoring system was used to implement the values for the graph. All of the tweets were subjected to POS tagging, which involved identifying the adjectives and adverbs in each tweet. After the tweets have been cleaned up, a list of separated terms is obtained and used to identify emotions in the NRC emotion lexicon. Words with their corresponding emotion scores made up the NRC emotion lexicon. A list of words that were often used in both tweets and the NRC emotion lexicon was compiled. With the aid of these often used words, a dictionary was made up of the words that appeared the most frequently in all tweets.

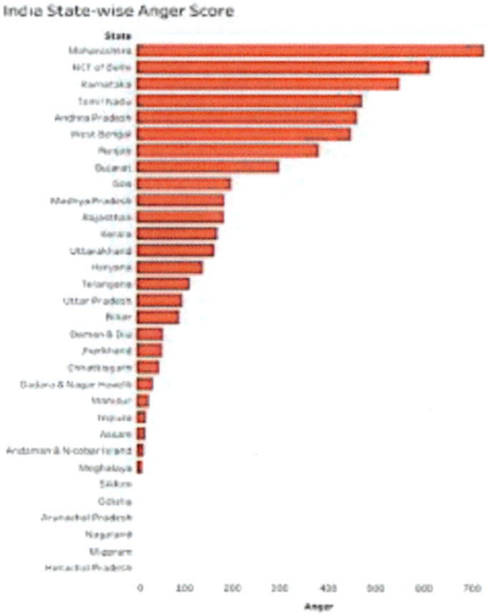
India State-wise Anger Score
State
Anger

(a)

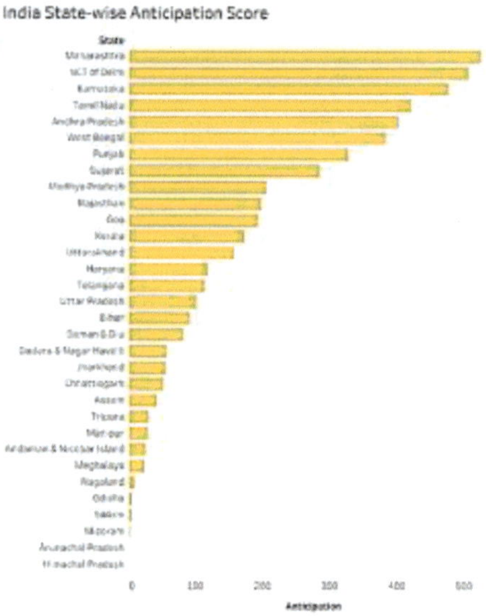
India State-wise Anticipation Score
State
Anticipation

(b)

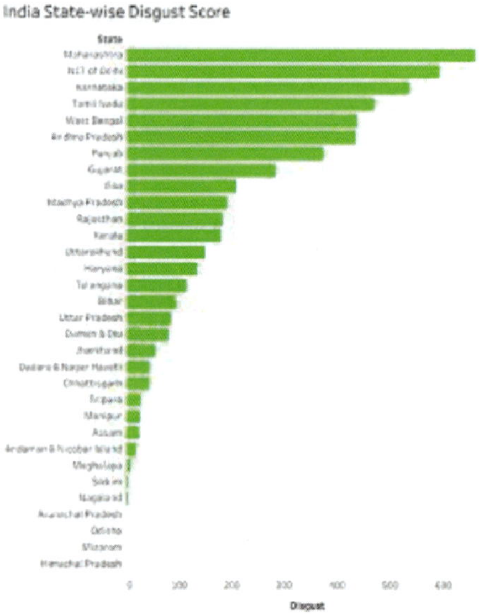
India State-wise Disgust Score
State
Disgust

(c)

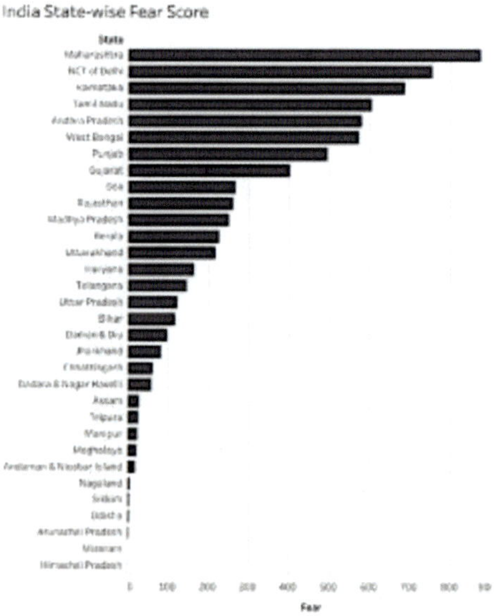
India State-wise Fear Score
State
Fear

(d)

Fig. 4. Indian State-wise Emotion Score: (a) Anger; (b) Anticipation; (c) Disgust; (d) Fear; (e) Joy; (f) Sadness; (g) Surprise; (h) Trust.

For each of the eight emotions examined in this analysis—anger, anticipation, disgust, fear, joy, sadness, surprise, and trust—a score system was developed. The scoring method determined the words in the NRC emotion lexicons for their respective emotions' values and used those results to calculate the emotion score. The term "state-wise-emotion-count-dictionary" was developed based on the values of emotions. It had state names and an emotion rating for each. Then, it was entered into a CSV file. Each state and the union territories were listed in this CSV file along with their corresponding emotion score.

Internet application

More studies are needed to fully comprehend the emotional unrest among the Indian population, although those that are now available focus more on the general emotional and behavioural analysis of the public during the COVID-19 attack than on lockdown-specific research. As a result of our research, we have also developed a website that uses Twitter streaming data to show the emotional turmoil that occurred in India during COVID-19. This website offers visualisations of emotional analysis by state and lockdown during COVID-19. Two alternative drop-down menu kinds, based on states and emotions, are provided for the users. The web platform updates its analysis in accordance with the user's selection. As seen in Fig. 2, the web site also features a section where the real-time tweets based on #COVID19 are regularly updated.

State-by-State Emotion Analysis of India

Figure 4 illustrates the feelings of the people in the various Indian states. Every emotion score places Maharashtra at the top, followed by the NCT of Delhi and Karnataka. The pandemic, which caused a sudden and significant increase in coronavirus cases, was most severe in these states. These states may have greater scores for fear, wrath, disgust, and melancholy. The number of recovered patients has also increased significantly, fostering greater public confidence and happiness. Other states like Tamil Nadu, West Bengal, and Andhra Pradesh also follow this tendency.

Outcomes

We can comprehend many aspects of the same topic that people are discussing thanks to the proposed multimodal emotion care method. Fig. In figure 6, the sentiments toward various modes are clearly shown. Due to the clear reduction in pollution, the emotion "joy" symbolised by the colour yellow has decreased towards everything (between ~9 and 15%) except for nature (~17%). The Fig. The emotional scanning of various modes is seen in figure 6. More trust (~29%) was placed in the educational system than any other area. The teachers' fraternity stood to declare that the students would not suffer as a result of this pandemic. As human lives were on the line, the health sector saw that fear (~18%) and grief (~16%) were the two most common emotions among the populace. Convincingly, the general population did not appear to be really upset about the situation.

One of the world's most unexpected events was the coronavirus epidemic. There has been anxiety and worry practically everywhere. Even the most powerful nations have given up to this issue because they were unable to adequately stop its expansion. While some nations, such as Sweden, South Korea, and Tajikistan, have decided to use herd immunity as a solution, other nations, such as China, the United States, India, and Italy, have decided that lockdown is the best option.

The world's economies were on the edge of collapse, millions of people were confined to their homes, and offices and businesses were closed. It is crucial to assess the mental health of the populace during these trying times. Checking people's attitudes toward various situations and events that are taking place around them is crucial since productivity cannot exist without a sound mental state.

The analysis is shown in this paragraph. People have voiced a wide range of feelings in response to the lockout. For this essay, a few of them are: revulsion, joy, disgust, anticipation, surprise, grief, and trust.

Maharashtra, Uttar Pradesh, Delhi, Tamil Nadu, Karnataka, Rajasthan, Madhya Pradesh, and Haryana have been the states most severely impacted by the coronavirus despite the huge efforts of the state and federal governments. This is how the analysis showed it. The majority of the populace has been extremely patient during the lockdown and has done their part to halt the COVID-19 spread chain. They have demonstrated trust in both their fellow citizens and in the policies and judgments of the government. Due to the virus's quick spread, individuals have continued to be quite afraid of getting sick despite everything. Another source of anxiety and despair may be the increasing death toll.

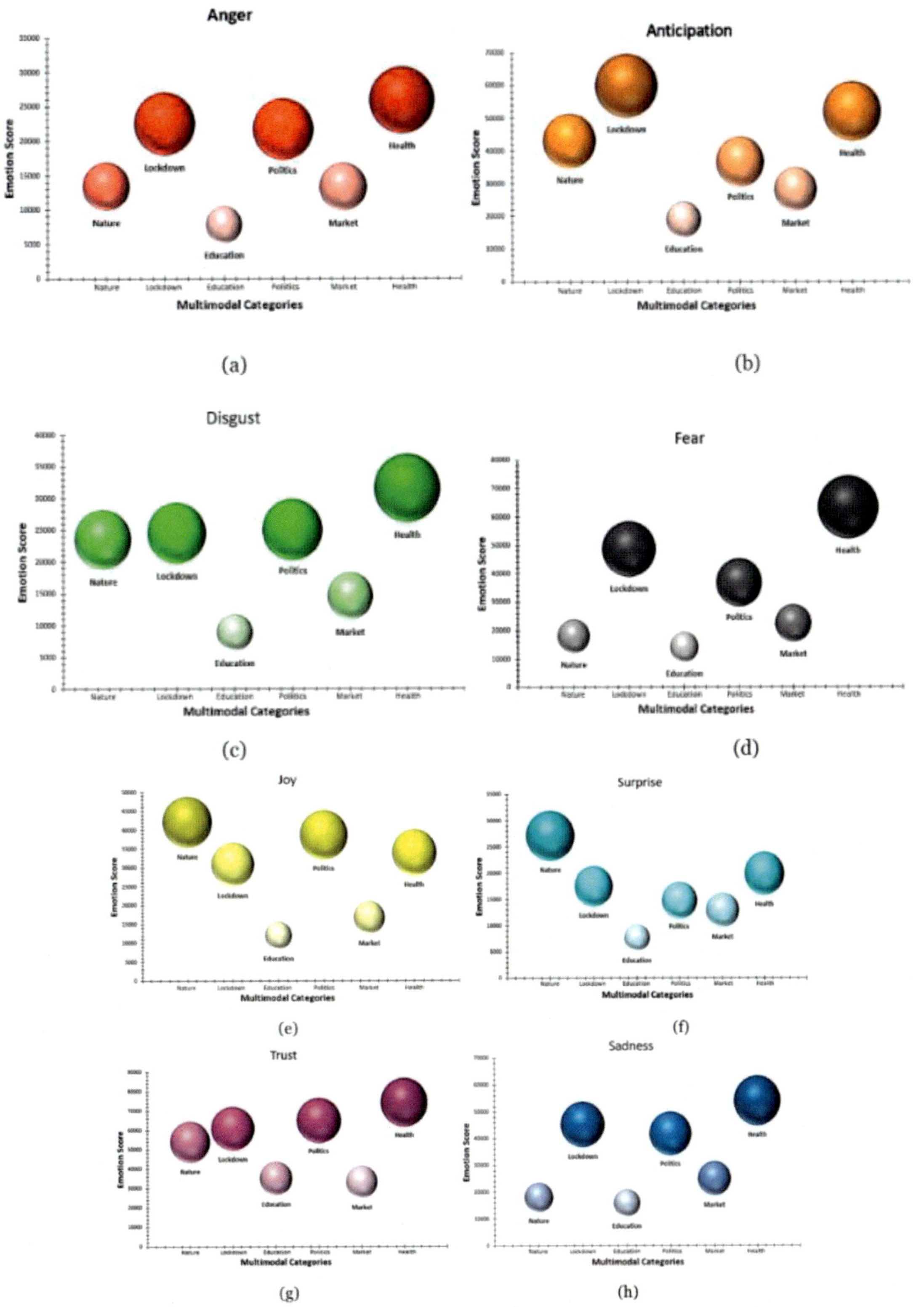

Fig. 6. Emotion intensity bubble plots pertaining to six modes: (a) Anger; (b) Anticipation; (c) Disgust; (d) Fear; (e) Joy; (f) Surprise; (g) Trust; (h) Sadness.

The majority of people have been afraid and unclear of what a lockdown will do. People's emotional well-being has been negatively impacted by factors like unemployment, working from home, a failing economy, and losing loved ones. People have made an effort to see the positive side of things despite all of the flaws. They have placed a lot of faith in the ability of schools and teachers to adapt to the evolving educational system. Another factor contributing to people's happiness has been the decline in pollution levels. The results of the lockdown and its effects on the economy have been eagerly anticipated. The government's unlocking policy has been eagerly anticipated by the public.

The mode-wise distribution of emotions during the lockdown is shown in Fig. 6. COVID-19 has obviously had a negative impact on people's mental health in addition to destroying jobs and the economy. It is difficult to adjust to being stuck in a foreign country far from your family, losing loved ones and missing their funerals, and having to wear a mask whenever you go outside. For people, the new normal is abnormal. However, a lot of people have been able to adapt to the changing environment. They are waiting patiently for everything to return to normal so they can concentrate on growing themselves.

Reflections

We continue to learn more about COVID-19's long-term effects on civilization as its roots spread throughout the globe. The pandemic not only had terrifying implications on the international economy and the physical health of people, but it also presented peculiar behavioural issues.

This essay examined the significance of collective feelings and how they affected people's mental health during this calamity. To determine the psychological well-being of the population, tweets from different states in India that were under different levels of lockdown were analysed. The strength of emotion in the top-affected states of the nation has been indicated by a plot of emotion analysis across various states. Additionally, the variations in various emotions experienced during each lockdown phase have been depicted. With the use of this analysis, policymakers may analyse the psychosomatic state of the public's health and take appropriate action to jointly combat this pandemic condition. Deep learning techniques may be used to improve the current system. The idea of sustainability rests in between finding long-term answers to today's problems and keeping an eye out for similar ones in the future.

Overall, if we had been intellectually, physically, financially, and emotionally prepared for such pandemic conditions, lockdown would not have been necessary. The system as a whole is strengthened by implementing the appropriate sustainability measures at the appropriate time. These preventive steps also search the world for long-term assistance facilities for people. The first step is to fully define the issues before tackling each one separately. Maintaining people's emotional and mental health is crucial since a nation is led by its population.

The Bottom Line

Using India as a case study, this paper proposes an emotion care programme and a web-based platform to identify people's emotional states throughout the ongoing COVID-19 issue. Health organisations and higher authorities will be able to better understand people's emotional health and interpret how people respond to varied daily decisions with the aid of this research. The proposed approach currently utilises data from Twitter. The plan can be expanded, though, if information from various social media networks is included. The model is fully functioning, but by incorporating additional languages, its scope might be expanded. Additionally, more emotions can be taken into account for a more thorough examination.

Chapter 14

An evolutionary-optimized Padé approximation method for studying the crowding impact in the Covid-19 model[14]

Introduction

SARS-nCoV2 produced Covid-19, which was spread by bats; SARS-nCoV1 and MERS-nCoV1 are related viruses. Its term, corona, comes from the fact that its genetic material, RNA, is enclosed in a lipid-layered surface with spike proteins that have the appearance of a crown. It was initially spotted in Wuhan, China, in December 2019. China, Italy, Iran, and South Korea were present in February 2020. Then, by March 2020's middle, it had taken over the whole world. Due to dramatically altered forms, it has now spread around the world in waves. The most at risk include the elderly, people with impaired immune systems, people with diabetes, cancer, and heart disease. Incubation takes 4 to 14 days. Most instances have moderate symptoms, including fever, sickness, and cough. In extreme cases, a cytokine storm can result in pneumonia, respiratory failure, body pains, nausea, shortness of breath, and even death. It spreads by the inhalation of respiratory droplets carrying the fatal virus that are generated by infected individuals and inhaled by nearby individuals. We utilize PCR testing to find suspected patients, and antibody tests to find suspected recovered patients. The illness is still being managed with the use of distancing, masking, hand washing, lockdowns, and widespread vaccinations. Vaccination has shown positive results ever since it was introduced.

In order to evaluate the effectiveness of the smallpox vaccination, Daniel Bernoulli created the first mathematical epidemic model in 1760. Today's modeling takes into account ongoing improvements in computational tools and medical data. This information is useful for understanding disease dynamics, assessing effective control methods, and forecasting next outbreaks. By foreseeing illness trends, they assist in flattening the country's Covid-19 pandemic curve. The mathematical modeling of biological processes enables the revision of epidemiological presumptions. As a consequence, by contrasting model results with observable patterns, we may evaluate our understanding of disease epidemiology.

Zeb et al. suggested an SEIQR mathematical model in 2020 to regulate Covid-19 transmission using strategies for optimum control. Several intricate epidemiological models have just been proposed for 2021. For instance, in Bangkok, Riyapan et al. presented an SEIIQRD mathematical model of Covid-19 that describes the suggested model's dynamical analysis. In

---

14 *Landmark paper: Javaid Ali, Ali Raza, Nauman Ahmed, Ali Ahmadian, Muhammad Rafiq, Massimiliano Ferrara, "Evolutionary optimized Padé approximation scheme for analysis of covid-19 model with crowding effect", Operations Research Perspectives, Volume 8, 2021, 100207, ISSN 2214-7160, https://doi.org/10.1016/j.orp.2021.100207.*

order to analyze the quarantine effect, which indicates how curable the vaccine for the terrifying virus is or which approach may be used during the vaccination, Oud et al. proposed an SEIAQHRM mathematical model for Covid-19. In order to monitor the coronavirus illness epidemic in India and use mathematical modeling to explain the virus strain, Shaikh et al. In order to investigate the link between the symptomatic and asymptomatic classes, Ahmed et al. created a SEQIR model of the coronavirus. Ullah et al. presented an SEIIQIIR model in 2020 to explain the utilization of various medications as vaccines. A SEIQR model was provided by Peter et al. (in 2021) to calculate the costs associated with a coronavirus outbreak in Pakistan. The efficiency of the Euler technique was recently quantitatively analyzed by Nazir et al. using an SEIARW model. In order to determine the spread of the coronavirus in Ukraine and the role that agents played in it, Kyrychko et al. created an SEIARD model.

In 2021, Wang et al. introduced an SEIRD model that takes into account the various methods of disease transmission. The SEIR approach was suggested by Baek et al. as a way to contain the spread of Covid-19 by hospitalization and quarantine. According to Ardila et al., the two most effective ways to stop Covid-19 from spreading are isolation and avoidance. In order to manage the illness in Nigeria, Peter et al. presented the susceptible (S), exposed (E), infected (I), quarantined (Q), carriers (C), and recovered (R) model. In 2020, Moyles et al. put out the theory that social isolation is very successful in stopping the transmission of disease. For the purpose of disease control in Moscow, Ko et al. recommended a link between the SEIR-HCD and SEIR-D models. Harjule recently mentioned the value of modeling in halting the spread of Covid-19. Staying at home, keeping your distance and early identification are the three main strategies for preventing the spread of Covid-19, according to a 2020 study by Kim et al.

The literature included in this study presents some well-known Covid-19 models using various mathematical techniques. One of the most cutting-edge approaches to obtaining trustworthy answers is to model differential equations as comparable optimization problems, particularly when the conventional approach cannot handle one or more features of the physical phenomenon. Solving inverse partial differential equations, nonlinear ordinary differential equations, and epidemiological models are a few instances of related modeling. For the purpose of resolving epidemiological models and nonlinear partial differential equations, Ali et al. suggested a brand-new evolutionary Pad'e approximation (EPA) method. Due to their extensive applicability across several scientific fields, Pad'e rational approximation functions are an important study topic. Even in cases where the Taylor series was unable to converge, Henri Eugene Pad'e created adequate Pad'e approximations for series expansion of functions. In earlier research, Pad'e approximations were used to improve the accuracy of the answer that could only be produced by other master approaches based on power series, differential transform, homotopy analysis, and Adomian decomposition.

Pad e-based optimization from differential equations may involve non-convexity, multimodality, and non-differentiability. Traditional mathematical programming cannot solve such situations. Evolutionary algorithms can solve most optimization issues. They're called metaheuristics. Metaheuristics imitate natural processes as firefly flashing, student-teacher learning, swarming, evolution, water dynamics, sport techniques, food gathering, animal hunting, etc.

Alexandros and Georgios' survey paper provide further details. Metaheuristics need theoretical validation. Metaheuristics applications have been criticized in the past. No Free Lunch (NFL) theorems show that a procedure that works for one set of trials may not work for another. Keeping the problem's complexity in mind, hybridization improves the global search optimizer's performance. In this work, we combined a widely used traditional form of the worldwide search Differential Evolution (DE) algorithm with a convergent variant of the Nelder-Mead Simplex (NMS) approach for superior results. This is the first EPA-based design and solution of the Covid-19 illness dynamical model with crowding impact as an optimization issue. In the initial EPA plan, optimization was little and the model was simpler. The current work adds additional elements to the EPA approach for solving crowding-effect epidemiological models. The EPA architecture has the following innovative elements not seen in earlier investigations.

(i) The influence of Pad e approximant order on cost function has been examined.
(ii)We compared the performance of many recent metaheuristics on analogous unconstrained optimization problems and described the hybrid evolutionary optimizer.
(iii)Mathematical programming and metaheuristics may solve complicated epidemiological models.
(iv)The EPA method retains essential qualities like positivity, boundedness, feasibility, convergence to equilibrium points, etc. by applying solution restrictions.
(v) The EPA scheme's convergence speed is high compared to a well-practiced NSFD approach.

Formulation of the model

Using the idea of population dynamics, we identify the subpopulations as Susceptible humans S(t), Infected humans I(t), and Recovered humans R. The whole population is represented by N. (t). Additionally, the model's fixed values are as follows:μ :(human death rate / recruitment rate), β: (force of infection), $\frac{1}{1+\alpha 1}$: (represents the crowding impact in a population), and γ: (the rate of recovery due to immunity or vaccination). The terrible situation will arise if the "α" keeps rising. The number of current cases eventually increases. As a result, there is a clear connection between the crowding factor and corona virus patients who are actively ill. Here, it becomes inevitable to adjust the parameter in order to regulate the dynamics of coronavirus sickness. From the perspective of mathematical modeling, we create the linked nonlinear dynamical system shown below:

$$\frac{dS}{dt} = \mu N - \frac{\beta SI}{1 + \alpha I} - \mu S \tag{1}$$

$$\frac{dI}{dt} = \frac{\beta SI}{1 + \alpha I} - -(\gamma + \mu)I \tag{2}$$

$$\frac{dR}{dt} = \gamma I - - \mu R \tag{3}$$

2.1. *Analysis of model*

2.1.1. *Positivity and boundedness*

The feasible region of the system (1–3) as follows:

$$H = \{(S, I, R)\epsilon\mathbb{R}_+^3 : S + I + R = N,\ S \geq 0, I\ \geq 0, R \geq 0\}$$

For this purpose, we will investigate the following results.

Theorem 1. *The solutions* $(S, I, R)\epsilon\mathbb{R}_+^3$ *of the system (1–3) are positive at any time* $t \geq 0$*, with given non-negative initial conditions.*

Proof: It is clear from the system (1–3) as follows:

$$\frac{dS}{dt}|_{S=0} = \mu N \geq 0,\ \frac{dI}{dt}|_{I=0} = 0 \geq 0,\ \frac{dR}{dt}|_{R=0} = \gamma I \geq 0.$$

Theorem 2. *The solutions* $(S, I, R)\epsilon\mathbb{R}_+^3$ *of the system (1–3) are bounded.*

Proof: Let us consider the population function as follows:

$$N(t) = S + I + R$$

$$\frac{dN}{dt} = \frac{dS}{dt} + \frac{dI}{dt} + \frac{dR}{dt}$$

$$\frac{dN}{dt} = \mu N - \mu(S + I + R),\ S + I + R = N$$

$$\frac{dN}{dt} = \mu N - \mu N$$

$$\frac{dN}{dt} = 0.$$

Since the total population is fixed, the system's solution (1–3) is bounded and lies in the feasible region H.

2.1.2. *Model equilibria*

The system (1–3) admits two types of equilibria as follows:

Disease free equilibrium (DFE) $E_0 = (N, 0, 0)$.

Endemic equilibrium (EE) $E_* = (S_*, I_*, R_*)$.

$$S^* = a_1 + a_2 I_*\ I_* = \frac{-A_2 + \sqrt{A_2^2 - 4A_1 A_3}}{2A_1},\ R^* = \frac{\gamma I_*}{\mu},$$

where, $a_1 = \frac{(\gamma + \mu)}{\beta}$, $a_2 = \frac{\alpha(\gamma + \mu)}{\beta}$, $A_2 = +(\beta a_1 + \mu(a_1 + a_2)\alpha - \mu N\alpha)$, $A_1 = a_2(\beta + \alpha)$, $A_3 = (\mu a_1 - - \mu N)$.

Note that, the reproduction number of the model $\mathscr{R}_0 = \rho(FV^{-1}) = \frac{\beta N}{\gamma + \mu}$.

2.2. Local stability analysis of the model

Theorem 3. *The system (1–3) is locally stable related to the virus-free equilibrium point E_0, if $\mathscr{R}_0 < 1$ and unstable if $\mathscr{R}_0 > 1$.*

Proof: For local stability, the Jacobian of the system (1–3) is as follows:

$$j = \begin{pmatrix} -\mu - \dfrac{\beta SI}{1 + \alpha I} & -\dfrac{\beta S}{(1 + \alpha I)^2} & 0 \\ \dfrac{\beta SI}{1 + \alpha I} & \dfrac{\beta S}{(1 + \alpha I)^2} - (\mu + \gamma) & 0 \\ 0 & \gamma & -\mu \end{pmatrix}.$$

At E_0, *the Jacobian becomes*

$$j(E_0) = \begin{pmatrix} -\mu & -\beta N & 0 \\ 0 & \beta N - (\gamma + \mu) & 0 \\ 0 & \gamma & -\mu \end{pmatrix}.$$

These are the following eigen values as

$\lambda_1 = -\mu < 0$, $\lambda_2 = \beta N - (\gamma + \mu) < 0$, if $\mathscr{R}_0 < 1$, if $\lambda_3 = -\mu < 0$.

Thus, point E_0 is locally asymptotically stable.

Theorem 4. *For $\mathscr{R}_0 > 1$, the system (1–3) at the positive endemic equilibrium E_* of the system (1–3) is locally stable.*

Proof: The Jacobean matrix of system (1–3) is as follows:

$$j = \begin{pmatrix} -\mu - \dfrac{\beta I}{1 + \alpha I} & -\dfrac{\beta S}{(1 + \alpha I)^2} & 0 \\ \dfrac{\beta I}{1 + \alpha I} & \dfrac{\beta S}{(1 + \alpha I)^2} - (\mu + \gamma) & 0 \\ 0 & \gamma & -\mu \end{pmatrix}.$$

At E_*, *the jacobian becomes*

$$j(E_*) = \begin{pmatrix} -\mu - \dfrac{\beta I_*}{1 + \alpha I_*} & -\dfrac{\beta S_*}{(1 + \alpha I_*)^2} & 0 \\ \dfrac{\beta I_*}{1 + \alpha I_*} & \dfrac{\beta S_*}{(1 + \alpha I_*)^2} - (\mu + \gamma) & 0 \\ 0 & \gamma & -\mu \end{pmatrix}.$$

Which yields one eigenvalue $\lambda = -\mu < 0$ and the characteristics equation

$$\lambda^2 + \left(\mu + \frac{\beta I_*}{1 + \alpha I_*} - - \frac{\beta S_*}{(1 + \alpha I_*)^2} + (\mu + \gamma)\right)\lambda + \left(\mu + \frac{\beta I_*}{1 + \alpha I_*}\right)\left(\frac{\beta S_*}{(1 + \alpha I_*)^2} + (\mu + \gamma)\right) + \left(\frac{\beta S_*}{(1 + \alpha I_*)^2}\right)\left(\frac{\beta I_*}{1 + \alpha I_*}\right) = 0.$$

It is clear, for $\mathscr{R}_0 > 1$, and by using Routh Hurwitz criteria for 2nd order $\left(\mu + \frac{\beta I_*}{1 + \alpha I_*} - \frac{\beta S_*}{(1 + \alpha I_*)^2} + (\mu + \gamma)\right) = \left(\mu + \frac{\beta I_*}{1 + \alpha I_*} - \frac{(\mu + \gamma)}{(1 + \alpha I_*)^2} + (\mu + \gamma)\right) > 0$.

And

$$\mu + \frac{\beta I_*}{1 + \alpha I_*})\left(\frac{\beta S_*}{(1 + \alpha I_*)^2} + (\mu + \gamma)\right) + \left(\frac{\beta S_*}{(1 + \alpha I_*)^2}\right)\left(\frac{\beta I_*}{1 + \alpha I_*}\right) > 0.$$

Hence, the system (1–3) is locally stable at E_* for $\mathscr{R}_0 > 1$. The proof is complete.

EPA for covid-19 model with crowding

This section describes the EPA approach for approximation model solving. The first part of the proposed technique models Eqs. (1–3) using the Pad e approximation to create an analogous optimization problem. The second component optimizes using a DE technique. DE is hybridized with a non-stagnated Nelder-Mead Simplex (NS-NMS) algorithm to yield global optimal solutions to the defined issue. Unconstrained minimization objective function ψ(x) may have discontinuities and local optima. As Pad e approximations' orders (M_v, N_v) grow, dimensionality curses. In such situations, a dependable optimization technique is helpful. We employ the DE method, which has been quite successful in practically all optimization tasks.

Optimization problem formulation

Formulation of an equivalent optimization problem involves approximating state variables with Pad e approximations, converting each governing equation to a residual function, using initial conditions as problem constraints, and using penalty functions to obtain an unconstrained global optimization problem. The global optimal solution of the unconstrained optimization issue is like the Covid-19 model with crowding.

Formulation of a similar optimization problem

Four essential steps go into the formulation of an equivalent optimization problem:

i. Pad'e approximations are used to approximate the state variables;

ii. each governing equation is transformed into a residual function;

iii. initial conditions are treated as problem constraints; and

iv. penalty functions are used to create an unconstrained global optimization problem.

The resultant unconstrained optimization problem's global optimal solution is comparable to that of the Covid-19 model with a crowding effect.

$$S(t) \approx p_S(t) = \frac{A_S(t)}{B_S(t)}, \ I(t) \approx p_I(t) = \frac{A_I(t)}{B_I(t)}, \ R(t) \approx p_R(t) = \frac{A_R(t)}{B_R(t)}.$$

Here $A_v(t)$ and $B_v(t)$ are polynomial functions with real coefficients a_{vj}, b_{vj} for each $j \in \mathbb{W}$ defined by:

$$A_v(t) = \sum_{j=0}^{M_v} a_{vj}t^j; \ B_v(t) = \sum_{j=0}^{N_v} b_{vj}t^j.$$

The derivative of $p_v(t)$ with respect to t can be expressed as under:

$$p'_v(t) = \frac{A'_v(t) - p_v(t)B'_v(t)}{B_v(t)} \forall v \in \{S, I, R\}$$

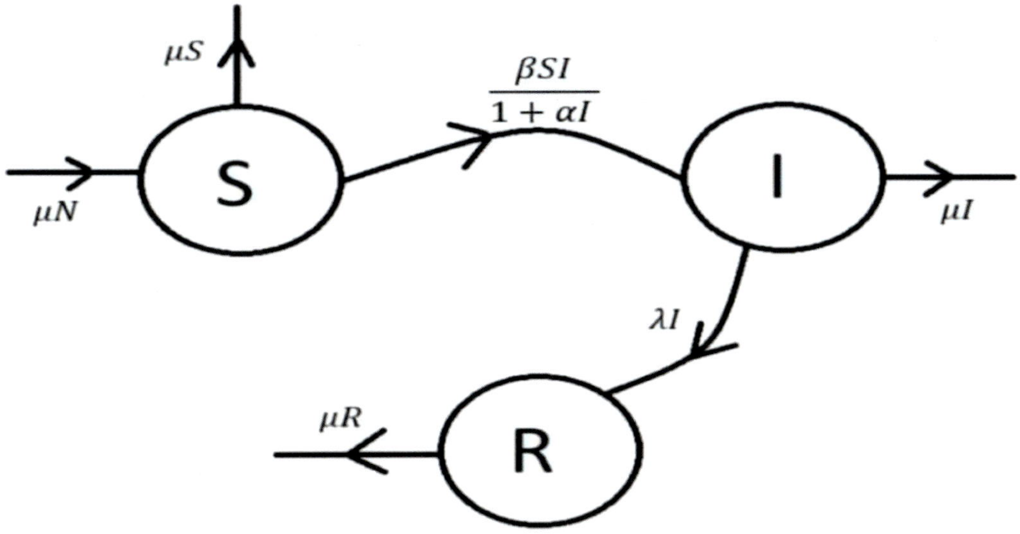

Fig 1: Covid-19 model flowchart with crowding impact

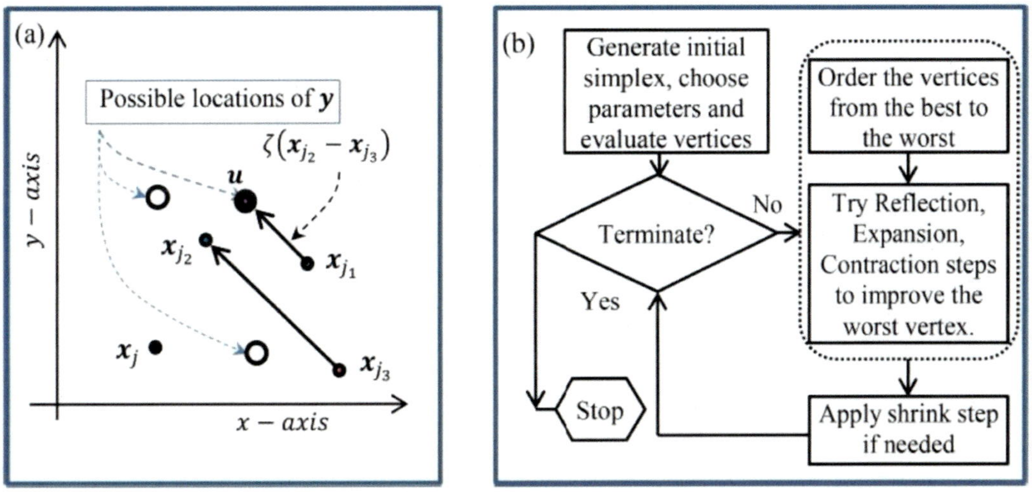

Fig 2: (a) R2's DE algorithm's geometry (b) Flowchart schematic for the NMS technique

Results and discussion

The main goal of the current work is to provide a highly accurate semi analytical solution to the model under consideration while maintaining essential dynamical features. It is crucial to look at the EPA scheme's precision, effectiveness, and dependability when used with the model under consideration. As a result, we do a double investigation of the solution produced by the EPA system in the subsections that follow. First, we examine the outcomes of our suggested EPA scheme's optimization. In order to emphasize the key features of the suggested technique, we compare the solutions produced by the EPA scheme with a well-established nonstandard finite difference (NSFD) scheme.

Analysis of the effects of optimization

We see that the objective function $\psi(x)$, which is defined by Eq. (11), has a global minimum value of zero, which equates to the global optimum point x^*. We have that:

$\psi(x^*) = 0 \leftrightarrow \varepsilon_v(x^*, t) = 0\ \forall\ v \in \{S, I, R\}$ and $P(x^*) = 0$ while keeping in mind the positivity of residual functions $\varepsilon_S(x, t)$, $\varepsilon_I(x, t)$, and $\varepsilon_R(x, t)$ and the penalty function $P(x)$ for all t and x.

While $P(x^*) = 0$ ensures that all initial conditions and the aforementioned structure-preserving features of the model are precisely met, the equation $\in_v(x^*, t) = 0$ suggests that x is the exact solution to the governing equation of $v \in \{S,I,R\}$.

The suggested EPA approach seeks to determine the model's approximate solution, let's say x, with tolerable accuracy. Therefore, the goal of the optimization process is to minimize (x) as much as feasible by making sure that all of the constraints imposed by the issue are met. The parameters utilized in the suggested EPA system have been listed in Table 1 in order to optimize the problem defined by NMS-DE.

Table 1: Parameters of EPA

Parameter	Description	Value	Reference
κ	Population size for DE algorithm	50	[49, 59]
c_r	The crossover acceptance rate of DE algorithm	0.9	[49, 59]
ζ	Differential weight of DE algorithm	0.5	[49, 59]
T_{max}	Maximum number of iterations for DE algorithm to produce the optimum solution	2000	Assumed
(M_v, N_v)	Order of Padé approximation for state variable v	(4,4), (5,5), (6,6)	
n	Problem dimension denoting the number of unknown Padé approximation coefficients	$\sum_{v\in\{S,I,R\}} (M_v + N_v)$	
L	The penalty factor of penalty function	10^6	
μ	Death rate	0.1	[29]
β	Bilinear incidence rate	0.2464 (EE) 0.1464 (DFE)	[29]
γ	Recovered rate	0.07	[29]
α	Infection rate	0.01	[29]
$V_{threshold}$	The threshold value for convergence speed	10^{-04}	Assumed

(i) The finding of a tiny value for x serves as a measure of the solution's correctness.

(ii) NMS-DE algorithm consistency is shown by calculating the best, mean, and standard deviations of the final optimal values over a number of optimizer efforts.

(iii) The number of iterations required to reach a threshold value represented by the V threshold is utilized to measure the NMS-convergence DE's speed.

(iv) By contrasting the obtained answers with several contemporary metaheuristics, the usefulness of the suggested technique is demonstrated.

Table 2: Results of optimization for two equilibrium states

Optimization results for two equilibrium states.

Order	DFE			EE		
	Best	Mean	SD	Best	Mean	SD
(4,4)	2.5e-07	**8.1e-06**	4.9e-04	8.9e-08	8.9e-06	3.1e-05
(5,5)	**1.7e-11**	3.6e-05	1.1e-05	4.2e-09	**1.2e-05**	1.6e-05
(6,6)	8.4e-07	9.4e-06	**5.3e-06**	**3.7e-08**	5.7e-05	**7.1e-06**

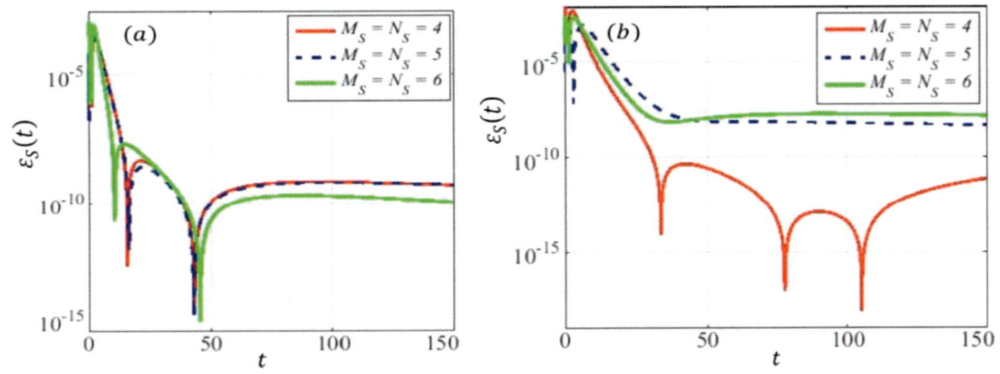

Fig 3: Mean DE-NMS convergence curves at the (a) DFE and (b) EE states.

We do not rely on the result of a single optimizer run to judge the consistency of NMS-DE. We conduct a statistical study of the marks acquired in many runs of the NMSE-DE algorithm in order to look into the dependability of the outcomes. According to the findings shown in Table 2, the mean of the best value of $\psi(x^{**})$ holds true for all orders taken into consideration and at both equilibrium points, with standard deviations falling within the range [5.3e-06, 4.9e-04]. These data show that NMS-DE consistently performs well in optimization tasks, and the results are trustworthy and accurate.

Table 3: Optimal coefficient values at the DFE state

Order	i	a_{Si}	b_{Si}	a_{Ii}	b_{Ii}	a_{Ri}	b_{Ri}
(4,4)	0	0.5	1	0.2	1	0.3	1
	1	11.62412	23.19136	−0.4410504	−1.99006	4.518759	15.1704
	2	17.96686	27.99012	21.62841	129.7301	41.81043	151.2964
	3	−4.589881	−4.792515	−0.5847947	−40.31095	−0.7980348	−13.7038
	4	3.214352	3.215415	0.0045273	71.09928	0.0038315	14.43962
(5,5)	0	0.5	1	0.2	1	0.3	1
	1	1.3390699	2.6037853	0.7072810	3.7697691	2.1501625	7.2888593
	2	788.49054	1570.245	−0.8496248	−5.7637786	1.4227432	4.0616136
	3	10.919599	36.620152	9.3823315	56.037332	7.9462428	30.799049
	4	4.7504681	3.9790506	−0.1915813	−7.5008662	−0.152888	−2.5337034
	5	4.7330172	4.7324437	0.0001154	5.4266051	−0.0001095	0.7767076
(6,6)	0	0.5	1	0.2	1	0.3	1
	1	1.08109	2.0329	1.2794	6.50122	0.452094	1.55232
	2	3.2641	8.91808	8.57519	47.9268	1.48791	5.34671
	3	10.8111	10.5012	6.6515	31.3825	6.66342	21.5409
	4	8.40516	26.7405	0.304318	20.9876	5.69837	24.053
	5	2.10008	1.75478	−0.0081925	−1.98912	−0.119462	−1.33771
	6	1.41142	1.41119	9.945e-05	1.2269	6.887e-05	0.603988

Table 4: Optimal coefficient values at the EE state

Order	i	a_{Si}	b_{Si}	a_{Ii}	b_{Ii}	a_{Ri}	b_{Ri}
(4,4)	0	0.5	1	0.2	1	0.3	1
	1	1.962976	3.873777	10.50587	52.57363	4.722648	115.74965
	2	5.110822	9.836035	16.82871	96.37293	32.34391	111.6259
	3	−0.2354903	−0.3935344	−14.07242	−77.26163	−0.5267137	−1.305307
	4	0.561096	0.8118427	3.553253	19.55911	.082824	8.514212
(5,5)	0	0.5	1	0.2	1	0.3	1
	1	−0.2527975	−0.5398225	4.208253	21.04604	2.752185	9.216065
	2	21.55926	43.33501	1.465227	11.21728	17.88936	64.84665
	3	71.79745	139.7148	−7.792861	−44.28272	16.88882	54.20429
	4	3.595083	4.53876	2.867689	15.78287	1.212053	11.0835
	5	8.729702	12.6298	1.85344	10.20357	0.6390833	5.025223
(6,6)	0	0.5	1	0.2	1	0.3	1
	1	−2.70156	−5.4178	4.88544	24.4964	7.69363	25.8147
	2	−6.08778	−12.5332	0.197156	8.6703	11.8406	39.6912
	3	−4.29643	−4.72722	9.74047	28.7846	9.08754	50.9515
	4	−8.35969	−17.1982	8.09084	66.408	7.75748	15.1099
	5	3.24166	4.79335	−0.899575	−5.46805	−0.0815287	0.269303
	6	−2.99372	−4.33166	1.66903	9.18781	1.07708	8.47145

Convergence speed

The mean convergence curves of the optimization procedure for all orders of Pad'e approximants are shown in Fig. 4 at two equilibrium locations.

Figure 4(a) shows that, for the (4, 4), (5, 5), and (6, 6) order solutions correspondingly, the threshold value $V_{threshold}$ is attained at the DFE point in fewer than 500, 600, and 900 iterations on average. Similar to how $V_{threshold}$ is reached for (4, 4) in equivalent solutions at EE point, it takes around 400, 500, and 750 iterations (please see Fig. 4(b)). These findings demonstrate how the rank of Pad'e approximants is inversely proportionate to the computing expense and convergence rate.

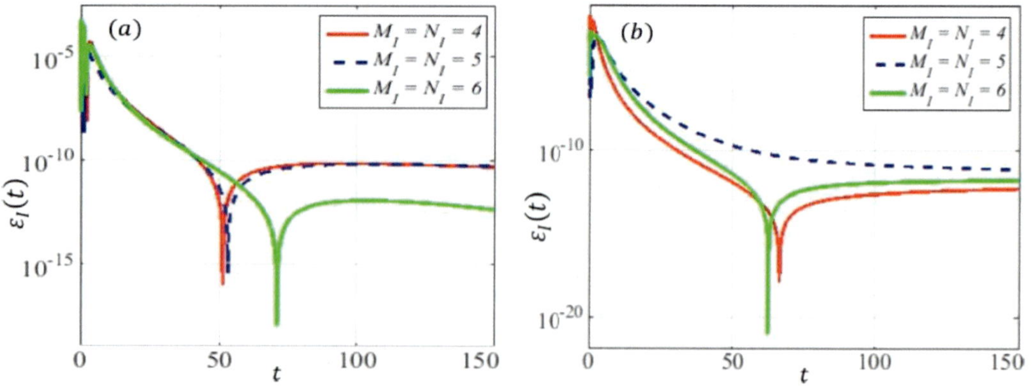

Fig 5: Squared residuals of the class S governing equation at the states of (a) EE and (b) DFE.

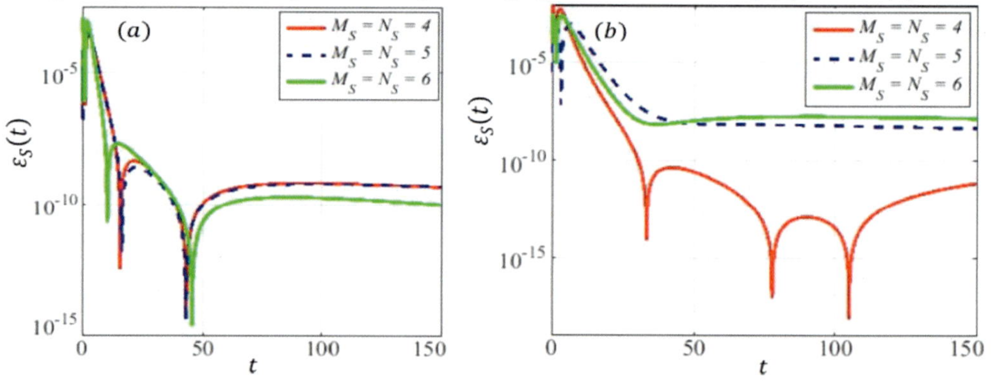

Fig 6: Squared residuals of class I's governing equation at (a) the EE and (b) the DFE states.

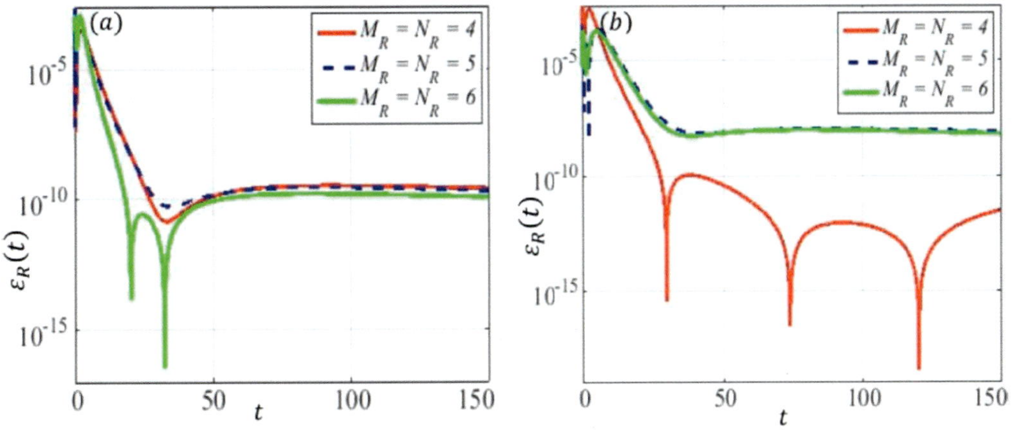

Fig 7: Squared residuals of class I's governing equation at (a) the EE and (b) the DFE states.

When TLBO, PSO, DE, CSO, and NMS-DE findings are compared, the following significant facts can be noted:

1. For all test cases, the DE algorithm produced the best minimal objective function values, outperforming TLBO, PSO, and CSO. NMS-best DE's minimum values are much superior than those of any of its rivals. For the corresponding situations of the DFE point, the NMS-DE optimum values are 92.42%, 99.998%, and 90.34% better than those of the DE algorithm. For three different situations of endemic equilibrium, NMSE obtained 85.41%, 99.65%, and 99.36% better values than the DE method at the EE point.

2. In terms of success rates (100%) of attaining pre-set accuracy Vthreshold in all circumstances, NMS-DE algorithm surpassed other metaheuristics. However, none of the rival metaheuristics managed to solve the CovidCE model's defined optimization issue with such a consistent performance. Only TLBO had success rates of 74% and 71%, respectively, greater than those of DE for the 5th order solution at the DFE point and the 6th order solution at the EE point; nevertheless, DE outperformed TLBO, PSO, and CSO on the remaining cases. This finding validates the choice of DE as a global solution and the requirement for additional hybridization in order to produce a more effective hybrid solver (NMS-DE).

3. The suggested NMS-speed DE's of convergence is quicker than those of TLBO, PSO, DE, and CSO, which is the final factor worth mentioning. The number of iterations necessary to reach the threshold value V threshold serves as a measure of the computing cost. For the fourth, fifth, and sixth order solutions, NMS-DE required around 413 (20.65%), 668 (33.4%), and 891 (44.55%) iterations at the DFE point. These figures are 973 (48.65%), 1023 (51.15%), and 1274 (63.2%) at the EE point. The competitive percentage measure of the NMS-quicker DE's or slower convergence speed across each successful metaheuristic is shown in Fig. 8. The positive and negative percentages show whether NMS-DE converges more quickly or more slowly than a rival algorithm. NMS-DE outperforms all of its rivals in terms of convergence speed, with the exception of the 6th order solution at the EE point, where TLBO outperformed NMS-DE.

Table 5: Results of competing metaheuristics' optimization at the DFE

Optimization results of competing metaheuristics at DFE point.

Algorithm	(4, 4) order solution			(5, 5) order solution			(6, 6) order solution		
	Best	P%	T_a	Best	P%	T_a	Best	P%	T_a
TLBO	1.4e-04	58	1078	5.3e-05	74	1142	1.5e-06	68	1212
PSO	3.8e-06	64	1685	1.0e-06	31	1715	7.1e-05	48	1729
DE	3.3e-06	71	1011	9.2e-07	70	1501	8.7e-06	81	1811
NMS	7.0e+06	0	-	3.5e+06	0	-	8.1e+06	0	-
CSO	7.1e-03	53	1623	4.6e-06	63	1495	5.6e-05	57	1677
WCA	5.1e-04	0	-	8.0e-04	0	-	1.4e-04	0	-
ABC	3.3e-01	0	-	2.2e00	0	-	9.1e-01	0	-
GWO	6.2e-02	0	-	2.8e-04	0	-	7.9e-03	0	-
NMS-DE	**2.5e-07**	**100**	**413**	**1.7e-11**	**100**	**668**	**8.4e-07**	**100**	**891**

Table 6: Results of competing metaheuristics' optimization at the EE

Optimization results of competing metaheuristics at EE point.

Algorithm	(4, 4) order solution			(5, 5) order solution			(6, 6) order solution		
	Best	P%	T_a	Best	P%	T_a	Best	P%	T_a
TLBO	2.3e-05	60	1053	1.7e-05	70	1083	1.5e-05	71	**976**
PSO	4.6e-06	60	1723	2.1e-05	20	1690	1.5e-05	70	1729
DE	6.1e-07	64	1303	1.2e-06	73	1429	5.8e-06	68	1691
NMS	3.4e+08	0	-	5.9e+06	0	-	7.7e+06	0	-
CSO	5.1e-05	50	1225	3.7e-05	60	1551	5.6e-05	60	1677
WCA	2.9e-04	0	-	4.0e-04	0	-	9.1e-04	0	-
ABC	4.0e00	0	-	1.8e00	0	-	2.4e01	0	-
GWO	3.7e-02	0	-	9.1e-03	0	-	1.5e-02	0	-
NMS-DE	**8.9e-08**	**100**	**973**	**4.2e-09**	**100**	**1023**	**3.7e-08**	**100**	1264

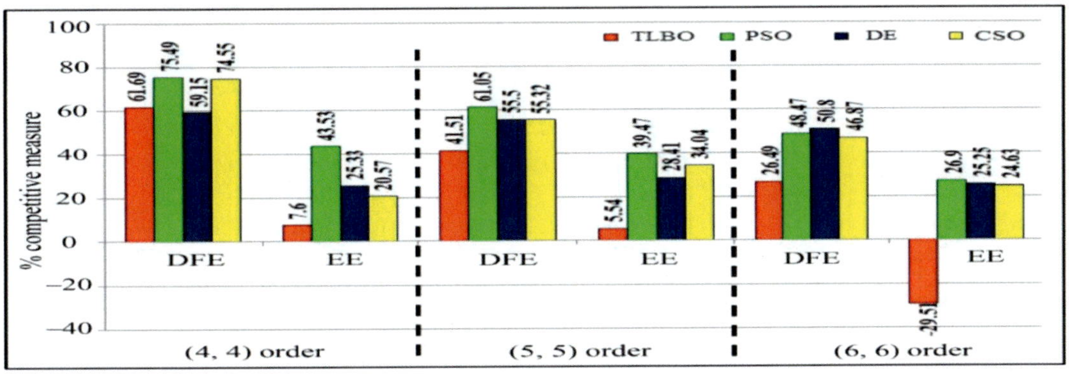

Fig 8: Competitive percentage metrics of NMS-DE convergence speed

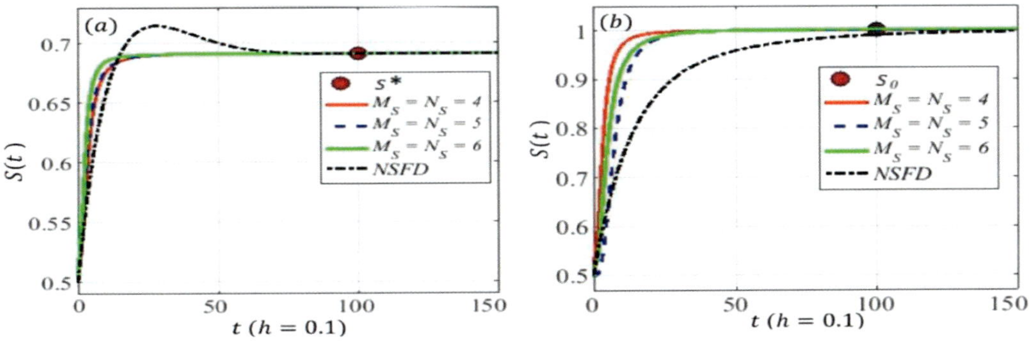

Fig 9: Dynamics of the vulnerable population in (a) EE and (b) DFE states

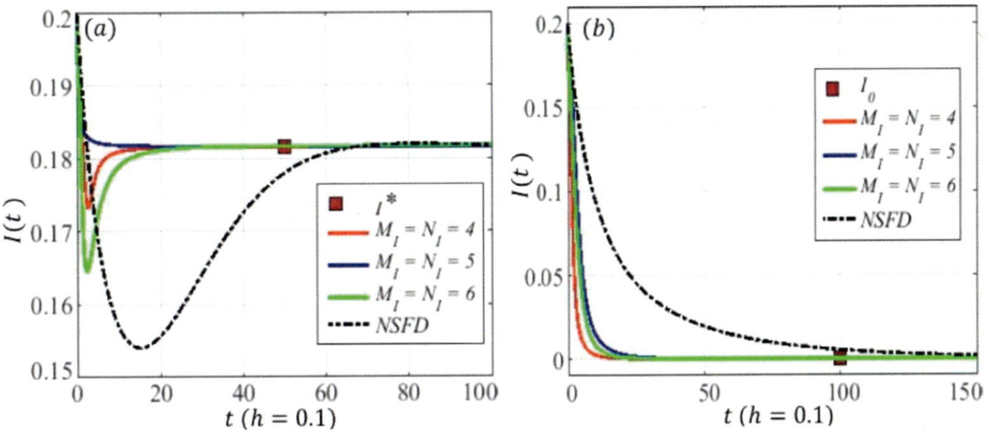

Fig 10: Dynamics of the vulnerable population in (a) EE and (b) DFE states

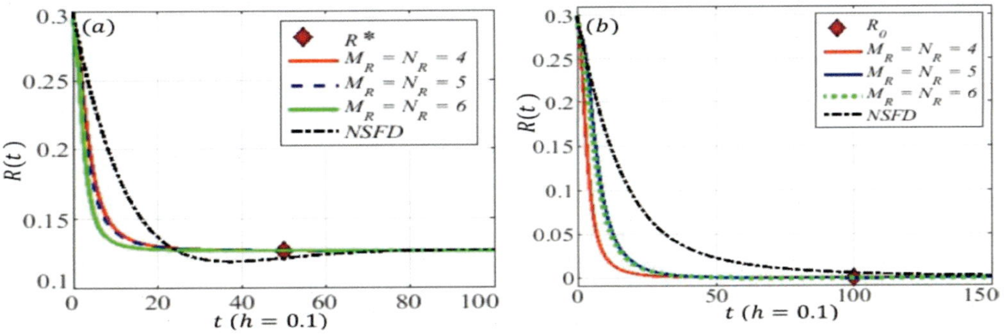

Fig 11: Dynamics of the restored population in the states of (a) EE and (b) DFE

Conclusion

The evolution of an evolutionary solution for a challenging Covid-19 model with a crowding effect (CovidCE) serves as the backdrop for the current investigation. The formulation and solution of the underlying CovidCE model as an analogous global optimization problem was the major goal of this study. This paper combines metaheuristics, epidemiology, and mathematical programming. The first contribution is to the theory of optimization, which contains two notable innovations:

(i) Formulation of a new general order Pad'e approximation-based equivalent global optimization problem that preserves the Covid CE model's crucial qualities (positivity, boundedness, and stability). This extension enables changing or modifying the ordering of Pad'e approximants to more precisely approximate the answer

(ii) The intricacy of the specified optimization issue prevented the employment of both deterministic optimizers and contemporary metaheuristics. In order to answer the described problem, a novel hybrid approach called NMS-DE was tuned as the second contribution of this study.

A statistical study of the outcomes of various solutions orders was done in conjunction with this stage. The comparison study demonstrated that the suggested hybrid technique handled the EPA scheme's optimization phase well and performed better than other metaheuristics in terms of accuracy, consistency, and convergence speed. The final contribution deals with the properties of the CovidCE model's derived solution. As far as we know, no one has yet published the precise analytical solution for such epidemiological models with all of their physical features. We can see an approximative closed-form solution to the CovidCE type model thanks to the recent work. The model simulation visuals further show that the EPA scheme's solution is in good agreement with NSFD in terms of convergence to equilibrium points and has a noticeably faster convergence time.

Chapter 15

Role of various nanomaterials in COVID-19 treatment, prevention, and diagnosis[15]

The COVID-19 pandemic, a new case of extremely severe respiratory syndrome brought on by a coronavirus, is putting global health in a high-risk situation. The highly contagious nature of the illness and the likelihood that around 6.89% of COVID-19 patients will die from pneumonia make this virus hazardous (April 27, 2020). Due of the infection's high rate of transmission, mobility, and fatality, it has caused alarm around the world. All individuals participating in the environmental system could be at risk if coronavirus were to exist in the environment, even for a brief period of time. In fact, the use of disposable items like facemasks and medical waste during the COVID-19 pandemic has increased the amount of Covid-19 pollution in urban garbage. In order to prevent the spread of viruses in the environment and urban life, the presence of nanomaterials with antiviral properties helps to kill the viruses. Rahmani and Mirmahaleh conducted a systematic literature research in 2020 to study COVID-19 preventive and treatment strategies as well as successful parameters. It's true that the author of this review paper suggested a taxonomy tree to look into the COVID-19 confronting approaches and impacts. A systematic literature evaluation based on the proposed taxonomy tree is also provided, and they conclude by highlighting the effectiveness of social and medical approaches in containing the COVID-19 outbreak. Another study examined how the antivirus-built environment stops the spread of viruses. Additionally, the significance of creating a healthy and sustainable built environment was examined in this study. More multidisciplinary study is needed to address many unsolved concerns. Therefore, understanding how to preserve nanomaterials that can be employed in the built environment is crucial.

Additionally, COVID-19 is spread from person to person mostly through respiratory droplets created during coughing, sneezing, and talking, similar to how the flu spreads (Huang et al., 2020). Without showing any symptoms, a healthy person may come into contact with an infected person or come into contact with an infected surface before touching their eyes, nose, or mouth. This new virus is the seventh coronavirus in the coronavirus genus, which has 30–40 species. The fifth and sixth coronaviruses, SARS-CoV and MERS, respectively, first emerged in 2002 and 2012. The symptoms of all three of these virus kinds are similar and include fever, coughing, and respiratory illness. The structure of coronaviruses must be understood in order to prepare for Covid-19. The coronavirus genome contains four main structural proteins with distinct roles: the spike protein (S) connects the virus to the host cell; the nucleocapsid protein (N) initiates the replication cycle; the membrane protein (M) determines the shape of the cell; and the envelope protein (E) is a hydrophobic viroporin (Fig.

---

15 *Landmark paper: Ferial Ghaemi, Amirhassan Amiri, Mohd Yazid Bajuri, Nor Yuliana Yuhana, Massimiliano Ferrara, "Role of different types of nanomaterials against diagnosis, prevention and therapy of COVID-19", Sustainable Cities and Society, Volume 72, 2021, 103046, ISSN 2210-6707, https://doi.org/10.1016/j.scs.2021.103046.*

1) Viroporins have a hydrophobic phospholipid coating on their outer layer, which causes them to interact with the host cell.

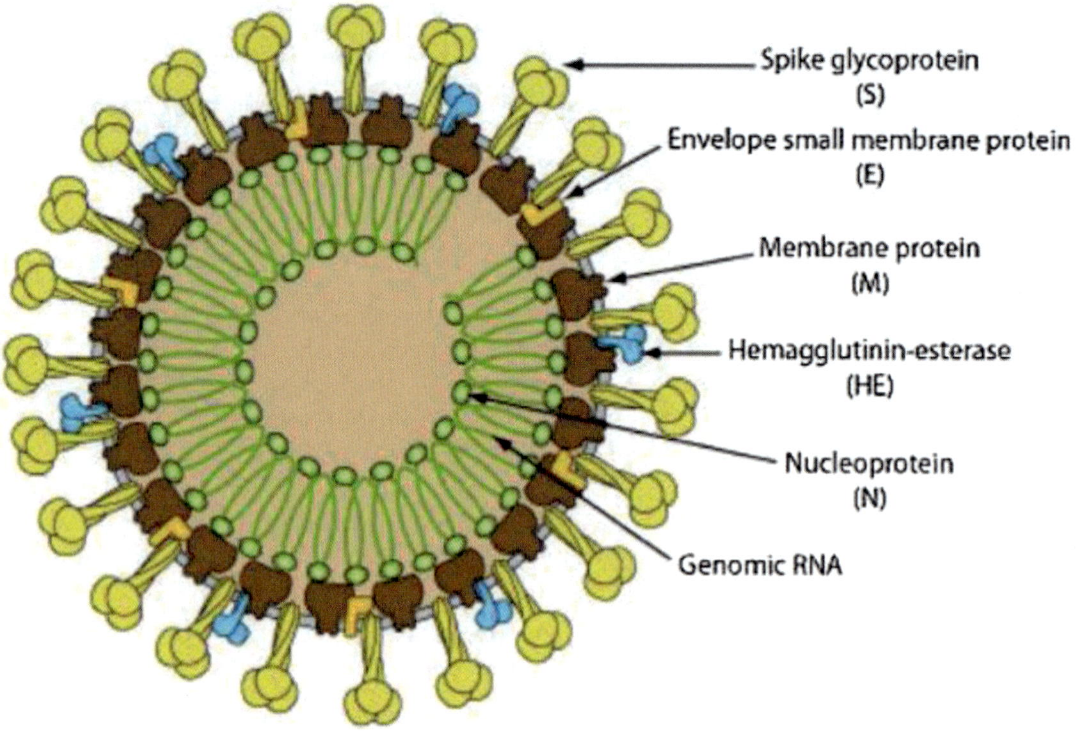

Figure 1. Coronavirus structure as shown in a schematic with structural proteins.

The fight against coronavirus sickness can benefit greatly from the nanotechnology community in 2019 (COVID-19). Nanoantimicrobials, or nanomaterials with antiviral capabilities, play a significant part in the detection, diagnosis, and treatment of viral diseases. More efforts could be made to stop the infection from spreading, even while serious resources are given to prevention, diagnosis, and treatment. As a result, coating surfaces with nanoparticles to act as antiviral coverings is a crucial step in preventing the spread of infection in the environment. This is not the first or last pandemic of the disease; the nanomaterials society may give some ground-breaking remedies to current and upcoming global health challenges. The strategies that have been studied to inactivate coronavirus often involve the contact of the virus's outer layer with nanomaterials, followed by a reduction in virus infection or complete eradication of the virus. In these circumstances, a nanosystem with hydrophobic and antiviral characteristics can engage with the surface of the virus.

Additionally, nanomaterials with noteworthy characteristics and a variety of advantages have lately been implemented into the fields of medicine such as vaccines, delivery systems, and formulations based on nanoparticles (NP). Nanoparticles can enter cells to enable the expression of antigens from supplied nucleic acids (mRNA and DNA vaccines), or they can directly target immune cells for the delivery of antigens because of their similar size to viruses (subunit vaccines). The virus antigen can either be encapsulated in the nanosystem during vaccine production or conjugated to the surfaces of nanocarriers for delivery alongside adjuvant. Antigen carriers include a variety of delivery nanocarriers include polymeric nanoparticles and lipid nanoparticles. The optimization of the nanoparticles' size, shape, and charge can increase the vaccine's efficacy. Recent great competition among scientists worldwide to develop COVID-19 vaccines has led to the production of numerous vaccine kinds. SARS-CoV-2 mRNA vaccines from Pfizer/BioNTech and Moderna use lipid nanoparticles as part of their nanotechnology-based formulations (McGill COVID19 Vaccine Tracker Team, 2021), whereas vaccines from the University of Oxford/Astrazeneca (hereinafter referred to as Oxford/Astrazeneca) and CanSino use antigen-encoding sequences found in the DNA carried by Adenoviruse Recombinant S proteins of SARS-CoV-2 are adorned by Novavax on their patented virus-like nanoparticles (Clinical Stage Pipeline, 2021).

As a result, we here emphasise the importance of nanomaterial-based technological solutions in a variety of potential applications of the virus-fighting process. In fact, to attach COVID-19, we looked at the many kinds of nanomaterials and their effects on the environment in this review paper. Safe, nontoxic, and biocompatible nanomaterials may therefore be the best option for viral prevention, detection, and treatment. In addition, this review study is separated into parts that discuss various nanomaterial types and their uses in biosensors, antiviral coating, airborne virus filtering, facemasks, medication delivery, and vaccinations to combat COVID-19.

Based on carbon nanomaterials

Although there aren't many studies available right now that discuss the potential uses of carbon-based nanomaterials in the fight against COVID-19 infection, these materials' remarkable physicochemical and antiviral properties strongly suggest that they play an important and active part in the fight against COVID-19. These nanomaterials, which have excellent sensing, antiviral, and antimicrobial properties, are perfect picks for potential applications against COVID-19 in biosensors for diagnosis, antiviral coating, airborne virus filtration, facemasks, and drug delivery. They also include graphene and graphene oxide, carbon quantum dots, carbon nanotubes, and fullerene.

In addition to graphene oxide

Due of their antibacterial and antiviral qualities, the two-dimensional nanomaterials graphene and graphene oxide have attracted a lot of attention. Antibody-conjugated graphene sheets are useful for improving environmental sensors and filters as well as for promptly identifying the virus's targeted proteins in large populations. Additionally, the functionalized graphene's acceptable virus capture capacity and heat- or light-mediated inactivation could be used to make disinfectants. Additionally, graphene sensor arrays can be used for drug efficacy testing and conventional utility textiles. There are, in fact, biosensing techniques that use antibodies to selectively detect the full infection. Furthermore, using a specialised antibody against its spike protein, graphene-based field-effect transistors (FET) have been developed as drinkable sensors to assess the COVID-19 viral load in clinical nasopharyngeal samples. In fact, by conjugating the SARS-CoV-2 spike antibody to the graphene sheet using a probe linker as an interface molecule, the antibody was fixed on the FET device (Fig. 2]). By testing the FET-based biosensing device's effectiveness using a cultivated virus, an antigen protein, and nasopharyngeal swab samples from sick people, it is able to identify SARS-CoV-2.

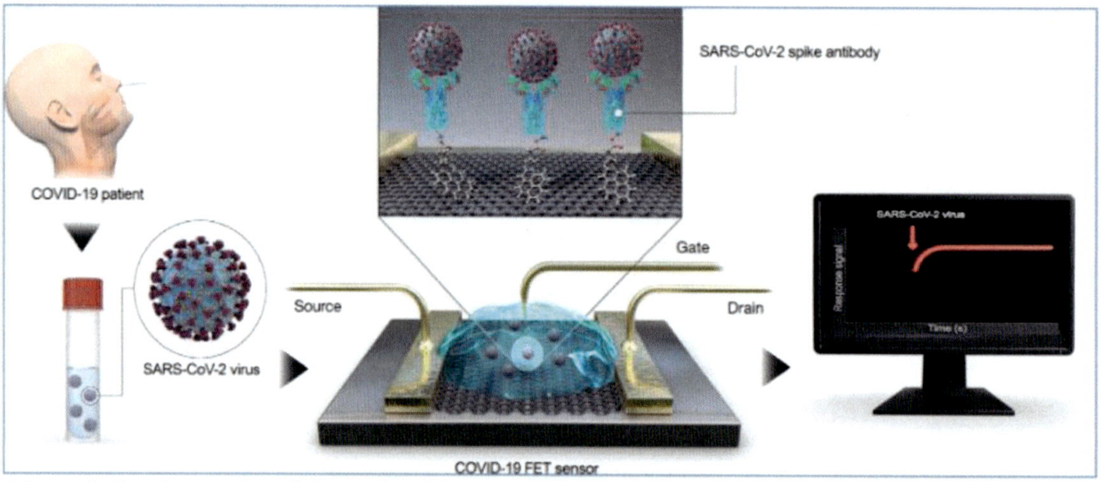

Figure 2. For the purpose of diagnosing COVID-19, a field-effect transistor (FET) sensor and its associated operational procedure

The COVID-19 antibody was applied to the graphene sheets using probe linker to create the graphene-based FET biosensors (1-pyrenebutyric acid N-hydroxysuccinimide ester).

According to the findings, the manufactured FET sensors are capable of detecting the SARS-CoV-2 spike protein at levels of 1 fg mL concentration and limits of detection of 1.6 101 pfu mL-1 for the cultured sample and 24.22 102 pfu mL-1 for the medical test, respectively, in phosphate-buffered saline and 100 fg mL-1 medical transfer system. Without sample pretreatment, this sensor demonstrates great sensitivity for new coronavirus disease diagnosis in 2019, and the use of graphene improves the signal to noise ratio (Seo et al. Additionally, Zhang and co-authors reported using graphene-based FET immunosensors to accurately, quickly, and simply diagnose COVID-19. The limit of detection was reached down to 0.2 pM in real-time and label-free fashion, with a detection speed of roughly 2 min. The graphene-based FET was also employed by Seo et al. (2020) to find the COVID-19. In nasopharyngeal swab samples, the LODs of this sensor were tested at concentrations of 1 fg/mL of phosphate buffer saline, 100 fg/mL of universal transport medium, and 1.6 101 pfu/mL of culture media, according to their research.

Ye et al. (Ye et al., 2015) used various graphene oxide (GO) derivatives to detect PEDV (porcine epidemic diarrhoea virus, strain CH/YNKM-8/2013, a DNA virus) and PRV. These derivatives included graphite (Gt), graphite oxide (GtO), graphene oxide (GO), reduced graphene oxide (rGO), graphene oxide/poly(diallyldimethylammonium chlor (pseudorabies virus, strain HNX, an RNA virus). According to the results, GtO, Go, and rGO were chosen as the best antiviral options, whereas Gt with the least amount of activity and GO-PDDA with no antiviral activity were disregarded. In fact, the existence of the materials' nanostructure has a direct bearing on this activity. Additionally, all GO materials except for the composite containing PDDA showed negative zeta potential. The required antiviral characteristics are then influenced by the particle charges.

The need for masks has grown all across the world as a means of preventing the spread of viruses. On the other side, the ecosystem is endangered by the large quantity of single-use masks that have already been used. Therefore, using graphene as permeable barrier layers on the facemasks reduces the danger of transmission while also enabling the creation of reusable facemasks. In addition, GO nanoparticles are utilised to inactivate viruses in filters, fabrics, and facemasks since they are hydrophobic materials. Since the maintenance of a facemask is impacted by the surface's susceptibility to water penetration, the protective layers are kept intact when the surface is hydrophobic and dry. This facemask can therefore be recycled using photocatalysis or heat. Additionally, the sun's irradiation and the mask's high surface temperature both effectively sterilise surface diseases. Indeed, after coming into touch with graphene at a low temperature of 56 °C for 30 minutes, viruses can be denatured. It has been discovered that several cutting-edge nanoparticles can be used to create multipurpose antiviral facemasks.

On the other hand, due to its - conjugation at every layer, graphene, a normal inorganic particle with a 2D structure, has a high drug loading capability to effectively adsorb small molecules and macromolecules of medicines. This property makes graphene a superior delivery platform for proteins and nucleic acids. Additionally, the development of vaccines may benefit from the usage of these nanoparticles. Using a self-made nano adjuvant loaded with carnosine graphene oxide adjuvant loaded with CpG molecule and RBD protein antigen, for instance, Gao et al. created a novel vaccination against COVID-19 in 2020. Their successes showed that this vaccination can produce high titer anti-SARS-CoV-2 RBD antibodies that neutralise SARS-CoV-2 in mice within two weeks.

Due to the unlimited permutations of dose, surface chemistry, and exposure route used for the test, the in vivo toxicity of graphene is still up for debate. According to one study, when GO comes into touch with the lungs of C57BL/6 mice, it causes excessive pulmonary inflammation. Another difficulty is that graphene aggregates and is unstable in solutions, whereas vaccination and medication solutions require stability.

Nanocarbon tube

Carbon nanotubes (CNTs) with dimensions of 10–100 nm, antiviral and antimicrobial activity, and good light–heat conversion efficiency have recently been widely used in biology and biomedical sciences due to their high surface–volume ratio, slight density, small pore size, flexibility, resistance to acids and bases, great mechanical strength, capacity to produce reactive oxygen species, resistance to respiratory droplets, and biological compatibility with a variety of drus. High storage capacity, high surface area, high biocompatibility, great permeability of biological barriers, good bioabsorption rate, multi-energy surface/tube chemical functional group capability, and targeted biomolecule modification potency are just a few of the excellent CNT properties that offer novel proposals facing COVID-19. Additionally, CNTs are used as a filtration, virus-inactivating, and diagnosing system. In addition, CNTs have been used to distribute medications, fight the HIV virus, and find and trap viruses and viral proteins. The potential utility of CNTs against numerous illnesses, including influenza and respiratory viruses like SARS-CoV-1 and SARS-CoV-2, is depicted in Fig. 3.

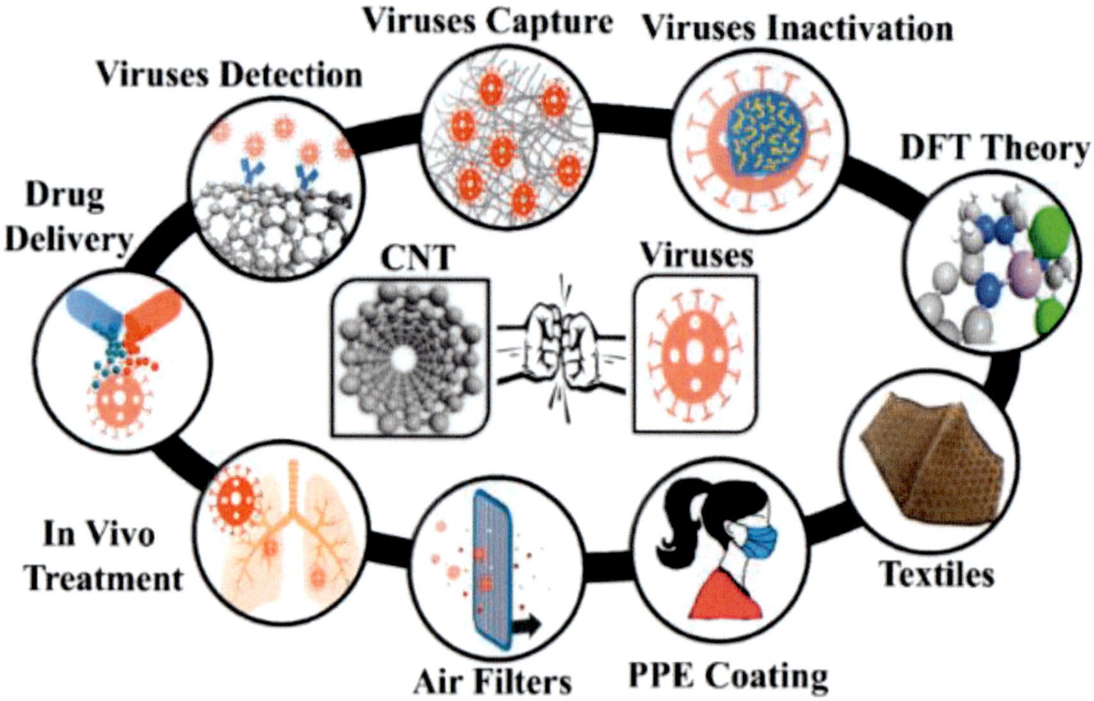

Figure 3. CNT in various viral capture/inactivation areas. Carbon nanotubes, personal protective equipment, and density functional theory.

The advancement of microfluidics allows for the management of small volumes of fluid (10–9–18 L), making it sensitive to the detection of viruses. A mobile and high-throughput microfluidic VIRRION platform with CNT arrays was proposed by Yeh et al. With the use of surface enhanced Raman spectroscopy (SERS) coupled to machine learning and a database, the VIRRION sensor successfully detected a variety of illnesses according to size while also performing continuous nondestructive virus and infection proof. In addition, Zheng et al. created portable CNT-based devices to accurately measure and capture infections. A factor of 100 can be used to selectively capture and identify infections in diluted samples using sensors that depend on the virus size in conjunction with CNT. Because no antibody is needed for viral identification, this approach has the most benefits in terms of both high sensitivity and ease of use in the isolation process.

Utilizing these nanoparticles in the creation of N95 facemasks, which stop virus transmission from person to person, is another potential use of CNT against COVID-19.

Although CNTs have many advantages, they also have certain drawbacks due to their genotoxic characteristics, which cause them to directly interact with DNA in vivo (in animal models) and at the cellular level. According to completed studies, pulmonary injection of these nanomaterials causes persistent oxidative stress by inducing chronic inflammation because of the genotoxicity of multi-walled CNTs.

Fullerene

The fullerene (C60) is a nanoparticle made of carbon with several qualities, such as antiviral activity, antioxidant and antiradical properties, as well as hydrophobic nature. In aqueous samples, fullerene takes on a colloidal form and has hydrophobic properties. This colloidal solution produces singlet oxygen when exposed to UVA light. The peroxidation phase of the oxidative reaction initiates the lipid destruction process. The degradation of the lipid layers is influenced by the fullerene concentration in solution. On the bacterial phospholipid membrane, lipid peroxidation by C60 was seen similarly. The damage to the virus's envelope caused by lipid peroxidation with fullerene coating is seen in Fig. 4.

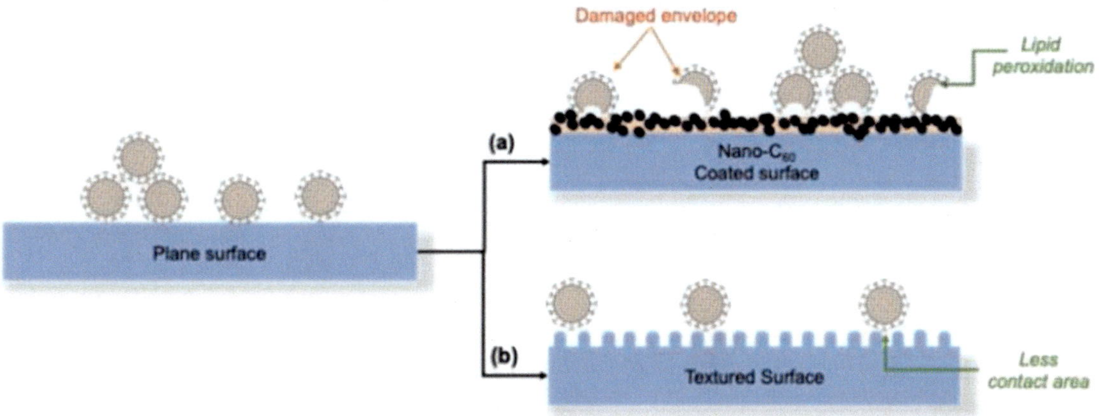

Figure 4. There are two alternative ways to combat COVID-19. (a) By covering the surface with nano-C60 and inactivating the lipid layer. (b) By surface texturing to minimise the area in contact with the virus.

Based on Fig. 4, the phospholipid layer that is present in the outer layer of COVID-19 is coated by C60, causing lipid peroxidation on the surface contact of the textured surface. Additionally, due to the presence of trapped air bubbles, the hydrophobic characteristics of C60 result in reducing contact between the texturing surface and virus outer layer. As a result, these nanomaterials as coating materials are offered as a potential remedy against COVID-19 since they will be hydrophobic as well as toxic to the virus's envelope. This is because C60 reduces the adherence between virus and texturing surfaces. However, due to the lipid's hydrophobic nature, lipid peroxidation by a water-soluble C60 causes the virus's outer layer of lipid to disintegrate.

According to the authors, research on carbon nanoparticles (G, GO, CNT, and F) has led to the conclusion that these types of nanomaterials are better suited for use in biosensor, filtration, and other applications that do not directly come into contact with living cells (like drug delivery system or vaccine). In fact, more research needs to be done on the toxicity and biocompatibility of various types of nanoparticles in living cells. Therefore, the manufacture of disposable facemasks is eliminated by the use of carbon nanomaterials as antiviral agents in facemasks.

Quantum dots (QDs)

To detect the long-term fluorescence imaging of various biological activities, quantum dots (QDs), semiconductor nanoparticles with 1–10 nm diameters and tunable optical wavelengths, were attached with high fluorescent probes. In fact, QDs, a novel nanoparticle, are employed as interception devices to stop COVID-19 from entering and interacting with the host cell membrane in addition to being used as fluorescent probes for molecular and cellular imaging. Due to their interaction with the S-protein of viruses, their ability to stop the genomic replication of viral RNA, and their use as fluorescent probes, QDs materials have the potential to inactivate viruses (Fig. 5).

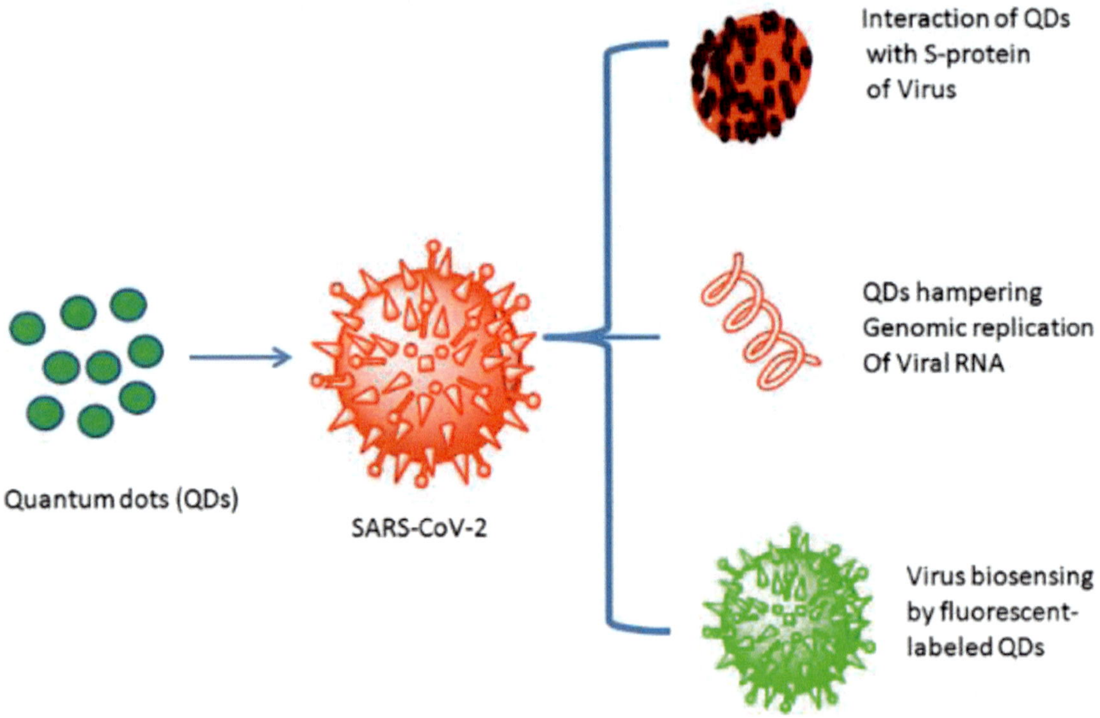

Figure 5. QD, or quantum dot, stands for spike protein; SARS-CoV-2, or severe acute respiratory syndrome coronavirus type 2, is shown in the diagram as being affected by QDs.

Additionally, the use of environmentally friendly technologies to create QDs makes them a good option for antiviral applications, particularly in vivo infection. Considering that SARS-CoV-2 will extrapolate nanostructures for COVID-19 restorative to inactivate the life-threatening diseases in the near future. QDs optimization and functionalization with innovative functional molecules.

Atomic carbon dots

Carbon quantum dots (CQDs), which are the most common imaging probes (chemosensors and biosensors) with antiviral activity, can be employed as a biocompatible inactivation system for pathogenic human coronavirus infections in addition to sensing microorganisms, biomolecules, and diseases. The CQDs, which have a high water solubility and have a diameter of roughly 10 nm, were made via hydrothermal carbonization of carbon precursors. Some cutting-edge methods have concentrated on the use of CQDs in the detection of coronaviruses. In one of the investigations, human coronavirus infections were treated using the antiviral properties of seven different types of CQDs. By combining boronic acid conjugation with hydrothermal carbonization, oczechin et al. generated various CQD kinds. It was discovered that the virus inhibition may be caused by a contact between the functional groups of CQDs and the virus' entrance receptors (Fig. 6). In fact, the positive charge on the surface of CQDs disables and separates the virus' spike protein, which then reacts with the COVID-19 virus's negative RNA.

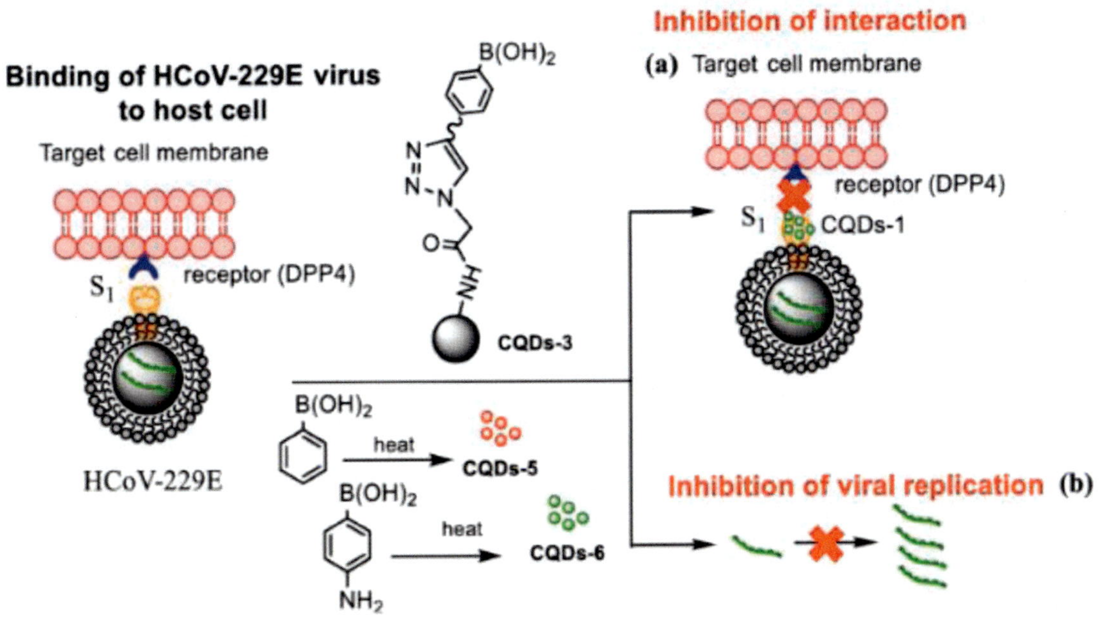

Figure 6. The effects of carbon quantum dots (CQDs) made by hydrothermal carbonization on the binding of the HCoV-229E virus to cells are as follows: (a) inhibition of the protein S receptor junction; (b) inhibition of viral RNA genome replication.

Atomic dots made of zirconium (Zr QDs)

Because of its characteristics, including UV light absorption, thermal stability, and mechanical strength, zirconium is a benign transition metal element that has been utilised in a variety of biological sectors. Additionally, because of its large surface area and the confinement of electronic states in comparison to its bulk regime, Zr nanoparticles exhibit unique physical and chemical properties.

Although some research focused on creating and characterising zirconium nanoparticles, zirconium quantum dots have not yet been reported on in any study (Zr QDs). Ahmed et al. investigated the usage of Zr QDs magnetoplasmonic (MP) NPs for the detection of infectious bronchitis virus (IBV) in one of the investigations. They described the use of an autoclave to facilitate the one-step production of Zr QDs from Zr nanoparticle (Ahmed, Kang, Oh, Lee, & Neethirajan, 2018). According to the results, Zr QDs have a blue fluorescence emission used to detect the infectious bronchitis virus (IBV). As shown in Fig. 7, coupled antibody-Zr QDs and antibody-MP NPs were initially shown individually before infections were added. The antibody-Zr QDs and antibody-MP NPs were then joined to form a nanocomposite (Zr QDs-MP NPs) to carry the viruses or infections, and the composite was afterwards separated using an external magnet.

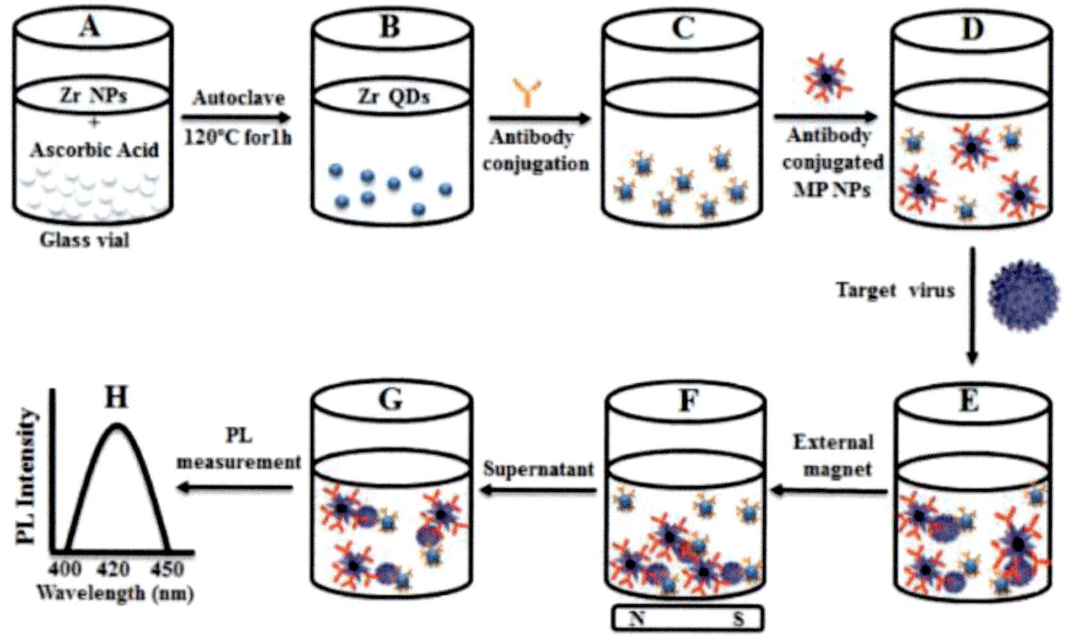

Figure 7. Virus sensor design depicted schematically using Zr nanomaterials. Zr nanoparticles and a reducing agent were kept in a vial for the following steps: (A) formation of Zr QDs; (B) antibody-conjugated QDs; (C) addition of MP NPs; (D) addition of antibody-conjugated QDs; (E) formation of nanostructured magnetoplasmonic-fluorescence with the addition of the target virus; (F) separation; and (G) dispersion of the nanoh (H). Magnetoplasmonic (MP)

In an alternative study, Weng and Neethirajan created a fast detection biosensor for IBV analysis based on antibody-functionalized MoS2. Their immunosensor offers important advantages over conventional testing, such as greater sensitivity and faster processing times, as well as appropriate linearity and ELISA technique validation. Therefore, the creation of novel QDs and their use as an optical-based bioassay may pave the way for new avenues of investigation and other optical and biological applications.

Overall, because QDs are very effective at treating coronavirus, using them is one of the best options. Additionally, QDs are an effective imaging probe and sensor for prognosis and diagnostics. In order to specifically target COVID-19, the medicines can also be coated on the surface of QDs. To prevent renal filtration and other side effects, vigilance should be taken.

Based on metal nanoparticles

Metal-based nanoparticles are one of the most significant nanomaterials with successful biomedical applications due to their capacity to serve as efficient drug delivery systems as well as to allow stimuli-responsive qualities and characteristic ability of some kinds (for example, magnetic or gold nanoparticles) to be observed after in vivo organisation to human body using noninvasive clinical imaging.

Even though metal-based NP is being thoroughly investigated in preclinical and clinical studies for the detection, diagnosis, and treatment of several infections, certain worries are still being raised concerning their safe use in medicine. Due to their harmless qualities, functionalized metal-based nanoparticles with various types of biocompatible materials are being researched as a potential solution to this issue.

Nanoparticles of gold

Gold nanoparticles (Au NP) have shown particular promise in the development of vaccines because they can easily trigger the immune system using cells that secretly introduce antigens.

Additionally, Au NPs may be administered intravenously before being released into the lymph nodes to stimulate the immune system's CD8+ (T-killer) cell response. Furthermore, the high atomic number of Au NP makes it possible to use this nanoparticle as a contrast agent for X-ray-based medical imaging, particularly in Computed Tomography (CT).

Papp and co-authors realised in 2010 that a composite of Au NPs-sialic acids (SA) prevents the virus from attaching to the host cells. The surface protein hemagglutinin of SA, which is a need for cellular entry on the target cell membrane, does, in fact, identify the infections. Furthermore, Staroverov et al. (2011) examined the protective immune response induced by the arrangement of gold nanoparticles (Au NPs) coupled with a particular coronavirus known as swine transmissible gastroenteritis virus (TGEV) in immunised mice and bunnies. In inoculated animals, TGEV-Au NP was found to elicit higher levels of interferon (a protein generated by host cells, typically in reaction to a virus entrance, which has the capability of blocking virus reproduction) and common titers of neutralising antibodies. In comparison to the response to the free antigen, the immunisation using antigen-Au nanoparticles increased the spread of T cells 10 times. In this manner, immune systems might regard AuNPs conjugated to infection as a potential antiviral candidate.

It has been investigated how to diagnose diseased cells using the electrocatalytic properties of hydrogen evolution in Au NPs. This biosensor functions by triggering reactions in host cell surface proteins to the conjugation of certain antibodies with gold nanoparticles. Using the known antigens and accessible antibodies, the same approach can be used to diagnose viruses.

Khater et al. (2017) carried out and reported SPCEs modification using AuNPs and thiolated nucleic acid immobilisation. The electrodes were first given a pretreatment by being subjected to oxidative potentials in an acetate solution, followed by rinsing and drying. Following that, carbon working electrodes were submerged in an Au solution and a continuous negative potential (0.4 V, 200 s) was used to produce spherical AuNPs with uniform morphologies. After that, SH-(AT7)-F1 made with MCH solution was incubated with AuNP-modified SPCEs for 2 hours at room temperature before being rinsed and dried. The target sequence of the (P20 gene) was then surface amplified and detected on the AuNP-modified SPCEs using Recombinase Polymerase Amplification (RPA) solutions. Additionally, the AuNP-modified SPCEs were assessed in comparison to RPA solutions containing water or other unrelated DNAs as negative controls. Figure 8 depicts the system's developed nucleic acid amplification and detection strategy.

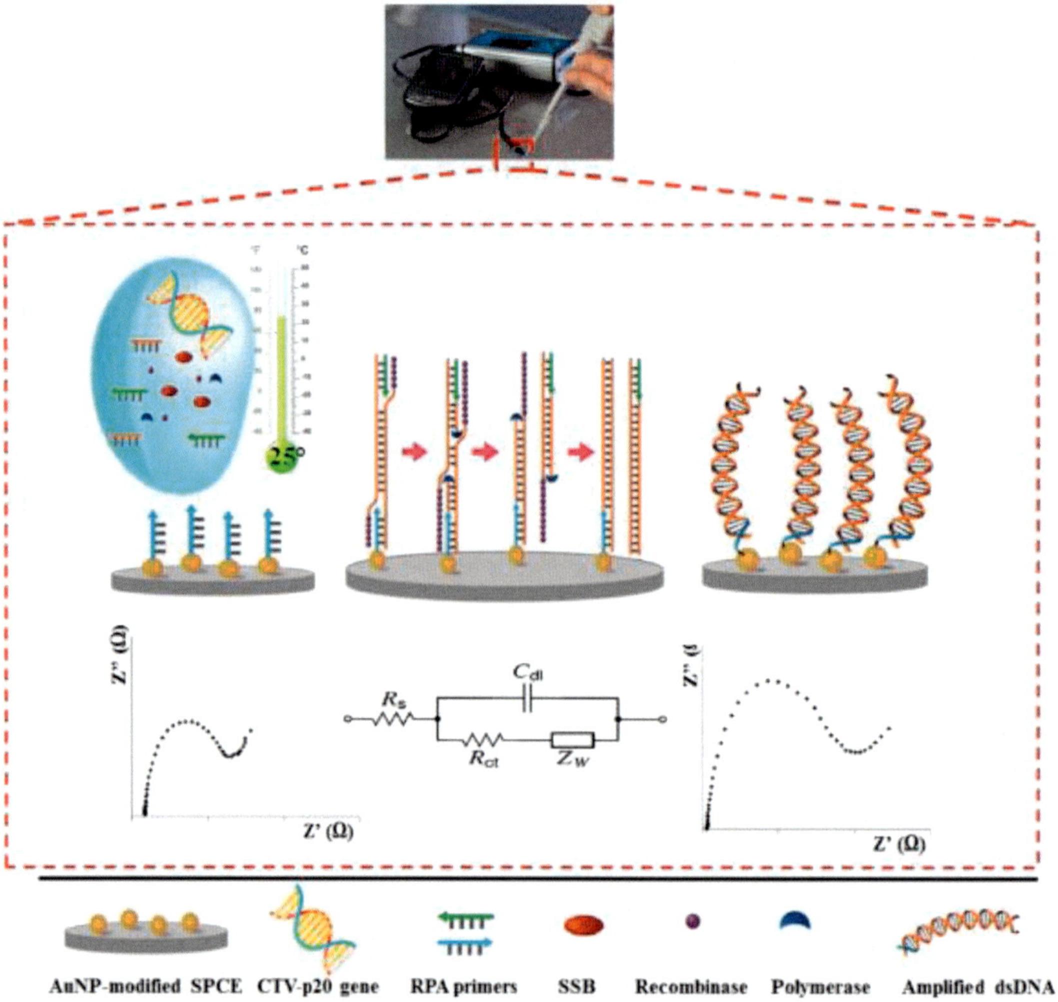

Figure 8. Schematic of electrochemical impedance spectroscopic tracing and Au NPs-modified DNA strands used in recombinase polymerase reinforcement-based diagnosis of Citrus tristeza virus.

To detect the 35S promoter from the cauliflower mosaic virus (CaMV 35S) gene in soybean, Ulianas et al. (2013) created a regenerable electrochemical DNA biosensor based on a new type of acrylic microspheres and gold nanoparticles (AuNPs) composite coated onto a screen printed electrode (SPE). The intercalated anthraquinone-2-sulfonic acid monohydrate sodium salt (AQMS) and the electrode surface were connected via the Au NPs, which helped with electron conductivity. Only a very small current response was seen in the composite without the addition of Au NPs.

Without the use of centralised infrastructure or laboratory organisation, point-of-care tests are used to identify positive cases. One point-of-care method for detecting COVID-19 is antigen lateral flow detection for SARS-CoV-2. This technique uses a membrane strip with two lines, one containing antibody-Au NPs and the other containing capture antibodies. The proteins are dragged across the membrane by capillary action after the blood or urine samples have been placed on it. The antibody-Au NPs and antigens bind to one another as the complex travels through the first line of the membrane. When the complex reaches the second line, the capture antibodies immobilise it, making a red or blue line visible. While individual gold nanoparticles are red, clustered gold nanoparticle solutions are blue as a result of the coupling of the plasmon band.

Recently, the diagnosis of COVID-19 nucleic acid has been performed using a dual-functional plasmonic biosensor that combines the effects of plasmonic photothermal (PPT) and localised surface plasmon resonance (LSPR) sensing transduction.

Two-dimensional gold nanoislands (AuNIs) and the polyprotein ORF1ab, thiol-cDNA receptor of RNA-dependent RNA polymerase (RdRp), or the E gene sequence form an Au-S link that unifies this system on a chip. This plasmonic device can provide local PPT heat, which improves the kinetics of fully matched strands' hybridization and creates quick and accurate recognition of nucleic acids. In another study, 2D AuNIs coated complementary DNA receptors were used to achieve sensitive detection of COVID-19 using nucleic acid hybridization. In this study, as in the previous one, thermos-plasmonic heat was created on the chip to improve detection execution. Illumination at their plasmonic resonance frequency and the resulting local PPT heat increased the in situ hybridization temperature and activated the precise diagnosis of two equivalent gene ordering. With a lower limit of detection of around 0.22 pM concentration, this biosensor displayed notable precision when analysing COVID-19 arrangements, which allows for the particular target recognition of many genes. In a different investigation, the antiviral drug Au NP coated with mercaptoethanesulfonate was employed to inactivate the HSV type 1 virus. This nanocomposite seduces the heparan sulphate cell surface receptor and competitively binds to the virus, preventing infections from attaching to the target cells.

Nanoparticles that are the same size as or greater than virus diameter effectively prevent virus infection. Larger nanoparticles may effectively cross-link virions, but ultra-fine nanoparticles only adorn viral surfaces. To more accurately predict the pharmacokinetic and pharmacodynamic properties of these nanomaterials, computational models show that healthy or diseased cells engulf the NPs. For example, Lunnoo and colleagues used a coarse-grained molecular dynamics (MD) simulation to understand the internalisation pathways of various gold nanoparticle shapes.

AuNPs have emerged as the vaccine technology of choice for immunotherapy applications due to their physicochemical characteristics that limit the formation of antibodies against the platform substance. In addition, some in vitro and in vivo investigations have shown that AuNPs stimulate a variety of immune cells. Sekimukai et al. evaluated the effectiveness of AuNPs as a vaccination adjuvant in 2020. Additionally, an additional study demonstrated a method to improve the COVID-19 vaccination technology by coupling viral antigens to gold nanoparticles. In fact, it is predicted that S or N coronavirus proteins can be linked to the AuNPs and then capped with polysaccharides to create coronavirus nanoparticle vaccines (Fig. 9).

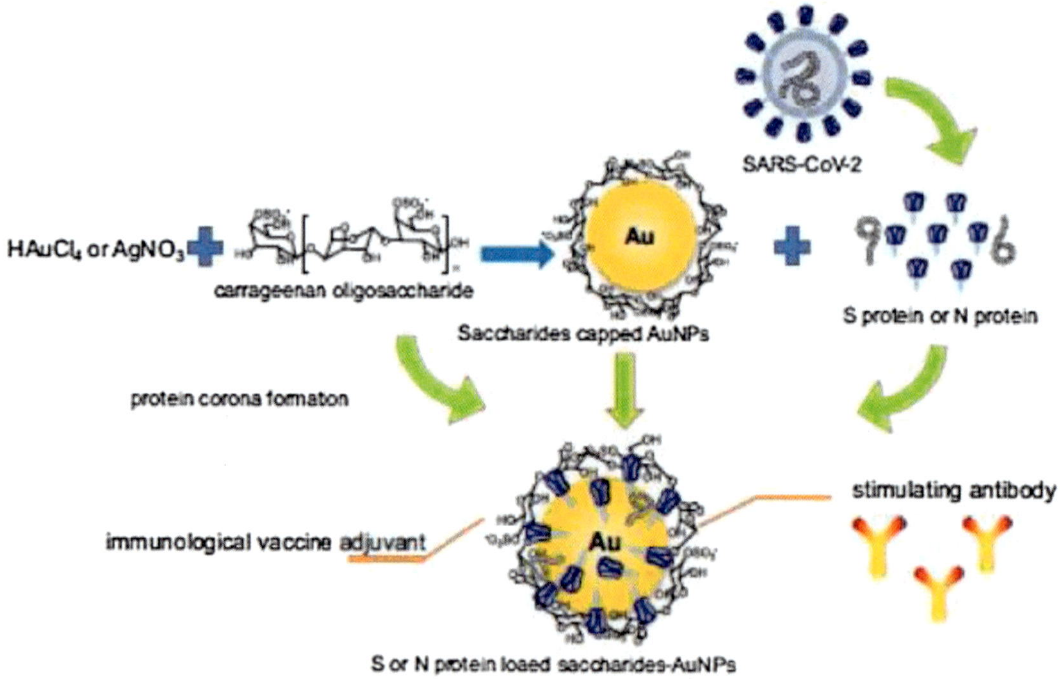

Figure 9. The suggested schematics showing coronavirus S or N protein loaded onto polysaccharides capped AuNPs.

Nanoparticles made of ferrites and iron oxide

Iron oxide nanoparticles (IONPs) have been approved by the US Food and Drug Administration (FDA) as a biocompatible material to treat anaemia in the past, and studies have demonstrated the in vitro antiviral properties of these nanomaterials. It has been frequently demonstrated that IONPs have antiviral properties. Rotavirus, dengue virus, and the H1N1 influenza virus have all been researched in terms of how well IONPs can eradicate them. The research suggests that the antiviral effect of IONPs results from interactions with virus surface proteins that prevent virus binding or penetration into the host cell, neutralising the virus. As a result, this nanoparticle can be employed as an appropriate and secure solution for the quick detection and treatment of patients with the SARS-COV-2 virus.

2020 saw the completion of a docking study by Abo-zied et al. to investigate the Fe2O3 and Fe3O4 as IONPs with the spike protein receptor-binding domain (S1- RBD) of SARS-CoV-2, which is necessary for virus attachment to the host cell receptors. Additionally, a comparable investigation on the antiviral activity of IONPs E1 and E2 HCV glycoproteins was conducted. Consequently, the S1-RBD of the SARS-CoV-2 virus and the glycoproteins E1 and E2 of the HCV were both successfully reacted with by Fe2O3 and Fe3O4. With S1-RBD, Fe3O4 produced a more stable complex, whereas Fe2O3 preferred HCV E1 and E2. The viral structural proteins' conformational changes and subsequent inactivation are linked to the interactions of IONPs that have been discovered.

Fe2O3 and Fe3O4's interactions with the important amino acids in the S1-RBD of SARS-CoV-2 are documented in Table 1 and depicted in Figs. 9 and 10. Fe3O4 has a lower binding free energy than Fe2O3, which indicates that the Fe3O4 S1-RBD complex is more stable. S1-RBD prefers contact with Fe3O4 over Fe2O3 as a result. Four hydrogen bonds were formed during the interaction of Fe3O4 with S1-RBD, with a total intermolecular energy of -11.40 Kcal/mol (Table 1). Additionally, interactions between Leu455, Ser494, and Phe497 and Fe3O4 were found to be hydrophobic (Table 1). In contrast, interactions with Fe2O3 involved the creation of three hydrogen bonds with a total intermolecular energy of -7.55 Kcal/mol, while interactions with Tyr495, Phe497, and Tyr505 were characterised as hydrophobic (Table 1).

Table 1
The Docking Interaction Parameters of Both Fe_2O_3 and Fe_3O_4 with S1-RDB of SARS-CoV-2 (Abo-Zeid et al., 2020).

Ligands	Binding free energy (Kcal/mol)	Total Intermolecular energy (Kcal/mol)	Interacting amino acids	Hydrogen bonds	Hydrophobic interactions
Fe_2O_3	−8.97	−7.55	Gly496, Gln493, Tyr 453	3	Tyr495, Phe497, Tyr505
Fe_3O_4	−10.66	−11.40	Gly496, Gln493, Tyr 453	4	Leu455, Ser494, Phe 497

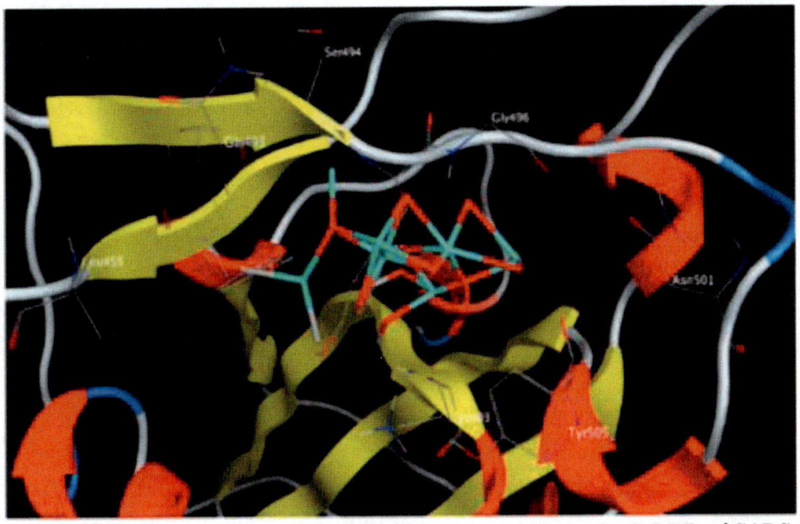

Figure 10. Fe_2O_3 docking interactions with the major amino acids in the S-RBD of SARS-COV-2 are depicted in a 3D interaction diagram.

Additionally, AuNPs and IONPs coated with organic ligands damage the ultrastructure of numerous viruses and degrade viral particles, which inhibits both encapsulated and naked viruses, according to Cagno and their colleagues.

Iron-oxides, which have proven beneficial in paleomagnetic research, are frequently found in cave sediments. Although HCO^{3-}, CO3-, H+, and OH- ions also contribute to surface chemistry, the surface charge of limestone is related to the cation Ca2+ and has been experimentally shown to have an isoelectric point (pI) between 8.0 and 9.5, with often seen pH values of 8.3. Iron-rich cave sediments and positively charged iron oxide surfaces have been shown to exhibit considerable poliovirus attraction, suggesting that limestone surfaces are also capable of binding significant amounts of SARS-CoV-2 particles. Additionally, surfaces made of calcareous or limestone will undoubtedly inhibit coronavirus activation due to the presence of bicarbonate and a pH higher than 8. Additionally, Singh and colleagues have unveiled an electrochemical DNA sensor for the detection of infection bacteria that is based on the chemical combination of chitosan and iron oxide.

Due to its outstanding properties, including a wide surface area, a high surface to volume ratio, a strong capacity for adsorption, ease of recovery, etc., ferrite-based nanomaterials (consisting of iron oxide) have been researched as an essential type of functional particles.

These kinds of nanoparticles have been employed in applications like catalysis, medication delivery, water treatment, sensors, memory technology, electrical components, etc. due to their unique features.

Utilizing Ferrite-based nanoparticles for biological and medicinal applications has grown significantly in recent years. Due to their ferromagnetic nature and insulation properties, ferrite-based materials have gained popularity. These materials are suitable in magnetic fields without eddy currents' undesirable effects thanks to these two sorts of properties.

Advances in magnetic materials and nanotechnology enable diagnostic methods at the nanoscale and lower the detection threshold for early infection diagnosis. Additionally, real-time PCR is used to detect the COVID-19 virus employing nasopharyngeal cells and functionalized magnetic nanoparticles to extract RNA. About 10,000 tests can be detected using this technology each day, covering a large portion of the population. The main disadvantage of this method is that it needs specialised magnetic nanoparticles with a large negative charge in order to purify viral RNA and detect the presence of the COVID-19 virus. In order to analyse approximately 50,000 COVID-19 tests, Edeas, Saleh, and Peyssonnaux (2020) developed a straightforward, low-cost method to create 100 g of magnetic nanoparticles in 1 L of the solution. This method helps to reduce the cost of obtained nanoparticles for various biomolecular applications, especially during the COVID-19 International Health Emergency.

Instead of other sorts of biosensors, magnetic biosensor areas have drawn specific attention. Magnetic biosensors that are surface- and volume-based have been used to diagnose metallic ions, cancer biomarkers, viruses, and other pathogens. Magnetic biosensors are in fact paired with antibodies or DNA/RNA probes that can precisely bind to the target cells, and the number of the target cells has an impact on the magnetic signals. Due to the lack of magnetic characteristics in the majority of biological ambient materials, this type of biosensor exhibits lower background noise than optical, plasmonic, and electrochemical biosensors. Moreover, the detection technique is extremely precise and dependable because signals are not influenced by the types of the analyte matrix.

Nanoparticles of copper

According to a 2015 investigation on CoV-229E, it was found that copper might significantly lessen the virus's activities in a relatively short period of time. Brasses and at least 70% copper were discovered to successfully inactivate the virus. The proportion of copper has an impact on the inactivation rate. Fig. 11 depicts the impact of Cu NPs on virus inactivation based on data gathered by Poggio et al (2020).

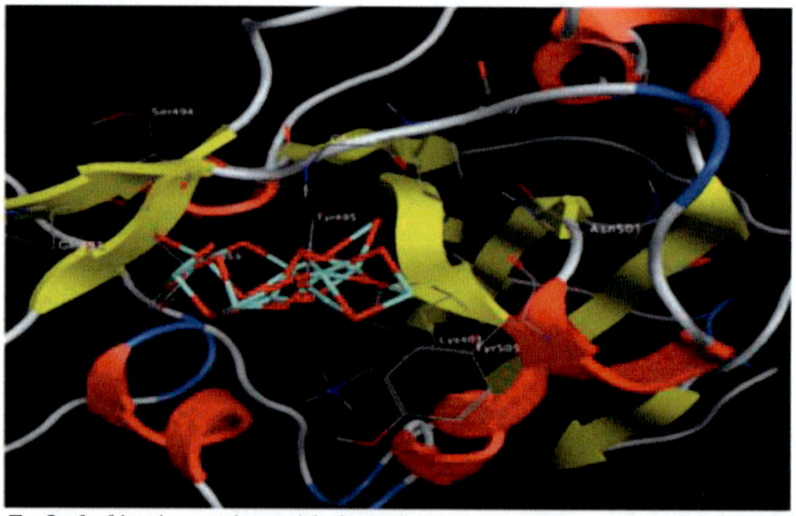

Figure 11. Fe_3O_4 docking interactions with the major amino acids in the S-RBD of SARS-COV-2 are depicted in a 3D interaction diagram.

To counteract COVID-19, the formulation could be altered to adjust its antibacterial capabilities utilising metal nanostructures. Use of copper salt, nanoparticles, metal salts, and/or solutions can help produce antiviral effects. This might help with the design of the PPE material. For instance, treating PPEs with copper ions may help to prevent virus scattering on the PPEs. Generally speaking, the metal ions may reduce CoV activity on certain substrates. Using copper brasses for the surface treatment in the interim is beneficial. The inactivation of the virus is influenced by the release of ionic metal. Reactive oxygen species and the release of the Cu ion are what cause the inactivation (ROS). Cu nanoparticle insertion in polymer matrices may change the metal release process and reduce the chance of environmental contamination. Additionally, by combining the copper core of nanoparticles with their quaternary ammonium shell, it is possible to generate a potent antiviral effect (Sportelli, Longano et al., 2020). A few studies reported on the PPE treatment utilising copper nanoparticles, copper oxides, and copper salts. It is clear that inadequate PPE may have contributed to the death of front-line personnel. In 2019, Bhattacharjee et al. investigated the subject by taking into account other pandemic illnesses. They stated that metal-grafted graphene oxide (GO), when used to modify non-woven tissues, demonstrated to have very potent antibacterial capabilities. When combined with metals like Cu, Fe, Zn, and Ag, graphene was employed as a photocatalyst and composite material. Studies have also looked into using GO with nanoparticles to treat PPE. It was discovered that nanometals like copper and silver, when placed onto GO, can function well as antiviral agents. Using a similar methodology, new anti-influenza respirators were created in 2010. Meanwhile, copper oxide-impregnated masks were created by Borkow et al., which can lower the risk of contracting the flu virus while retaining effective filtration. However, masks and other PPE did not yet use comparable techniques. Cu(II) ions were discovered to have little toxicity in eukaryotic cells. Recently, it was discovered that polyurethane/CuO nanocomposites can function well as antimicrobial air filters. In addition, CuO microparticles were preferred to CuO nanoparticles as an additive for PU filters. Consequently, the nano element's potential for harm is reducing. An example of an antiviral air filtration was the use of the SiO2 -Ag active material against the MS2 bacteriophage.

The antibacterial properties of copper have been recognised since antiquity, and surfaces with a high concentration of copper have been shown to be effective against viruses. This demonstrates the poliovirus's efficacy. Recently, the ability of Cu to neutralise coronaviruses has shown that Cu might also be useful against SARS-CoV-2. In contrast to other smooth surfaces, it was discovered that the deactivation of the virus occurs significantly more quickly on brasses with Cu content. The findings demonstrated that the viral genome suffers damage. This might guarantee that the inactivation is irreversible. This is because the liberated copper ions are poisonous, and the oxidising agents (ROS) that Cu produces target viral proteins and lipids. In addition, compared to other examined surfaces, SARS-CoV-1 and SARS-CoV-2 deactivate on Cu surfaces more quickly. The viral proteins and lipids are damaged, which results in the deactivation process. In addition to stainless steel, using Cu alloys could result in more effective antiviral surfaces. The supported catalysts Al2O3 impregnated Cu and Ag were discovered to be capable of deactivating viruses for air disinfection.

It is possible for Cu and CuO nanoparticles to release metal ions. Due to the high aspect ratio and increased reactivity, the release of Cu ions proceeded more quickly. These nanoparticles might be incorporated into textiles. Consequently, a product with antiviral qualities could be created. Masks impregnated with CuO have been found to have anti-influenza viral properties (H1N1 and H9N2). Therefore, it is important to look at how these materials might be used to combat the SARS-CoV-2 virus.

Nanoparticles of silver

The antiviral effects of Ag nanoparticles are widely recognised. This is because it can prevent viral entrance into host cells. Additionally, it was discovered that the metal's interaction with a viral genome prevents viral replication. It was discovered that gold nanoparticles wrapped in silver nanoparticles might attach to the HIV envelope glycoprotein gp120 and so prevent infection. It was also researched how the virus interacts differently depending on its size. The functionalized AgNPs may also be able to prevent virus infection through a variety of methods. It has been discovered that smaller particles would enter the cell membrane more readily. As a result, this might prevent virus replication. For instance, it has been reported to evaluate the effective minimal inhibitory concentration using nano-titanium dioxide and silver ions (MIC). Included in this is research on how well it works in various respiratory system target organs. Early home therapy is one of them, as is reducing the incidence of ventilator-associated pneumonia (VAP) in hospital intensive care units. The size of the Ag nanoparticle affects the dosage. After taking into consideration deposition losses, it was determined that MIC could be reached (Van Doremalen et al., 2020). Silver nanoparticles' antiviral and antibacterial properties have been widely adopted in medical applications, such as silver-containing paint and food plates as a biocide. Many diseases, including HIV-1, the monkeypox virus, the bacteriophages UZ1 and MS2, the murine norovirus MNV1, the HSV and HBV, and, more recently, the swine epidemic diarrhoea virus, are rendered inactive by these characteristics (PEDV). There were three methods anticipated to have an antiviral effect. The first step is the release of some hazardous Ag(I) forms, such as Ag + ions. Additionally, it demonstrates a strong attraction for sulphur. Since thiol is present in the active areas of enzymes, it interacts well with it. Additionally, Ag NPs have the potential to assemble in host cells and interact with viral protein spikes. Viral propagation will be resisted by further interactions with the enzymes. This was proposed by Zodrow et al. (2010) as well as De Gusseme et al. (2010). (2009). Additionally, Ag_2S nanoclusters (NCs) demonstrated efficient suppression of the Porcine Epidemic Diarrhea Virus's RNA copy. Additionally, it was discovered that exposing living cells to silver ions at a comparable concentration did not prevent viral replication. It can be said that the Ag(I) release had no effect on the antiviral property. However, it is important to remember that Ag + ions and Ag particles reach the cells through many ways. As a result, the distribution within cells would differ, which would result in a varied virus-toxic response. Whereas Ag(I) may aggregate in other cell regions or be swiftly removed, Ag NCs may accumulate in intracellular regions. Second, since Ag NPs' antiviral activity would result from direct physical contact with virus surfaces, this might prevent viruses from docking with host cells and reduce their infectiousness. For the HIV-1 example, this was investigated by Elechiguerra et al., and for the HSV-2 case, by Orlowski et al. From the findings of Elechiguerra et al., they deduced that the physical contact between the nanoparticles and the virus was unaffected by their size. According to Orlowski et al., the greater size would be desirable to act as an antiviral agent. They came to the conclusion that this may be done by preventing the virus from attaching to the host cell. When the release of Ag was combined, De Gusseme et al. postulated the same mechanism (I). It was also claimed that the Ag nanoparticles' docking on the virus surface caused the local release of ROS, which in turn could harm the virus's membrane and/or envelope. Ag nanoparticles are used in numerous medical devices and equipment. Additionally, the use of Ag can be viewed as fillers in paints, air filter materials, and face masks. Additionally, it was discovered that filters containing Ag NPs have effective antiviral properties against bacteriophage MS2.

Nanoparticles of zinc

Due to its versatility as a physical element, cofactor, and signalling molecule, zinc is utilised in numerous biological processes. The component involved lipid and carbohydrate metabolism. additionally important in maintaining proper cardiovascular, reproductive, and nervous system function. Our immune system depends heavily on zinc, which controls the maturation, differentiation, proliferation, and function of leukocytes and lymphocytes. Additionally, zinc exhibits a signalling function in the control of the inflammatory response. Additionally, it is a part of dietary immunity. Modifying the zinc status can have a substantial impact on the immune system. Increased exposure to illnesses including measles, pneumonia, and malaria will come from this. The topic of zinc's potential use during the pandemic is intriguing. Zinc has potent antiviral and immune-modulating effects. To the best of our knowledge, there is no analysis or data on the effectiveness of using zinc to treat COVID-19. It was discovered that Zn2+ cations and Zn ionophore pyrithione might stop the growth of viruses. This suggested that Zn2+ might have antiviral properties. It has been discovered that chloroquine may function as an antiviral medication for the treatment of COVID-19. To understand the antiviral mechanism, more research is necessary. Chloroquine has been demonstrated to function as a zinc ionophore in earlier research. The scientists also suggested that zinc influx mediated by chloroquine might function as anticancer agents. Additionally, it was projected that using chloroquine to raise intracellular Zn2+ content would help fight SARS-CoV-2. When using zinc supplementation without chloroquine, similar beneficial outcomes can be anticipated. Applying alternative zinc ionophores with reduced toxicity is supposed to have a similar effect. It took more research to confirm the forecast in this case.

Targeting Zn ions as a defence against COVID-19 is an alternative strategy. Mainly, it was found that protein instability in both MERS-CoV and SARS-CoV can be caused by disulfiram-induced Zn2+ release from papain-like protease. Zn-ejector medications may also serve as targeted oxidation strategies in the treatment of viruses and as antiviral medicines. Both SARS-CoV-2 and SARS-CoV have a comparable need for angiotensin-converting enzyme 2 (ACE2) to enter target cells (Hoffmann et al., 2020). In order to treat COVID-19, it might be said that ACE2 receptor modification is a good therapeutic approach. According to Speth, Carrera, Jean-Baptiste, Joachim, and Linares (2014), exposure to 100 M zinc could reduce the activity of recombinant human ACE-2 in rat lungs. The moderating effect of zinc, however, seems speculative in their investigations. Although HCoV 229E or HCoV-OC43 infection did not clearly reduce the frequency of ciliary beat, it was shown that HCoV 229E-induced ciliary dyskinesia would lead to reduced mucociliary clearance. Not only may this affect the elimination of the viral particle, but it could also increase the risk of bacterial co-infection. Zn supplementation was observed to increase ciliary length in bronchial epithelium in a study on Zn-deficient rats. Additionally, it can raise the frequency of ciliary beats in vitro. Zinc may therefore help to alleviate the dysfunctional mucociliary clearance caused by nCo-2019. Due to its anti-inflammatory and antioxidant properties, as well as the regulation of the tight junction proteins ZO-1 and Claudin-1, zinc has been shown to be essential for the respiratory epithelium. Consequently, this might improve the barrier functions. The viral inflammatory processes are progressively made worse by a decrease in barrier function and a downregulation of tight junction protein complexes. Additionally, the selectivity of TJ perm loss in the airways may contribute to the development of ARDS and alveolar edoema. High molecular weight proteins and water were able to leak into the airways without restriction as a result of this.

Although there have only been a few research on the effects of zinc on COVID-19, its antiviral qualities have been proven for other viral diseases. This is accomplished via modulating viral particle entrance, replication, viral protein translation, fusion, and, for some viruses, extra release. The increase in internal Zn levels caused by the use of Zn ionophores was found to significantly alter picornavirus replication. These findings came from earlier research conducted in the 1970s. Zn therapy led to a rise in interferon (IFN) production by leukocytes. It amplifies its antiviral effect in cells that are also infected with rhinoviruses. Zn2+ was found to have the ability to stimulate the antiviral activity mechanism. These results raised awareness of Zn's potential role in the prevention and treatment of the common cold. In a review article by Singh and Das, it was demonstrated that Zn supplementation can be utilised as a successful cold remedy. The best form was zinc acetate. Some studies link the presence of zinc to respiratory syncytial virus infection (RSV). It has been noted that kids with RSV pneumonia have reduced zinc levels in their whole blood. Additionally, decreased zinc metabolism might expose more people to RSV infection. Zn compounds were found to stop the replication of the respiratory syncytial virus as a result. It has been demonstrated in a study on influenza that Zn deficiency may raise mortality. Additionally, the potential of bacterial coinfection must be taken into account. To treat respiratory viral infections with zinc supplements, additional clinical evidence must be examined.

Few research have, however, documented the antibacterial effects of zinc oxide nanoparticles. It has been shown that S. pneumoniae cannot form or grow biofilms in the presence of ZnO. Other bacterial agents, including P. aeruginosa, methicillin-resistant S. aureus, and K. pneumoniae, showed a comparable effect (Ann et al., 2014). ZnO nanoparticles, however, are toxic to the lungs, which restricts their use as an antibacterial agent and reduces the phagocytic activity of macrophages in the respiratory system. It is crucial to keep in mind that when the study involves S. pneumonia and Zn, Zn is required for bacteria to grow and colonise. Zn bioavailability was also necessary for biofilm development.

Nanoparticles of TiO2

SARS-CoV-2 could be inactivated by photocatalytic nanoparticles, according to research. The most prevalent one is titanium dioxide (TiO2). The substance is non-toxic, inert, and resistant to photocorrosion when exposed to UV radiation. TiO2 is used for self-cleaning windows, water filtration, and paints. The capacity of photocatalytic TiO2 to eliminate volatile organic compounds (VOCs) under UV light makes it possible for paints with nanoparticles to purify the air. However, the release of poisons into the air from its use in paint could be an issue. TiO2 photocatalysis may, if possible, help in the deactivation of the SARS-CoV-2 virus by surface decontamination employing aerosol, paint, water, and air treatment systems that contain these particles. The excitation of an electron from the valence band (VB) to the conduction band (CB), which starts reactions to produce ROS like superoxide anion and hydroxyl radical, is the mechanism of this photocatalytic process and is well understood. TiO2's ability to disinfect surfaces was aided by the hydroxyl radicals that resulted from the oxidation of water molecules. This occurs as a result of protein changes, DNA damage, virus cell wall damage, and virus membrane damage. TiO2 can also be utilised as a bacterial inhibitor. In contrast to bacteria, Bogdan et al. discovered that numerous research had demonstrated that viruses would be more vulnerable to inactivation. According to studies, enveloped viruses pose a greater threat than non-enveloped viruses. However, there were also contradictory results. To the author's knowledge, only one journal paper has discussed the use of a photocatalytic titanium apatite filter (PTAF) to fend against SARS-CoV-2. It demonstrated that the therapeutic approach may be used.

Additionally, efforts were made to create second-generation photocatalysts that incorporate N- and S-doped TiO2 in addition to other components. Bacteria and several viruses were effectively rendered inactive as a result of this. These papers contain the review work completed by other researchers. To the best of our knowledge, the second generation photocatalyst treatment has not yet been tested on viruses. It was discovered that the Ag nanoparticle on the TiO2 particle might boost the antiviral productivity against MS2 by producing hydroxyl. Additionally, it has been suggested that employing Ag- and Cu-doped

TiO_2 nanowires instead of Ag-, TiO_2, or Cu-TiO_2 when subjected to UV light will help to eradicate bacteria from drinking water.

This is caused by a combination of increased photoactivity and (Ag, Cu)-TiO_2's smaller bandgap. The free Ag and Cu in treated water may also have an antiviral effect. TiO_2 and SiO_2 nanoparticles can be combined as an alternative method. Due to SiO_2's higher specific surface area than TiO_2 alone, this gave TiO_2 an efficient antiviral action. Additionally, it was discovered that TiO_2 coated on glass slides and doped with Pt was more effective at preventing influenza. aerosols contain a presence. It's wonderful to see that Byrnes et al(Byrne .'s et al., 2015) research on photocatalytic materials for the deactivation of SARS-CoV-2 has already involved a lot of work. The fact that the materials are safe for us to utilise is very crucial. It was discovered that nanofibers coated with TiO_2 and electrospun onto the surface of the filter were capable of deactivating viruses when exposed to UV and sunshine. In this study, NPs were electrospray-deposited onto the nanofibers. The results of the experiments shown that the materials have remarkable photoinduced hydrophilicity, photocatalytic activity, and antibacterial activity.

Carbides and nitrides in two dimensions (MXenes)

Two-Dimensional Carbides and Nitrides (MXENES), a newly developed material, is utilised as a coating for facemasks to catch and inactivate viruses since it is hydrophilic and has a large negative charge. MXenes have the formula $M_{n+1}X_nT_x$, where M is an early transition metal (such as Ti, Zr, V, or Mo), X is either C or N, T_x denotes the surface functional groups (such as O, OH, F, or C———l), and n is between 1 and 4. $Ti_3C_2T_x$, $Ta_4C_3T_x$, and Nb_2CT_x are only a few of the many MXenes that are biocompatible. Additionally, the high surface area and porosity of MXenes cause them to bind to viral spike peplomers and immobilise the virus in addition to significantly adsorbing amino acids. Indeed, MXenes are used as a potent protein magnet. Additionally, it has been demonstrated that these substances are photocatalytically active, which means that when viruses bind to their surface, they simultaneously employ light to kill the adsorbed virus. MXenes with visible or IR plasmon resonance are capable to effectively converting light to heat. Depending on the type, MXene can be sterilised with certain light wavelengths and can also be stimulated by certain wavelengths to kill viruses that have been left on the surface. For instance, $Ti_3C_2T_x$ is sterilised using solar light and a red/infrared lamp while being stimulated by red light (780 nm plasmon resonance). Furthermore, due to the interaction of their charge transferability and hydrophilicity, MXenes have antimicrobial properties. Furthermore, the most prevalent and affordable form of titanium carbide MXenes has no harmful or adverse environmental or toxicological consequences on the ecosystem.

The estimated 30–40% of COVID-19 patients with kidney illness who require hemodialysis therapy to prevent uremic toxins in the blood that may cause death, in addition to the recognised pulmonary abnormalities (US Renal Data System 2018 Annual Data Report: Epidemiology of Kidney Disease in the United States, 2019). MXenes are able to regenerate dialysate by eliminating toxins that accumulate in renal failure situations. The negatively charged MXene sheets in MXene, which is biocompatible, have slit holes that may easily absorb urea that was removed from dialysate by rigorous dialysis (Fig. 12). Therefore, due to their effective urea adsorption, compact design, and light weight, MXenes are presumably qualified to overcome some of the major drawbacks of present mobile dialysis systems.

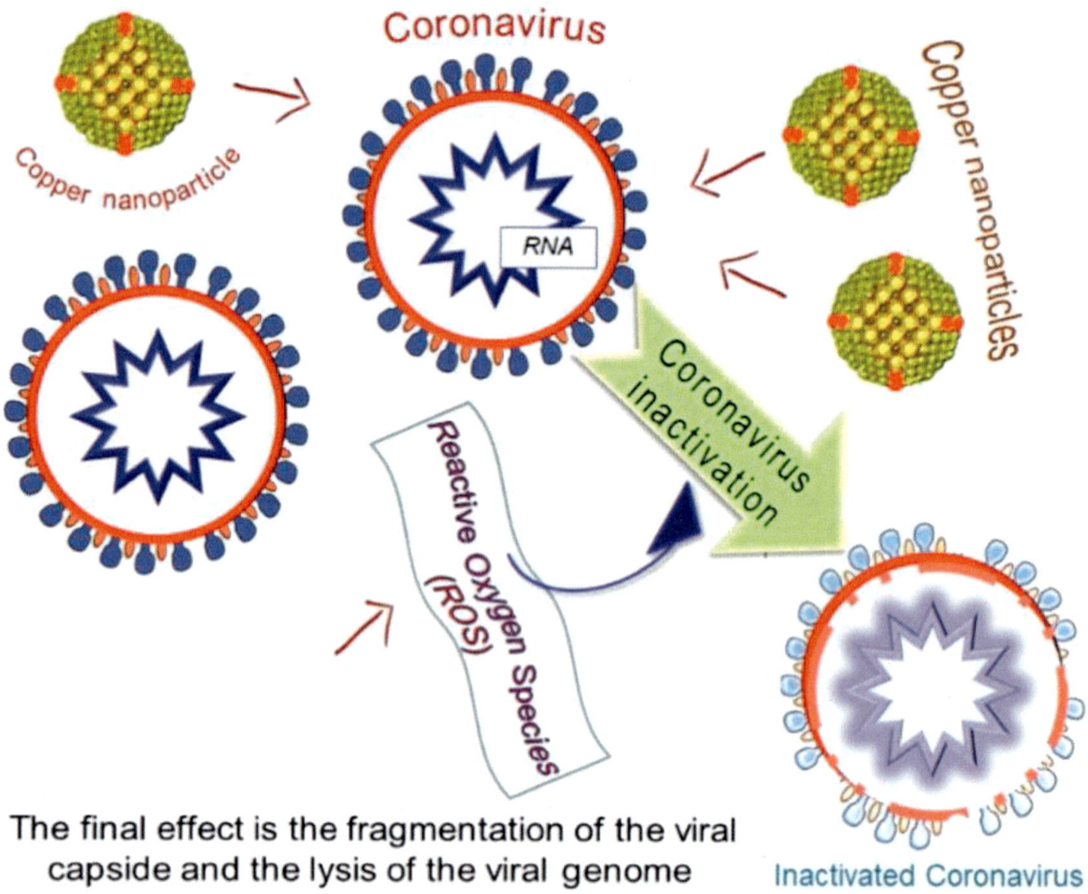

Figure 12. Copper nanoparticles inhibit the growth of the coronavirus

Organic Metal Framework (MOF)

The use of air filtration as a control measure against the viral disease could be viewed as ineffective. However, a lot of purifiers on the market simply use dense fibrous filters, which are good at removing particles but lack any antibacterial or antimicrobial qualities. In order to create a nanofiber membrane, Li and colleagues created a variety of metal-organic frameworks (MOFs) that are super adsorbents with bacterial and photocatalytic properties. When not exposed to sunlight, this substance can effectively produce biocidal reactive oxygen species (ROS) (see Fig. 13 A). For two hours in a saline solution under simulated solar radiation, Zn-based MOF (ZIF-8) in particular inactivates approximately 99.999% of Escherichia coli (E.Coli). To stop the spread of COVID-19, this extremely adsorbent material can be utilised as an antimicrobial filter in facemasks, clothing, ventilators, and air purifiers.

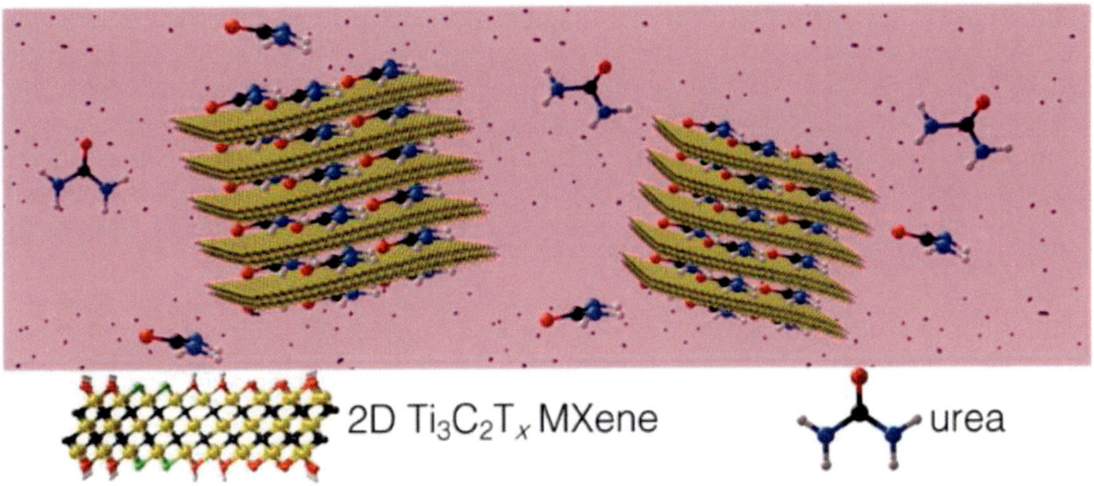

Figure 13. MXenes' urea adsorption from aqueous solution. Diagram of the MXene nanosheets employed as the adsorbent in (a).

In fact, MOFs exposed to ultraviolet light were able to inactivate SARS-COV-2 by removing spike proteins with a crown-like shape, puncturing the lipid membrane, and extracting the RNA contents for around three hours. In contrast, a large number of hydroxyl radicals are produced when the photocatalytic capabilities of MOF under solar light target the viral RNA, which causes damage to the spike proteins.

In conclusion, the majority of metal NPs-based virus diagnosis methods were developed based on the special features of metal nanoparticles in the context of metal nanoparticles (NPs) applications against COVID-19. Most of them have been employed in antiviral coatings to stop virus transmission in any community due to their antiviral characteristics. Noble metal NPs, such as Au, Ag, and Cu, in particular, have unique optical and electrical properties that make them ideal for use in biosensing applications. Additionally, due to AuNPs' biocompatibility, it may be possible to use it in vaccine technologies.

Based on a polymer, nanoparticles

The adjustable features, practical synthesis procedures, and strong biocompatibility of polymer-based nanoparticles made of synthetic and natural polymers make them a potential choice for biomedical applications. Viral delivery systems, in vivo delivery, and controlled release of viral vaccines are only a few biological applications that make use of these kinds of nanomaterials with biosafety features. Viral vaccines can be given as DNA, mRNA, or proteins, all of which are easily enzymatically broken down when they enter the bloodstream.

synthetic nanoparticles made of polymer

The best nanoparticles for the delivery system are synthetic polymer-based ones that can have their properties and functionalities customised. They feature a variety of architectures, including branching, linear, and three-dimensional networks, which were created by combining multiple monomers. Their size, morphology, and surface charge might all be improved to control how much cargo they release when exposed to external factors (Kamaly, Xiao, Valencia, Radovic-Moreno, & Farokhzad, 2012). One of the most well-known polymers in this group, poly (lactic-co-glycolic acid) (PLGA), has been given FDA approval for use in human applications due to its high biocompatibility and biodegradability qualities. Zhao and colleagues explored the creation of poly (amino ester) with carboxyl groups (PC)-coated magnetic nanoparticles (pcMNPs) and created a pcMNPs-based viral RNA extraction technology in order to identify the COVID-19. The lysis and binding procedures that result in the pcMNPs-RNA complex, which was added to ensuing RT-PCR experiments, are combined in this one-step, streamlined technique. During this procedure, the viral RNA was separated from several samples using a straightforward manual method or an automated high-throughput method within 20 minutes. A 10-COpy sensitivity and a high linear association between 10 and 105 copies of SARS-COV-2 pseudovirus particles are attained by detecting two components of viral RNA (ORFlab and N gene). The turnaround time and operational requirements in the present molecular detection of SARS-COV-2 can be significantly reduced by using this innovative, straightforward, and highly effective technique for viral RNA extraction, especially for the rapid clinical diagnosis.

Additionally, polymer nanoparticles can be employed to create protective facemasks (Fig. 13B). Based on a poly (vinylidene fluoride) electrospun nanofiber film and a triboelectric nanogenerator, Liu et al. developed a new self-powered electrostatic adsorption facemask with the potential to be more effective than a commercial mask at 99.2% particles removal.
Nanocellulose

As a natural polymer, cellulose-based materials can be utilised to make a variety of goods for personal hygiene as well as medical uses such filtration, absorption, paper electrodes, paper-based microfluidic chips, biosensors, and biological tests. Crystallites, nanocrystals, whiskers, and nanofibers are among the several cellulose forms that are frequently used in biomedical applications. Due to its unique qualities, including a large surface area and strong mechanical strength, cellulose nanofibers with nano dimensions extracted from cellulose fibres have been a focus of research. This is because they have attracted attention as a method for filtration and infection diagnosis.

Another advancement in nanocellulose-based kits is the installation of electrical elements like various sensors and displays to boost the kits' sensitivity and accuracy.

In order to create a sterile deactivation region that may further aid in limiting the transmission of COVID-19, Johnson and co-authors provided a model for thermoplastic 3D printing facemasks coated with sodium chloride or clay/biocellulose impregnated with sodium chloride.

A non-woven, m-thick filter paper made of cellulose nanofiber was introduced by Metreveli et al. in 2014 to create a membrane made of nanofibrous polymer. With a log 10 reduction value (LRV) of 6.3, this 100% natural membrane can remove viral particles according to the size-exclusion principle, matching the effectiveness of commercial synthetic polymer virus removal filters. The use of these active filters to remove viruses in public places is very effective at reducing the harm and dangers of influenza and coronaviruses both now and in the future because of the frequent mutations of these viruses and, on the other hand, because there isn't an effective vaccine against these types of virus.

Nanoparticles of chitosan

Chitosan, the second-most prevalent naturally occurring polymer-based nanoparticle, is greatly sought after for use in biomedical applications because it can be altered to the required size and form. Due to its biocompatibility, biodegradability, and non-toxicity qualities, chitosan with the linear and partly acetylated (1-4)-2-amino-2-deoxy-d-glucan structure is frequently used as drug carriers and excellent nucleic acid delivery vehicles. The solubility and stability of drugs, as well as their effectiveness and toxicity, are all improved by the slow/controlled release of chitosan nanoparticles. Chitosan also has an immediate impact on tumour cells, interfering with their metabolism and either slowing down their growth or inducing apoptosis. Chitosan can enhance the persistence of polymeric NP in the mucosal environment and penetration to mucosal tissue when combined with medicinal chemicals.

Chitosan's cationic charge makes it more likely to bind tightly to nucleic acids, which can be employed for successful gene transfer. Chitosan's ability to deliver genes can be utilised in the creation of gene-based antiviral vaccines. In order to administer a vaccination through the nasal passage, Raghuwanshi and colleagues created dendritic cell-targeted chitosan nanoparticles. They employ a combination of chitosan's ability to transport pDNA and bfFp's selective targeting specificity for respiratory Dendritic cells (DCs). To create pVAXN-loaded nanoparticles, ultrapure water-soluble biotinylated chitosan hydrochloride was used. Bifunctional fusion protein was used to surface-functionalize these pVAXN-loaded biotinylated chitosan nanoparticles in order to accomplish nasal DC targeting (Fig. 14).

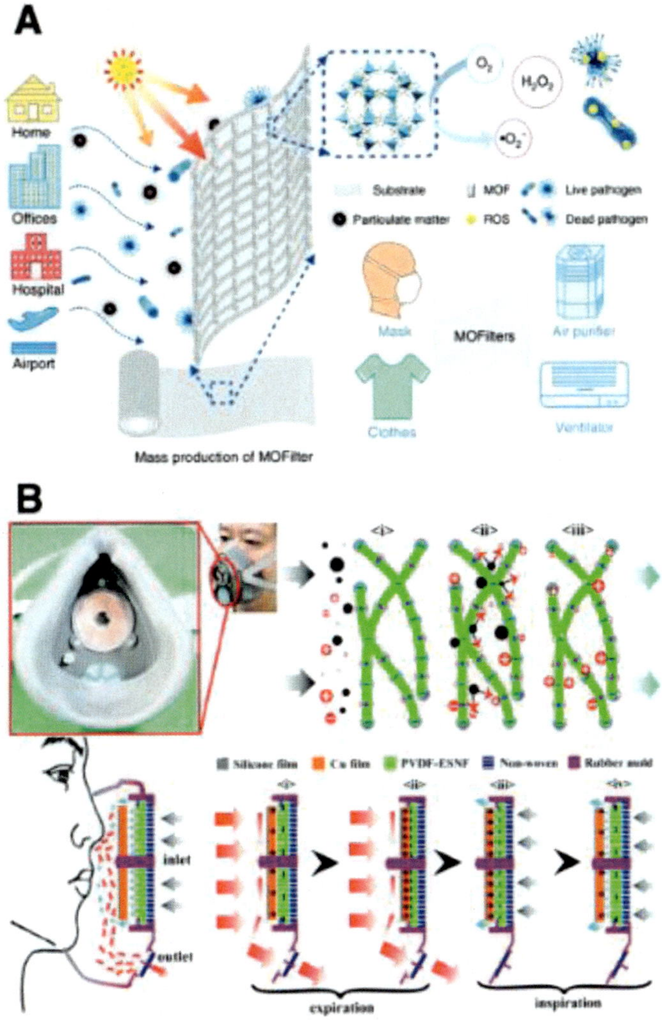

Figure 14. Antimicrobial biosafety materials for personal protective equipment. Metal-organic framework (MOF)-based filter schematic shown in (A); polymeric material mask filtration mechanism schematic shown in (B).

The improvement in delivery with chitosan nanoparticles, which have offered an excellent way for prevention of DNA vaccine degradation while the cationic nature enables binding to the negative charge of DNA, is one of the most significant advancements in DNA-based vaccination technology. For the delivery of DNA vaccines to the mucosal surface, chitosan offers a number of desirable benefits, including mucoadhesion, high solubility, inertness, and non-immunogenicity. Since mucosal surfaces are the primary location for the majority of viruses that infect humans, DNA vaccination at the mucosal surfaces using chitosan nanoparticles is strongly advised. With the establishment of mucosal and systemic immunity, vaccination sites do indeed experience strong immunological reactions. Additionally, it was discovered that the intranasal delivery of plasmid DNA expressing nucleocapsid COVID-19 loaded into chitosan nanoparticles produces favourable and efficient effects (Fig. 15).

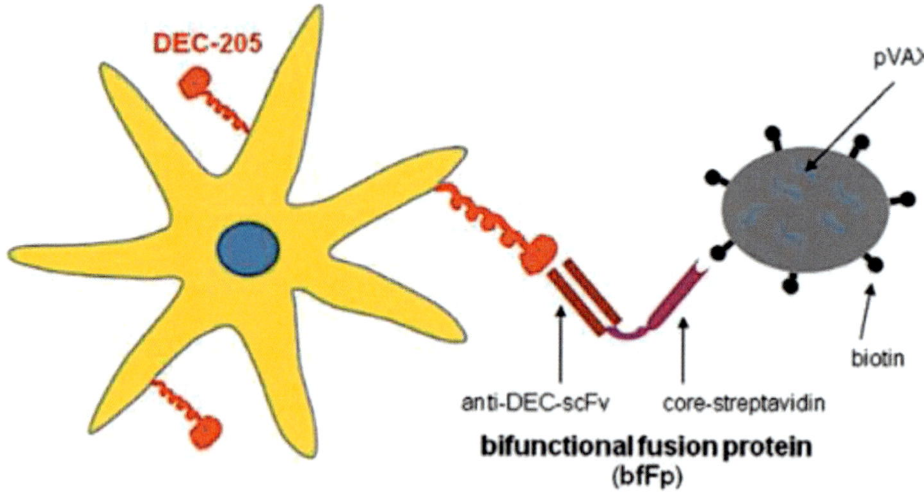

Figure 15. Bifunctional fusion protein targeting approach for dendritic cells is shown schematically (bfFp). The bfFp is a recombinant fusion protein made up of anti-DEC-205 single chain antibody and truncated core-streptavidin (scFv). While the anti-DEC-205 scFv provides targeting specificity to the DC DEC-205 receptor, the core-streptavidin arm of the fusion protein binds with biotinylated nanoparticles.

Some materials have an adverse impact on the environment and ecological system. Therefore, it is crucial to use biocompatible and harmless nanoparticles against COVID-19 for a long time to minimise the harmful effects of COVID-19 on the environment. Chitosan and cellulose nanoparticles are excellent options to employ against COVID-19 because they come from a natural source.

Nanoparticles of lipid

However, certain nanoparticles have been used for effective nucleic acid delivery; lipid nanoparticles (LNPs) are a clinically advanced one that has received approval from the U.S. Food and Drug Administration (FDA). LNPs may also be effective mRNA delivery platforms in the future. These nanoparticles are made up of a variety of lipids, including phospholipid, cholesterol, ionizable amine lipid, and PEG lipid. Ionizable amine lipids have the largest function in the endosomal escape of nucleic acid among them. Numerous studies have been conducted on mRNA-based lipid nanoparticle vaccines against a variety of infectious illnesses, including HIV, CMV, rabies, influenza, zika, and most recently COVID-19. For instance, Elia et al. created an mRNA-based vaccination in 2021 using the SARS-CoV-2 human Fc-conjugated receptor binding domain encapsulated in LNPs (RBD-hFc). Two top LNPs formulations have been chosen for the future RBD-hFc mRNA vaccine technology after various ionizable lipids have been evaluated in vivo in a luciferase (luc) mRNA reporter experiment. The results of the current study demonstrate that these nanoparticles have the potential to be used in COVID-19 LNP-based mRNA vaccination technology.

Analysis

Researchers are turning to nanotechnology in place of conventional approaches to combat COVID-19 due to the global demand for clever and innovative solutions. Coronavirus treatment, prevention, detection, and diagnosis are all successfully accomplished using nanotechnology. Nanomaterials' antiviral characteristics are useful for coating layers on things like facemasks and medical apparel. Nanomaterials in biosensors have several advantages, including a high detection capacity, stability, straightforward design, dependability, and affordability. Utilizing nanomaterials in textile, facemask, and filters, such as carbon nanomaterials, Cu, Ag, TiO2, MXene, MOFs, and polymer nanoparticles, has various benefits that not only reduce the danger of transmission but also make the facemask, textile, and filters reusable. In addition, because they have demonstrated their potential for detecting other viruses, nanoparticles such as graphene and graphene oxide, carbon nanotube, quantum dots, gold nanoparticles, iron oxide, and polymer nanoparticles significantly enhance biosensors' performance for detecting the SARSCoV-2 virus. Nanomedicine has the potential to significantly increase (or enable) the safety and effectiveness of vaccine and medication technology. Since lipid nanoparticles are very biocompatible and biodegradable, there haven't been many instances of immune system complications up to this point. Although polymeric and metallic nanoparticles often biodegrade more slowly, depending on the condition being treated and the medicine being administered, they may potentially be advantageous. In addition, the nontoxicity and high surface area to volume ratio of nanomaterials utilised in nanomedicine enable extremely effective medication packing. In fact, more research needs to be done on the toxicity and biocompatibility of nanoparticles in living cells. In short, the mRNA- and DNA-based vaccinations wouldn't be as effective without the nanoparticles. Old nanoparticles, chitosan, and lipid nanoparticles play a significant role in vaccination technology among other types of nanoparticles. As a result, the COVID-19 can be better and more quickly managed in the environment and society by using nanomaterials.

The Bottom Line

With the alarming risk of the new respiratory virus COVID-19, global health is in catastrophic condition. This review examined and evaluated various nanomaterial kinds that might be used in antivirus software to combat COVID-19. Some topics, however, require more study and care. First, we discussed many kinds of nanomaterials and their prospective uses, including drug delivery, COVID-19 vaccination technology, facemasks, antiviral coatings, airborne virus filtering, and detecting biosensors. These nanoparticles are routinely utilised to treat, diagnose, and infiltrate many illnesses. Nanotechnology-based biosensors for COVID-19 detection have recently entered the commercial market. The toxicity of these kinds of nanoparticles in vivo, however, poses a significant obstacle to their use in sustainable built environments. The use of standard amounts of nanomaterials with the least hazardous and most antiviral effects is a significant challenge that requires additional research. However, investigating the toxicity of these chemicals in vivo is still a major concern in this direction.

Last but not least, the components of nanoparticles play a significant role in mRNA- and DNA-based vaccinations. A massive phase 4 clinical trial is in underway to test a notion about how to use nanomedicine to solve the clinical issue. The unidentified risk of lipid nanoparticles in COVID-19 vaccination technology was then resolved by the phase 4 clinical test. Since nanomedicine is crucial to the development of COVID-19 vaccines, translational nanomedicine has finally advanced from its early stages. Future developments and uses for nanomedicine are certain to be unexpected. Therefore, gathering useful information and examining the adverse effects of each COVID-19 vaccination will appear to be a great route for the development of more complicated and non-lipid nanomedicines in the future. The use of antiviral nanomaterials is a useful and crucial step in reducing the frequency of Covid-19, even if ultimate eradication of this virus necessitates much more thorough research. Accordingly, antiviral nanomaterials should be used in medical devices, nanotechnology-enhanced fabrics, facemasks, and other products. Additionally, disinfectants based on nanomaterials have higher inactivation rates and faster inactivation rates, which are particularly useful at boosting safety in hospitals and public areas. This chemical can be employed in the creation of diagnostic kits, vaccinations, and treatments because to the incredibly helpful features of nanoparticles in the eradication of viruses. As a result, using nanomaterials in biomedical applications is a successful strategy for containing the viral pandemic epidemic at the local, national, and global levels.

Made in the USA
Columbia, SC
04 March 2023

4a0c81a6-7674-4301-9cec-33a8ba3c79a8R04